RÓBERT CHOVANCULIAK
PROGRESS without PERMISSION
HOW SHARING ECONOMY, CROWDFUNDING, AND CRYPTOCURRENCIES TRANSFORM OUR SOCIETY

Chovanculiak, Róbert: Progress without permission

How sharing economy, crowdfunding, and cryptocurrencies transform our society

From the Slovak original

Pokrok bez povolenia
Ako zdieľaná ekonomika, crowdfunding a kryptomeny zmenili svet

translated by Barbora Tricoire

Published in 2023 by INESS
ISBN 978-80-89820-10-8

Josef Sima | professor of economics, Chair of the Department of International Business at Metropolitan University, Prague

"I have been privileged to read Robert Chovanculiak's wonderful book " Progress without Permission" and write an introduction to the Czech translation thereof. The book is really cool. It builds on "old" arguments for pure markets and shows how new technologies strengthen that argument (or overcome the objections based on mainstream "market failure" approach). The reader hence learns how the existence and functioning of Airbnb, Uber, Bitcoin, crowdfunding platforms, conflict resolution on Blockchain etc. modifies our understanding of political economy. There is a lot of things in the book for both students and general public, it is full of historical examples and stories of success and failure of "populating the new world of digital technologies", of "digital anarchy", of the "Wild West" of the new frontier. It is simply a great read and I highly recommend it to all curious readers."

Pavol Luptak | CEO of Nethemba, ethical hacker

"In times of trial-and-error policies and desperation in society, Progress without Permission represents a clear vision of our society's future steps towards higher economic efficiency... You don't have to be a libertarian to be convinced by the purely economic arguments in this book that future technologies will enable the private sector to much better compete with the public sector at providing of all its current services."

Juraj Bednar | serial entrepreneur and ethical hacker

"Progress without Permission describes what people do when they are unsatisfied with traditional solutions or a lack thereof. It's not a philosophical work, but rather an overview of today's reality and its impact. For me, this book is a look into the future, which is already here yet not evenly distributed. Róbert Chovanculiak takes a look into those fragments of the glimmer of the future which is reflected in today's reality."

Juraj Karpis | founder of INESS, author of the economic bestseller Bad Money

"Reduction of transaction costs powered by information technology has triggered a social revolution. This book represents a suspenseful journey through its battles. Free interaction of members on emerging platforms has created space for feedback and has extended selective pressure to the rules of cohabitation. Services provided by the government monopoly are now freely up for sale which makes it possible to improve them."

Matej Galvanek | director of Sigil Fund, Crypto Investor

"This book opens a window to a world where technology trumps bureaucracy, people networks win against official authorities and free market beats regulation. You will get to read about age-old economic debates put into modern context and get an overview of modern technologies and their potential to change our society. All of this is illustrated by many well-known and also less-known examples. Very inspiring indeed."

Marek Hudik | lecturer at the University of Economics, Prague, economist

"Progress without Permission is a fascinating book about how new technologies can improve the world if we let them. It is a book for those who want to better understand today's world and at the same time take a sneak peek into the world of tomorrow."

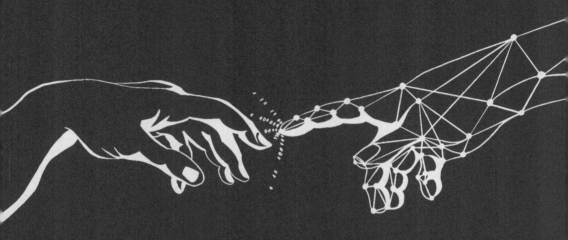

"The growth of the internet will slow drastically [...]. By 2005, it will become clear that the internet's impact on the economy has been no greater than the fax machine's."
   Paul Krugman, 1998

"I think that the internet is going to be one of the major forces for reducing the role of government."
   Milton Friedman, 1999

to Mária, Zuzana and Emily

CONTENTS

INTRODUCTION — 13

This book describes the clash between old institutions and new technologies.; Uber is not in competition with taxis – it is in competition with the Ministry of Transport; Why did I write this book?; How to read this book

SHARING ECONOMY AND INFORMATION ASYMMETRY — 21

INTRODUCTION – NIGHTHAWKS — 22
Analogue Information Traders; Who's Going to Protect Customers from Customer Protection?; Conclusion

HOW A YOUNG CIVIL ENGINEER ALMOST GOT RICH, BUT ONLY MANAGED TO SAVE SOME MONEY — 31
Sharing Doesn't Always Equal Sharing Economy and Sharing Economy Doesn't Always Have to Be About Sharing; What Did Sharing Economy Bring?; Why Are Economists So Excited about Sharing Economy?

NOT ALL REGULATION IS THE SAME — 57
Incentives Matter – or, as Our Fathers Would Say – Opportunity Makes the Thief; Who regulates the regulator?; Private regulators are like the baker from Smith's quote; What happened to Uber?; What happened to Airbnb?; Lack of Knowledge – or as They Say: Nobody is Born Knowing Everything; Public regulators are deaf and blind; When platform entrepreneurs become law-makers; Enforcing Good Behavior; Conclusion

FORBIDDEN PROGRESS — 87
Let the Competition Decide; Sharing Economy as a Litmus Test; Litmus Test that Can Bite; The best Possible World ; When it's Easier to Beg for Forgiveness than Asking for Permission; A Christmas Story about Forbidden Fruit; Progress without Permission – Conclusion

CROWDFUNDING AND PUBLIC GOODS — 117

INTRODUCTION – THE DARK SIDE OF RATIONALITY — 118
Soldier's Dilemma; Market Failure – Public Goods

CROWDFUNDING — 122

THERE ARE THREE PROBLEMS WITH PUBLIC GOODS; CROWDFUNDING OFFERS THREE SOLUTIONS — 127
Eliminating the Short Straw; Binding Free-riders; Organization Costs and the Internet; Conclusion

STATE FAILURES WHEN SOLVING THE PROBLEM OF PUBLIC GOODS — 148
Public Good: a Solution to the Public Good Problem; Homebody Turns into Free-rider; Conclusion

LAW AND ORDER IN INTERNET ANARCHY — 171

INTRODUCTION – PRISONER'S DILEMMA — 172
Small-scale Informal Anarchy; Limited Anarchy ; Was Hobbes Right after all?

INFORMATION EVOLUTION IN BRIEF — 183

GLOBAL INTERNET CLUBS WITH SUPER-MEMBERSHIP — 186
Reputation on Internet Steroids; First set of parameters: from quality to quantity; Second set of parameters: from raw data to applicable statistics; Third set of parameters: from operational statistics to their correct interpretation; Super-membership Cards on Internet Steroids; Two Big Advantages of Non-territorial Provision of Law and Order Services ; Forgotten Idea – Panarchy; Halfway to Anarchy: Lack of Policemen; Halfway to Anarchy: Absence of the Judiciary; Halfway to Anarchy: When Laws Are Written by Entrepreneurs

DIGITAL CRYPTO ANARCHY ON THE DARKNET   **213**
    Tor – the Internet's Dark Alley; Bitcoin – the Digital Cash

CRYPTO MARKETS OF THE INTERNET'S "WILD WEST"   **232**
    Dread Pirate Roberts vs. Thomas Hobbes; Drugs: Quality and Safety; Protection against Public Order Protectors; Even an Expert Makes Mistakes; CryptoHydra; Conclusion – Thomas Hobbes Must Be Turning in His Grave

DECENTRALIZED CRYPTO MARKET   **245**
    What Doesn't Kill You Makes You Stronger – OpenBazaar; The Future of Trading – Smart Contracts? ; Kleros: Two Heads Are Better Than One; Conclusion – Are You Against us If You Don't Decentralize?

CONCLUSION – REFLECTIONS   269
    What this book wasn't about; If you don't like it, move to Somalia!; Tutorial for a benevolent ruler; If I had to...

REFERENCE   276
    Sharing Economy and Information Asymmetry; Crowdfunding and Public Goods; Law and Order in Internet Anarchy; Conclusion – Reflections; Footnote references

INTRODUCTION

"...we have paleolithic emotions, medieval institutions, and god-like technology."

E.O. Wilson

INTRODUCTION

THIS BOOK DESCRIBES THE CLASH BETWEEN OLD INSTITUTIONS AND NEW TECHNOLOGIES.

Had I written it 12 thousand years ago, I would have described new technologies resulting from the agricultural revolution and told you about their impact on hunters and gatherers. I would have written about how the organization of life changed after the transition from a migrating nomadic lifestyle to more stable settlements and also about new social rules brought about by the plough and the domestication of animals.

If I had written it 250 years ago, I would have written about the new technologies of the industrial revolution and their impact on feudalism. It would have been a story about the change in the organization of the lifestyle of people who moved to cities from rural areas and also about new social rules brought about by the steam engine and the loom.

Nevertheless, I am writing it in today's digital era. I will be describing the clash between 21st century digital technologies and 20th century brick-and-mortar institutions. I will write about how the organization of life changed after the transition from the offline to the online world. If you are one of those who are fascinated by the internet and its social impact, you have picked up the right book.

UBER IS NOT IN COMPETITION WITH TAXIS – IT IS IN COMPETITION WITH THE MINISTRY OF TRANSPORT

People often view the arrival of internet technologies through the eyes of the past. They focus on small battles between new companies and their analogue predecessors and miss the main point.

As newspapers publish articles about sharing economy stealing taxi drivers' jobs, Uber is working on improving their own private regulations in an effort to protect their consumers. While analysts are complaining that eBay and Amazon are pushing out brick-and-mortar stores, both of these platforms are operating as the biggest courts of justice in the world solving thousands of cases every day.

The progress that came with the internet is therefore not only in competition with analogue businessmen and brick-and-mortar stores but mostly with the world of regulators, officials and politicians. This is what this book is about – how the role of the state and the market changed in society after the arrival of the internet.

The following pages will reveal whether Airbnb can protect guests and hosts better than state inspectors, whether Kickstarter can manage to collect sufficient means for the provision of public services such as private police or an army. You will learn when it is more reasonable to ask for forgiveness rather than for permission, about how each of you can become an internet judge and also about the rules of internet anarchy. You will discover the story of how Bitcoin brought the first digital cash into the world of state money and enabled the building of a parallel society without "bosses" and where we can all be movers and shakers.

INTRODUCTION

Long story short, this book is about how the internet and entrepreneurs helped overcome many textbook-example market failures. They did not have a choice – if they wanted to succeed and win over the hearts and minds of their customers, they had to start competing with state machinery.

Writing this book was a small adventure in which I was constantly testing, examining and discovering new ecosystems growing around internet technology. Every now and then I felt like a modern anthropologist who got the chance to gaze into the busy world of digital communities. Sometimes, these were small groups of people who wanted to get funding for public benches and sometimes the digital community would look more like an internet realm extending to various continents.

The results of my exploratory mission are these several hundreds of pages which can serve as a guide to internet technology seen through the eyes of an economists. This is not a futuristic book. I don't know how the coevolution of new technologies and social institutions will end and exactly what it will bring. Rather than a prediction, this text is an acknowledgement. An acknowledgement which is not tinted by any specific values of its author – an economist-scientist who at one time t=0 had a certain idea about the right role of state and market in society and with the arrival of internet technology, decided to rethink this idea at another time t=1.

This economist is not me and I don't know such person. But I imagine they exist. They are pure scientists, pragmatic and unbiased by ideologies and normative ideas about right and wrong. They are Ok with abandoning and rethinking their views. The point of the book is to show that if such an economist existed, the world of new technologies should make them reconsider their opinion on the role of the state in society because thanks to the internet, the market works better than it ever did.

WHY DID I WRITE THIS BOOK?

I would not have to write all of this if the development of institutions kept up with the development of technology – meaning constitutions, laws, regulations but also informal rules, such as norms, customs and traditions. However, the coevolution between institutions and new technologies is not that smooth. Both phenomena form part of a broader cultural evolution but each of them has their own "evolutionary" pace.

These days it is widely accepted to consider technological development as an evolutionary phenomenon[1]. Each new technology sits on the shoulders of their predecessor and it develops through a gradual accumulation of new "mutations". Technological evolution is fairly exact, which means, that in the world of new technologies, you get feedback as to whether a new mutation brings the expected result or not. When Alexander Fleming discovered penicillin, when Norman Borlaug introduced his new variety of wheat and when Jonas Salk successfully came up with the polio vaccine, they all knew whether their "mutation" was effective quite early on.

Technological mutations spread rapidly across society. When these men came up with their inventions, others were able to successfully replicate them and therefore saved millions of human lives. This was also true for some less-sophisticated technologies such as the use of fire, the wheel or horse stirrups. The spreading of technologies doesn't require a collective agreement and every individual has their own motivation for using them. Technology spreads like a virus – once one person starts using it, it doesn't take long for the rest to catch up.

In comparison, the evolution of institutions is a lot slower, more limited and imprecise. Society and its functioning represent a complex and dynamic system where it is very difficult to track the causal threads between actions and reactions. This is one of the reasons why knowledge from this area of scientific expertise is often the subject of conflicts. Many historical and social events can be interpreted according to one's beliefs.

Ideology also plays its part – people don't seek the truth; they simply want to be right. The result of this is that institutional evolution gets stuck in a multitude of one-way streets and is much less precise than its technological counterpart. There is no direct feedback for institutions and therefore, it is impossible to know whether specific activities yield the expected results. Even if they do somehow find out what they do right or wrong, they have a problem replicating them. Unlike technology, institutions need to be accepted by a critical mass of people and require collective action which renders institutional evolution inefficient and slow.

This doesn't mean that these two kinds of evolution are completely independent and that with time they will not start to influence each other. Technologies and institutions develop hand in hand, but technology is more innovative and dynamic while social institutions remain more conservative. Consequently, there are certain "limbos" where institutions could afford an upgrade to keep pace with results of technological development, but this either doesn't happen or is delayed by the conservative tendencies of institutions.

Today we are experiencing such "limbo" where internet technology is developing exponentially while institutions often take one step forward and one step back. The way E.O. Wilson puts it: "We have Paleolithic emotions, medieval institutions and god-like technology."

HOW TO READ THIS BOOK

Apart from its introduction and concluding remarks, the book is divided into three main sections with the same basic structure. I start by identifying a problem because this is the basic step in any search for a solution. By problem, I mean a market failure: information asymmetry, public goods or law and order services. You can often find these problems in economics textbooks together with explanations of why we need the state and its interventions. Where I present a market problem, I also show the solutions the state has to offer. This means regulation of business, collecting compulsory taxes and public provision of the services of police, judges and politicians.

After identifying the problem, we must find a solution. In each chapter, I present a new technology which solves or at least mitigates the given problem. At this stage, I will show you how sharing economy platforms remove the issue of information asymmetry thanks to private regulations. Together, we will take a look at how crowdfunding platforms make it possible for people to voluntarily chip in and thus obtain funding for public goods previously financed involuntarily – with taxes. You will read about how internet entrepreneurs provide police and judicial services to people who, for some reason, could not rely on traditional public providers (for instance because their internet business model is illegal). In the last part of the book, I address the topic of cryptocurrencies and explain how they helped people assure internal cooperation and external security and privacy.

Although this book is written in layman's terms, the difficulty gradually increases as you progress. From the first part about sharing economy, which is based on fundamental economic principles, through the second part, which employs more sophisticated economic concepts, to the third part, which deals with cryptographic topics such as asymmetric encryption or hash function, a determined layman should be able to get through all of them. If there are parts that you find incomprehensible, disagree with or feel that what I have written is not true, please contact me at: chovanculiak@gmail.com because feedback is the cornerstone of progress.

INTRODUCTION

SHORT INSTRUCTIONS FOR USE

In the book you will find sections of text marked with yellow strips. This is supplementary information – if you skip it, you won't miss the main message of the book, but you may miss out on a lot of fun.

In the book you will find two types of notes. The first type refers to a footnote where you will find a short explanation, the second type refers to the references used at the end of the book where you will find citations and sources.

In addition, you will find the following superscripts in the footnotes: A1, A2, A3 – these refer to the literature used in the note itself. The latter can be found at the very end of the book. So much for the technical side of reading.

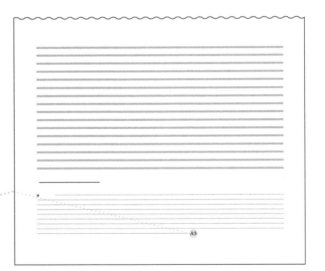

SHARING ECONOMY AND INFORMATION ASYMMETRY

"You never change things by fighting the existing reality. To change something, build a new model that makes the existing model obsolete."

Buckminster Fuller

1. INTRODUCTION – NIGHTHAWKS

On a warm evening in 1889, a respectable citizen of San Francisco named F.S. Chadbourne got off a ferry and made his way to the nearest taxi. In late 19th century California, this meant a horse-drawn carriage and at its reins sat James "Nosey" Brown, a local taxi driver known as a "nighthawk". These men were not ashamed to ask a high surcharge for their services, especially from non-locals. When a fare refused to pay, nighthawks drove them to a deserted spot and gave them the choice to get out or pay. In other words, nighthawks were the predecessors of taxi drivers circling around airports and big train stations almost anywhere in the world.

It was an unlucky night for our nighthawk, James "Nosey" Brown, because the out-of-towner that got in his taxi was not just any out-of-towner. It was a man by the name of Chadbourne – a successful businessman with connections to politicians in the highest offices in town, who also knew the rates for local taxi services. Chadbourne refused to pay the exorbitantly high surcharge, so Brown drove him to a deserted place and left him there. On the walk home, Chadbourne planned his vengeance and in the following months, proposed and implemented a new regulation designed to clip the wings of Brown-like hawks.

The new regulation allowed only licensed taxi drivers to work in San Francisco and limited one vehicle per driver. In other words, the number of granted licenses had to be the same as the number of registered carriages. It became known as "Chadbourne's Ordinance".[2]

The San Francisco Morning Call newspaper wrote the following lines on the 18th of September, 1890:

"The crying nuisance that this law aimed to remedy, and in a wonderful measure has remedied, was the practice that irresponsible carriage-owners and carriage companies had of procuring blank licenses for a few drivers, not designating any particular carriage [...] it allowed two or more drivers to run with one vehicle, by means of which every now and then some rascally trick was perpetrated on an innocent unsuspecting traveler."[3]

In order to be granted a license, a potential taxi driver had to convince a police committee that they were an "honest law-abiding citizen". James "Nosey" Brown ended up being one of the drivers who never managed to obtain a license. Chadbourne's vengeance worked perfectly.

To the experienced eye of an economist, this story is a classic example of market failure addressed by state intervention. The market failure is information asymmetry and the solution is public regulation. The principal behind this was described by the Nobel Prize winning economist George Akerlof, who, in his renowned article[4], explained the problem of information asymmetry with vehicles – this time using the example of selling second-hand cars.

Personally, I will never forget when I bought my first second-hand car and how each family member, colleague, friend or enemy of mine had their own opinion on which brands, years and types of cars break easily and which are reliable. These opinions did not tend to overlap. Once I had chosen the approximate parameters and established my budget limit, the internet search engines inundated my screen with a plethora of offers from many different sellers which only multiplied my suffering. I was able to see pictures of these cars or read about their features but I had no way of knowing whether the previous owner of a Toyota Auris handled the clutch gently, whether they changed the oil as they should have or if, perhaps, the car had been in an accident and photographed only after a skillful auto body shop had worked its magic.

This is all private information available to the seller but not to me. At the same time, sellers probably would not be very keen to list this information in their advertisements because they know that if they disclose it, buyers might become less interested. It's not that honest sellers and good used cars don't exist, but the problem was that I could not tell them apart. I could not separate wheat from the tares just as Mr. Chadbourne who, upon his arrival in San Francisco, could not tell an honest taxi driver from a nighthawk.

George Akerlof explained that the customer's inability to separate the wheat from the tares reduces their willingness to pay and how it influences the market. If you are buying a car with a real value of somewhere between $10,000 and $15,000 and the probability that the provided information is true is 50:50, most people are willing to pay maximum $12,500. Of course, nobody thinks explicitly like this, but when market processes influence the decision-making of millions of sellers and buyers, this is more or less the result we may expect. If the customer is not sure about quality, their willingness to pay diminishes.

How will honest sellers, who know that their car is worth $15,000, react when the customer is only willing to pay $12,500? They leave the market, which contaminates it even more and leads to an even greater decrease in the customers' willingness to pay. Sellers lose motivation and the second-hand car market collapses into a terrifying spiral. Where there is information advantage, bad and dishonest sellers push out the good ones from the market.*

This is how a market failure is born. There are indeed buyers who are interested in quality cars just as there are sellers who possess such cars, but informa-

---

* When George Akerlof sent this argument to different economic journals, he got several negative responses. Some rejected him saying they would not publish such a trivial article and others objected that if what he was claiming was true, economics as they knew it would be incorrect. Finally, he managed to have his article published in The Quarterly Journal of Economics in 1970. 31 years later, he got a Nobel Prize for it. [A1]

tion asymmetry prevents these world-improving exchanges from happening and these cars stay parked in a garage.

And so, when economists see the invisible hand of the market failing, they sneakily start to consider the involvement of the state's visible hand. Quotes such as this by Nobel Laureate E. Stiglitz started to appear in economics textbooks: "The fact that when there are asymmetries of information, markets are not, in general constrained Pareto efficient implies there is a potentially important role for government." And legislators then started to use the term of information asymmetry to justify the state protection of customers.[5]

Suddenly, the public sector saw an increase of agencies or justified the existence of offices, bodies and institutions that protected the customers against all things imaginable. In addition, there is a spreading license mania for all possible professions. The U.S. has the best processed data in this area but our situation is not much different. In the 1950s, 5% of U.S. workers needed a license to carry out their profession while today it is more than 30%. You need a license to be a grave digger, hair dresser, florist, interior designer, nail designer, and the list goes on.

It was not only the numbers of authorities and licenses that increased – piles of paper and red tape regulations were accumulated as well. In the U.S., the second half of the 20th century brought tens of thousands of these per year. As a result, at the end of 2016, according to the Code of Federal Regulations (CFR), there were in total 1,080,000 regulations, restrictions and other decrees consisting of bans and orders.[6]

Of course, things would have probably developed the same way even without an economist writing a Nobel-Prize-winning article about information asymmetry which introduced his theory to every economics textbook. The public sector, with its politicians and officials, has a natural tendency towards expansion.[7] Nevertheless, the theory of information asymmetry contributed to this becoming a one-way process.

These days, if you want to criticize the amount of regulation or, God forbid, call for reducing them, you'll be bombarded by arguments involving information asymmetry and customer protection from academics, journalists and lobbyists and even the general public. Today, the issue of information asymmetry is, if nothing else, a powerful tool for the retrospective rationalization of existing public regulation.

However, we don't live in a black-and-white world. Without public regulation, we would not be consumed by a black hole of chaos where customers would be afraid to take out their wallets because evil sellers are waiting to use the information advantage to rip them off.

Moreover, we also have to admit that the world of public regulations is not exactly a paradise where officials and politicians float on pink clouds and sprinkle the world with vital manna in the form of laws and regulations that protect the vulnerable and punish the fraudsters.

1.1 ANALOGUE INFORMATION TRADERS

Akerlof did, of course, notice that the used car market works despite his theory. In his article, he included several ways in which people attempted to address the issue he identified. He mentioned guarantees, trademarks and business chains.

Apart from this, entrepreneurs came up with many other ways to fight information asymmetry. Make no mistake – their motivation was not to make the world a better place. It was simply a way to earn more money. It turned out that entrepreneurs who offer quality assurance on top of a good product earn more than those who don't. The consumer wants to be assured about the quality of their purchase.

Trying to solve the problem of information asymmetry thus became a profitable opportunity despite the skepticism of another Nobel Laureate – Kenneth J. Arrow who wrote: "Trust and similar values, loyalty or truth-telling, are examples of what the economist would call externalities [...]. But they are not commodities for which trade on the open market is technically possible or even meaningful." Nobody is more successful at refuting theories written by economists than people who decided to improve their lives.[8]

The most common quality assurance approach is to include all your products under one brand. This way an entrepreneur gives the customer leverage for purchasing a poor-quality products or services. The brand is the customer's hostage after the purchase and can be sacrificed whenever they are not content – next time, they will opt for a different brand or they will tell all their friends about their bad experience. Thanks to the existence of a brand, the news about its quality will travel fast and let's be honest – building a brand on bad quality products and dangerous services is hardly a sustainable business model.

Yet another Nobel Laureate, Friedrich Hayek, thought that competition is to a large extent a competition for reputation: "The competition is here precisely to teach us who will serve us well."

We all possess brands – take for example your name and surname. I have a theory that this cultural artifact – hereditary label (surname) with a variable component (name) became so popular in almost all societies worldwide because it pressured people into good behavior and nobody even stops to think about it today. Where people had no names, it was more difficult to enforce good and safe behavior towards others and such societies did not make it very far.

The second way of providing customers with quality assurance (mainly in case of one-off and expensive interactions) is to put an intermediary between them and the entrepreneur. If you need an appendectomy, you only need it done once and, in this case, the hospital can serve as an intermediary who will build a bridge of trust between you as the patient, and the surgeon. A person usually falls ill more than once in their lifetime and therefore has repeating experiences with hospitals. Just like a surgeon who performs an appendectomy repeatedly, the hospital becomes a player who turns one-off interactions into a repeated game with an ever-arising pressure to provide good service. A similar role is played by retail vendors or different dealers and brokers.

In some cases, one bad experience can be a deal-breaker and some products and services can be dangerous to even try despite having an intermediary as well as the possibility to execute the hostage in the form of a brand. To address such situations, new institutions and organizations were established. Their competitive advantage is that they are able to collect and assess costly information and then sell it to those who are interested but cannot obtain such information on their own. Fortunately, there are independent assessors or consumer associations with their own labs and product analyses, who are able to provide their potential customers with certified information about products and services before they even try them.

In my region, the company dTest publishes a monthly magazine and also has its own TV show where it tests tens of thousands of products. Originally, dTest was a civic association of consumers and two of its basic rules are the independence in product choice, which is guided by market research and consumers' demands, and the independence in testing – it avoids all connections with producers and doesn't have a single advertisement published in a magazine or on a web page. The organization is financed by subscriptions to its own services. Nevertheless, my personal favorite collector and assessor of information is Labdoor. They independently test everything from food supplements and vitamins to fish oil.

In the case of organizations like dTest or Labdoor, the initiative comes from the customer. The customer searches, subscribes or requests information about products and services they plan to use. However, various certification and accreditation bodies are approached by producers themselves in their effort to diminish information asymmetry. Once they have passed the test, they get a certificate which will serve as a seal of trust. This sends the consumer a signal that the products are OK and nobody is trying to trick them.

My favorite examples are certification bodies which test kosher food. To people of the Jewish faith, information asymmetry is an important issue due to their religious dietary restrictions. If they want to find something kosher, not even the best chemical analysis can help but, luckily for them, there are certification bodies which ensure compliance from every link in the chain of production. They have elaborate quality management and compete for reputation among themselves. More importantly, customers are extremely satisfied with their results.[9]

A university degree can also be considered a "certified quality seal", since it signifies that an individual possesses qualities required by employers: the ability to work under pressure, completing tasks on time, disciplined attendance, certain level of intelligence, and so on. A university degree helps to lower the information asymmetry faced by employers upon purchasing the services of employees. In this case, it is the employer who is disadvantaged in terms of information.[10]

Another commonly used mechanism for decreasing information asymmetry is creating business chains or franchises because the quality of their services is a constant. In Slovakia, you can be sure to get lunch in every big town and be 100% sure of the quality you are getting, or a lack thereof. McDonald's restaurants, for example, have to comply with certain rules down to the exact parameters of trays or the quantity of pickles in a hamburger if they want to get a license from the owners of the McDonald's network. A franchise means a possibility to rent a place under the auspices of a brand built by somebody else and you can be sure that it is in the interest of the brand owner not to have his wheat mixed up with the tares.

Apart from the above-mentioned mechanisms, entrepreneurs have come up with many other tools which serve to "reassure" the customer and lower information asymmetry. One of the most popular is the refund, which serves as an expensive seal of quality only top producers can afford. Another such signal would be the guarantee and returns policy. These tools aim to transfer the risk of buying a bad quality product from consumers to producers, assuring the former that the latter are not up to no good, for if they are, they will pay for it in the form of a warehouse full of returned goods.

In the same category of assurance tools, we also find the possibility to try before you buy or commercials, which lower information asymmetry and are a costly way to signal that the company and its products are here to stay. We should also mention competition, which ensures that different producers and service providers review each other and share information about possible shortcomings or fraud.

By now it is clear that people are often more creative than economists who come up with theories. This doesn't mean that the issue of information asymmetry is not real. It means that if we think about public policies and compare alternatives, we should at least consider this other spectrum of solutions created voluntarily by people who are subject to the pressure of competition and who, at the same time, seek to improve their lives. These solutions are not perfect but neither are the solutions proposed by the opposite party – state regulators.

1.2 WHO'S GOING TO PROTECT CUSTOMERS FROM CUSTOMER PROTECTION?

Now let's go back to the nighthawks we met in the introduction of this chapter. The development of social events tends to be a bit more complicated than what can be captured in fairytales about the battles between good and evil. Social events are usually more like a chaotic ball of relations, conflicts, intended and unintended consequences.

Chadbourne's Ordinance, which meant the end for nighthawk James "Nosey" Brown, was supported and co-created by the Carriage Drivers' Protective Union. It represented independent carriage owners and it strongly emphasized the part of the regulation that limited the use of one carriage for one driver and license only.

This was no random request. The Union's members picked up on a new trend that started to appear in the U.S. Up until then, taxis were big and relatively slow four-wheeled carriages pulled by two horses (the hacks), while new taxis were lighter, faster, had only two wheels and were pulled by one horse (the cabs). They were invented by J. Theodore Gurney from Boston, who in 1890, attempted to expand to the west and established an operation in San Francisco.

Apart from faster and more flexible carriages, his business model consisted of lower prices. He managed to do this by having more drivers alternate on one carriage so they could operate almost the entire day without a break. Independent carriage owners could not and did not want to do such thing and so, also thanks to them, such practices became illegal in San Francisco.

But Gurney did not worry too much about regulations. He ignored the licenses and operated his taxies as usual. When the Carriage Drivers' Protective Union started to protest, he reacted by saying that he would in no way stop his activities and that he considered the regulation to be anti-constitutional. Consequently, he informed his lawyer, Alfred Clark, that if they had to, they would take the case to the Supreme Court.

The story of Gurney and his taxis finally ended up buried by the strictest and most objective regulator mankind has seen so far: loss winning over profit. First, Gurney set prices that were unsustainably low and when he began to increase them, it led to him losing customers and his business failed.

For Gurney, that was the end of the story. However, it did not mean the end of regulations. Unlike entrepreneurs, regulations cannot go bankrupt and are not subject to the already-mentioned strictest punishment/regulator. On the contrary, they are often ruled by the willingness of entrepreneurs to pay (bribe), which brings along many juicy stories.

The situation with taxi regulations in New York has become legendary. Surprisingly, the history of New York taxis can be traced back to Stuttgart, Germany where, in 1897, a local engineer and industrialist named Gottlieb Daimler came up with a new invention – motorized taxis with taximeters. Businessman Harry N. Allen noticed these, bought one and brought it with him to New York in 1907. Later, he managed to get sufficient resources for an entire car fleet and his new marketing strategy changed the taxi industry forever – to distinguish his cars from other cars, he painted them yellow.

That is not to say that everything went smooth with Allen. His innovation did not meet with admiration on the side of the original service providers. They blamed him for unfair competition, breaking the rules, amoral behavior and the list goes on (any resemblance with the present is purely coincidental).

As if the taxi drivers were not tense enough, they were further irritated by John Daniel Hertz – a Slovak from the city of Martin. Hertz was a young amateur boxer, horse breeder and car dealer who gradually came to establish taxi companies in Chicago, New York and other towns in the 1920s.

His competitive advantage was the economy of scale – he tried to bring as many taxi drivers as possible to each town. He used this advantage to charge lower prices, and that is how he made taxis accessible to the middle class and was able to increase drivers' benefits so that he not only paid them their wage but also covered other social benefits, health services and dentists' appointments. His drivers even had a share in the company profit.

Hertz's competitors were not big fans of his new approach and they were incapable of uttering one positive word about him. Exchanges of sharp words would sometimes turn to exchanges of bullets.[11]

During the Big Depression (1929-1941), this highly competitive environment started to change and the number of taxi drivers rapidly increased. It was not easy to earn a living in times of extensive unemployment and almost anybody who owned or rented a car could work as a taxi driver. Of course, along with this came heavier traffic, more accidents, the quality of cars decreased and so did the drivers' profits. Local politicians jumped straight into tackling the issue and their proposed solution was simple: limit supply.

This was far from being an unusual solution for decreasing profits and wages during the Big Depression. Back in those days, many industries formed cartels with the help of politicians in order to keep product prices up and ensure the profit for producers.

In no other area was this policy as obvious and as damaging as it was to agriculture. President Roosevelt introduced a program aimed at fighting the crisis known as the New Deal and in 1933, he adopted the Agricultural Adjustment Act. The events that followed are now taught at economics classes as "political market failure".

You don't need to attend economics classes to realize how nonsensical such a policy is. It imposed the destruction of food, even of entire harvests and herds of cattle in order to maintain high food prices in times, when just a few miles away, people were starving. And so, it happened that in one country you could simultaneously see farmers who were injecting oranges with kerosene to prevent them from entering the market and people who had literally nothing to put in their hungry mouths. The result? In 1935, the farms' profits were 50% higher than one year before the adoption of Roosevelt's Act.[12]

We no longer burn food or coat it in kerosene (although we do still pay farmers for leaving land idle in the European Union), but regulations concerning taxi drivers have remained in force in many countries. Namely in New York, there was the Haas Act which created a system of permits to operate taxis called medallions. More than 13,000 medallions were issued in 1937.

However, in the following years, their number dropped because not all taxi drivers were interested in renewing their licenses for a $10 annual fee (these days this would correspond to approximately $170) at the end of the Big Depression.¹³ Those who decided not to renew it made one of the worst investment decisions because the value of licenses started to skyrocket. In 1950, it cost $5,000 for one license, at the end of the 70s it went up to $50,000, in 2004 they cost over $300,000 and the sum climbed up to the striking number of 1.3 million dollars.¹⁴ The average growth of the medallions' value beat the growth of stock exchange and precious metals.

New York was, of course, not the only place where the prices of licenses climbed so high. Up until recently, you could buy a $200,000 license in Paris and the prices in Australia ranged between $250,000 and $500,000.

The interesting part is that this system did not up helping the taxi drivers themselves but rather the medallion holders. The medallion value soaked up the entire political rent created by limited supply and high prices. If a potential taxi driver wanted to start working, his higher earnings were automatically offset by higher costs to purchase or the rent of a medallion. Medallions thus became a regular cost item for drivers – just like the purchase of a vehicle or gasoline, which were gradually payed off via higher monopoly rates per ride. Therefore, their earnings remained at the average level of the competitive market, as it was stated also in a report by OECD.¹⁵

Evgeny Freidman, who became known as the Taxi King, was one of the medallion beneficiaries. In 1996, he inherited a taxi business from his father with approximately 60 medallions. Their price started to rapidly increase, which enabled Evgeny to take a loan and buy more medallions. By repeating this strategy, he managed to get over 1,100 medallions by 2015 with a value of almost $1.5 billion. During one interview, he openly confessed the following words:

"Every day that I wake up, you know, I'm like, this is great [...] You know, I live on Park Avenue, got a bunch of, like, Ferraris, that I drive. I have a house in the south of France. I can have breakfast, like, at Cipriani. And it's like, you know, pinch me. Is this real?"¹⁶

Reality did kick in in the end because as he was giving the interview, the number of drivers of the Uber and Lyft platforms already topped the number of taxi drivers and two years later, the medallion price dropped from $1.3 million to 300. Not only did the unbelievable wealth Freidman found hard to believe vanish, banks started to touch his property and, in addition, tax officials accused his companies of tax fraud. He also had problems at court for not paying drivers' wages and threatening his business partners. On top of all that, authorities refused to renew many of his medallion licenses. In June 2017, he was arrested and charged with several crimes for which he can get up to 25 years of prison.¹⁷

1.3 CONCLUSION

The problem of information asymmetry is the cornerstone of the "new theory of market failure" which was born in the 1970s and in 2001 grew into two Nobel Prizes – for George Akerlof and for Joseph Stiglitz. As illustrated by the story of San Francisco nighthawks and my own trauma from buying a used car, this is not an imaginary problem. It's a sad part of our imperfect world where one possesses information and others don't and where the former is not afraid to use it to their advantage. At the same time, the multiple tools and mechanisms that have been created by people to solve this issue are just as real and solving the issue brings what comes first on the market: profit. And profit is a strong temptation.

On the contrary, what turned out to be very much imaginary is the idea that if we encounter a situation resembling a market failure, all it takes is political intervention. Not all politicians belong amongst the most skilled and diligent common-good-seekers. Their endeavors often result in wealth for a few chosen ones. Take, for example, "Taxi Kings".

All these variables (gravity of market failure, human creativity when finding a solution or the (in)capability of politicians) transform as time passes. One of the reasons behind such transformations is new technologies. The way in which technologies, mainly the internet, have been transforming the issue of information asymmetry over the last decades is precisely what we are going to talk about in the following part.

2. HOW A YOUNG CIVIL ENGINEER ALMOST GOT RICH, BUT ONLY MANAGED TO SAVE SOME MONEY

When I finished primary school, I continued my studies at a secondary technical school of civil engineering. This meant I had to take a four-mile-long bus ride on public transport from my neighborhood to the city center. As I waited for the bus holding my ticket, I would notice many cars going in the same direction I was headed. Practically all of them had at least one free seat and in most cases, the driver was alone in the vehicle. I spent my time thinking about how many of them would eventually pass my school. And would anybody be willing to give me a ride if they knew where I was heading? Back then, a student ticket cost six Slovak crowns, so I told myself that I would pay maximum 5 crowns for such ride. I did not care about comfort – I wanted to earn money by saving it. I suppose it was as early as then that the economist imprisoned in the body of a young civil engineer started to manifest himself. Unfortunately, I did not manage to rake in the potential profit that was passing before my eyes every day.

I imagined different coordination schemes of putting people together in cars with passengers waiting at bus stops. I remember to this day the best idea I came up with: we could create a big computer where all passengers enter where and when they want to go the following day and when they want to return. The computer would then generate results – travel plans for each person – in order to prevent two people from going in two half-empty cars to the same place or not pick up a passenger going their direction from a bus stop – just like me.*

Later, when I started university, I had to use inter-city transport. The chances that I would stop a car going in the same direction got significantly lower, but the new city had a new problem ready for me: I had nowhere to live. Sixty miles wasn't enough for me to get a room in the university dorm but it was too long a distance for a daily commute.

During the first year, I solved the problem by sharing a flat with some friends with whom I shared a similar faith. But in the following years, I managed to optimize the time I spent at the faculty and I did not need to stay over more than one, maximum two nights per week. My heart broke at the thought of spending several thousand crowns to rent a place that I only used a few nights per month. Paying for a hotel room would amount to pretty much the same, so I decided to start commuting.

My classmates quickly gave me the nickname of a "distance-learner" and it turned out that commuting had its unintended positive consequences. The boredom it often led to made me start to deeply contemplate the economics books and articles I was reading. Every time I left the city, in the distance I saw a big neighborhood with tens of thousands of inhabitants. I was sure that there were at least a few people – pensioners, families whose children left home to study in my home town, who would be willing to let me stay over the night for a small fee. They could get some extra money and I would save on accommodation. This time I did not manage to solve the problem either but I started to get an idea of why I was failing repeatedly – and that was some progress.

One day when I was going home, I came across a legendary article written by Nobel Laureate Ronald Coase under the title "The Nature of the Firm". It is still one of the most frequently quoted articles in economics and written in very understandable language that can be understood even by a curious layman. Dear reader, I hope I have sufficiently stirred your interest and that you will look it up

---

* An experienced reader will, of course, immediately notice the flaws in such a solution. How do we fix the problem with transferring information from several places to a centralized computer? How do we coordinate constant updates and assessments of new decisions and the corresponding changes in the plan? And what if people don't like to share their car or they only want specific types of passengers? Who would operate this computer and why would they do it? And so, the idea only remained in my imagination. The closest anybody got to using my idea was in Cuba, where the so-called Amarillo-vía (state employees in yellow uniforms) stopped passing cars and assigned them passengers who wanted to go the same way. A similar system used to be common until recently in St Petersburg.

too. If you are still hesitant, let me add that Coase wrote it when he was 21 and got the Nobel Prize for it almost six decades later.

What was so genius about the article then? First, Coase asked himself the right question and second, he looked around. He wondered why companies existed if the market was so efficient. In other words, why couldn't we meet at a marketplace each morning where entrepreneurs can buy all activities and services from people for market prices? These prices would ensure that everybody performs their specific activities as long as it is efficiently possible. Everybody would follow the prices and their own interests and the invisible hand of the market would ensure that everything will just click at a minimum cost. Why don't we live in a world where an entrepreneur rents a warehouseman when he realizes he needs to store his stock in the morning? Why do we see big companies that resemble islands of socialism – islands of central planning without prices but with commands and bureaucracy and arbitrary hands of managers instead of the efficient invisible hand of the market? Entrepreneurs would rather rent the services of a warehouseman for eight hours per day five days a week, even if the warehouseman will not always have work to do or if there will be many unnecessary job positions.

In the days when Coase wrote this article, few economists asked themselves these questions and they looked at companies like black boxes where input somehow transformed into output. In economics textbooks, a company would look like a graphically displayed cost function.

The answer came to Coase during his internships at various U.S. companies. He came to the realization that market transactions come at certain costs. The market is not a perfect place where everybody knows everything immediately, where deals are made easily and cheating and disappointment don't exist. If we look at the reality, we see that there are some costs to the functioning of the market and if we create a company, we suppress the market and save these costs. All it takes is to replace a decentralized decision-making system with a hierarchical one, where the fuel doesn't come in the form of supply and demand but rather in that of orders and compliance.

In that case, why doesn't the entire world work as one big post office? This was, after all, Lenin's idea and the crazy dream of many past and present socialists. It is because the internal operation of a company has costs that appear at the point when a company starts to employ hundreds, thousands, or even tens of thousands of persons.

The great contribution Coase made consisted in pointing out a new type of cost – transaction costs he himself referred to as the costs of using the price mechanism. This is how he explained them:

"In order to carry out a market transaction, it is necessary to discover who it is that one wishes to deal with, to inform people that one wishes to deal and on what terms, to conduct negotiations leading up to a bargain, to draw up a contract, to

undertake the inspection needed to make sure that the terms of the contract are being observed, and so on."

It was precisely these costs that prevented me from finding accommodation for one or two nights per week in that neighborhood and made it impossible for me to get a ride to school from that bus stop. Although there was obviously room for gaining profit and reaching a win-win deal in both situations, the wheels of a voluntary exchange were not turning because they were hindered by transaction costs that Coase described.

We simply did not know about each other and even if we had known, we would have had to meet somehow to make a deal and then trust each other that later everyone involved would stick to everything we agreed on.

In order for me to better remember the concept of transaction costs, I made up a mnemonic tool to define them. I classified them into three types:

- discovering
- deal-making
- doing it right (developing trust)

Or three Ds, if you will. In Coase' article, you can read that the level of these costs determined the extent to which companies would grow, what they could manage to do on their own with the help of their in-house staff and what they would have to outsource or, in other words, buy on the market.

Transaction costs don't only influence the actions taken by companies and the lives of broke students trying to save a buck. In the following chapter, I will also explain the impact this theory had on public goods (in the second chapter I refer to them as "organization costs").

Transaction costs represent what physics would aptly label as friction because of how they obstruct the smooth functioning of the market as a whole. Historically, the mechanisms that most obviously decrease transaction costs (apart from technology) are social institutions — a set of formal and informal rules that form our interactions. I would even venture to say that if we study them deeper, we will discover that many institutions helped to lower transaction costs. It is what their adaptive advantage in cultural evolution consisted of.

Private ownership has been one of the most successful institutions enabling transactions. In the absence of at least an implicit agreement that A is mine and B is yours, it is difficult to exchange A for B. Without that, many mutually beneficial transactions will never be carried out in the world.

Religion used to play (and undoubtedly continues to play in some places) a similar role – it has an extensive set of rules (thou shalt not steal, commit adultery, kill…) and in charge of their compliance is a perfect omniscient but most importantly, punishing God.[18] In the 9th and 10th centuries, Islam helped merchants in North Africa lower their transaction costs[19] and Judaism fulfilled the same function for Maghreb merchants in the Mediterranean.[20] Coffee and coffee houses played a similar role in establishing financial stock exchanges and first insurance companies (we will talk about it more in the upcoming sections of this chapter).

Money has been another key transaction-costs-lowering institution. Thanks to money we no longer need to rely on a rare state referred to by economists as the "double coincidence of wants". Let me illustrate it with an example: if I bake bread and you make shoes, an exchange can only happen if you are currently hungry and I have a hole in my loafers. In this case, we can simply exchange X amount of bread for Y pairs of shoes. But if I have money, I can buy shoes even when the shoemaker is not hungry. I can pay him with money and he can use it to buy something else.

Economist and Nobel laureate Douglass North once said that no matter what the question is, the answer will always be transaction costs[21], and the truth is that apart from all that has been described, transaction costs also influence consumers' decision-making. More specifically, decisions about whether to buy something or just rent it from someone. Transaction costs equally impact the owners of various assets when they decide whether to keep them unused or rent them to somebody.

In reality, you don't necessarily want to own things so much as you want to use the services they provide you with. I, for example, don't desire to have a drill at home but I want to be able to make a hole in the wall every time my wife decides to hang a new painting. Similarly, I don't need to own a car but I want to be able to get a ride to the gym and back every time my baby takes a nap. So far, in present days, the simplest and also the cheapest way of drilling holes and getting a ride was to own a drill and a car.[22]

But this was not always the case. Most people may not realize this, but our not so ancient ancestors were much poorer than we are. The possibility to "buy and own" was not as common as it is today. People lived in smaller villages and settlements where everyone knew everyone. So, as much as the possibility to buy was unavailable, it was common to exchange and put things to common use or, in other words, "share" them, be it within individual villages or multi-generational houses. A household represents the basic sharing unit.

As society became richer, people moved to bigger towns that were more anonymous. Back then, every young family desired an independent home, so the importance of buying and owning property started to gradually increase. Nowadays, the tables are slowly beginning to turn because the accumulation of new technologies such as the internet, GPS or smartphones has made people start sharing more again. This new trend got the name of sharing economy.

Think of sharing economy as kind of a virtual marketplace where people who have something to offer meet those who are interested in using it. For instance, people could simply create an account in a specific application that focuses on personal transport in a specific city or on accommodation in unoccupied rooms and the application then helps lower all three components of transaction costs –

our three Ds: people discovering each other, the deal-making process, and doing things right – complying with the agreed conditions.*

If I was a high school student waiting at a bus stop today, I could create an account on the UberPool platform and join somebody who passes my school on the way to work. University students can now use Airbnb to find a family who lives near the university and who is happy to rent them a free room a couple of times per month. Currently, these are the two biggest sharing economy platforms used by hundreds of millions of people around the world and if we add up their value, we get more than $100 billion.

In my student years, it never occurred to me to create something this genius despite having been aware of practically all technologies necessary for running such platforms. It would have been enough to put the pieces together, which is basically what genius entrepreneurs do.

I ended up solving my problem of spending the night in my university town during my PhD studies by bringing an old collapsible armchair into my office and when my colleagues left work in late afternoon, my office became my bedroom. I used to be proud of this but now I regret not coming up with Airbnb instead.

Marx would be delighted with sharing economy

Employment as most people know it today is not the "natural state of things". The organization of labor changed many times over the course of history. It was different in the times of hunters and gatherers, ancient towns, in medieval kingdoms and because of technological advances, another different form started to arise in the beginning of the 19th century. It was precisely this change in labor organization that motivated Karl Marx's intellectual reflections. If we wanted to summarize one of his conclusions in a word, it would be alienation: the alienation of a person from work in capitalism. Marx mentions the following to explain this alienation:

"First, the fact that labor is external to the worker, i.e., it does not belong to his intrinsic nature; that in his work, therefore, he does not affirm himself but deny himself, does not feel content but unhappy, does not develop freely his physical and mental energy but mortifies his body and ruins his mind. The worker therefore only feels himself outside his work, and in his work feels outside himself. He feels at home when he is not working, and when he is working, he does not feel at home. His work is therefore not voluntary but coerced; it is forced labor. It is therefore not the satisfaction of a need; it is merely a means to satisfy needs external to it. Its alien char-

---

* Finding a life partner is another area where high transaction costs cause significant problems and where new technologies have brought means of lowering them.

acter emerges clearly in the fact as soon as no physical or other compulsion exists, labor is shunned like a plague."

Why did people become estranged from their work? Even though Marx used the expression "forced labor", employers did not actually stand in front of factories and threaten people in order to make them come in. People went there on their own accord. What changed for them to start voluntarily filling up factories? The simple answer would be the start of the industrial revolution. In economic terms, we would say high specialization and economy of scale. These two phenomena started to motivate people to exchange their freedom to decide what they will do each day and every hour for money and to commit to something we now call the "work week". Why did employers insist on a work week? Well, the answer would again be: transaction costs.

It would be too costly for a factory owner to hope to buy enough "work services" for each of his machines every morning. He would be nervously biting his finger nails wondering whether the two guys who worked all day yesterday would also show up the next morning. They might get a better offer the following day or simply decide they don't feel like working.

Economically speaking, there is a complementary relationship between work and capital and also among different workers. If an employer has stable employees who are coordinated at a specific time, they can produce products and services more efficiently. They save transaction costs, which enable them to offer higher wages to his workers that serve as a compensation for their "loss of freedom". If Marx could see today's Western European wage workers and what the "alienation of work" resulted in, he would not believe his own eyes – this is definitely not how he imagined the result of exploitation.

The world is changing. Sharing economy sells the lowering of transaction costs even for matching work supply with demand. And so, the so-called gig economy becomes more and more common.

It isn't a breakthrough – gigs have always been present. Lowered transaction costs merely expand the areas and extent of activities you can do on a gig basis. Take, for instance, platforms like TaskRabbit through which you can find someone to build your furniture, mow your lawn, cut your trees, install your washing machine, repair your dishwasher or pack your things before moving your house. Globally, you can find specialized platforms: for shopping (Shipt), delivery and mail services (Postmates or Flex by Amazon), domestic chores (Handy), taking dogs for a walk (Dogvacay), and so on. These platforms can offer you some truly interesting gigs, such as changing lightbulbs, building a puzzle, writing an article for an Alaskan newspaper, decorating a hall for a Christmas party or writing a best man's speech.[23]

In a certain sense, sharing economy means going back to the times before the Industrial Revolution, when work was not organized into permanent employment contracts. In other words, reliving the times before capitalism alienated people from work. This shift literally fulfills Marx's words where it is "possible for me to do one thing today and another thing tomorrow, to hunt in the morning, fish in the afternoon, rear cattle in the evening, criticize after dinner, just as I have a mind, without ever becoming hunter, fisherman, herdsman or critic." Only it was not brought by communist comrades but by capitalism and entrepreneurs.

Work within sharing economy doesn't have to suit everyone, just like not everyone is happy with a typical employment contract. Sharing economy doesn't force anybody to do anything but it offers an extra possibility. Take, for example, a woman on maternity leave who needs to earn some extra cash, a starting entrepreneur who needs to compensate their initial absence of income, a pensioner who lost touch with people, a teacher who wants to afford a luxurious summer holiday or the unemployed who are still searching for their dream jobs.

These are not just merely hypothetical examples; these are real people I met when I started to use sharing economy as a customer. Apart from anecdotal evidence, now there are also empirical studies which confirm what has been said earlier in this chapter. People used sharing economy mostly to compensate a temporary absence of income.* It also tends to serve different marginalized groups well, including immigrants.[24] Those who use sharing economy mostly value its flexibility and the possibility to work as much as they want without having a boss telling them what to do.**

Bosses are precisely those who should be most worried by the arrival of sharing economy because platforms often substitute for various managerial positions. Thanks to application software, everything is automated and there is no need for an HR department, task management and regular surveillance of employees' work. The application takes care of everything and the tasks are delegated to algorithms or individual platform users.

This is also one of the competitive advantages of platforms like Uber, Lyft or Bolt in comparison with traditional taxi services. Organization costs slow the growth of traditional taxi services which is why they often only operate on a local level. For example, in the U.S. there are approximately

---

* One US study has shown that sharing economy is used by workers mainly in order to cover a drop in their income, for example, when they are in between jobs.[A2]

** Economists from Princeton analyzed the US labor market on the Uber platform and they concluded that what workers appreciate the most about sharing economy is flexibility. As much as 87% of drivers stated that their reason for working within sharing economy is being able to be their own boss and work whenever they want. Three quarters of drivers would rather have a flexible job than a typical full-time job with employee benefits. In fact, more than two thirds of drivers have other jobs in addition to Uber and half of all drivers spend less than 16 hours per week working via Uber.[A3]

6,300 taxi companies who manage about 170 thousand taxis. Over 80% of these companies own only 1-50 taxis and only 6% percent own more than 100 vehicles. The vast majority of taxi drivers (almost 90%) work as independent contractors within these companies – they are not employees.

Apart from taxi drivers, these thousands of companies employ multiple levels of managers, dispatchers, admin workers and accountants. In the world of online platforms, all of these jobs are replaced with software. And that means lower prices for customers. What is more, the online world is not exempt to innovation – Lyft beat Uber at lowering costs and they even delegated the recruitment of new drivers to experienced drivers with excellent ratings.

Not everyone is thrilled with the new flexibility that comes with working via sharing economy platforms, which is natural. However, it's strange that those who decided to work this way and willingly accepted all the related conditions complain too. They forfeit the regulations and obligations connected with a typical employment contract. At the same time, they want the platform to guarantee minimum wage, pay their sick leave and they also want some paid leave, compulsory breaks and other social benefits. These dissatisfied individuals were anything but idle and sued the platforms in the U.K., California, New York, Texas and even in Nigeria.

I would recommend these people submit their requirements to a true-false test. It could look something like this: they find a full-time job and take a good look at their employer's facial expression when they announce that next week they will come to work only when they feel like it and also, they will only work as much as they want to. I am guessing their boss's expression is not going to be pleasant. But this is exactly what they are doing to sharing economy platforms – only the other way around. They feel platforms should employ people but they cannot tell them when, where and how much they should work.

From the platforms' point of view, it makes no sense. And it doesn't make sense from the platform workers' point of view either. It is always just a loud minority of workers who sue platforms. In London, it was only several drivers that sued Uber. The thing is that the court not only decides on their situations, but potentially also on the remaining 40 thousand drivers who did not sue Uber and who seem to be content with the current state of things (which can be backed up by numerous studies). These drivers freely decided to start working for Uber under the given conditions and if they don't like them, they can try the competition, do a different job or get a fulltime job.

However, if the loud minority manages to push their requirements through, the remaining majority will very likely lose the opportunity to earn extra money because the functioning of sharing economy platforms will have to change. If platforms provide their workers with minimum wage and various social benefits including paid leave, they will have to establish a minimum number of working hours or performance norms and also dictate who should work where, when and how much. Let's also factor in the necessary recruitment, managerial and supervisory functions and we are back to traditional employers. Gig – workers would become employees which would completely erase the business model behind platforms and all the advantages of the auto-coordination of workers via apps and internet would be lost.

Also, the platform would have to ensure that drivers would work for it exclusively. This would destroy one of the biggest advantages of sharing economy – the intense competitive struggle for workers. Today you can install several platform apps and choose who you will work for at a particular moment according to what is most beneficial for you. This is why platforms need to compete for their workers, which is what they are doing through offering different bonuses and benefits.

There is no doubt that people who are trying to fight for "employees' rights" on sharing economy platforms mean well for themselves and for the rest of the workers too. The problem is that their requirements are based on the faith in free lunches for everybody promised by a politicians and officials. They think that if we increase wages and establish social benefits for workers today, the world will be the same tomorrow, only workers will be doing better.

Even if we put the above-mentioned problems connected with the misunderstanding of the business model aside, politicians are not able to use laws to increase platform workers' productivity and thus increase their paychecks. Imagine if politicians or courts forced platforms to pay for their drivers' fuel. Is there really anybody who thinks drivers would suddenly start to earn more? Does anyone believe that Uber and Lyft would in such case not increase their fees to make up for the fuel costs? In reality, drivers' income would probably even go down because people would start using inefficient cars in a more inefficient way just because they could have their costs reimbursed. There is no such thing as free lunch.

Labor code, minimum wage and social benefits may have had their theoretical purpose when there was only one big employer in a region and it was too costly for the employees to go to competition in a different region. Today, we are only a couple of clicks away from going to the competition. We can even have several "employers" at a time. Broad labor laws are not the best social protection for workers, but having many possibilities for employment is. That is exactly what sharing economy brings. Competition for platform workers makes labor laws an obsolete way of providing protection and social benefits for workers.

It is interesting to observe today's socialists fighting against the changes which shift work towards the state that Marx considered natural and how they, on the contrary, try to stick to the employment system based on the alienation of work. Left-wing politicians therefore de-facto become conservatives who refuse a change which would lead to more freedom of workers from bosses, entrepreneurs and capital.

The current trend triggered by sharing economy may in the end completely change the nature of many professions. And it wion'thappen as the result of conscious planning but, as I mentioned in the beginning, rather as adaptation to the change in economic conditions and transaction costs. Today's form of employment is not a historical necessity. Michael Munger even considers the thought that people in the future would see 20th century employment as we now see medieval servitude. People are no longer tied to a piece of land for their lifetime, but they are often tied to their employer. This is changing. Let us see how long the legislative straight jacket of employment will resist new technologies and economic pressure.

2.1 SHARING DOESN'T ALWAYS EQUAL SHARING ECONOMY AND SHARING ECONOMY DOESN'T ALWAYS HAVE TO BE ABOUT SHARING

How would we define sharing economy? Unfortunately, there is no general consensus on the matter and there is a lot of debate about what falls under sharing economy and what does not. This dispute is not merely an academic exercise; there is a normative tint to it. So, l have decided to contribute a few paragraphs to the debate on the definition of sharing economy while hoping not to scare off those readers who, just like me, have had their share of intense and negative experience with reading and memorizing definitions at school.

Some people define sharing economy in quite a narrow sense. They are of the opinion that true sharing happens only when people share things – meaning they exchange them and put them to common use without expecting anything in return and without the involvement of money. They say Uber and Airbnb are not about sharing but rather about earning money and that these platforms just stole the label of sharing economy to take advantage of the positive connotations of the term to make profit.

There are also those, who say sharing economy is basically "neoliberalism on steroids", which is how they try to associate it with negative connotations (even though this had quite the opposite effect on me and, I dare say, I am probably not alone).[25] They think that sharing economy is no longer what it used to be in its beginnings and they call for a radical purification of the term.[26]

Others, on the contrary, have quite a broad definition for sharing economy. Typical examples of these are articles about the growth of the sharing economy sector in China. However, when we look closely, we can see that their authors talk about companies who bought thousands or hundreds of thousands of bicycles, balls, sleeping capsules or umbrellas to distribute them to cities and connect them to mobile applications. Another such example would be that of WeWork – a platform labelled as a sharing economy platform by Forbes magazine – which rents office spaces, modifies them and rents them to startups.[27]

Though it isn't a golden rule that the truth is somewhere in the middle and it is a widely overused statement, when it comes to defining sharing economy, I would place myself somewhere between these two approaches. I consider the first one to be too narrow and the second one to be too broad, as you might have figured out when I described them as such to begin with.

What bothers me with the first approach is that it excludes money from the equation of human cooperation as if it was something that would "stain" it. When I travel with my family, I actually prefer to choose accommodation from people who do it for money – they share their home in order to earn something extra, so I know that I can expect a certain level of service while people who do it "just like that", for free, raise my suspicion.

Plus, money is a great transaction cost lowering tool. If Uber and Airbnb had ruled out money from their business model, we would not be talking about them today because they would either not exist or they would be negligible. An example of such "non-existence" is Couchsurfing, which is about "true sharing" – with no money involved. Sharing economy is therefore not only a question of pure sharing; it involves rent, exchange, cooperation or provision of services. To put it simply, it is also a question of earning some extra money.

Another problem of the first approach is that it mistakes an incorrect prediction for a normative ideal. When sharing economy came around in 2010, its supporters labeled it as a new movement and they embellished it with adjectives such as democratic, egalitarian, non-hierarchical, uplifting for the human soul, social and anti-consumerist.[28] However, the sharing economy industry took a slightly different route and gave rise to startups worth billions where people could earn some extra money or pay for services. The supporters of the "true-sharing-approach" did not simply admit their predictions were wrong but turned them into normative ideals so that they could criticize the real world for not being in line with their personal values.

As for the second definition, I don't like the idea of companies whose business model was working even before the term sharing economy started to be used, to be labelled as such. Indeed, buying a lot of cars or electric drills and renting them can be considered a form of sharing, but I think this cannot be considered sharing economy only because you put a mobile app between buying and renting.

So, according to which criteria would I personally define sharing economy? What is the defining quality? It is the activation of unused resources through lowering transaction costs. For me, a sharing economy platform is one that converts consumer goods, that were formerly being used only a couple of hours per day (car, house, electric drill and during free time), into capital goods that generate value. An empty room in a house is therefore no longer a mere liability that needs heating but an asset that generates income. There is nothing wrong with improving traditional business models using various platforms and the internet. However, the sharing economy innovation happens when you convert an empty garage into a storage space for your neighbors via Spacer.

Of course, Uber or Airbnb are generally not against you buying a car or a house for the purpose of generating income (which no longer makes it an activation of unused resources), but, in reality, the vast majority of Airbnb hosts own only one property and most Uber drivers work more or less occasionally. That is why, in my way of seeing things, Airbnb and Uber are without a doubt sharing economy platforms.

I am not saying my definition is better than the two previous ones because definitions are always arbitrary. The important thing is for definitions to overlap in human minds so that we know what we are talking about when we talk about sharing economy. If I was an important linguistic authority and had influence on the development of this aspect of cultural evolution, perhaps I would choose a more fitting name than sharing economy, like, matching economy – in the sense of matching supply and demand through an internet platform. But at the end of the day, it doesn't matter what things are called and how they are defined. What matters is that this new phenomenon with its added value continues to develop without being banned.

Well, enough with the definitions – let's now take a look at how the world actually works.

2.2 WHAT DID SHARING ECONOMY BRING?

As I have already indicated, the main benefit of sharing economy is that it lowers transaction costs. But that is not all. Sharing economy platforms have learned how to sell the lowering of transaction costs.[29]

The short-term accommodation platform Airbnb has passed the milestone of three million offers in 2017, which is more than the five biggest hotel chains combined. It also managed to do it without owning hotels! The only thing Airbnb owns is a virtual infrastructure for the lowering of transaction costs. Uber is in a similar situation – it has the biggest number of drivers globally (three million) without owning practically any cars. Therefore, both platforms offer the services of physical capital with a value of billions of dollars – none of which they had to buy. They merely revived what already exists.

The arrival of sharing economy showed ordinary people that in fact, they have a lot more capital and work opportunities than they thought. Sharing economy platforms managed to turn consumer goods that were lying abandoned during most of their life cycle into valuable assets and thus satisfy other people's needs. Put simply, they increased the amount of capital in the economy even though it cannot be captured by any statistics. The results are market expansion with all consumer goods and services and growing competition. This means greater well-being, wider selection for consumers, more innovation, higher differentiation of products and higher specialization and efficiency on the side of the supply.

From an economic point of view, sharing economy is a step closer to what economists consider to be the Holy Grail – the Pareto optimality. It is a state where all mutually beneficial transactions are carried out and there is no more room left in society for a change that would help at least one person without harming anybody.

Some economists might therefore view sharing economy as a small miracle. Before it made its appearance, they could not even begin to imagine the presence of so many potential (yet never realized) mutually beneficial exchanges. Otherwise they would have to label it "market failure" and start thinking about state intervention. However, the market has once again surpassed the imagination of economists and solved the problem before they even managed to identify it.

Sharing economy makes it possible to serve free lunch without cooking anything new. The best way of appreciating its added value is to imagine a world without it. Imagine two parallel worlds in 2005. In one world, entrepreneurs would in a few years' time, invent sharing economy platforms and in the other one, they would not (or they would be banned as soon as the state would figure it out – which is not a complete dystopia as we will see further on in this chapter).

Physically, both of these worlds would have the same number of cars, houses and drills. The difference is that in one world, the number of people who benefit from all of these material goods changes. To put it differently, the overall well-being of this world would change while there would be the same number of physical objects.* Sharing economy would transform the state of these things from a less meaningful use (a drill lying in a garage cabinet) into more meaningful ones (a drill in the hands of a neighbor who happens to need it). An empty room where children used to live when they were still at home could now serve a university student who needs a place to sleep a couple of nights per month.

As I have already said, sharing is nothing new in human history.[30] In the past, people were more pushed to it by poverty and social closeness. Today, sharing economy makes it possible to expand the benefits of mutual exchanges even to an anonymous metropolis filled with strangers who have never met, who may not even be from the same continent or speak the same language. Sharing economy helps create global villages and thus change informal norms and patterns of behavior our mothers were trying to instill into us since our early childhood.

Ten years ago, nobody would even think that it would soon be completely normal and common to let a stranger into one's house or spend a night at a stranger's house. If we were to translate our mothers' warnings: "Never get into a stranger's car!", into economic language, we would arrive at the concept we already know – information asymmetry. We simply don't know whether the driver is an honest man seeking to earn some extra money or a nighthawk with dishonest inten-

---

* After some time, these worlds would probably start to differ physically as well. In the world of functional sharing economy, the demand for mass production will decrease – not every household is going to need to buy a drill or a lawn-mower. Also, the demand for more quality and long-lasting products will increase.

tions. People even used to pay to keep strangers away from their homes. Thanks to sharing economy, today we are paid for letting them in.

Sharing economy thus changes our fossilized ideas about what is normal and what is not. Actually, one of the biggest problems of Airbnb founders was to convince investors to invest in their first platforms. Investors just found it difficult to believe in the idea that sharing economy could manage to reach what it has today. These things were unimaginable before.

> **What does a taxi driver have in common with an encyclopedia writer and what does Airbnb have in common with a cruise ship?**

Some people doubt the added value of sharing economy platforms. They blame Uber that they do the exact same thing as taxis, only illegally. You will read more about breaking the law in the following part of this chapter. Now, I would like to show you the main difference between Uber – a sharing economy platform – and traditional taxi services that may even have their own application (just like Curb) but don't fall under the sharing economy category.

First of all, the difference can be found in the drivers' point of view. Uber offers something no one did before: anybody who has a car and some spare time can basically become a transport service provider overnight and earn some additional income. Uber activated unused work capacity by providing a platform for people to work in their free time. If you need money today, you can become an Uber driver tomorrow, the day after tomorrow you can work instead of watching evening TV, you earn what you need and you can stop it the day after. As long as you offer good quality services that are convenient for your customers and yourself.

Actually, most Uber drivers work less than 10-15 hours per week via the platform and 68% of them stop in less than six months.[31] This is the added value of Uber that was impossible before sharing economy appeared. If you don't believe me, try and pull over next to a young lady and ask her if she needs a lift since you have some free time and need some extra money. In the best-case scenario, you will get no extra money, in the worse one you will have to explain your proposal to the police.

The flexibility of sharing economy also makes the supply of Uber drivers slightly "inflatable".* People in cities need a lift in specific times and at specific spots, such as a Friday night ride downtown and back. Employed taxi

---

* Taxi apps such as Curb require a taxi license from their drivers. Obtaining it and fulfilling all the related conditions takes months and costs hundreds of euros. In addition, taxi drivers often have inflexible contracts with dispatch services. These companies usually ask drivers to pay a fixed daily fee. Given these conditions, taxi drivers are motivated to work as many hours as possible in order to lower their average daily costs. Contrary to traditional taxis, sharing economy platforms ask for

drivers are unable to cover these rush hours purely because of the nature of their work. If there were enough drivers to cover such situations, it would mean that during the week when the demand is lower, there would be too many of them and there would be nobody they could give a ride to. If we turn it upside down, the same logic will apply: if there are to be just enough taxi drivers to cover the demand during the week, it is understandable that there will not be enough of them during rush hours. The "inflatable" Uber has tackled the issue and they can not only easily get new drivers but also convince registered drivers that it is time to get behind the steering wheel.

To do this, apply the so called "surge pricing" – a dynamic mechanism of price adaptation according to current supply and demand. In 2014, one unfortunate event in New York put surge pricing to the test when due to technical issues, it stopped working for 26 minutes. This created room for a "natural experiment" which enabled economists to examine what happens to supply and demand once prices freeze.

Before the technical issue, there was a 100% rate of completed customer requests. Each customer got where they needed to go. But when the algorithm broke and the prices stopped reacting, the rate got under 25%. This is how customers in New York got to experience socialism for a few minutes and the queuing that comes with it.[32] Surge pricing works similarly when it starts to rain. In New York, the number of Uber rides goes up by 25%, while that of taxi rides only increase by 4%. Most people don't feel like working when the weather is nasty, but they might if somebody is willing to pay a few percent extra like Uber does.[33]

Taxi drivers are now unlucky because their job can suddenly be done by everyone in their free time without becoming a taxi driver: a pensioner who can no longer sleep in the morning, a mum on maternity leave who wants to get some air, a teacher who needs some extra money, an entrepreneur who needs to pay for the initial costs of his new business. Thanks to the platforms, all these people can now do what taxi drivers used to do as a full-time job in their free time, and they are willing to do it cheaper because they already own a car. All they need is some extra pocket money (to cover marginal costs instead of average ones).

Something similar already happened in the past to some other professions. Of course, this is very unpleasant – I myself would hate to wake up one morning only to discover that there is a new app where people can share their clever economic insights in the evening. Even though I have to say that such platform already exists, it is called "pub" (cafeteria) and instead of the internet, people are connected by beer (coffee).

But seriously, the last time this happened, it happened to encyclopedists. Their important work was substituted by millions of people who, in their

---

a fee that is in proportion with daily earnings, which makes them avoid such problems. Now we know that drivers from such platforms appreciate this flexibility.[A4]

free time and without getting paid, started to co-create the biggest encyclopedia in the world: Wikipedia. Wikipedia has more than 44 million pages today. In comparison, the 15th edition of the most famous encyclopedia Britannica has "only" 32 thousand pages. Encyclopedia authors are lucky enough that their work doesn't need to undergo the test of the consumers' willingness to pay. Their wages are often paid from state budgets and the demand for their work is generated by officials and politicians. Taxi drivers, however, are unlikely to share their destiny.

Those who share a similar fate with encyclopedists are traditional media: TV, radio stations and newspapers. Amateur vloggers, podcasters and bloggers became their competition. These days, presenters lose their viewers to youtubers and journalists lose their readers to bloggers. People have replaced prearranged TV reality shows with the authentic reality show they can observe on Facebook, Twitter or Instagram.

The same arguments and counter-arguments that apply for Uber can be applied to Airbnb. Airbnb activates unused accommodation resources, such as an empty room, cabin or house. Just like Uber, Airbnb's supply is also inflatable (no wonder – the initial name of the platform was Airbed and Breakfast). It helps provide accommodation during different events, like conferences, concerts or Olympic games, or simply put: when the demand for accommodation in a certain area goes up rapidly.

Until recently, the inflatable supply in port cities was ensured by big cruise ships capable to increase the city's accommodation capacity by tens of thousands of beds. This was the case of the Olympic games in Barcelona (1992) or in Athens (2004). But during the Summer Olympics in London (2012) and in Rio de Janeiro (2016), it was Airbnb who catered to the inflated offer of accommodation – they were even the official partner of the Rio Olympics.

Apart from new opportunities for occasional service providers who work in their free time, sharing economy also offers benefits to customers. It gives them the option to choose from a bigger palette of services which are often of better quality. Plus, sharing economy services are cheaper than those offered by traditional service providers. This applies mostly to the two biggest industries: accommodation and transport.

Sharing economy platforms can afford low prices simply because they are using capital which would otherwise not be used. Nobody had to build a new hotel to provide accommodation through Airbnb the same as nobody had to buy a new car to work for Uber. Economically speaking, professional service providers have average costs which also include fixed costs such as purchasing a hotel or a vehicle. Sharing economy service providers only have marginal costs: they bought their car and house for their personal use.

In addition, sharing economy is not trying to impress the average customer. While you cannot beat traditional providers when it comes to standardized services, sharing economy offers uniqueness. For example, via Airbnb you can spend a night at some very interesting places – be it a castle, treehouse, igloo, tent or a cave. When it comes to sharing economy travel services, one can chose from several levels (you want to travel alone or with someone, you need more comfort or you don't care about it). Also, on each platform you meet new people from various different areas of expertise – teachers, investors, entrepreneurs, pensioners.

What is the added value of sharing economy? It depends whom you ask. An economist will tell you that sharing economy gets you closer to the production-possibility frontier. A philosopher will tell you about the spreading of peaceful cooperation among people in the world. An ecologist will appreciate the better use of available resources, less production and therefore less damage to the environment. An ordinary person will be happy about having a flexible opportunity to earn some extra money and also better and cheaper services. To put it simply, sharing economy increases the well-being of society.

But if we want to truly understand its added value, we have to ask what prevented us from getting into a stranger's car before sharing economy came.

2.3 WHY ARE ECONOMISTS SO EXCITED ABOUT SHARING ECONOMY?

"Many of these (sharing economy) companies have us engaging in behaviors that would have seemed foolhardy as recently as five years ago." [34]

Janos Tanz

We already know that the innovative aspect of sharing economy is that it can sell the lowering of transaction costs. We also know that transaction costs are the costs connected with the three Ds: discovering, deal-making, and doing it right (developing trust). This part will explore the individual Ds in more detail and we will talk about why sharing economy makes economists so excited. We will also have a look at what all of this has in common with information asymmetry.

Sharing economy sells the lowering of transaction costs: discovering, deal-making, doing-it right and developing trust.

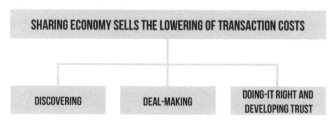

SHARING ECONOMY AND INFORMATION ASYMMETRY
HOW A YOUNG CIVIL ENGINEER ALMOST GOT RICH, BUT ONLY MANAGED TO SAVE SOME MONEY

DISCOVERING

The first step to any transaction is discovering and obtaining information about a potential partner. There are many mutually beneficial transactions that never take place just because demand has not discovered supply and vice versa. This problem is as old as society itself and the solutions are too. In addition, this is not only an issue for business interactions – it concerns romantic ones too. One traditional solution for lowering the costs of discovering romantic partners is a night club or a disco which connects single people.

Before Uber and Lyft entered the scene, traditional taxi drivers used to visually differentiate their vehicles from others (yellow in the U.S. and black in the U.K.), they had their fixed spots (e.g., in front of airports or train stations) and a dispatcher would coordinate them via walkie-talkie. Traditionally, customers called them with a wave of a hand or by dialing the taxi company number, but Uber and Lyft have significantly upgraded these traditions.

Now a platform driver looks at a map on their cellphone display and it indicates their route straight to the customer, who only a few seconds before, used a couple of clicks to insert the address of the place they want to go to. The rest is all taken care of by algorithms and GPS navigation. Similarly, Airbnb is also simplifying the discovery process between supply and demand.

This is not the part that I find particularly interesting but it can't be denied that behind algorithm and localization services there is an enormous bit of science and if this book was written by an engineer, they would talk about it in detail. But I am an economist and the way I see it is that sharing economy "simply" brought the concept of the yellow pages on internet steroids. In fact, this is not the first time we've seen it happen.

Google existed years before sharing economy made its appearance and it lowered the costs of discovering more than any other thing or concept in the history of transaction costs. As for accommodation, remember Booking.com? It was here at least ten years before Airbnb was launched. And when it comes to taxis, before Uber, there were already other apps, such as Magic Taxi or Cabulous. After all, even the mentioned night clubs and discos were later substituted to a large extent by chat rooms and social media and today they are being replaced by platforms such as Tinder, Match.com, Grindr, or Bumble.*

---

* Tinder is interesting because it completely understood the nature of the costs involved in asking someone on a first date. These transactions are represented by information asymmetry – the one who is asking doesn't know whether the other person is also interested. Tinder has lowered these costs by enabling one party to show interest in the other party without them having to, or being able to communicate. The possibility to communicate appears when the other party reciprocates the interest based on the first party's profile picture or bio. The fact that this way of lowering information asymmetry actually works is confirmed by the stunning number of 50 million users of the app.

DEAL-MAKING

When supply and demand meet, the transaction needs to go through necessary steps to be complete. The parties involved have to agree on the conditions and the price, and then payment must take place. This is where it gets interesting for economists. Economists like to talk about prices. But that is not all, we have to go even deeper and look at transaction costs in the form of the price of pricing. To put it differently: how much it costs to agree on how much it is going to cost. Let me give you an example:

Platforms like Uber and Lyft don't make it possible for drivers and passengers to agree on the price. Pricing is centralized and left up to algorithms that adjust it according to the current situation on the market. That is why during the hostage drama in Sydney or the snowstorm in New York, prices multiplied several times. There was a huge demand and insufficient supply on the market.

Some Uber critics consider the centralized approach to be treason to sharing economy and cite examples like Blablacar, where pricing is done on the basis of a deal between the driver and the rider. However, their criticism reflects their lack of understanding of the platform's role because platforms make money by lowering transaction costs, which vary according to circumstances.

While deal-making and decentralized pricing may have their advantages, they also come at a certain cost. This is true mostly for short-distance city transport, which primarily needs to be fast and easy. An indication of this being true is the story of Sidecar – a platform who did not offer algorithm-generated pricing and left the deal-making part up to its members, and failed as result.

It seems like city people are not willing to waste their time and argue about a few cents' difference – they want readily and easily accessible means of transport. This is why after some time, Lyft also started to apply centralized pricing like Uber, and it reduced the whole process of drafting a contract and paying down to one click. Airbnb also radically lowered the transaction costs of deal-making connected with short-term rent – there is no longer any need to meet in advance or to compose, print, sign, and make copies of contracts. Everything, including payment, is now a matter of one click.

However, I don't want to overestimate sharing economy's innovation in this regard either. Apart from its ancestors who came up with it before (Booking.com), we should not forget about payment platforms such as PayPal, which also lowered the transaction costs of deal-making.

> **Uber does not determine nor is able to determine transport fares; if you don't like how much you earn, uninstall the app**

Uber drivers complain from time to time because they are not happy with how much they earn. Or, what is even more frequent, different "industry experts" start to calculate how much Uber drivers make and start to complain for them.

But these complaints reflect a misunderstanding of how Uber works and what it can and can't do. In reality, Uber has no say in how much drivers make in a specific town – all it does is find a price which clears the market. This means that there won't be a single customer on the streets who wants to get a ride but cannot find a driver, just like you won't find a driver running in circles around town in an empty car

Transport fares in a city are determined by many factors, such as functional public transport and its accessibility, cost and accessibility of parking, morning traffic jams, or number of people working in the city center. Other important factors include: population age structure, city nightlife, or number of tourists. Prices also largely depend on the unemployment rate in a city, number of job offers for low-qualification labor and how many people are willing to do them, number of car owners, etc. All of these variables impact supply and demand for transportation in a city.

When Uber comes to a new town, it starts to set up their price policy – often by trial and error (in Bratislava, for example, three different price quotes have already been tried). In its earlier stages, Uber subsidizes prices for both, drivers and customers – this is a temporary phase which aims to get a sufficient customer base in the city and teach people to use its services. After this, pricing starts to approach the market balance, meaning a price that would ensure that customers don't wait long and drivers are very busy.

Once Uber has found a price, it doesn't make any sense to change it. Not only from the point of view of efficiency, but also regarding the hourly rate of drivers since the supply of them is very elastic. This means, that every time the rate increases, they are willing to work longer (Mike, who under different circumstances would watch his favorite reality show in the evening, will get into his car and drive customers), or new drivers come to work (Ben, who was too lazy to register in the platform will finally do so and start working).

And now imagine a politician with a halo around their head, or an "industry expert" who enters the scene and decides to increase the wages of Uber drivers by 30%. What will happen next? Mike, Ben, and many other people start working through the platform. At the same time, many customers stop using it and will prefer to use public transport, go on foot, drive their own car, or simply stay at home. The result of increased drivers' rates will be that they will be less busy, it will take them longer to find a customer, and their hourly earnings will go down as a result. They may earn more per ride, but they will have way fewer rides. Plus, such political or "expert" intervention would result in fewer carried out mutually beneficial transactions (and therefore decrease the well-being in society) and at the same time, mean higher prices for customers.

A recent study has confirmed that this is not just some "naïve economic theory".[35] It showed that when Uber increased their fares, the drivers' earnings grew only temporarily and in eight weeks dropped to the original level before the increase. How can that be possible? The conclusion of the study is similar to what we explained above: drivers were less occupied and their vehicles were empty more often. It's sad news for politicians and experts but also for union activists and unhappy drivers: if you don't like your hourly rate, you just have to find work elsewhere.

There are some exceptional situations when a fare increase is due to increased demand from customers – for example, on a Friday night when many people need a ride home from the city center. In such situations, Uber uses surge pricing and it temporarily increases its fairs. In such cases, drivers do earn more because the key market conditions are temporarily changed. It is true that customers tend to complain under such circumstances but again, there is nothing they can do about it. Uber doesn't determine prices. It merely tries to find a price which is as close to the market balance as possible. The motivation for it is simple – when drivers earn more, more customers get a ride and this means more profit for Uber.

The only number Uber can modify is its own commission. Uber charges a 25% commission from the price for a ride. But it isn't as free to determine the commission rate as you might think. Its biggest U.S. competition, Lyft, charges only 20% and its European competitor, Bolt, even made it 15%. So, you can see that platforms also compete when it comes to commission.

DOING IT RIGHT AND DEVELOPING TRUST

An attentive reader has surely figured out that the third part of transaction costs is the most exciting part for economists (or at least for the author of this book). This is what is known as ex ante development of trust and doing it right ex post – complying with the agreed conditions.

All of the aforementioned ancestors of sharing economy platforms (Magic Taxi, Booking.com) or other online services (PayPal) have been focused on professional providers or traditional business and act as intermediaries between professionals and customers. But that is not true for sharing economy, which I have defined as the revival of dead capital within a peer-to-peer economy. This is why sharing economy had to work harder than its traditional competitors to push itself in the area of transaction costs.

Ordering the services of a certified taxi driver and getting into a stranger's car are two completely different things. Spending a night in a hotel is not the same as sleeping at a stranger's house because with the latter you cannot rely on traditional regulations such as inspections, brand, customer service, or a fixed company seat. It is therefore much harder to develop trust ex ante and ensure that they will comply with the agreed conditions and be on their best behavior ex post.

Before sharing economy, the absence of technology that enabled low-cost discovering and deal-making was not such a big issue in comparison with developing trust and sticking to rules and good manners. Therefore, entrepreneurs from the sharing economy area had to come up with new innovative solutions to assure both parties that the other one would not abuse their position. They had to find ways of assuring the demand that the supply is not up to no good and vice versa. In other words, they had to find solutions to the problem of information asymmetry.*

When sharing economy platforms were born, investors did not doubt they would be capable of creating sufficient "discovery" algorithms or an environment for deal-making when it comes to prices and conditions or that the platforms would be able to automatically generate the price themselves. Their concern was whether people would be willing to let strangers in.

Platforms came up with numerous tools, mechanisms, and ways of achieving that. They have built an entire trust-development infrastructure, which ensures efficient compliance and good manners. They include: rules allowing access, identity verification, cross-linking social media accounts and phone numbers, insurance for platform members, applied reputation mechanisms, the star-ranking mechanism or written evaluation, checking and filtering dangerous activities, big data analysis, conflict resolution, or establishing entire bodies which deal with inappropriate behavior. Simply put, they started to provide private regulation services, which traditionally used to be provided exclusively by the state.

Most people see Uber as a competitor of taxis or public transport. Just like most people view Airbnb as competition for hotels. In reality, sharing economy platforms, with their provision of private regulation services and attempts to find solutions to the problem of information asymmetry, started to compete with the state and its regulations. This is partly why we may observe so many conflicts between them.

The state suddenly de facto started to lose the monopoly over establishing rules and their enforcement even though de jure it still holds it tightly in its hands. After the arrival of sharing economy, we can no longer seriously believe that what we are facing is a binary choice between state regulation and no regulation because now there is a third possibility: private regulation.

---

* Different authors who write about sharing economy noticed the importance of trust. For example, Rogers and Botsman wrote an article about sharing economy in 2010, where they say that trust is key for sharing economy. They even labelled it the currency of platforms. Similarly to that, Ronald Berger claims that sharing is trusting. A year after that, the authors of a frequently quoted study by PwC said that comfort and saving money is what is tempting about sharing economy, but trust is what at the end of the day turns its wheels and helps it grow. Developing trust is therefore the cornerstone of each sharing economy platform.

Although private regulation has always been present to a certain extent, sharing economy platforms launched an open competitive fight in the area of customer safety and protection. That was the second reason why investors were not too sure about these platforms. They had the feeling that the state is not going to welcome such a competitor with open arms but rather by saying: "Don't move or I´ll shoot."

The World is sharing road workers, dogs, priests, planes, and ice hockey rink workers

What will we share besides an Uber ride or Airbnb accommodation? That is the most popular question from journalists about sharing economy. This part is therefore specifically dedicated to journalists and to all those who like to share curiosities from the world over a meal. Although not all of the following platforms are in line with my narrow definition of sharing economy, I have decided to list them anyway because they are interesting.

If you have a car that you aren't using but you don't want to become an Uber driver, you can rent it to somebody via Turo, Getaround or Drivemycar. Once your car starts earning money, you can get some more money from a free parking spot via Justpark or Parkindigo. Speaking of parking spots, you can also rent your garage equipment with the help of Toolsity, Jelouetout, Allovoisins or Open Shed, and once all your garage items have been lent, you can rent the freed space to your neighbor by using Spacer.com or StoreAtMyHouse. You don't even need to own a closet because on Rent the Runway you can rent clothes of all kinds for a monthly fee. If you happen to have some things you no longer need, use the app LetGo – it makes it literally easier to sell an item than throwing it away. You can, for example, sell your furniture and replace it with rented furniture from Ikea, which is testing its first furniture sharing app.

After you put your car, parking spot, closet, and garage to good use, you can stay in and cook a tasty meal and share it with your neighbors or travelers who are passing by via dedicated platforms like MealSharing, EatWith, Withlocals or AirDnd. If you prefer traditional restaurants, try apps like LoveYourLeftovers or TooGoodToGo where restaurants share leftovers from meals somebody ordered but did not manage to finish and left them untouched on their plate.

You can digest an excellent lunch while walking your neighbor's dog via DogVacay or Wagwalking and earn some cash at the same time. Or, if you are a dog owner, you can use the BorrowMyDoggy app to lend it to somebody whose parents won't let them have one. In the meantime, you can go for a ride on a bike that you borrow on Cycle.land or Spinlister.

If you suddenly feel like working, Pivotdesk and Sharedesk will help you rent an office at somebody's house. Once you are in your new temporary office, you may log in to a unique Slovak platform called Hacktrophy – it is an open community of talented hackers and web developers who test internet safety. You may also indulge yourself in planning a more pleasant activity and browse the Ohlala app which connects people who are willing to pay for sex with those who are willing to be paid for it.

After work you need to get some rest and there is nothing better than the peace and quiet nature has to offer. Platforms like YouCamp, Shacky, or Unyoked connect people who want to go camping, do sports, or experience the local ambience of remote places together with owners of land that makes all of this possible. These platforms offer everything – from beaches and deserts, to mountains and forests. In addition to that, some landlords offer "experiences" – you can try out life on a farm, go fishing, or learn how to start a fire and track wild animals. If you felt that some destinations are a bit too remote, you used to be able to "hitchhike" a plane ride on Flytenow. Flight sharing was eventually forbidden by the Aircrafts Owners and Pilots Association (AOPA).

If you end up on a farm, inform the owner about Mermix, a platform where people rent all sorts of agricultural machines and mechanisms. They may even be interested in Teambrella, a risk sharing platform – a poor harvest doesn't have to mean the end anymore.

In case the end is near after all, the ConfesorGo platform may come in handy. It connects people whose sins weigh heavily on their conscience and have the need to confess to a priest. And if, God forbid, there is an accident, GoodSam will send you a qualified person who can quickly provide you with first aid. If you are a doctor, fireman or if you simply passed a first aid course, you may register as a volunteer worker whom they call responders. First, the platform verifies your abilities and then you can start helping people in need.

But you can also help without any special training. For example, you can support the visually-impaired via BeMyEyes. In the app, you can select whether you need an eye-sight aid or you can provide assistance. The software will then automatically connect a visually-impaired person with a volunteer and the volunteer will be able to see live video through the smartphone of the person they are helping. They point the camera to a place or object that they need and the volunteer on the other side makes up for their eyesight.

If you want to help, but you don't have internet access, you may use the Fon platform, where people from all around the world share Wi-Fi hotspots. Did you miss a bus? Use the time you would otherwise spend waiting and earn money for your ticket: you can profit from this extra time and log in to Spare5, which is a platform where you can get some pocket money by doing tiny gigs, such as tagging, photo description, adding key words, or filling in questionnaires. If you have decent reflexes, you can earn an extra buck on GoalieUp, a platform which connects hockey teams with free-time goalies. It's most popular in Canada.

This is also the country of the first "Uber for snow plow workers". I'm talking about Plowme.com where you can order a truck with a snow plow similar to how you order a ride via Uber. There is another app for sharing other road equipment and maintenance vehicles – MuniRent, which is even used by municipalities in the U.S. A similar principle is applied by the CoHealo app, which is used to share medical equipment. This tends to be very expensive, so its efficient sharing may save lives.

Sharing economy in the U.S. started to work even in an area which is traditionally fully controlled by the state – education. Teachers can use the TeachersPayTeachers platform which enables them to share and sell their work methods and lesson plans to other educators. The website is currently used by 4 million teachers who paid their colleagues the total sum of almost $220 million (12 of the best teachers have become millionaires).

An extreme form of sharing economy is represented by the Omni platform, which could be characterized as "storage with fractional reserves". Its founder originally wanted to create a platform that would enable people to share storage spaces. But then he thought: why should the stored items just lie there if they can be further used and generate additional income? The platform shares this income with the owners of the items.

Did I miss any interesting platforms? I will be happy if you share your tips with me at chovanculiak@gmail.com

3. NOT ALL REGULATION IS THE SAME

"A lot of economic theories about asymmetric information, while logically correct, have been rendered empirically obsolete."[36]

Alex Tabarrok and Tyler Cowen

There is a legend that says that one day, a Roman emperor announced a grand singing competition. Something like an ancient version of the American Idol. Among his subjects, singers were selected and sent to sing in front of a professional jury who ended up choosing two best singers out of the contestants. These two singers then went to sing in front of the emperor, who requested the first of them to show him what they could do.

It was terrible. The emperor must have looked like Simon Cowell after watching an awful performance. The poor guy's singing was simply unbearable. The moment he stopped, the emperor stood up and announced that the winner of the competition was singer number two without even listening to him. He based his decision on the supposition that it could not possibly be worse.

What is the moral of the story? It can always be worse. Never choose the winner without comparing both alternatives.

Well, this is exactly what happened to economists in the second half of the 20th century when they came up with theories about market failure and proposed state interventions as a solution. They too only got to listen to the first singer (the market) and without any hesitation named the second singer (the state) the winner. The economists, who consequently pointed out this error, are now referred to as Public Choice Theory economists.

As the title indicated, they applied economics not only to private choice, but also to public choices - political ones. The best of them, James M. Buchanan, got a Nobel Prize in 1986. In this chapter, I am going to use economic tools elaborated by the above-mentioned economists and I will compare two different regulatory services providers: the state (public regulation) and sharing economy platforms (private regulation). But first, let us clarify what is meant by public and private regulation.

Public regulation is created by a public authority with a territorial monopoly – the state. It is the result of a political process and it is created by politicians who were elected by people. The characteristic feature of public regulation is that it applies equally to an entire sector in a given territory. In other words, at any given time, only one set of regulations that applies to all members of the economy can be functional. Public regulation tends to put some restrictions on entering specific industry sectors, which take the form of license requirements and established norms and rules, the compliance with which is supervised by different inspectorates.

On the other side there is the alternative of private regulation, which has recently become popular mostly thanks to sharing economy. Actually, it did not just make it more popular; it also brought it to a whole new level. It suddenly gave us platforms with their own "laws" and safety infrastructures. The difference between them and state providers is that they have owners and they can't force the whole economy to comply with their regulations. Their private regulations only apply to those who decide to enter their platform.

The following comparison is not going to put the mentioned alternatives in contrast with an ideal world. That was the favorite modus operandi among the economists of the first half of the 20th century when they tried to compare the actual functioning market with a flawless world of perfect competition. They labelled the differences they identified as market failures and consequently prescribed state intervention as a cure. Today we describe such working methods by using the term "nirvana fallacy".[37]

In order to avoid it, we are going to compare both alternatives just as they are and how we can expect them to function in a world inhabited by imperfect people. People, who are sometimes selfish, every now and then they make mistakes, and their knowledge is never perfect.

So, we will have a look at how humans create regulations in the frameworks of two different institutional settings. Specifically, I am going to focus on three areas: first, I will compare the incentives for the creators of public/private regulations; then I will explain what knowledge problems they face; and finally, I will list the options and capabilities that they have when it comes to the enforcement of their regulations in practical life.

3.1 INCENTIVES MATTER – OR, AS OUR FATHERS WOULD SAY – OPPORTUNITY MAKES THE THIEF

"You have, in the legislatures, representatives of wheat, of meat, of silver and of oil, but first of all, of the various unions. Only one thing is not represented in the legislature: the nation as a whole."[38]

Ludwig von Mises

WHO REGULATES THE REGULATOR?

DESK PERSPECTIVE*

The first problem faced by public regulation is the way the structure of incentives and motivations of their creators is set. If we want to truly understand how public regulations a+++re created, the first thing we need to do is give up the idea of a benevolent creator of rules and regulations in the public sector. All we need to do is to apply the same (and realistic) expectation to our legislators as we do for all other individuals within the economy. That is, their interest comes first.

By saying this, economists are not saying that all people are selfish or that we should be or want to be selfish. This supposition only points out a simple empirical conclusion that with increasing social distance, the willingness to act altruistically goes down and minding one's own interests becomes more prominent.

This fact was picked up on by Adam Smith when in his often-disregarded work titled The Theory of Moral Sentiments, he wrote that people tend to be more concerned about the loss of their own pinky than about a natural disaster that took place on the other side of the planet and took millions of lives. What the eyes don't see, the heart does not grieve over and people always put themselves first.

---

* Subchapters labelled "Desk perspective" deal with theoretical ideas. They are always followed by subchapters titled "Window perspective", which apply these theories to real world examples.

It would therefore be naive to suppose that politicians and bureaucrats automatically create regulations that are beneficial for society as such.[39] It came to the attention of the economists of the second half of the 20th century, and since then they have come up with several explanations as to why regulations don't "protect customers" but seek political rent for selected companies. In other words, the regulator is kidnapped by companies they were originally supposed to regulate.[40]

The principal problem of public regulation is that the right to regulate entire industries is in the hands of temporary administrators – politicians who won elections or bureaucrats who work in the name of politicians. After being elected, a politician has to choose between two ways of acting. Namely in parliament, this means choosing between two types of laws.

The first option is to try and draft laws that would increase the well-being of society as a whole – the same society that they and their families are members of. In practical terms, this often means the annulment of already existing laws that were adopted by the politicians before them. They may, for example, cancel all counterproductive regulations from price regulations to protectionist measures and legislation that impairs competition in different sectors of the economy. With every such step, their family, themselves, and to a large extent all the citizens of their country, would do a little bit better. Let's call these types of laws good laws.

And then there is the second option. They can draft laws that would be beneficial for small interest groups and lower the level of well-being in society as a whole. The result of these types of laws is the dispersion of costs to broad masses of people (e.g., consumers) and concentration of the benefits of political rent to limited interest groups (e.g., established service providers). It often happens that such groups include the family members and close friends of our politicians. Let us call such laws bad laws.

So which type of laws will politicians adopt more frequently? Who are they more likely to meet and who is more likely to benefit from their actions? Will it be large groups of the population or small lobbying groups?

Unfortunately, it is the small organized groups of lobbyists who are capable of coordinating amongst themselves to knock on the politicians' doors as opposed to big, dispersed groups of population. Mancur Olson calls them "distribution coalitions" and he wrote a book about them where he explains how their multiplication caused the decline of entire nations and end of civilizations. As soon as a small group within society creates their own "distribution coalition" with the aim to act to the detriment of others, things start to go wrong in society.

From these theories we may conclude that politicians are only humans with their own best interest at heart. In their position, this means adopting bad laws which only limited interest groups benefit from. The rest of the population that doesn't profit from them has a problem – these people don't all know each other and just one bad law can cost them a significant fraction of their budget. They don't see how and why they should approach the politicians regarding every silly law.*

The results of such political failure, and therefore also of public regulation failure, are several types of inefficiency:

- Deadweight loss: fewer business transactions are carried out and fewer services are provided in comparison with how things could be without the existing regulation (e.g., limiting the number of taxi drivers in a city).
- Seeking rent: entrepreneurs use their resources to get political advantages instead of ensuring customer satisfaction (e.g., the millions of dollars the taxi lobby contributes to political campaigns and the amount of human capital used for the purposes of lobbying).
- Inefficiency X: there is no competitive pressure that would ensure efficient company management and create innovation (e.g., obsolete taxi services which have not undergone a significant innovation for decades).

WINDOW PERSPECTIVE

Here is an economic riddle for you: how come taxi drivers complain about how little they earn while costumers complain about how much they have to pay for their services, and how come both of them are right? The answer is simple: politicians and their regulations.

In the beginning of this chapter, I briefly described the rise of the medallion system in New York and what beneficial effects it had on the self-proclaimed taxi kings. Of course, taxi kings never sat in a taxi and unlike how they were unskilled when it came to driving a taxi, they were very much skilled when it came to maintaining a functional cartel covered by politicians and the state. And they indeed managed to keep it that way for years. Over the span of half a century there were many attempts at banning or restricting this system, but they were to no avail.

One of the first attempts at ending the taxi monopoly in New York was the appearance of the so-called pirate taxies from the beginning of the 60s. In the 70s, their number was almost four times higher than the number of yellow taxis. While yellow taxis would only move in densely populated parts of Manhattan and ignored the rest of the city, pirate taxies focused on the forgotten parts (Brooklyn, Queens and the Bronx). Their drivers were often Afro-American or Puerto Rican and yellow taxis did not take any interest in them. When confronted with the police or the authorities, their request was simple: let us step outside of the grey economy and work normally.

---

* Such conclusion would be a paradoxical one for the first critics of democracy among whom we find Plato, Aristotle and even the Founding Fathers. They were worried about the contrary – that democracy would create the tyranny of the majority.

Of course, yellow taxis were against that. In the end they won and convinced those in power to keep their "street customer monopoly" untouched. Pirate taxis got authorization to work within contracted transport (they couldn't take customers directly form the street) and gradually developed into some kind of community minibuses.

There were also some attempts to increase the number of medallions, with the aim to at least get to their original number in 1937, since it was gradually dropping and got to the bottom in the 90s (11,787 licenses). Even though the number of New Yorkers and tourists was growing, yellow taxis managed to resist change for six whole decades. During these decades, different proposals popped up: selling new licenses at auctions, selling old ones, giving each taxi driver a second medallion or awarding them in a lottery. But they all met with big resistance from the part of medallion owners who pulled out different weapons: from the official support of political campaigns (that is, unofficial bribery) to engaging the best lobbyists and taking things to court. Their lobbying partner was a part of the financial sector that started to specialize in giving credits and financing the medallion business. At its peak, this sector had a value of $5 billion.[41] There was nothing that would indicate change and economists were skeptical. In a report from the *Washington, D. C.* Finance Office from 2009, they wrote:

"A taxi medallion system is nearly impossible to end even if it proves to be providing unfairly high gains to a limited number of original medallion owners. Medallion owners fiercely resist any possible threat that may challenge their advantage."[42]

An Analyst from The American Enterprise Institute was of the same opinion when he asked the following: *"What are the chances of any major changes to the taxi cartel? Probably none, as public choice economics would predict. The medallion owners are too well organized, too entrenched in the status quo, and they have the financial resources available for rent seeking to protect their cartel status. Taxi customers are dispersed and disorganized, and have limited resources to fight the taxi cartel so nothing will change."*[43]

Textbook conclusions about politicians who serve only small interest groups and ignore consumers were interrupted only by the arrival of Uber. It inconspicuously snuck into New York in 2011. In its first year, Uber had around a thousand drivers, the number tripled in two years' time and in 2015, there were already slightly more Uber drivers than yellow taxi drivers. In 2017, sharing economy platforms combined had more than 60 thousand drivers.[44] In comparison with taxis, the overall number of rides on platforms doubled.

Economically speaking, before sharing economy came to New York, there was a deadweight loss amounting to approximately 12 million rides per month, which means that there were drivers who wanted to work and customers who wanted to get a ride but couldn't do so because of politicians who were taking care of their own interests.

What about the wealth of the "Taxi King" that ended up disappearing into thin air? No wonder it did – the price of medallions reflects the capitalized values of the estimated future profits connected with the protection from free entry in the industry. This sort of protection is what started to disappear when Uber, Lyft and similar platforms made their appearance. This was something that could not be stopped, not even by corrupt politicians.

PRIVATE REGULATORS ARE LIKE THE BAKER FROM SMITH'S QUOTE

DESK PERSPECTIVE

It is the platform owners who create private regulations. Unlike politicians, who are only temporary administrators responsible for creating public regulation, private regulators own the capital value of their platform. When it comes to providing regulation services, they have substantial skin in the game. It is therefore in their interest to adopt such rules and regulations that will maximize the value of their platform in the long run.

When platform owners want to act in their own interest, they must consider the interest of all the participants of their platform – both service providers and consumers. The only way for them to gain profit is to create an environment (rules and regulations) that will ensure the highest possible number of carried out transactions.

This is why it's in private regulators' interests to make sure their platforms are safe so that customers don't have to be afraid to get into a stranger's car, and tourists are comfortable with sleeping at a stranger's house. They make sure that individuals on platforms are more willing to do business, share, rent, and provide services.

That's how platforms get their income and also why they cannot be kidnapped by lobbyists. Their incentives are in line with their customers' interests, just like the famous example of the baker that Adam Smith, the father of economy, wrote about: "It is not from the benevolence of the butcher, the brewer, or the baker that we expect our dinner, but from their regard to their own self-interest. We address ourselves not to their humanity but to their self-love, and never talk to them of our own necessities, but of their advantages."

We may therefore expect from private regulators nothing but that they will act in their own self-interest. In the case of public regulation, it is to the contrary, and adopting a public regulation that would increase social well-being would require good intention from politicians and regulators which is, of course, theoretically possible but practically very rare.

WINDOW PERSPECTIVE

Of course, in their beginnings, sharing economy platforms were not providing the same services of regulation and customer safety as they do now. Both of the world's biggest sharing economy platforms – Uber and Airbnb – underwent various tests that decided their future. They came in the form of tragic incidents that unveiled the shortcomings in their regulations.

Both platforms had basically only two options in such cases: they would either wash their hands and say to the world that the tragedy is not their problem since they are merely internet yellow pages (just like Craiglist did in the past) or admit their errors, accept responsibility, and change the rules of the platform in a way that would minimalize the possibility of these tragic incidents happening again. Airbnb and Uber both chose the second option.

WHAT HAPPENED TO UBER?

On December 31st, 2013, approximately 8 hours before New Year, a young woman named Huan Kuang and her two children were crossing a road in San Francisco when suddenly, a grey Honda appeared and crashed into them. One of the children did not survive the accident. The driver was 57 years old Syed Muzaffar who, at that time, had been working for UberX for a month.

This may sound cynical, but if you have million drivers on the road giving hundreds of rides per day, an accident will happen sooner or later. But in this case the problem was somewhere else: the driver did have the app on but there was no customer in his vehicle. Although Uber immediately deactivated his account, the platform's insurance up to 1 million dollars did not apply to him because it only covered accidents that happened if there was a paying customer in the car. And so, the Kuangs had to cover high medical costs from the driver's insufficient personal insurance.

Shortly after that, in 2014, another tragedy happened – an Uber driver in India allegedly raped one of his customers. The tragic events were even more accentuated by the fact that Uber's reaction was neither timely nor direct. Despite that, it did adopt some measures in the end. Three months from the San Francisco accident, Uber introduced complementary insurance for drivers, by which they are covered even in the time between searching for a customer and finding them. Lyft did the same. That year, Uber established their new safety department led by Joey Sullivan, a safety expert from Facebook.

The first results of his team's work were new requirements for the verification of the authenticity of accounts as well as the creation of a new telematics tool that enabled them to collect and assess detailed data from gyroscope sensors in cellphones. Thanks to this, Uber could monitor how their drivers use their phones and see if drivers are holding it in their hands while driving. The team could also see if drivers were driving too fast or braking too suddenly. This data helped the platform better enforce the compliance with rules and to be a fairer judge in case of customers' complaints.

Recently, Uber has patented a new system. This system enables the detection of the level of drunkenness of customers and the expected time for them to sober up. The input data are supposed to be speed of walking, the angle of holding a phone, speed and precision with which data are entered, or place and time. Artificial intelligence assesses all of this and notifies the driver that there is a problem with the customer. When testing this, Uber also added a special SOS button that can be used by the customer if they are in trouble and in the need of immediate help. The app is then able to instantly share such customer's exact coordinates. This function was especially popular in Asian countries where women face danger more often.[45]

The most popular function in practice came to be SafetyNet. With Safetynet, a customer can select five contacts to receive exact information about the current bearings of their daughter/father/wife, in which car they are, and the expected time of arrival. It all happens in real time.[46]

Judging by the numerous new functions, it is clear that Uber took its role as a private regulator very seriously. In the following parts of this chapter, I will talk more about some other safety elements within the trust infrastructure built not only by Uber but also by its competitors like Ola, Lyft, Bolt, Didi, or Grab.

WHAT HAPPENED TO AIRBNB?

Essentially, the same series of events happened to Airbnb. There was also a tragedy in San Francisco, only a couple of years earlier (2011). A woman came from a business trip, during which she rented her apartment through Airbnb. All she found were literally the remnants of her apartment – her guest was wearing her clothes, he made holes in doors, stole valuables the owner inherited from her mother, used furniture to feed the fireplace, and demolished the kitchen.

When the media became interested in her case, it triggered one of the biggest media avalanches Airbnb could experience. The sharing economy platform found itself at a crossroads again: will they pretend it's not their problem since their task is only to help discover and close a deal? Or will they accept their responsibility and try to tackle the issue? Airbnb's co-founder and CEO, Brian Chesky, opted for the second choice. In his letter addressed to the public he wrote: "…over the last four weeks, we have really screwed things up."[47]

Right after that, Airbnb doubled the number of their customer service employees, implemented a 24/7 help line and created a special safety department. The new team immediately started to work on tools for the authentication of hosts and guests via phone numbers, social media, or official documents.

The main improvement was supposed to be the implementation of insurance against material damage for hosts. At first, Chesky was considering insurance of up to 5 thousand dollars but his advisor, a safety expert from eBay, convinced him to add at least one zero to that. The following year, Airbnb increased the insurance to one million dollars.

In addition to all this, Airbnb created a special investigation body in charge of preventing and taking care of tragic incidents. It monitors all suspicious transactions and its workers even call bigger groups of guests who booked accommodation during big sports events to remind them that they are at somebody else's house and they should act accordingly.[48]

Another story from Spain provided a valuable case study about the efficiency of the Airbnb safety department, when a 19-year-old man from the U.S. traveled to Spain and was locked up by the host who demanded sex from him.

The young man did not appreciate his host's proposal and started to defend himself. He managed to send a text message to his mother and asked her for help. She called Airbnb, but they refused to give her the exact address of her son's accommodation or call the police. They were not allowed to do either of these things. In the end, they just gave her the phone number for the police in Madrid, and when she called, all she heard was their answering machine in Spanish. In the meantime, her son managed to escape the flat and the story ended well.

Later, when Airbnb had a dedicated department to these types of incidents, they retroactively investigated the situation and took action. First, the safety department reconstructed the entire series of events and assessed at which points there should be protection mechanisms and internal rules in order to handle similar situations. This was their basis for amending their internal rules so that their employees are authorized to call the police in case there is an emergency. Also, their app developers started to work on a new function that would enable a traveler to add a list of contacts of selected people to have simple access to information about their accommodation.

Just like what we said about Uber, if during one weekend 1 million people use Airbnb to spend a night somewhere, there is a certain probability that something might go wrong. But the important thing is that it is in the interest of the regulators to learn from the past because at any moment, they are only one step away from losing the trust of their customers and the risk that they will either go to new competition or back to traditional service providers.

Apart from creating a safer environment, by acting in their self-interest, the platforms cannot be "kidnapped" by the interests of different individuals as is the case with public regulators. A nice example of this took place in 2013 when Uber introduced the UberX service in San Francisco, which meant that amateur drivers with their own vehicles were now welcome to join the platform.

UberX was cheaper and more accessible than the service that was up until then provided by the original Uber drivers. The entering conditions for their vehicles were stricter and they were professional drivers with licenses to drive limousines. No wonder they did not like the new UberX, but there was absolutely nothing they could do about it. The rules of Uber are not just created by temporary administrators but also by its owners who would not accept bribes from "interest groups". Not even when this group consists of their own limo drivers. They would go against their own self-interest. That is why the original drivers had to accept the new competition within the platform as well as lower earnings. Today they work under the UberBlack category.

3.2 LACK OF KNOWLEDGE – OR AS THEY SAY: NOBODY IS BORN KNOWING EVERYTHING

"The peculiar character of the problem of a rational economic order is determined precisely by the fact that the knowledge of the circumstances of which we must make use never exists in concentrated or integrated form but solely as the dispersed bits of incomplete and frequently contradictory knowledge which all the separate individuals possess."[49]

Friedrich A. Hayek

PUBLIC REGULATORS ARE DEAF AND BLIND

DESK PERSPECTIVE

Although the selective pressure of the political process has a preference for politicians with poor personality traits such as string-pulling, careerism or pathological lying, we cannot deny that from time to time, an exception appears to the rule in the form of an altruistic politician with society's best interests at heart.

But that still doesn't mean that problems related to politics and public regulation are solved. It's not enough to have a good person occupying the right position. Even if we supposed that a politician or a regulator has the best intentions there is still the problem of identifying what the right regulation in its appropriate form is. When it comes to this, we lack knowledge.

Different regulations create different costs and revenues for individual contractual parties. The same regulation may bring more costs than revenues to one party and more revenues than costs to the other. How does a public regulator decide whether they should adopt such regulation?

If they adopt strict requirements for obtaining a license to the industry (such as: each hotel room must have air conditioning), it generates high costs for service providers. However, at the same time, consumers get to benefit from better-quality service. Public authorities have to face a problem related to lack of knowledge: to what point are the providers' costs of strict regulation justified by being more than compensated by the consumer benefits? And to what point would the contrary be true?

The principal challenge of any central public regulatory body is to create regulation that brings more overall benefits than overall costs to all parties – or in other words, the maximum overall net benefit. To put it in the language of economic connoisseurs: marginal costs of additional regulation equal its marginal benefits. It doesn't matter how we formulate it; it is basically about seeking maximum value with minimum costs.

The thing is, that when a regulator is creating regulations, they generally don't possess all the necessary knowledge about a specific place in a specific time that they would need in order to correctly assess the costs and benefits for individual contractual parties. Also, public regulatory bodies that have a monopoly on regulations that apply to the entire economy only get minimum feedback that helps them find out whether the additional regulation brought net profit or loss ex post. On top of that, there is no competition pressure that would help reveal bad regulations.

Let's not forget that market conditions change fast and constantly, which also impacts the relative costs and benefits of regulations and thus brings many new ways of solving the problems of asymmetric information and opportunistic behavior. However, public authorities are not able to react flexibly enough to such changes because they cannot assess their relative benefits and they don't have enough feedback at hand. When a politician adopts a bad regulation, they don't lose customers. Public regulations apply to everybody with no exceptions. And don't even get me started on the length of legislative procedures, which are rigid by definition.

WINDOW PERSPECTIVE

Even if we suppose politicians are benevolent, we have to admit they sometimes lack important knowledge related to the issues they're trying to resolve. Let's have a look at the example of regulation of taxi services in Slovakia.

According to the local transport law, it isn't allowed to register cars older than eight years for the provision of taxi services. This regulation apparently brings costs for (some) service providers who are forced to buy newer cars which they wouldn't do if it wasn't for this regulation. On the other hand, it brings certain advantages to customers who get to travel in newer cars thanks to this. The question is, if it really brings net revenues. Maybe customers would be happier to get a ride in an older vehicle provided they pay less.

But public regulators have no way of knowing whether their decisions about the 8-year-old limit for taxis is correct or not because they have no feedback that would help them overcome this lack of knowledge. Their public regulations apply to the entire state territory and there is no competition pressure that would allow questioning it.

However, this is not the case of Uber or Bolt. When they came to Slovakia, they required that their drivers have a vehicle no older than 10 years. Gradually, they discovered that this requirement limits the supply too much and they also noticed that the average Slovak customer cares more about price than quality. They used this feedback to change their regulations and adapt them to the specific conditions of place and time – they increased the maximum age of vehicles to 15 years (Uber) and 13 years (Bolt).

Licenses provide another very nice example. A license tells you under what conditions you can do business within a certain industry. They determine the fee you must pay, exams you have to pass, your minimum age, education, training or experience. Their objective is to decrease information asymmetry and ensure that the customer will get good quality, safe service. Let's take a look at the development of licensing in the U.S., since most available data and studies come from there:

In 1950, 5% of U.S. workforce needed to have a license to work in their profession, in 2000 the number went up to 20% and today, we are approaching almost one third of all professions.[50] This is not so much due to the fact that more people now chose to work in licensed professions, but rather because the number of licensed professions has gone up. It seems that in the absence of a compass, politicians have the systemic tendency to prefer a one-way path – adding more regulations. There is some logic in this – it is difficult for a politician to boast regulations they did not adopt when they get to the end of their electoral term.

The fact that the number of regulations is growing doesn't necessarily have to mean that they are inefficient or redundant. Maybe it was the original state, when only every 20th worker was licensed that was inefficient. However, there is a lot of evidence proving the contrary to be true.

First of all, it makes one wonder when they see the overall number of licensed professions: 1,100. This means that now, it isn't only professions like the medical industry where we would expect a license. These days you need a license to become a hairdresser, manicurist, cosmetician (maybe somebody thought their job has to do something with the cosmos?), make-up artist, hair washer, funeral services provider, interior designer, fortune teller, upholsterer, florist or equine masseur. It is a paradox that California, as the state with the highest number of licensed professions (177), doesn't regulate the remaining 900 professions that are licensed in other U.S. states.[51] The strictness of requirements for individual licenses varies as well. For example, the job of a manicurist is regulated in 49 states and the necessary training for this profession can last 3 days (Alaska), 9 days (Iowa) up to 162 days (Alabama).

Research on the impact of occupational licensing on the quality and safety of services only revealed a negligible correlation. An economist called Kleiner summed it up with the following words: "There is little to show that occupational regulation has a major effect on the quality of service received by consumers or on the demand for the service other than thorough potential price effects."[52]

In their report on occupational licensing, Obama's administration came to a similar conclusion: "With the caveats that the literature focuses on specific examples and quality is difficult to measure, most research doesn't find that licensing improves quality or public health and safety."[53]

Even if we were so generous as to suppose that the research in question was unable to capture the subtle, yet important nuances responsible for quality improvement, it would not automatically mean that licensing increases the well-being of society. Just imagine the improvement in the quality and safety of vehicles if we banned all cars except SUVs. But that would not automatically mean an increase in the well-being of society since only the privileged ones could afford to buy a car.

Economists discovered this effect through examining the licensing of electricians. In states that had a stricter regulation in place, there were fewer electricians per capita which lead to a higher number of deaths caused by electricity because people started to rely more on their own abilities. Better qualified electricians don't equal better quality of electrical wiring in your house.[54]

While there is a lack of evidence about the impact of licensing on quality and safety, there is plenty of it when it comes to the impact on these three variables: wages, prices, and employment. Obtaining a license presents an obstacle for entering into an industry and where there are obstacles, you also find fewer people. And where there are fewer providers, there are also higher prices. Empirical studies estimate licensing surcharges to be somewhere between 5% to 33%, depending on how strict regulations are and on the conditions of the specific market. These higher prices for customers naturally mean higher earnings for licensed providers. Political rent reaches on average 14-18%. The biggest "rent-catchers" are lawyers who inflate their earnings by as much as 50% (as many as 40% of Congress members were lawyers). Inflated earnings only reflect lower employment or its slower growth. It's estimated that the U.S has a lack of 2.85 million workers caused precisely by licensing.

What is interesting is that most studies conclude that licenses present obstacles to employment mostly for marginalized groups like different minorities or ex-convicts. Vietnamese nail technicians who cannot speak English well are an example of a group on which licensing has negative impact since a strong command of the English language is one of the conditions for obtaining a license.[55]

So, even if we choose to believe that most politicians are not selfish and that they care about the well-being of others, we can see that having a good heart is not enough for good policy-making. Wanting to create good regulations will not suffice – you also need to know how to do it.

WHEN PLATFORM ENTREPRENEURS BECOME LAW-MAKERS

DESK PERSPECTIVE

We must first of all realize that there is no such thing as objectively correct regulation. Just like there is no objectively optimal quality, color or size. Market conditions change with time, there is constantly new innovation and people's preferences change too. This is why it is necessary to keep on discovering the right regulation.

Private regulators are not generally smarter, better, or more gifted than public regulators. They were not born knowing everything either. The skills of individuals are not the deciding factor – it is rather the type of mechanisms and feedback that various institutional settings can offer to imperfect human beings. This way it's not people who make the difference but the pressure generated by the given environment.

The first very important feature of private regulation is that unlike public regulators, platform owners don't have the possibility of forcing their ideas of the right regulation onto all other participants of the economy. All they can do is limit access to their platform for those who don't comply with the rules and regulations they have established. They can therefore only regulate conditions within their own platforms.

It creates room for two mechanisms that generate the necessary knowledge: competition between decentralized platforms in the area of creating private regulation (free entry into the industry) and feedback from consumers who either join or quit the platform (the consumer has the option of saying no).

Competition between platforms helps generate the right regulation by trial and error. "Trial" in this context means that any platform can implement different ways of tackling the issue of asymmetric information at any time. This is the freedom of trying new things. Such trials may even take place simultaneously (unlike public regulations where reforms only happen consecutively – one after another). If these trials are parallel, it means that those that turn out to be efficient will quickly spread to other platforms.

Errors, on the contrary, will be pushed out by competitive pressure. This is thanks to the second feedback mechanism which drives unhappy customers to use their option of saying "no, thanks" (unlike with public regulations that are obligatory for everybody). Both mechanisms thus help generate knowledge necessary for avoiding bad regulatory practices and imitating successful ones.

As I have already mentioned, there are several attributes that must be present in order to call a regulation good. The same regulation can bring benefits to customers but at the same time generate unjustifiably high costs for providers and vice versa. Thanks to competition and feedback, private regulators tend to discover a degree of regulation, where marginal costs equal marginal benefits.

If entrepreneurs adopted regulations that would be too lax, there would still be a profit opportunity in the form of tightening regulation on the platform since customers would be willing to pay more for higher safety than is the cost that comes with such regulation. The examples of such situations would be the regulation of rider insurance on Uber and Bolt platforms, where we can see that private regulation is stricter than the public one. In Florida, for example, a customer of Uber or Lyft is insured by over 400% more than a taxi passenger.[56]

While these regulations may create costs for some service providers (there are also drivers who would be willing to work on the platform before they are 21, without a driver's license or with no insurance), we may also expect that they will generate greater benefits for customers who will feel safer (they are willing to pay higher charges in the presence of these regulations). Private regulators tend to introduce regulations with costs fully compensated by the benefits they bring. They see it as the only way to obtain profit.

When, on the contrary, regulations are too strict, there is a profit opportunity in cancelling them. Let's imagine a platform that would require its drivers to undergo psychological tests where they would measure their reflexes by how fast they can press a key on a keyboard or professional competences tests where they would ask them, for instance, what the maximum speed allowed in Ukrainian towns and villages is. These are the real examples of taxi services regulations in Slovakia. However, competition and feedback would very likely quickly show the platform that the costs of these regulations (hundreds of dollars and months of waiting) are not justified because they don't bring sufficient improvement in terms of benefits for customers. From the platform's perspective, it makes no sense to comply with such regulation, so they circumvent it, as it happened in Slovakia.

The same goes for the proposal made by one U.S. civic association for each Uber driver to install a camera in his car. Obligatory cameras would probably increase the customers' feeling of safety but they would certainly significantly increase the drivers' costs which would have an impact on their supply and therefore also on the prices. If Uber as platform owner believed that the benefits from installing those cameras are substantial enough to compensate elevated costs and related higher prices, they would have a reason to introduce this regulation or its more capable competitors would do it. Given that no platform introduced cameras in vehicles, we have quite a strong indication that the request is unjustified.

To sum it up, unlike public regulators, private regulators have enough reasons to avoid exaggerated or unnecessary regulations. A platform owner doesn't have to show their members in a few years' time what regulations they adopted in order to be re-elected. In private regulation, there is a tendency to create regulations to an optimal degree.

When even the public sector is aware that regulation is wrong but there is nothing to be done

On the 27th of March, 2018 at 10 PM, Uber turned off its application in Bratislava. It was a result of a decision issued by Bratislava District Court to take immediate action against Uber based on the request of the Civic Association of Licensed Taxi Drivers. The Court examined current regulations and the practices of Uber and concluded that Uber's activities are illegal and they have to stop. In his indication of reasons, the judge basically admitted that Uber works better than traditional taxi services and people (drivers and customers) prefer it, but he was bound by the law to decide the way he did.

To quote the judge: "The defendant's (Uber) innovative idea in the area of providing transport services via an application through which they organize and operate a taxi service on the territory of the Slovak Republic may generally be very popular, welcomed by drivers and customers, and definitely have the potential to contribute towards the development and quality improvement in this area, however, it must provide and operate its services primarily in accordance with the laws of the Slovak Republic."

The same judge then even admitted that current public regulations are bureaucratic and don't function optimally, but there is nothing he can do about it:

"The establishment of legal conditions, requirements, knowledge, or skills (licenses, medical checks, professional capability, and others) for exercising an activity (including providing taxi services) is the exclusive responsibility of the legislature, or in some cases the executive (e.g., Decrees). The court therefore adds that objections concerning the unjustifiability of some requirements or exaggerated bureaucracy when it comes to obtaining the necessary permits for operating a business will have to be addressed by these authorities."*

So, it seems some parts of the public sector may be aware that forbidden innovation makes society progress, but it doesn't help. Three years of Uber's operation were not enough for the key players – politicians who make legislation – to adapt 20th century regulations to the current reality.

WINDOW PERSPECTIVE

The ecosystem of tools and mechanisms platforms use to provide their services in the areas of safety, protection and quality is vast. What is more, it develops with time. Within platforms, entire teams are responsible for their development. In the following lines, I will try to describe some of the most interesting tools coming from the most interesting platforms.

First of all, platforms choose who they let in. Every manager of a disco club as a meeting platform for single people knows, that good bouncers constitute the most important part of his business because they check that only those who are welcome enter and make sure that the unwanted guests are "escorted" from the club. Similarly, platforms don't let everyone enter their club either – they must first comply with their conditions.

For example, if you want to be an Uber or Lyft driver, you must fulfill a lot of requirements related to you personally (you must be older than 21 and have had a driver's license for at least three years or older than 23 and had a driver's li-

---

* The Court decision was analyzed by Paul Loan.[A5]

cense for one year) as well as your car (year of manufacture, equipment, technical check-up, number plate, etc.).

Platforms also check if your criminal record is clean, if you have caused a traffic accident in the past or if you have been caught drink driving. Their bouncer in the form of an algorithm will not let you in if for the past three years: you had more than three car accidents (without victims), you broke traffic regulations, you were speeding, or if you went through a red light. You are also not allowed to enter if your driver's license was suspended or withdrawn. Your history of sexual or violent criminal offences or drink driving is also checked for a period of the past 7 years.

In addition, platforms have several "subsections" with a varying level of strictness of some rules. Uber, for example, has UberX (accepts older cars and less experienced drivers) or UberBlack (requires newer, better quality cars and experienced, even certified drivers). The key question is whether the rules and requirements for being accepted to the platform are too strict or, on the contrary, too lax. Nobody can answer this with complete certainty but within the competition of private regulations we have a feedback mechanism that allows us to approach the hypothetical optimal level.

Lyft is Uber's main competitor. In some cities, it has almost a tenth of the overall market of shared transport services and in 2017 it even grew at Uber's expense. Unlike Uber, Lyft doesn't care for corporate appearance and prefers to build a community image. Their process of drivers' recruitment is more focused on their personality. A potential driver has to undergo a 45-minute-long introductory ride with an experienced Lyft driver, who then reports on how it went so the decision can be made whether the new driver becomes a member of the Lyft community or not.

During the onboarding process, drivers are informed about community norms and traditions aimed at increasing trust. One of Lyft's traditions is that a rider sits on the passenger seat and greets the driver with a fist bump before they start chatting. Originally, Lyft drivers were supposed to place Lyft's pink moustache sticker on the front part of their car – today it's enough to have it on their window. Even the car has to undergo a detailed exam where up to 19 specific items are being checked – ranging from tire tread pattern to the functioning of their air conditioning.[57] Also, Lyft allowed drivers to be tipped since the very beginning.

Entry rules and regulations for Lyft and Uber drivers overlap to large extent – we may suppose that the market generated rules that under today's conditions, approach the optimal level. However, there are still differences in their regulations and only time and the market will tell who did better.

Once people are successfully established on a platform, there is another tool aimed at increasing their trustworthiness – matching their virtual and real identity. Platforms like Airbnb usually verify user profiles via an SMS and then connect it with their accounts on social media or the credit card number they inserted. Hosts have the right (not obligation) to ask guests for a scan of their ID or driver's license.

These signals of trustworthiness are combined into some sort of a virtual CV. This CV is composed of important trust generating elements such as a photo of a member (which hugely influences the success on a platform)*, short bio, ratings from other users, information about how long they have been on the platform (this piece of information is a great signal of trustworthiness), how responsive they are, or what their house rules and safety elements are. Hosts can also get a certificate of quality and trustworthiness in the form of a virtual badge of a "Superhost".[58] A similar certification system has also recently been launched for guests.

All published information helps potential guests in choosing a host they can trust and is used reciprocally by hosts to make the decision whether to let a particular guest into their home or not. This second step is a very important part of Airbnb's rules. Hosts on other platforms cannot simply say 'no' and Airbnb hosts really use this feature. In one questionnaire, 75% of hosts said that they refused a reservation at least once due to not being sure about the "quality" of the guest.

Airbnb therefore created the unusual situation where the customer needs to "sell himself" and try to gain trust of his service provider. What sells best here is the above-mentioned good quality virtual CV.

As has been already said, it's a standard requirement for platform members to be insured. Airbnb offers property damage liability insurance up to 1 million dollars but also accident insurance for guests during their stay. Airbnb also guarantees a refund or accommodation replacement if a guest is unable to stay at the accommodation they booked, if the place doesn't correspond with the description, if it's dirty, dangerous, or if there are animals and this information wasn't previously disclosed.

The platform also processes guests' payments. The guest pays upon booking, Airbnb holds it as a guarantee and pays the host the day after the guest has checked in provided there are no unexpected problems. This is a smart feature that comes in handy if it turns out that the accommodation isn't prepared or doesn't exist.

The innovative character and entrepreneurial creativity of Airbnb manifests itself even in such details as the first contact form between the host and the guest. It's a result of cooperation between Airbnb and external researchers who studied its optimal form and length. An internal survey showed them that if guests gave too many unimportant details ("Hi, I'm looking for accommodation because last

---

* Several experiments conducted by economists showed that users' pictures have the potential of increasing their trustworthiness in the eyes of strangers and therefore also their success on a platform. The good news is, that attractiveness doesn't play such a significant part as trustworthiness. The best way of increasing your trustworthiness is by having a positive or neutral expression on your photo. Another effective signal of trustworthiness seems to be being a woman. Women receive more requests for accommodation in comparison with men.[46]

week I had a fight with my mum who doesn't understand my life goals…"), it was rather off-putting for the host. The same was true if the message was too brief ("Hi, I'll come with some friends. See ya.").

The result of their testing was a precisely calibrated space for three questions that should be answered by the guest upon first contact: "Let your host know a little about yourself and why you are coming." The communication between the guest and the host is archived in case of a potential (court) dispute.

One of the ways in which Airbnb protects hosts is by not displaying their precise address but only the approximate location of the accommodation. This is how hosts are protected from fraudsters and people with bad intentions who want to take advantage of knowing which house will be empty at what time.

Platforms aren't only helpful before you enter or before you interact with someone on them, but also during the provision of the service itself. Each platform has its own "game rules" which create interactions between members and if you break them, there are several punishments ready – from lowering your reputation, to blocking your account or charging you a certain amount, up to the highest punishment: expulsion from the platform.

Uber, for instance, doesn't allow customers to have any physical contact with the drivers and fellow passengers, to use rude words or gestures, carry a gun, unwanted contact with the driver once the ride is over, or trying to manipulate the driver into breaking the law. If a customer damages or makes a mess in the car (e.g., spills beer), Uber charges 80 dollars from their account and sends it to the account of the driver in question. In cases of a big mess (e.g., vomit or urine) the driver is entitled to compensation in the amount of 150 dollars.[59] Similar rules apply to drivers with an addendum about drug and alcohol consumption.

In cases when Uber is informed that somebody broke its rules, it begins by temporarily deactivating the account of the alleged culprit and then launches its own investigation. If a serious breach of rules is confirmed, the account is deactivated permanently and the member in question will never take another ride through the platform.

Airbnb has their already-mentioned safety and trust department to take care of improving safety features. Today it has three big centers worldwide (Oregon, Dublin and Singapore) with almost 300 employees divided into an operational team, law enforcement team, production team and community safety team, which is responsible for monitoring suspicious and dangerous activities within the platform. The department also includes crisis managers and specialists of first contact with potential victims. On top of that, Airbnb organizes a regular safety workshop for hosts and operates a nonstop customer call center in 11 languages where it employs its internally trained staff.

Innovation in the area of building an infrastructure of safety and trust doesn't take place exclusively on the two biggest platforms. There's an interesting example of a startup from India called Shuttl. It's a bus transport platform that came up with many ideas for increasing safety for its members in more dangerous parts of

Indian cities. Apart from what are now traditional functions like the reputation mechanism or the SOS button, the platform also introduced an alcohol test for drivers, which automatically blocks the driving controls of the bus if it comes out positive.

Shuttl also has an application feature where you can upload a photo of your face to be used by facial recognition software installed on the bus, to recognize and automatically register you once you get in. You can also opt for sound identification with a short audio clip of a specific frequency – the so called "chirp". Another feature you may activate is HomeCheck, which uses GPS to track your route even several minutes after you get off the bus to verify if you get home safely. If it isn't able to do so, it sends a notification to confirm whether everything is OK and if it's not, it calls for help to arrive at your GPS coordinates. This platform's services are mostly used by employers to guarantee safe transport to work for their employees.

The platform SafeMotos in Rwanda had another issue to deal with. This African state is known for its motorcycle taxi drivers who are extremely dangerous. In Rwanda, motorcycles cause 80% of all traffic accidents and traffic fatalities are the most frequent cause of death right after AIDS and malaria. As is indicated by the name of the platform, SafeMotos wanted to tackle precisely this issue.

Apart from traditional procedures, such as verifying a driver's age and driving experience, the platform also monitored a lot of detailed information about a driver's behavior on the road: average speed, acceleration, braking, and sections of the road where they have a tendency to speed. This data is then processed and as a result they get some sort of driver's score. Top score is 100 and if you are under 90, you have a problem – your standing within the platform is in jeopardy.[60]

These are all tools, mechanisms, and rules that platforms came up with in the process of their competition for customers and profit.* Nobody's saying that they're perfect and that nothing bad can ever happen within the platforms. The only zero accident platform is a platform with zero members. Perfection cannot be a criterion when comparing real alternatives. What matters more is the ability to learn and adapt to new challenges. And that's what platforms do all the time. They update their applications several times per month and are constantly trying to remove mistakes. For instance, Uber regularly publishes calls and offers financial rewards to those who reveal bugs in its security systems.[61]

---

* This is what makes sharing economy platforms different from regular service providers like Booking.com. These connect supply and demand but with the disclaimer that they aren't accountable, don't offer any insurance, don't meddle with payments, don't have safety departments and teams, don't have special profiles for customers who would be evaluated by the other party, and their service providers don't have the option to refuse a customer, etc.

3.3 ENFORCING GOOD BEHAVIOR

"Covenants, without the sword, are just words."

Thomas Hobbes

PUBLIC REGULATION- PAPER REALLY ADDS UP

DESK PERSPECTIVE

We can also move the analytical game of generous assumptions to a deeper level. Even if we suppose that public regulations are created by politicians who have halos around their heads and their ideas about good regulations simply came to them because they're enlightened, it still wouldn't ensure their optimal functioning. There are costs connected with the enforcement of their compliance and because of this, even beneficial regulations sometimes don't work the way they should.

Paper can add up and regulations are far from being "self-enforceable". They require an active approach to monitor provider and customer compliance. Sometimes it's even difficult to catch non-compliance with regulations. Customers aren't familiar with every existing regulation, there are never enough inspectors and those who break rules won't always feel like reporting it. Tourists don't feel like going to different town offices and filling in a mountain of forms. Even inspectors may look away if they're motivated to do so. The result? Regulation that doesn't work the way it should.

Public regulators can therefore define the correct quality standards and rules for the provision of services de jure but if they lack sufficient monitoring and enforcement mechanisms to ensure compliance, the regulation de facto, has little real influence.

WINDOW PERSPECTIVE

Watch out for the taxi driver from Las Vegas! That could be the title of a new Hollywood comedy or thriller that was written by life itself and also by the local administration[62]. Las Vegas has had problems with taxi drivers for years.

In the capital of gambling, taxi drivers used to regularly lie to tourists when they drove them from the airport by choosing unnecessarily long routes in order to earn more. Once the issue became unbearable, the local administration decided to take action, but it turned out to be not such an easy task.

Their plan A was to have more policemen present on the roads. In 2012, the local administration decided to introduce police checks for taxi drivers to make sure they weren't trying to rip off tourists. The first immediate result was the slowing down of road circulation and a drop in the quality of transport services. What was worse, in addition to traffic jams, the plan didn't work.

It turns out that tourists who spend their holidays in Las Vegas aren't willing to fill in complaints and spend time to reclaim a few dollars (the success rate was about 5%) but without this, the measures were pointless.

Then they implemented plan B: provide tourists with information. The local administration decided to install big information boards at the airport that listed the local taxi service laws and the calculation of correct prices for many possible routes.

Again, tourists would rather not start their holiday by studying information boards. What's stunning, was how quickly the (in the end pointless) boards were put up. It took two whole years for the local administration to install them. The main reason for this delay was that they had to discuss the contents with local taxi services.

Get ready for plan C: When paper fails you, try Excel! Due to the failure of traditional methods, the local administration decided to take advantage of revolutionary modern technologies. Unless you're a programmer, you can skip the / following lines.

The local administration of Las Vegas created a special Excel file which included a blacklist of naughty taxi drivers and they uploaded it to the internet. Unfortunately, not even this plan turned out the way they wanted it to. For some reason, tourists weren't keen on downloading the current list of local taxi drivers and saving the numbers of their licenses in order to pick the right one once they were on holiday.

Let's continue to plan D: When Excel fails you, try PDF! The administration decided to create their own taxi evaluation system consisting of three simple steps:

1. Print a PDF file titled "Declaration of voluntary witness".
2. Fill in all the required boxes; sign the document in the presence of a notary.
3. Send it by post or fax to the corresponding department.

What could possibly go wrong? It's enough to have a computer, printer, envelopes, stamp and fax machine on you. Then you just note the driver's name during the ride together with their license number, name of the company, license plate number, and your driver's physical appearance (you can take a selfie with them). If they then charge you, say, 10 dollars more, you can visit a notary with your completed form and they will charge you 10 dollars for a signature. Next you send everything to the authorities. Easy.

And finally, plan E: When software fails, try hardware! Originally, they approved a procedure to be designed to set up a system that would monitor the movement of all taxis in Las Vegas online – the so called RideIntegrity. The estimated costs amounted to six million dollars and they included the installation of special tracking devices inside all taxis. I suppose no further commentary is necessary here.

In the end, the Las Vegas thriller finished with a happy ending. Uber solved the problem with its own private regulation and enforcement mechanisms which we will talk about a few pages later. It was temporarily banned in the city as a result of pressure from taxi drivers, but in the end, it was the customer who won and Uber keeps happily providing its services there.

Taxi drivers aren't the only group where law enforcement and compliance are tricky. We find similar examples in practically every other industry and they range from relatively harmless to truly dangerous. For example, my favorite cooking show Ano, šéfe!, (translator's note: the Slovak and Czech equivalent of Yes, chef!) made it possible for TV viewers to sneak a peek into the kitchens of Czech and Slovak chefs. And it wasn't always a pretty picture. The Public Health Authority would be surprised about several things if they could see all there is to be found in a restaurant kitchen.

Sadly, the enforcement of regulations can also fail in more serious cases, for example in the area of air transport. As we know, there's a list of items you cannot bring onboard a plane: guns, knives, explosives, bottles of water or manicure scissors. And because there will always be those who try to circumvent these rules, we have security checks at airports where we're asked to take off our shoes, undergo a body search and we walk through a scanner so that security staff can make sure that we aren't carrying any forbidden items.

It is very surprising to know that not even these strictly enforced regulations work the way most people think they do. Secret tests of airport security checks success rates showed that in 70% of cases people managed to smuggle dangerous items on board and in 2015 the figure was 95%.[63]

The situation with prisons is very similar. Despite the strictest regulations that determine what prisoners can or cannot have in their cells, prisons are filled with contraband items and prisoners trade them as they please.[64]

The lessons to be learned from this are obvious. You should not rely on regulation just because it was written by serious-looking politicians and published in thick collections of laws. It may even save your life. One fourth of pedestrians who were killed on the road in 2016, were on a pedestrian crossing at the moment of their death. I suppose they thought they had the right of way.[65]

PRIVATE REGULATORS HAVE SUBSTANTIAL SKIN IN THE GAME

DESK PERSPECTIVE

The experience of the public regulators from Las Vegas shows us how problematic it can be to enforce compliance with regulations (even good ones) in real life. It also illustrates how easy it is for regulations to be in place *de jure*, but not *de facto*.

Private regulators cannot afford such things. They aren't temporary administrators on their platforms but the owners of capital. They have no monopoly or right to force customers to use their services and customers can turn their back on them at any time. Platforms have no right to arrest somebody for not behaving the way they feel they should.

However, their entrepreneurial exploration helped them discover other mechanisms that encourage good behavior and enforce compliance with their rules. They mostly include reputation mechanisms, big data analyses and the possibility to say: *"you no longer belong to this platform."*

Let's start with reputation mechanisms. Platforms used them to outsource the services of inspectors, investigators and supervisors to their active members. Instead of an employee of the state trade inspection, it's the customer who checks quality and safety. Should they find a problem, they can strictly punish the service provider by lowering their reputation.

The same thing applies the other way around – customers are being checked by providers, which is unprecedented in traditional industries. The first company to come up with this revolutionary online evaluation system was eBay. Star rating and comments to express the level of satisfaction with a service have become a standard used by practically every platform.

Reputation creates double pressure. First, we have people who are ex ante motivated to search for those with a good evaluation because it shows them that in the past they behaved in accordance with good manners. Second, once people have established contact, they are ex post motivated to obey the rules and avoid opportunist behavior because they are afraid it might hurt their rating and therefore lose future transaction opportunities.

Reputation is information about past decisions which influence present behavior and decides future success (or lack of it). The loss of reputation is like the Sword of Damocles hanging over the head of every potential fraudster who wants to benefit from asymmetrical information. We can best understand the added value of this method of enforcement of compliance and good behavior if we compare it with the approach adopted by most public regulations.

In the world of public regulations, rules are meant to apply to all service providers in a given industry (e.g., taxi drivers). Such regulated providers then randomly provide their services to customers. Because the interactions are random and usually one-off, (like when you randomly stop a taxi on a street) you have no way of knowing in advance how the taxi driver behaved in the past, just like you can't hurt their reputation in the eyes of others if it turns out they act rudely and abuse their position of being on the better end of information asymmetry. That's exactly what happened to our gentleman from San Francisco. Such taxi drivers can feel free to be rude to their customers, have a car that smells of cigarette smoke or charge 40 dollars for a five minute's ride. Yes, they will make their customer angry but the costs of their hurt reputation will be externalized to all other taxi drivers and end up damaging their reputation in general.

From the economic point of view, we're talking about a typical example of the tragedy of commons. Instead of people who throw their garbage into the common lake and hurt the environment, we have taxi drivers who are rude to their customers to the detriment of all their fellow taxi drivers.

Then there is the system of platforms and private regulation which tracks all previous interactions, creates their complete history, aggregates it and distributes it to all other platform members. A platform customer therefore knows about the driver's history and drivers can no longer affect their fellow drivers by behaving rudely to customers – everybody bears the consequences of their own behavior. This is what creates the aforementioned double pressure on good behavior both, ex ante and ex post.

However, not all academics are excited about sharing economy's reputation mechanisms. Some of them looked into the distribution of star ratings and reputation and found out that the vast majority of them are positive. For example, as many as 90% Airbnb providers' rating is between 4.5 to 5 stars. They discovered a similar situation with eBay where 70% of sellers had a flawless reputation.

Academics then concluded that evaluation mechanisms don't work.[66] To have some sort of comparison, they put them in contrast with, for instance, Netflix, the rating of which is, according to Gauss's criterion, more normal. The rating of most films and series is somewhere around the middle but you can also find some top-quality things to watch as well as some real junk.

Nevertheless, this academic conclusion reflects the misunderstanding of the theory about the role of reputation mechanisms as well as the empirical trivialization of the influence of rating on the fate of platform members. The primary objective of sharing economy's reputation mechanisms is not to capture the nuances or differences of quality between individual products (like films), but to reveal and punish the black sheep of platforms. In other words, when it comes to platforms, people aren't evaluating the absolute quality but rather the relative fulfillment of their expectations.

Airbnb rankings aren't there so you can distinguish a luxuriously equipped apartment in the city center of Paris from a below-average suburban apartment, but for you to find out if somebody is likely to cheat, lie or, in the worst of cases, hurt you. In other words, avoiding disappointment is the biggest fear and obstacle when creating trust between complete strangers. Airbnb ratings won't tell you if there was one towel instead of two or whether the mugs were chipped.

What is surprising about this mechanism is that even though it works, it may seem as though it doesn't. Or it may seem useless because if it works, it means that there aren't any black sheep on the platform. Wheat was separated from the tares and everybody who remains on the platform has an excellent reputation. This may confuse some academics. Plus, even if the ratings were too optimistic, the platform can very easily adjust the evaluation criteria.

That is exactly what Uber does, and most drivers' average reputation is somewhere between 4 and 5 stars. According to data from an official report issued by Uber, only 2-3% of drivers have their average rating lower than 4.6 stars.[67] Uber solved this optimistic distribution by making the evaluation criteria stricter. This way a driver gets in trouble once their rating drops under 4.7 stars. First, they will send them a notification. Then they will talk to them and if their rating keeps dropping and goes under 4.6, they deactivate their account.*

This was Uber's simple solution to tackle the inflation of positive ratings. From the point of view of the above-mentioned academics, it must be strange that this platform boasts its "distorted" ratings when they say that only 1% of all rides in San Francisco were rated with one star. On top of that, Uber guarantees that if you rate a driver with three stars or worse, you'll never meet them again on the platform – their algorithm will take care of it.

Also, Uber gives riders the opportunity to specify what they (dis)liked. They can comment on the five following categories: cleanliness, driving, pickup, level of service, and car quality. The answers are evaluated by local teams who have the right to "deactivate" a dangerous or a clumsy driver or suspend their account while the issue is being investigated.

Long story short, sharing economy platforms don't organize beauty contests but instead provide the services of a safety agency. Their objective isn't to rank their members from the prettiest ones to the least but rather to identify black sheep and filter them out. The almost complete absence of negative experience, and therefore also negative ratings, can be seen as proof of their success.

The deal breaker for all reputation mechanism skeptics is a study that proves that even relatively small differences between the ratings of individual Airbnb accommodation providers have a substantial influence on their success on the platform. A host with a published rating (after three ratings) can, for example, charge more. Also, according to data collected by Airbnb, the probability that somebody chooses a host with feedback by one guest is 4 times higher than for hosts with zero feedback. Hosts with a good rating can choose better guests. A similar effect was observed on eBay, where better-rated sellers could charge more and had a brighter future ahead of them.

Empirical experience also confirmed that the evaluation mechanism helps overcome what's known as homophilia, which has nothing to do with what you are probably thinking. In this context, it is the inclination to trust those who are similar to us more than those who aren't. Social psychologists from Stanford discovered this inclination on Airbnb, but they also found out that positive feedback can suppress it. Their conclusion was preceded by an experiment and by data obtained from one million interactions on the platform itself.[68]

---

* The level differs from city to city depending on the local average. This is Uber's effort to reflect cultural differences when it comes to evaluating.

WINDOW PERSPECTIVE

It isn't that easy to create an reputation mechanism and correctly implement it, so it is no wonder that platforms didn't get it right on their first shot.

In the beginning, Airbnb published feedback as soon as it was written by both, guests and hosts, but that created room for reciprocity and revenge. In July 2014, the platform carried out an internal investigation to solve the issue. The result of this was a mutually-blind evaluation system: you can see what others wrote about you once you have written something about them or after the end of the 14-day period when you are allowed to add feedback. This is how they removed the issue of reciprocity and revenge.

This change of rules led to a 7% increase of ratings and a 2% increase of negative ratings – black sheep being filtered out. At first glance, it may not seem like a lot, but this increase is growing and at the end of the day, thanks to this, millions of people have safer and better-quality accommodation owned by nicer guests.

Today, 75% of all stays are rated on Airbnb.[69] Economists must find this number surprising since giving feedback is basically like contributing to public goods – it's the others who reap the benefits. In case of Airbnb, you're doing a favor for those who visit your host after you. When it comes to traditional hotels, only 10-15% of guests fill in their satisfaction forms.[70]

So, Airbnb isn't only about passive transactions like traditional hotels or platforms like booking.com. Airbnb is more of a global village with its own behavioral standards that uses and provides feedback to maintain itself. Its information value is increased by the rule that you can only give feedback once you have stayed at somebody's place or hosted someone.

Airbnb's reputation mechanism also has plenty of other, less visible, elements. Apart from publicly available feedback within different categories (cleanliness, communication, punctuality, overall experience), you can also provide some private feedback to your party in transaction. Even more importantly, once your transaction is over, Airbnb will ask you as a guest to provide anonymous feedback exclusively for Airbnb, where you can either recommend the host to future guests or say why they were a good choice or not.

This step represents a very important data source for the platform, because it enables its teams to discover suspicious activities on the part of hosts – for example, they may have a lot of positive public feedback but may not be recommended anonymously. The same goes the other way around when hosts evaluate their guests on several levels. After each transaction, a host has the opportunity to report a guest's dangerous behavior, such as damaging property, sexual proposals, discrimination, or any other issue. This sort of feedback isn't public.

Uber faces other limitations and conditions which is why its evaluation mechanism is set up differently. The platform is aware that every driver can have a bad day or have an extremely critical rider, so it only uses the last 500 rides to calculate drivers' average ratings. This way, even a driver who had a bad evaluation in the past can do better.

Of course, research and innovation in the field of reputation mechanisms continues. In 2017, Airbnb published a study which consisted of an experiment in collaboration with economists from the National Institute of Economic Research. They examined the influence of rewards for feedback on people.

The results showed that rewards attracted more people and motivated them to give feedback, which was not surprising. What was surprising indeed was that negative feedback increased too. The authors of the study interpreted it as a step towards more objective evaluation because these people would otherwise probably not share their bad experience.[71] Only time will tell if Airbnb is really going to offer some kind of reward.

Reputation mechanisms improve cooperation and function as control and enforcement mechanisms, help signal trustworthiness and quality, lower risk, and motivate good behavior while punishing out bad behavior, which helps solve the issue of information asymmetry.

Apart from outsourcing inspectors, policemen and supervisors to individual platform members, sharing economy also uses the services of e-inspectors, e-policemen and e-supervisors in the form of algorithms, learning machines, behavioral models, analyses and big data. They're responsible for prevention – they make sure black sheep won't even get the opportunity to do something nasty. Each problem generates costs for the platform – whether it's in the form of money or lost reputation. Problem prevention is therefore the holy grail of safety on platforms.

Before receiving final confirmation, each Airbnb reservation is assessed for potential risk by all the technologies listed above. Based on the amount of collected data and hundreds of millions of stays, the platform is able to estimate which reservations are potentially risky. If such reservations are found, Airbnb can freeze them, demand additional verification or contact the risk guests or host.

Airbnb's software assesses hundreds of signals for every potential transaction in real time and marks them according to the level of the risk they pose. These assessments are also connected to algorithmic processing of natural language which makes it possible to "read between the lines" and pick important comments to be further analyzed.[72] This way, the platform doesn't rely exclusively on the number of stars but analyzes written comments as well. The platform's safety team is trying to get as much data as possible from what is available.

Airbnb elaborated a four-level system of seriousness and urgency of incidents. The first level consists of fraudulent payments and stolen credit cards. This is a less pressing issue and Airbnb is one of the victims because it guarantees that all payments will be processed through its system and bears the cost connected with fraud. The highest – fourth level – includes cases where health and safety of a guest or host are at stake. The sorting system classifies individual issues and assigns them to specific employees. Airbnb also has a special team which monitors Facebook and Twitter for posts in which people are calling for help.

All of this happens under the supervision of their advisory board composed of experts on safety and protection. They're professionals who used to work for safety and security agencies but also safety experts from Facebook and Google. The body convenes four times a year to discuss and evaluate all their tools and procedures.

Punishments for naughty platform users differ. They can be less painful, such as a damaged reputation or a drop in the platform's search engine ranking, or they can be strict: like freezing transactions, deactivating accounts, or expulsion from the platform.

One of the potential problems of internet platforms is that if they kick out a black sheep who broke the rules at their front door, they can come in through the back. There's nothing easier than creating a new account and registering your property under a different name. This is where Airbnb uses the services of AI, which is able to recognize hosts' offers according to photos of their homes and recognize them even if the same property is registered under a different name and with brand new photos.[73]

Uber faces a similar problem. Some drivers lend their account and identity to someone else and riders then get into the car of a different person from the one promised by the application. Uber is already experimenting with random checks during which they ask a driver to take a selfie via the Uber app which is then compared with the driver's photo in their system.[74]

Uber is strict with drivers who break their rules or fail to provide the quality of service expected of them. That's why avoiding the suspension or deletion of an account is a frequent topic on various discussion forums for drivers. The same goes for riders – they also need to behave and if they break the rules, their account can be deactivated too.

Platforms are therefore more efficient when it comes to getting rid of black sheep than traditional service providers. In fact, they are so efficient that some are starting to consider mechanisms like "reputational bankruptcy", which would mean institutionalizing a second chance for those who didn't do well during their first time on the platform.[75]

Today Uber gives the opportunity to appeal against the deactivation of an account and offers a second chance to drivers and riders who didn't commit a serious offence (involving violence, for example) and had their accounts blocked because of a low reputation. They can attend a course on how to improve their driving skills and increase the quality of their services. These courses are organized by third parties whose methods are fully approved by Uber. Once you have completed the course, all it takes is to upload the certificate into Uber's system and you can have your account re-activated.

3.4 CONCLUSION

"Imagine if every plumber, manufactured product, cell phone provider, home builder, professor, hair stylist, accountant, attorney, golf pro, and taxi driver were rated... In such a world, there would be diminished need for regulatory oversight and legal remedies because consumers would police misconduct themselves."

Lior Strahilevitz

The aim of this section of the book was my modest attempt at convincing you to be a bit more optimistic towards private regulations and at the same time a bit more skeptical towards public ones. In all three problematic areas (incentives, knowledge and enforcement), private regulations have the theoretical tendency and empirical indications of outperforming public regulations. In other words, sharing economy brought new additional solutions to the issue of asymmetric information and when we compare the state and the market, the market seems to be closer to the optimum. If the world of politics truly reflected the actual need for state interventions (decreasing due to new technologies), we should rely on private solutions (platforms) more than public solutions (regulations).

The situation in the public sector is never that simple, though. Those who steer the wheel and those who feed them and choose what they want aren't happy to see that somebody is trying to intervene with the status quo they've been building for years. Politicians, interest groups and entrepreneurs who manipulate regulators are fighting to keep their power tooth and nail. They don't want change that would mean freshly dealt cards. Especially when they see there are new players with aces up their sleeves.

If take the trends and experiences described in this section into serious consideration, sharing economy will no longer represent a mere tool for sharing and thus use resources more efficiently, but it will also identify and circumvent obsolete, dysfunctional, and inefficient public regulations. Let's call it creative destruction in politics. It is also the topic of the following section.

4. FORBIDDEN PROGRESS

"The reasonable man adapts himself to the world: the unreasonable one persists in trying to adapt the world to himself. Therefore, all progress depends on the unreasonable man."

George Bernard Shaw

4.1 LET THE COMPETITION DECIDE

Society is a dynamic and complex system. Despite the systematic tendencies of both ways of regulating, it's difficult to say "this is better, let's do it this way" in a specific situation. Even economists with their excel spreadsheets find it difficult. But how do we identify the right regulation and the right providers? Should we keep on insisting on licenses and psychological tests for taxi drivers or should we just leave it up to Uber star ratings?

We already know that just because regulation exists, it doesn't automatically mean that it's economically or socially beneficial. But who can guarantee that canceling public regulations in a specific sector will bring better results? In the real world, it's not easy to determine when the cost of public regulation outweighs its benefits and when it's beneficial only for concentrated interest groups instead of dispersed costumers.

To solve this problem, we can try relying on political processes and democratic mechanisms but this could take a long time and, in some cases, we may never see the end of it. Just like the establishment of public regulation itself, its transformation is a process that suffers from the problems we already mentioned. Luckily, there is another way of choosing better regulations and their providers: good old competition.

Competition is an evolutionary process of discovering functional solutions. We can also apply the power of competition to the discovery of the right regulation. Thanks to the arrival of sharing economy platforms that didn't worry too much about sticking to existing regulations and brought their own ways of lowering information asymmetry, we suddenly have several parallel functioning ways of regulation. Suddenly, we no longer have to take part in those academic exercises where people compete over who has better empirical data and excel spreadsheets or lead philosophical debates about contrafactual states of the world – all the what ifs. These days the strictest and most appropriate judge is the customer who has access to simple and direct comparison of regulations of their favorite services. They decide which ones bring the best value for their money. Unlike academics, policy-makers and politicians, customers have their skin in the game, so they need to think properly about the choices they are making.

This is why the competition for customers can easily decide who is doing things better between traditional, publicly regulated services and new sharing economy platforms. We can see that the platforms' value is growing rapidly and they are used by millions of satisfied customers who happily choose them over traditional providers bound by private regulations.

This is a strong indicator of what the real situation is. If public regulation was really justified, private regulation that ignores real issues should collapse in a spiral of dysfunction and disappear for reasons described by the theory of asymmetric information.

Some traditional providers complain and think it is unfair that they have to obey so many regulations and rules that cost them money and thus they are obliged to charge more than their sharing economy competitors. They are right, that's extremely unfair. But the injustice is committed against customers. Why should they be forced by law to pay a surcharge for the service of regulation which brings them no value?

The fact that there are regulations that lead customers to simply refuse to "buy" and opt for a cheaper alternative not bound by them instead, should serve as a red flag. It is direct evidence that suggests public regulations generate high costs without delivering the corresponding value. It also shows that somebody else is able to ensure service safety differently and with much better results.

But this is far from the way many states and governments think. On the contrary, they look for all the ways possible to ban their competition or at least hurt them.

What we (don't) know today about (lack of) safety on platforms

What is safer: hotels or Airbnb? Taxis or Uber? These are excellent questions but to answer them we unfortunately lack comparative data. However, there are many indications that can give us some answers.

Taxi services generally have to face several problems: anonymousness, the absence of records and payment in cash. This results in taxi driving being one of the most dangerous professions in the world. When considering the murder rates for taxi drivers, it is the most dangerous in the U.S. and nearly twice as high as those for policeman. This is perhaps also why there is only a negligible percentage of female taxi drivers (0.5–2%).

However, such problems don't apply to Uber: it isn't anonymous, they have records about rides including the precise location and everything is paid electronically. The result: one third of Uber drivers are women. Their numbers are even higher on Airbnb where female hosts are more numerous than male hosts. The same goes for earnings.[76] So, if we can consider women, or rather their absence, as some kind of indicator of potential danger, it seems that sharing economy platforms represent a relatively safe environment in comparison with their traditional alternatives.

Of course, I'm not trying to say that nothing bad can ever happen in an Uber vehicle or at an Airbnb accommodation. With so many rides and stays, there will always be someone with bad intentions and when this happens, you can be sure it will be widely publicized. However, in case of accidents it is necessary to put emotions aside and stop creating public policies according to the news in the media. Instead, we need to look at the issue pragmatically and compare the realistic alternatives.

Last year in London, Uber was facing accusations from the media regarding unpleasant incidents caused by their drivers. The local regulator listened to what his heart and taxi drivers were telling him and decided not to renew the platform's license. They didn't have to wait long for feedback – apart from the hundreds of thousands of customers and tens of thousands of drivers, the End Violence against Women Coalition was strongly against it, saying that thanks to Uber, women felt safer when travelling at night in London. Although we don't have data that would compare the feelings of the Coalition and impressions of the regulator, the U.K.'s institute of Economic Affairs didn't find any correlation between the increase of drivers on the platform and the number of sexual assaults in London.[77]

When I say there is no comparable data, I mostly mean taxis. When it comes to Uber, we know that during three years of its existence, (2012-2015) there were 170 sexual assaults globally. That means one sexual assault per 3.3 million rides. So, the probability that you will become the victim of an assault during an Uber ride is 0.0000009 %. It is a much lower probability than that of being hit by a lightning and still lower than dying the next time you travel by plane (1:5.5 million).

We have similar data for Airbnb. In 2016, out of 30 million stays, only 0.009 % of them had incidents where damage worth more than 1,000 dollars was incurred. With this probability, you can rent your apartment every day for the next 27 years without suffering substantial damage.[78]

How safe is sharing economy in comparison with traditional alternatives? If you want a precise answer, it is hard to say. If you are convinced by the available indications, it seems that sharing economy isn't some sort of unregulated anarchy filled with lunatics. As an economist, I consider repeated customer satisfaction to be the best proof. 15 million rides in 80 countries take place every day through Uber. Airbnb provides more accommodation capacity than the five biggest hotel networks in 191 countries and has so far provided accommodation to more than 200 million guests. If these platforms were really dangerous, people would gradually start avoiding them, but we only see the contrary.

4.2 SHARING ECONOMY AS A LITMUS TEST

"When buying and selling are controlled by legislation, the first things to be bought and sold are legislators."

P. J. O'Rourke

"Thou shalt not forbid free exchange", should be the first commandment of every regulator. Or at least it shouldn't be the first thing they actually do. Many world governments disrespected this commandment and quickly banned sharing economy. They shot first, and asked questions later. They rarely asked the relevant groups involved. They asked competitors from the traditional sector instead of asking the ones they should have been asking – satisfied customers and platform service providers.

Actually, sharing economy can also tell us something about local politicians and officials. It turns out that Uber and Aibnb are a sensible litmus test for how much local administrations and governments care about the well-being of their citizens as opposed to the well-being of narrow interest groups.

TFL (Transport for London), the administrative organ of London's local government responsible for transport in this British metropolis and the surrounding region, issued a document in September 2015, in which it proposed new regulations in the area of personal transport. One of the suggested measures was supposed to bring an unusual obligation to sharing economy drivers – they were supposed to wait at least five minutes between accepting the order and letting their customer into the car, regardless of how far the customer is. That means that if you order a ride via Uber and your driver arrives within two minutes, you have to spend the remaining three pacing next to the car.

If you think this is crazy, take Paris where they adopted similar measures before London and their minimum waiting period was supposed to be 15 minutes.[79] You can't beat the French at beating the competition.

Any reasonable person can tell that regulators in London and Paris weren't trying to solve the issues of asymmetrical information and customer protection. They had a different motive – they were trying to find a way to insulate traditional service providers from their innovative competitors.

Apart from the time limit, London also tried to impose a regulation that the costumers can't see the location of surrounding cars in the application. To put it differently, the regulator was consciously trying to limit information available to customers. In the end the regulation didn't pass in London and was withdrawn in Paris. But this is far from meaning that Uber works just fine in these cities. In Paris, they were burning Uber drivers' cars, they imprisoned their managers and, in the end, they managed to chase Uber out of the city (only a limited version remained there). In London, they are fighting for Uber to be forbidden as I write these lines.

Regulators in Washington had different methods to reach the same objective. They decided to "help" Uber by imposing an increase of prices. To be specific, a five-times increase in comparison with what taxi drivers charged. Their reasoning was that if Uber wants to provide good quality service, it should charge accordingly. In a draft of the regulation that became public, there was a strange section titled Uber Amendments. It said: "these requirements would ensure that sedan service is a premium class of service with a substantially higher cost that doesn't directly compete with or undercut taxicab service."[80] Regulators couldn't have been more honest.

As for Airbnb and the reactions of governing bodies, regulators and hotel operators weren't as aggressive as they were in the case of Uber. Apart from other factors, it is also thanks to the global growth of tourism.[81] Despite this, several conflicts arose between Airbnb and local politicians.

In Japan, for example, politicians originally limited the functioning of the platform and forbade it to rent accommodation for less than one week. Most tourists were in the less-than-one-week category.[82] The author of the law was well aware that this was a significant restriction, but his argument was that it was in the interest of his voters – namely hotel operators who started to raise concerns over the growing requests for accommodation via Airbnb – their yearly increase in Japan was 500%.[83]

New York had a similar approach and in 2016, it adopted an even stricter regulation which made it impossible to rent accommodation for less than 30 days in case of absence of the host and it also limited the number of guests to two per accommodation.[84] It was again the result of Hotel operators' lobby.

As I have already said, the main advantage of Airbnb consists in the "inflatable" supply during large events, holidays, or in the middle of a tourist season. Hotel operators don't like this. They are not so much concerned about having empty rooms as much as they mind that they cannot increase their prices as much as they used to. At least that was the complaint of the president of a hotel's association in New York.[85]

Towards the end of 2017, The New York Times got hold of a document which contained an action plan of hotel operators to fight Airbnb across the U.S. Their main argument consists of a good old reproach: "Airbnb operates within the accommodation industry, but its hosts are not subject to the same regulations as hotels!"[86]

Hotel operators established three points they wanted to focus on: 1. Hire lobbyists who would influence politicians and administrators to limit the number of Airbnb hosts (the document even states specific names); 2. Finance studies that would show that Airbnb operates hotels in residential areas; 3. Emphasize that Airbnb doesn't pay taxes and avoids safety regulations. Also, 2017 was the year of a planned campaign where victims of tragedies that happened in connection with Airbnb were shown. The American Hotel and Lodging Association allocated a decent amount of money to finance this plan – over $6 million.[87]

Australian hotel operators felt similar problems and that is why their association of the biggest hotel networks contributed 500 thousand dollars to the financing of the campaigns of their two biggest political parties. They had a simple request: Level the conditions so that the same rules apply to Airbnb hosts.[88] Same story, different background.*

---

* A frequently used argument against Airbnb in big cities is that it increases the prices of long-term rent for the locals. However, this argument has no empirical ground. The cities in question already had problems with rent which was too high before Airbnb even existed (San Francisco, New

Although many states and cities allow Airbnb to operate in their area, they still limit the maximum number of nights during which hosts can rent their accommodation. Politicians thus force people to leave their own flat unused instead of allowing them the opportunity to earn some extra money and perhaps pay off their mortgage earlier.

4.3 LITMUS TEST THAT CAN BITE

"You either want to be below the radar or big enough that you are an institution. The worst is being somewhere in between. All your opposition knows about you but you are not a big enough community that people will listen to you yet."

Brian Chesky

In political battles, consumers tend to get the short end of the stick rather than producers. At least backstage. That also used to be true for industries that sharing economy entered into. Even a report on taxi businesses by OECD says that it is generally unlikely that consumers will go lobbying for the regulator to decrease taxi rates or increase the number of drivers. In this situation, regulators are willing to yield to the pressure of providers (maybe even with good intentions) at the price of increased rates and a more restrictive policy regarding entry into the industry. Politicians tend to protect already existing service providers by keeping them under thick ice, sometimes even to the detriment of dispersed consumers. Or at least that used to be the way things were before the sharing economy icebreakers appeared.

The mayor of New York City, Bill de Blasio, announced a plan in 2015 aimed at reducing the number of the for-hire vehicles. That means he was going to limit the number of Uber and Lyft drivers. Nobody is able to see inside de Blasio's mind so it is pointless to discuss whether he was acting in good faith or got "bought out" by taxi drivers. But the truth is that they gave him a donation of more than half a million dollars during his last campaign.[89]

Uber may have not had its mayor in New York, but it had hundreds of thousands of drivers and riders who had first-hand experience with privately regulated transport services where there are no parasite "kings". In the course of a few days, it managed to coordinate this mass of people through its app and organize massive protests. In addition to that, Uber also built in a new special feature into the app. It was called the "de Blasio" and it showed riders what the adoption of

---

York, Berlin). Plus, Airbnb rent in these cities constitutes a very small part of the overall supply of apartments for rent– 1% in New York and 0,4% in Berlin. The real problem of these cities is their regulatory policy concerning the construction of new houses and apartments. According to the current territorial regulations, 40% of existing buildings should not have been built in New York today. Not to mention rent price regulations that bend the market and prevent new construction.

the mayor's restrictions would bring. This feature showed that a very large part of free vehicles would disappear and the waiting time would go up from a few minutes to almost half an hour. This new function also allowed customers to automatically sign a petition against the proposal and within a couple of days, tens of thousands of people did so.

This strategy became a classic. When the representatives for the State of Illinois voted yes for restrictive measures, Uber managed to get 25 thousand signatures from all over the state for a protest petition within one hour. Uber repeated the procedure in tens of other cities and states across the world. In London, it created a masterpiece – in 24 hours half a million people signed the petition against the decision not to renew Uber's license![90] Nobody in history had managed to mobilize such dispersed forces as fast as that.

A case from Sarasota, Florida represents an interesting climax. The local commissioners were supposed to vote on a proposal for regulating Uber. According to the original proposal, all existing regulation applicable to traditional taxi drivers should apply to Uber as well. Uber reacted by threating to leave the city and the public was outraged. What happened in the end? Not only that Uber wasn't regulated as proposed by the city commissioner, Susan Chapman, but the unnecessary regulation of traditional taxis was unanimously withdrawn too.[91]

Airbnb uses the same strategy. It even institutionalized this form of member coordination in some cities. In the US, it supported the creation of hundreds of clubs that connected local hosts. Airbnb supports the clubs who aim to defend themselves against restrictive measures on the platform.[92] The platform tears down the restrictions in a similar way in Japan and Germany.

In their attempts to protect their businesses, sharing economy platforms also used conventional strategies like hiring lobbyists and convincing politicians backstage. But it wasn't enough. Their competitors had their own lobbyists and in addition to that, they had years of experience and relationships with politicians. That's why it was key for sharing economy to mobilize people and thus create public pressure on politicians. It cut their maneuvering space and they were forced to bend more to the will of consumers.

This doesn't only concern Uber and Airbnb – eBay took the same steps when it asked its members to take part in political meetings. EBay even prepared a letter for them where consumers asked law-makers no to regulate eBay as a traditional auction.[93]

This tool for mobilizing masses doesn't work both ways. Coordination and protests by traditional service providers are more likely to have negative feedback which helps sharing economy platforms. In Prague, for example, taxi drivers organized a huge protest after which Uber drivers and riders multiplied.[94] The same scenario occurred in London, Paris, New York and other big cities.

As an economist, I must admit that sharing economy platforms are a lot more efficient than the work of all the world's analysts and academics. For a long time now, they have agreed that taxi lobbies and regulation in different states represent big political rent but they were unable to do anything about it. They wrote professional articles and studies and also meta-professional studies, but it didn't make politicians, regulators, or consumers make any moves.[95] At the end of the day, within a few years, sharing economy managed to do what economists talked and wrote about for years.

How do you profit from a gold rush? You sell shovels.

So far, I have mostly written about the relationship between sharing economy, service providers, customers and competition from the traditional sector. However, sharing economy can also produce what we call externalities – external influences on other people in society who, at first glance, seem to have nothing to do with sharing economy. Just like everything else in life, externalities can be positive and negative.

One of the first external effects brought about by Uber and Lyft was a decrease of fatal traffic accidents caused by alcohol, which is backed up by several studies.[96] According to the authors, the reasons why sharing economy contributes to the reduction of the number of such accidents are lower prices and accessibility at a given time and place, even though it has to be said that this effect isn't always true for every city.[97]

Another one of Uber's unexpected external effects was the impact it had on ambulance rides. In more than 700 cities where it started to operate, the number of ambulance rides decreased by an average of 7% after certain time.[98] New Yorkers even half-jokingly started to suggest that Uber should have its own integrated ambulance system since the average time of the arrival of an ambulance is 6.1 minutes after an emergency call while Uber's average is 2.42 minutes.[99] What makes this externality positive is not only cost-savings for ambulance vehicles but also the fact that when somebody needed an ambulance urgently, it was more likely they would get it faster and for free.

Uber has also left its mark in the behavior of its traditional competitors. In his study, Scott Wallsten showed that everywhere where Uber operates within the US, taxi drivers miraculously started to treat their customers better. Suddenly, there were fewer complaints regarding the quality of the interior of their vehicles and payment terminals for credit cards started to work too.[100]

Accommodation platforms also bring their positive externalities. When hurricane Sandy came in 2012, one Airbnb host from New York made his accommodation free in his effort to help the unfortunate ones who lost the roof over their head. Airbnb immediately adopted the idea and it programmed a special regime into their system that is launched when mass unfortunate events happen and there are many people in need of accommodation. In such events, Airbnb charges zero commission and looks for hosts who are able to help. Now this is a standard procedure that helped mitigate many tragedies, such as the earthquake in Nepal, EU migration crisis, terrorist attacks in Paris, or tropical storm in Fiji.

Airbnb also has some environmental benefits. The carbon footprint of staying in somebody else's home is much lower in comparison with a traditional hotel stay during which more water and electricity is consumed.[101]

Of course, not all externalities are positive. When it comes to Airbnb, those who feel its negative externalities most are people who live in the proximity of its hosts. Tourism brings along a certain level of noise, strangers, denser traffic and fuller streets, which can make the life of locals somehow less pleasant, not to mention the situations when guests decide to organize a party in their rented apartment.

How should one deal with such a problem? The general rule is that the most efficient way of solving negative externalities is to address them on the level they arise without going beyond the reach of their impact. Tackling global warming and ocean pollution requires a different level of cooperation and regulation than the issue of a stinking local waste dump. In the case of the former, we need transnational organizations and decisions on the state level while the latter requires rather the actions of a local government or citizens' initiatives.*

So, these problems should be addressed by institutions that are able to best cover the externality's impact. We also tend to refer to it as the principle of subsidiarity. From this point of view, Airbnb's problems resemble the case of a local waste dump more than the issue of global warming from our previous comparison. Should a problem arise, it should be addressed by local government, housing developer or at the flat owners' meetings where rules of renting out flats in the building can be established. It can even be solved by hosts themselves since they are the ones who establish the rules for using their flat or a house. They, for instance, have the possibility to forbid any parties and gatherings already at the point of offering accommodation.

Today, sharing economy entrepreneurs also care about what is beyond their platform. Airbnb launched a special website for the hosts' neighbors. An unhappy neighbor can select from various types of complaints according to the type of problem (noisy parties, lack of parking space, waste lying around, safety, or crime) and submit it anonymously. Airbnb team will then contact the problematic host to try and solve the matter with them and inform the neighbor about the result of their dialogue. If a host actual-

---

* And we shouldn't forget that nothing produces more negative externalities than the effort to eliminate all negative externalities. Sometimes, letting a negative externality be is the right decision.

ly breaks the rules, Airbnb can expel them from the platform. To give you an example, in 2016, 300 houses and flats were deleted from the platform in San Francisco and in South Korea the number reached 1,500.[102]

Apart from direct externalities, sharing economy created an entire ecosystem of additional services. Some entrepreneurs got rich by selling shovels during this gold rush. Harry Campbell became an expert on transport via Uber, Lyft and other platforms. Before he established the world-known website The Rideshare Guy, he used to work as aviation engineer. Thousands of people read his blog now and he has recorded over 70 podcasts. He shares different tips with drivers: how to ride most efficiently, how and when to switch between platforms, what type of cars to use, and how to pay taxes. He also talks about legislative changes and comments on the latest trends and changes within platforms. Uber regularly invites him for consultancy and is interested in his views on the life of a driver.

A similar story is that of Chip Conley, who became an expert on renting homes via Airbnb. He provides hosts with different tips, gives lectures, courses and mentor programs, and also established good practice rules for hosts. He ended up working for Airbnb.

But this isn't only about individuals. Airbnb enabled the rise of new companies and platforms which offer additional services: changing bed sheets, dusting cushions, handing over keys, managing the flat, minibar services, tax consulting, data analysis and price strategy setting.

4.4 THE BEST POSSIBLE WORLD

"Imperfections of one arrangement must be weighed against the imperfections of another."[103]

Paul Samuelson

Even after all that has been said so far, you will still find those who remain unconvinced whether sharing economy platforms have the right to live. For them, it's not enough that:

- Sharing economy doesn't circumvent public regulations but substitutes them with its own security elements.
- It gives us the opportunity to evaluate the functioning and added value of public regulations.
- It tells us something about the character of politicians and their actual interests.
- It enables the coordination of consumers in the fight against narrow interest groups.

These people only care about one thing: according to current laws, Uber belongs under the category of "taxi services" which is why it should respect the current related regulations unconditionally. Similarly, Airbnb falls under the category of "provision of accommodation" and should therefore comply with all the applicable rules and conditions hotel operators have to stick to. These nonbelievers find it inexcusable that a platform should doubt the validity of laws and regulations even to the point of breaking them. In their world, platforms should first fulfill all the conditions required by the law and only then try to explain to politicians how their business model works and eventually maybe also ask them to adapt 19th and 20th century regulations to the technologies of the 21st century. And of course, according to them, politicians will do just that. Nobody should circumvent the law; everybody should obey the rules.

There is no doubt it should work like this in an ideal world. But we don't live in one, so we have to make do with the best possible world. What are the alternatives then? In one realistic scenario, Uber could have decided to develop an application and present it to all the states and local governments in the world. Its team would use a PowerPoint presentation to show politicians how amazingly it will all work even without things like taximeter, marking of vehicles, tests, exams and licenses. They would explain that they can offer an alternative solution and even improve the current state of things.

How many politicians would Uber's team have to visit? How many of them would be willing to meet them and betray taxi drivers who contribute to finance their campaigns? How many would believe that people are willing to get into strangers' cars or even sleep in strangers' homes? How many would draft up a new regulation and how much of it would actually get through the parliament? And most importantly: how long would this all take and who would pay for it? The answer is fairly obvious. Uber and Airbnb would not exist in such world and I would not be writing this book.

Another realistic scenario would be if Uber came to a state or city and began focusing on satisfying customers and drivers, while not worrying too much about complying with all regulations (which is impossible when it comes to Uber's business model. It would be like forcing taxi drivers to comply with regulations applicable to carriage drivers). Once Uber has enough customers to whom it has proven the functionality and safety of its business model, it will try to explain to politicians that maybe it's time to change regulations. If it manages to do so, it's usually because it already has a solid base of drivers and customers.

As an economist, I would definitely opt for the second scenario – the second possible world. In the first one, sharing economy wouldn't even exist and we would lose a significant part of the aforementioned benefits. Insisting that sharing economy platforms should under no circumstances try to search for legal loopholes and comply with all regulations, is a typical example of the nirvana fallacy. Those who talk about an ideal world filled with unicorns lose touch with reality and fail to notice that their favorite solution is actually the worst one. It is shortsighted to obsessively insist on everything going according to the law. When handling public finances, it is no longer enough for everything to be accordance with the law, but we also try to find the value for money of individual costs. We should act similarly when it comes to regulations.

Looking for a gray zone and avoiding regulations was like the purchase of an option for startups. They couldn't lose much because they were startups. At the same time, they could gain a lot provided they manage to survive. Most people have no idea that Uber wasn't the first platform to choose such a strategy. Before 2013, Uber only authorized professional limousine drivers who possessed all the necessary licenses to work within the platform. Startups like Lyft and Sidecar were the first to come up with the idea to allow access to ordinary people with their personal vehicles. At first, Uber refused this business model and even brought this kind of practices to the attention of California's regulator. However, once Uber realized the regulators weren't going to react, it also ventured into forbidden waters where it has remained up to this day.

Then there are platforms like Bolt, who openly admit that their strategy is to let a big player (usually Uber) enter a local market first, fight all regulatory battles and spend a lot of resources on the fight with politicians, and only then expand to a country where they can already operate legally. Thanks to the costs it saved, Bolt can charge lower prices for its services.

Today we even have evidence about what would happen if sharing economy platforms obeyed the laws to the foot of the letter. To put it briefly – nobody would know their names now. Taxi Magic and Cabulous are the ancestors of Uber and Lyft and Couchsurfing or HomeAway were here before Airbnb. Owners of those platforms set their business models into the framework of the applicable laws or at least they tried not to go beyond what everybody in the industry was doing. Today they are, at the best, merely weak competitors of big platforms. Some even regret retrospectively that they were way too careful and failed to see the opportunity that was lying off the official beaten track.[104]

Yishan Wong, an investor from Silicon Valley who used to work for PayPal, summarized it best when he said:

"If you are a startup who feels that the violation of a law (or an excursion into a grey and questionable/undefined area of the law) will allow you to create a business that provides enormous value to people, the tactically wise thing to do is to move forward and try to build the business. Moreover, if your business is not doing something morally egregious (e.g., killing people) but simply violating the law in a somewhat more minor way, the officers of the company bear little more risk than the company being sued out of existence."

4.5 WHEN IT'S EASIER TO BEG FOR FORGIVENESS THAN ASKING FOR PERMISSION

I am not so naïve as to think that the previous part convinced all readers that a strict compliance with law isn't always the best idea. I suppose that especially lawyers or judges remained unconvinced. However, I do believe that they also have their limits up to which they are willing to admit there are exceptions. One of those exceptions can be illustrated by the fate of those who tried to cross the borders of the iron curtain. Nowadays we commemorate those who were brave enough to try but didn't make it and paid with their lives. I am aware of course, that this is an extreme example.[105]

What I am saying is that people with legal education often tend to underestimate how many innovations had to go through a period of prohibition, accusations from breaking the law and fighting the regulatory windmills. In other words, they underestimate the contribution of what academics today call regulatory or evasive entrepreneurship.[106] Society benefits from the ability and willingness of these entrepreneurs to go against the status quo in the area of regulations.

Things change rapidly these days and we live in an era of high inflation of laws and regulations. The combination of these two factors can threaten the ability of humans to innovate and that's why some economists are calling for permissionless innovation. Some even consider it the most important concept of political economy.[107]

It may not seem like it today, but every era had its Uber or Airbnb. The problem is that people die and laws change, so these examples often fall into oblivion. One doesn't even realize how many services and goods which are taken for granted today had to go through regulatory hell and were also considered illegal at some point in the past.*

4.6 A CHRISTMAS STORY ABOUT FORBIDDEN FRUIT

"The natural effort of every individual to better his own condition, when suffered to exert itself with freedom and security is so powerful a principle that it is alone, and without any assistance, not only capable of carrying on the society to wealth and prosperity, but of surmounting a hundred impertinent obstructions with which the folly of human laws too often incumbers its operations; though the effect

---

* The problem of breaking the law isn't only the issue for innovative entrepreneurs. According to Harvey Silvargate, a U.S. lawyer, the inflation of laws is so high in the U.S., that an average person who wakes up, has a cup of coffee, goes to work and eats his dinner when he gets back home, has unknowingly committed several felonies during that day.[A7]

of these obstructions is always more or less either to encroach upon its freedom, or to diminish its security."[108]

Adam Smith

I am not an expert on buying presents. Perhaps it's because I always leave it to the last moment. I know somebody for whom buying presents means an all-year-long observation process of his wife's looks into shop windows (today this observation includes the analysis of cookies in the internet search engine). Last year, when I was ordering my wife's Christmas present, I realized something interesting. Practically every step of the order included a service that wouldn't be here had the wrong party (officials, politicians or lobbyist groups) won.

I ordered the present on eBay and paid through PayPal. It travelled to Europe in a shipping container and was delivered by a FedEx car. At some point in the past, someone wanted to either ban or strictly limit each of these steps: eBay, PayPal, shipping containers, cars and FedEx. It wasn't enough for innovators who brought these inventions to just gain the customers' hearts and wallets, they also had to win the battle against regulators. They faced officials and politicians who were a tool to fight competition in the hands of already established entrepreneurs.

EBAY, THE "AUCTION HOUSE"

As I said, I ordered my wife's Christmas present via eBay. On eBay, you can find things that you wouldn't find in a brick-and-mortar store. It's like a global garage sale where we're all just a couple of clicks away from each other. In a few seconds you can show the contents of your garage to a collector in Japan or peek into the garage of a German pensioner. Originally, prices on this platform were purely the results of auctions.

In order for you to better imagine how successful eBay is, let me just say that only three years passed between the moment its founder, Pierre Omidyar, got the idea of creating a digital garage sale and sold his first item – a broken laser pointer – for $14.83 and the point when he became a billionaire in dollars. He was as old as I am now – 30.

However, not everybody appreciated the idea of a digital garage sale where anybody can become the auctioneer of their own things. Like the supply chain of antique collectors, who used to physically visit remote corners of the world in order to find hidden treasure in various garage sales, or dealers who acted as intermediaries between them and antique store owners. All of these links of the chain blew their tops when they saw how the platform made it possible for a Buck from Minnesota to sell his grandmother's iron to a Kevin from New York City. A lot of people with their worn shoes, small stores and warehouses were substituted by zeros and ones which lowered transaction costs. They were unlucky because back then, there were no regulations applicable to this sort of business. They therefore had no leverage and had to adapt to the evolutionary pressure of the profit or loss statement.

Professional auctioneers were luckier. They had a regulatory stick at hand and it didn't take them long to find a dog to beat it with. In 2004 and 2005, eBay was flooded with a wave of regulations, new laws and accusations of breaking the law. Back in those days, regulators in many US states started to propose new auction regulations or extend the scope of the existing ones to users of the new platform.

In Ohio, for example, this meant that if somebody wanted to sell items via eBay, they had to become an officially accredited auctioneer, which meant they had to pay 200 dollars, pay a $50,000 guarantee, pass the exams and carry out 12 "testing" auctions. Otherwise they would face a one thousand dollars fee and 90 days in prison.[109] Of course, all of this was done in the name of security and protection of customers. As one of the defenders of regulations put it: "While it's true that the law will require additional controls, it's all a good thing for consumers, despite the resistance from online sellers."[110]

Back then, about 430 thousand people in the US made their living or had some sort of financial dependency on eBay. The situation was similar in other countries. For example, an auction house in France sued eBay because its sellers don't have an auctioneer's license. It accused eBay of unfair competition, endangering the interests of consumers and not paying taxes.

The main argument of all regulators and licensed auctioneers was that eBay presented itself as a place where auctions are conducted and an auction can't be conducted just like that – by anyone and anywhere. Auction forms a specific category and that's why eBay and all who sell there have to hold a license. An attentive reader will find the situation somehow familiar.

After a lot of convincing, many verbal attacks and legal battles, eBay managed to succeed in basically all countries and today we only smile about the idea of it having licensed auctioneers.

PAYPAL, THE "BANK"

PayPal, the next hero of my Christmas shopping, had to undergo a similar regulatory detox. When eBay started, people used to pay their purchased items by checks or in cash that they sent in envelopes. That's why the first eBay employees were people who opened envelopes. Paying via a credit card wasn't that common back then – people didn't use to give their bank details just like that, to anybody on the internet. Also, most eBay sellers were ordinary people and not big stores, so they didn't even have the option to register as sellers in banks.

PayPal was the one who started to try and solve complications related to transferring money via the internet. And they indeed solved it in a very handy way – all you needed was an e-mail address. Later in the book I explain how it worked exactly and what problems PayPal had to face. What's important for now, is that it worked and customers were happy.

Those who were not happy were established banks because they could see that suddenly, somebody had figured out how to send money via the internet quickly and safely, while avoiding slow yet fairly expensive services. An attentive reader won't be surprised to learn about the tools big banking chose for the competitive fight against PayPal.

Literally a couple of days before PayPal tried to offer a part of its shares to the public in an initial public offering (IPO), it got noticed by several regulators from various US states. Four years after the launch of the platform, the Office of Financial Institutions in Louisiana leveled accusations that the platform does its business without the necessary banking license and sent PayPal a letter with a call for an immediate termination of their activities.

Up until that point, at PayPal they thought they didn't need such license because they don't conduct commercial bank activities. But for some reason, regulators across the country suddenly changed their opinions and similar letters started coming from various states. As a result, PayPal was seriously threatened. One of the people who saw the beginnings of PayPal expressed his disappointment:

"Squaring off in a competitive match with eBay was one thing—at least in that situation we could adjust our product and marketing and then allow the marketplace to decide. Even combating the Russian mafia was within our comfort zone; we could challenge them head-to-head with our wits and our moxie. But trial lawyers and regulators drawn to our pending success were an entirely different type of opponent. The entrepreneurial traits of creativity, energy, and flexibility might not be enough to get us out of these jams."[111]

So, what was the problem? Well, it's the same old story – consumer protection and safety. When the director of eStrategies of the American Bankers Association commented on the whole issue of regulation, he declared a growing consensus among bankers that online payment companies should be regulated the same way as banks. How else could we assure that the consumer will get safe, quality service? The CEO wasn't saying that PayPal and similar companies lie to their customers, but to quote him: "If they're not regulated then are they going to voluntarily abide by all these things? I'm not saying that PayPal's not doing these things, but who's looking over their shoulder to be sure they are?"[112]

If PayPal had been obliged to get a banking license in the end, it would have meant paying huge fees, fulfilling a multitude of bureaucratic duties, and adapting their business model to new rules and requirements that were applicable to banks. This means, for example, having a much higher cash reserve or fulfill the requirements for the registration of transactions and their privacy. The life of PayPal was in danger. To put it in the words of Eric Jackson: "If regulators continue with their hunt on our young business in the name of customer protection, in the end we may not be able to provide any services to our consumers whatsoever."

In the end, PayPal managed to defend itself from bans and hard regulation when the Federal Deposit Insurance Corporation declared it doesn't consider the company to be a bank. Even though the decision wasn't binding for individual states, it helped a lot in the argument and contributed to the fact that after all, no state required a banking license from PayPal.[113]

"EXTREMELY URGENT" FEDEX

New startups, online websites and platforms weren't the first ones to be obstructed by regulators. The Sword of Damocles with an official stamp on it was also hanging over the other three heroes from my Christmas shopping story: FedEx, shipping containers, and cars.

FedEx was born in the mind of a Yale student in the 1960s. He drafted his idea and concept in the form of an essay. Rumor has it, he received a bad mark for it and the professor laughed at his work. As popular as this part of the story is among students with bad marks, it's made-up. However, what isn't made-up is the monopoly of the US mail service for the delivery of letters and packages that young Frederick W. Smith had to cope with. And he coped just brilliantly.

In the mail law, there is a section § 320.6 – Suspension for extremely urgent letters – which made it possible for him to circumvent the state monopoly.[114] As the name of the section indicates, an exemption is applicable to those cases when the delivery is extremely urgent. That's why FedEx has been marking its mail "extremely urgent" up to this day. And so, this successful company with revenues in millions exists only thanks to somebody who in the 18th century added a suspension into the law and thanks to the young Frederick who didn't hesitate to use it.

ILLEGAL CONTAINER

Another example of a forbidden innovation is the standardized shipping container. Today, there are more than 20 million of them transporting practically anything, anywhere, at any given time. This innovation from the late 1920s changed the world. It transformed the way shipping ports look and work, the way port towns look, where factories are built, and the development of international commerce and globalization. The shipping container is the unsung hero of our time.

Before shipping containers came along, goods were transported in all sorts of packaging: pallets, wooden boxes, barrels, cardboard boxes, crates, sacks, and so on. The transport of goods in the first half of the 20th century wasn't so different from the way goods were delivered in previous centuries. Yes, ships and trains were more modern and trucks appeared too, but the goods still went through the hands of loaders and unloaders to a large extent. This job was present in every port in the world. However, this way of handling transported goods had its shortcomings.

First of all, it was generating high costs. More than a half of all costs of transporting goods from point A to point B could be attributed to loading them from the factory onto the train, from the train to the port and then onto a ship, from the ship onto a truck, and from the truck into a warehouse. This wasn't just an issue of money but also of time. A cargo ship would spend more than a week in the port before it was completely unloaded and then fully loaded again. At the same time, things would get lost or even stolen from time to time. Sometimes, the ship had to wait to be unloaded because the local loaders and unloaders were on strike, which used to happen quite frequently. Ship transport was getting weaker after the Second World War.

Malcom McLean, a successful entrepreneur in truck transport, decided to change the situation. Of course, he wasn't the first to notice the high costs and risks related to loading and unloading goods and neither was he the first to see the solution in standardized containers. But he was indeed the first to understand the importance of a comprehensive approach and came up with paradigm shift in transport.

He stopped looking at cargo transport industry as the management of trucks and ships and coordination of trains and instead started to see it simply as transporting cargo. This made him approach the concept of "containerization" from a completely different angle than his contemporaries.

McLean created a completely new ecosystem of container manipulation. He adapted the berths, ships, cranes, warehouses, trucks, trains, and the entire management system of all components. With his vision, he topped everybody, even experts from various committees and offices who were surprised by his new approach and the radical change he brought about.*

Nevertheless, it wasn't that easy to implement the change in paradigm. The US transport industry was strictly regulated in the first half of the 20th century. Public institutions and regulators divided their responsibilities according to different means of transport and together they regulated everything: from delimited routes and number of participants to prices for individual transported items. On top of that, it wasn't possible for one company to be involved in different activities within all parts of the industry, in other words – to manage trucks, ships, and, in addition to that, rent a berth with cranes and warehouses.

McLean together with his team of lawyers and accountants knew about all of this, but he needed to integrate all the aforementioned components into his business model. That's why before launching the container transport model, his lawyers carried out several legal and finance operations that shifted around ownership relationships in McLean's companies in order to circumvent the strict regulation. The ink on the contracts didn't even have the time to dry when McLean's

---

* You can read more about McLeans story in The Box by Marc Levinson.[A8]

competitors from truck and railway transport started to attack him and request the suspension of his business activities.

What followed were two years of disputes between his companies and the International Commerce Commission (ICC). Truck and railway companies' representatives were protesting saying McLean got his shipping company illegally. So, his business was declared illegal and therefore banned. They almost managed to achieve their goal when in November, 1956, an ICC investigator said they were right. But in the end, ICC didn't accept the investigator's conclusion and in 1957 they granted McLean's companies a permit to operate. This happened at the time when McLean had already been transporting his containers for a year and a half.

The first ship loaded with McLean containers set off from a port in New Jersey to sail into a port in Texas in 1956. It took eight hours to load the entire ship, which was extremely quick compared to the several days it took when it was done the traditional way. Soon they managed to make it even faster thanks to better cranes and mostly due to loading and unloading the ship simultaneously. Despite all that, McLean was solely interested in one piece of information – the cost of transporting one ton of goods. In 1956 it was about $5.83. MacLean's ship Ideal-X managed it for 15.8 cents per ton.

OVERREGULATED CARS

My last example of a previously limited yet these days vastly spread innovation is the car. Back in the days when the power of pistons started to replace horse muscles, the U.K. government adopted what they called the "Locomotive Acts". The strictest of these was the Red Flag Act. It was 1865 and the government set the speed limit for "road locomotives" to 4 mph in the country and 2 mph in the city. The government also ordered that a person holding a red flag should run 55 meters in front of the vehicle. Some of you may find it funny but perhaps back then it made sense. After all, road motorized vehicles were still in their infancy in those times.

However, it is very likely that the intention of these regulations was slightly different than what they claimed. Only four years before adopting this series of regulations, the government had adopted a different regulation according to which there were no flags required and the maximum speed limit was double. So, the 1865 law was going in a different direction than modern progress. According to a historian named Smith[115], two groups were responsible for this: English railways and the owners of carriages and horses. But their plan failed. Some car owners circumvented the law risking a fine of 10 pounds (today approx. 1,300 dollars). The difference between reality and regulations was smoothed out as late as in 1898 upon the adoption of a new law.

The equivalent of the Red Flag Act also existed in some US states.[116] In Pennsylvania, they even adopted a law in 1896 which required a motorized vehicle driver to conduct the following three steps should he cross paths with cattle or livestock:

immediately stop the vehicle, disassemble the automobile as quickly as possible, and conceal the various components out of sight behind nearby bushes until the equestrian or livestock have been sufficiently pacified.[117]

If you think such regulation is obsolete and could not be found in today's times, the case of Tesla electro mobiles will prove you wrong. For over ten years, Tesla has not only been fighting to gain the hearts of customers but also the minds of regulators. Tesla's business model is built on direct sale to customers, which was originally forbidden by practically all US states. In the past, U.S. car dealers successfully lobbied for a law that forbade car manufacturers to sell their vehicles without an intermediary. When the internet spread, car manufacturers started to fight against it, but to no avail. Car dealers won't ignore their interests and neither will politicians, since car dealers regularly contribute to their campaigns.[118] According to them, a lot is at stake, when it comes to customer protection: "a dealer who has invested a significant amount of capital in a community is more committed to taking care of that area's customers".[119] The props change while the plot remains the same.

Although Tesla didn't convince politicians, they at least managed to find legal loopholes. In New York and Massachusetts, they opened what they call "galleries" where they display their vehicles. In Texas, where they have to face the strongest resistance, they have nine of these. They claim that they aren't breaking the Sale of Goods Act, since there are no price tags on the cars. Car dealers complain that these galleries happen to be in shopping malls and they react with legal action.[120]

Today Tesla has to face not only car dealers but also other big car manufacturers. For example, General Motors wrote an open letter to the government in Ohio where they explain that an exemption for Tesla would constitute an unfair competitive advantage and deform the market. Tesla is currently involved in court disputes and other attempts to solve the problem with regulations in eight different US states.[121]

THE PRESENT ARRIVED AND IT TASTED GOOD

So, what did I buy for my wife on eBay?* Coffee. Four pouns of Nicaraguan coffee. This beverage didn't have it easy when it came to Europe through Ethiopia, Yemen, and the Ottoman Empire in the 16th century. In its early days, politicians, kings, the clergy and even the competitors – winemakers – cursed coffee and fought against it.

First, Pope Clement VIII declared that coffee was Satan's beverage, but since it tasted so good, they tried to baptize it and thus convert it into a Christian beverage. That, of course, didn't thrill winemakers and poet Belighi sighed: "this seditious disturber of the world has, by its unparalleled virtue, sup-

---

* If I wanted to be really consistent, I would add a mini chapter about the bans and restrictions the internet went through. Until 1992, it was forbidden in the U.S. to carry out any commercial activities on the internet. The internet could be legally used for academic and military purposes only.

planted all wines from this blessed day." In France, doctors warned against coffee, saying it should only be available on prescription because it attacks the lymph vessels and dries out the kidneys. Sure enough, there were many winemakers in France, so attempts to ban coffee were very much present. At least dairy farmers managed to found a compromise in the fight for the consumers' taste buds – they called it café au lait, known simply as latte today".*

Before the arrival of coffee, Germany was a bastion of beer. Beer is a very nutritious liquid and, in the past, it would accompany practically every meal in Germany. So, coffee wasn't successful here at first. There were some attempts to incorporate it into soups, but unlike latte, it didn't become popular. Later, when the locals started to like coffee, their rulers who practiced faith in mercantilism did not approve of it. It was simply not popular to export precious metals and import black grains. Friedrich the Great, a Prussian king, was literally disgusted when he saw his subjects enjoying coffee and he ordered them to drink beer. He even hired professional "noses" who went around sniffing to identify those who smell of coffee, and once they did, the person in question received a fine.

After one heated exchange of opinions in the Swedish parliament, the representatives of local peasants decided to take their revenge for being banned from making their own homemade moonshine. They voted against a higher social class to ban the import of coffee. They were even supported by King Gustav III who decided to prove the harmful effects of coffee with an elaborate experiment. He ordered a murderer sentenced for life in prison to drink coffee regularly. As a control sample, he took another convicted murderer who was ordered to drink tea. Then they observed them to find out which one would live longer. The results of the experiment are difficult to assess; two doctors were hired to observe the convicts, but they both died before them. Even the king himself was unfortunate enough to not see the results – he was murdered before the experiment was concluded. The last one standing was one of the prisoners – the coffee drinker.

Coffee had a rocky start in England too. Anthony Wood, an academic from Oxford, complained that because of cafés, the level of education was worsening since scholars were spending too much time there sharing the news and saying nasty things about their superiors. At the University of Cambridge, they issued a decree according to which students were only allowed to visit cafés in the company of their tutors. Publications saying that drinking coffee turns you into a Turk started to spread throughout London. A belief that coffee is merely a gateway to hard drugs and that one is only a couple of cups of coffee away from eating spiders were also popular. On top of that, local women launched a petition claiming that men become impotent as a result of drinking coffee and they recommended that anyone younger than 60 should be forbidden to drink it. King

---

* Although I have to say that Filip Vačko, my friend, wrote to me on Facebook saying café au lait and latte are two different things and you can get both in coffeeshops.

Charles II joined the crowd and in 1675, he banned cafés since unpleasant rumors about him were spreading there and coffee drinkers were undermining the public order which threatened national security. That could not be tolerated.[122]

The same negative attitude towards coffee and cafés could be found in other countries' rulers and clergy representatives. The already mentioned Friedrich the Great would complain that one simply couldn't rely on coffee drinkers when it came to defending the country. It's no wonder – coffee and cafés suddenly created a space where everyday folks could exchange ideas, news and gossip, engage in political or religious agitation, and coordinate themselves. Until then, there were only beerhouses, which didn't have a good reputation, and they were places where alcohol was consumed (once you drink alcohol you feel like you have solved the world's problems already anyway) or churches where most of the time, all one could hear was one person's monologue. Alternatively, there were spas but they were for the higher class only.

So, cafés became the place where people could share their ideas. Soon, the first results of this beneficial activity appeared. In 1655, young English students talked pharmacist Arthur Tillyard into standing up against Oxford and preparing and selling them coffee. The pharmacist didn't hesitate and founded a café called Oxford Coffee Club, which, together with its visitors, later renamed itself to the famous Royal Society of London for the Improvement of Natural Knowledge. Until this day it is the world's oldest scientific establishment.

Another café, called Jonathan's Coffeehouse, gradually turned into an exchange which was later renamed to Stock Exchange – the most famous stock exchange where you too are probably saving up for your retirement. A similar café in New York turned into the no less famous New York Stock Exchange.[123]

Also, let's not forget to mention the café on Tower Street in London, where in 1687, sailors started to chat and gossip about ships and expeditions. The more courageous ones were even willing to bet on some of the rumors – for example, whether the incompetent admiral John Byng would be shot during his voyage. The café was founded by Edward Lloyd and all the rumors and betting resulted in an insurance company. And not just any insurance company; later it was renamed to Lloyd's of London – the world leader in the insurance industry today.[124]

Author William H. Ukers said that coffee shook the ground everywhere it went: "It has been the world's most radical drink in that its function has always been to make people think. And when people began to think, they became dangerous to tyrants and to foes of liberty of thought and action." Cheers then!

Urban mobility

Does the arrival of sharing economy solve the question of urban mobility or does it only worsen it? The answer is that there is no universally correct answer. Every city is different. Manhattan is a nice example. The number of platform drivers has quickly become the same as the number of licensed drivers there. A study published in 2016 concluded that the worsening traffic situation isn't caused by these "additional" drivers but rather by tourism, construction, and delivery services.[125] But a year later, another study appeared and it pointed the finger at sharing economy.[126]

From the economic point of view, traffic jams are a source of pollution. Each driver is like a small chimney that contributes to a traffic jam. When there are fewer, it is no problem. The problem appears when the density of drivers reaches the breaking point. After that, every additional driver makes traffic worse and by deciding to get into their cars they increase their own and all other drivers' costs caused by waiting in a traffic jam. It's a typical example of a negative externality.

That is exactly what happened in Manhattan. It's not like the traffic was smooth before Uber and Lyft appeared. Traffic jams had already been a part of the daily lives of New Yorkers. However, the situation got worse with the arrival of platforms. The question is: how do we react? Some find the answer in an accounting method called LIFO (last in, first out). Taxi drivers were here first. So if somebody should be asked to leave, it's those who came last – Uber and Lyft.

But economics isn't accounting. An economist would ask a simple question: how do we reach the goal (improving traffic) at the lowest costs? To put it differently: how do we eliminate the so called "least cost avoiders", or those who lose the least by not driving around Manhattan? Given the almost double efficiency and occupancy of sharing economy platform vehicles compared to traditional taxi drivers, it could mean bad news for those who were there first.

So, how do we best find out who gets the shortest straw? First of all, it would help to stop treating busy roads like common pastures open to everybody. This means that those who rush to the hospital to save lives have the same traffic conditions as those who are off to buy a new doormat or a toy for their favorite pet. We need a system that ensures that those who can spare a ride decide to do it later or opt for public transport or Uber instead. Historically, the best system is a price mechanism. Some cities are already experimenting with different models of road charges or privatization. However, setting the right parameters is quite a tricky task.

(Un)Fortunately, not every city is Manhattan and sharing economy can generate completely different challenges and opportunities for other cities. Some North-American cities concluded agreements with platforms in order to create cooperation in the area of public transport. For example, in the city of Summit, in the state of New Jersey, public money is being used to subsidize transport fares for Uber customers. The city chose to do this instead of investing $20 million into a new parking garage. The city's spokesperson even said that it made no sense for the city to invest so much capital into garages because people will use cars differently in the future. A similar situation happened in the Canadian city of Innisfil near Toronto, which decided to subsidize transport fares for Uber customers instead of introducing two new bus lines. Their calculations showed that it it's economically more efficient. Similar stories can be found in other US cities.[127]

The platforms themselves are also launching several initiatives in this area and develop special "sub apps". For example, Shuttle by Lyft or Uberhopp which both provide something like bus transport for fixed fares on fixed routes. In Seattle, drivers can drive on a special route with fourteen fixed points. Another version of this is UberCommute which works like coordinated hitchhiking. If somebody regularly drives on the same route, they can pick up people along the route. UberPool or LyftLine work somehow more freely and enable several customers to share a ride in order to save money.

Express Pool is Uber's latest idea aimed at optimizing routes and rides while actively involving customers. Customers get recommendations as to when and where they should go before getting into the car so that they better fit into the rides timetable. What do they get in return? They pay 50% less.[128]

But today, we already know that even "traditional" Uber and Lyft can have a positive impact on traffic in most cities. Economist Ziru Li from Arizona and his team conducted an empirical study which proved that in the areas where Uber started to operate, there was a significant decrease of traffic jams and air pollution.[129] In order to measure the impact, they benefited from the experimental conditions found in cities where Uber was gradually entering its individual neighborhoods. That way economists were able to statistically clear Uber's influence on the indicators in question.

One of the reasons why sharing economy platforms can decrease the level of pollution and number of traffic accidents is the fact that its drivers have 30% higher vehicle occupancy than traditional taxi drivers and 50% more miles of rides with a paying customer.[130]

According to the authors of the study, this result can be attributed to four factors: Uber's technology of contact between customers and drivers is better and more elaborate than that of traditional taxi companies; Uber makes better use of economies of scale, which leads to connecting drivers and customers faster; Uber isn't bound by inefficient regulation; and its job supply and dynamic pricing mechanism are flexible.

Another potential reason is the average number of riders per ride. According to one survey, the average occupancy of Uber vehicles was 1.8 customers while for traditional taxies it was only 1.1.[131]

One of the indicators that things change with the arrival of platforms on the scene of urban transport is the dropping revenues and problems of companies that provide parking places. Ace Parking, one of the leaders in the provision of parking in the US, experienced a two-digit occupancy decrease in several different areas (nightclubs, restaurants, hotels). This doesn't mean that people stopped going downtown; it just means that they are beginning to leave their cars at home more and more often.[132]

4.7 PROGRESS WITHOUT PERMISSION – CONCLUSION

Throughout history, many innovative ideas had to fight for their place under the sun – not only against competitors and picky consumers but also against regulators. It's no wonder – public regulation is static by principle. Based on their knowledge from the past, a regulator defines conditions for the present. However, they have no way of knowing what the future will bring. The definition of innovation is the complete opposite of that. An innovator doesn't care how people did things in the past, neither do they examine the present state. Innovation is the projection of the future. When these two concepts clash in the real world, problems start to rise. Innovators propose innovation based on its future usefulness, but regulators assess it according to old standards.

As the examples in this book illustrate, this isn't only a matter of our old history but can be found in the recent past as well. Today we may even expect more such clashes to come. Our world gets more and more classified and bound by thousands of regulations yet at the same time, we live in times of rapid changes and constant innovation. We should therefore be ready to see progress without permission becoming a more frequent phenomenon than in the past.

This is why it's necessary to take a step back when looking at conflicts between regulation and innovation and look at it from a more distant perspective. It would be naïve to ask ourselves whether some new technology falls under one of the established official categories and if it doesn't, we automatically forbid it or wait until somebody changes a definition of a specific official category. Had our ancestors obligingly repeated this process, our lives would be very different now. The arrival of the new automobile by Carl Benz wasn't preceded by a legislative change – it was the other way around. Nor did the Wright brothers ask state institutions for permission to carry out their first flight. If every innovation had been required to pass through the parliament first, we would now live in a very sad world – a world without innovation.

The topic of progress without permission isn't being avoided by academics either. They conduct studies which explain the potential societal benefits generated by regulatory or evasive entrepreneurs. They conclude that where there are bad state laws and regulations, brave entrepreneurs who circumvent them and build competition can actually contribute towards the growth of well-being in society.*

This, of course, doesn't mean that defending progress without permission gives regulatory or evasive entrepreneurs an authorization to do whatever they like. None of the examples of controversial innovation that I mentioned included the breach of basic social norms. There was no stealing or physical violence. The same goes for sharing economy platforms. Their motto isn't "build a platform and you can do everything". These entrepreneurs also act in accordance with the fundamental laws and values our society is built on: they respect property rights, health, and lives of their members and comply with agreed conditions. To put it simply, they are faithful to the rule of law. The point where they cross the line usually represents specific regulations, which aren't fundamental to the western civilization but are rather a result of a conscious effort of politicians and lobbyists.**

What should a "unicorn state" do to achieve a just and prosperous society that doesn't seek to help selected interest groups? It should enable one simple thing: opting out from the system of regulations. It should let entrepreneurs openly and explicitly admit that their services aren't supervised by trade inspections, regulators, and different officials and clerks. It should also let them publicly show that they consider it their competitive advantage.

Some customers may be of the opposite opinion. Some people may decide to not step into a restaurant where no Public Health Authority has set foot. I would risk it without any problem. If I see hipsters in checked shirts working in

---

* Elert and Henrekson say the following about evasive entrepreneurs: "In such cases, evasive entrepreneurship becomes a welfare-enhancing second-best substitute for inefficient institutions, enabling the reallocation of resources to the pursuit of profitable business activities that are productive and would not have occurred without the evasion."

Pollman a Barry wrote about regulatory entrepreneurs: "Regulatory entrepreneurship provides a way to combat some of these socially inefficient laws. In certain instances, it is possible to build a business that stands to benefit from repealing inefficient legislation and replacing it with a more economically efficient regime."[9]

** This doesn't mean that these companies are saints and were founded by angels. Uber is a typical example of a troublemaker. Its employees and owners are also only human and make mistakes. Sometimes they act immorally and their working methods may not be approved by everybody. Unfortunately, there was even a case when the working environment and setting of the company lead to the harassment of female managers. This is sad and it is very important to point it out. But when we assess the phenomenon of sharing economy, it is irrelevant. We must separate the management of a specific firm from the concept of sharing economy which breaks existing regulations. These two things aren't related and an individual human failure doesn't mean that the concept as such isn't working. Similar things happened in the Oxfam charity during their humanitarian aid project on Haiti. Oxfam's employees took advantage of the locals being in need and paid them for sexual services. Yet nobody is calling for a general ban of the concept of humanitarian aid in the world.

a restaurant where a small glass of homemade lemonade costs $4, I consider it sufficient quality assurance.

The possibility to explicitly opt out from the official system brings competition with all its positive effects to the regulation services. The incentives of creators will improve, the evolution of progress will be defrosted, and rules will stop existing only on paper.

Some may find such policy too radical. They want to be sure that the restaurant they decide to eat in is compliant with all regulations. They're even convinced that everybody else is like them – wanting the certainty that comes with regulation. An evolutionary biologist would call them domesticated people. However, their objections are a misunderstanding of the proposed policy. As opposed to a one-off annulment of publicly provided regulation or a radical deregulation, the possibility to opt out from the regulatory system doesn't cancel anything. If somebody wants to choose a restaurant that sticks to regulations, they can choose one that complies with the standards of the Trade Inspection, Public Hygienist, and all other public regulations. And if most people are like that, then the majority will opt for such restaurants.

Policy that allows to opt out from the system doesn't ban regulations – it only creates sufficient market in the area of providing regulation services. It equalizes the conditions for public and private providers. It removes the monopoly everywhere it's unnecessary.

Personally, I am convinced that when private providers join their forces with the internet, they can substitute and even outperform public regulators. But I may be wrong and today's public regulations actually provide an excellent value and money ratio. It's important for a provision of regulation services or, in more general terms, quality assurance to become a regular service where market principles apply and where the customer is the boss instead of a temporarily elected politician or lobbyist start to apply.

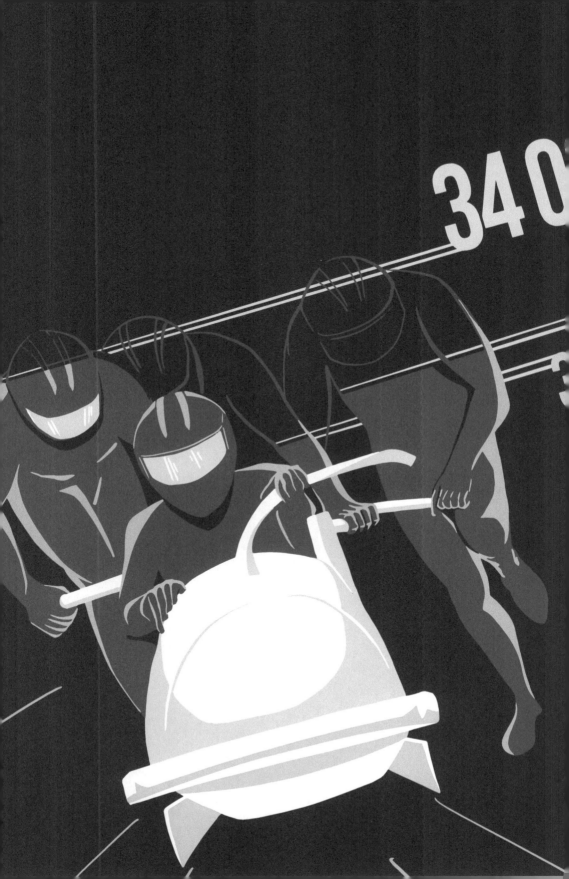

CROWDFUNDING AND PUBLIC GOODS

"Americans of all ages, all conditions, all minds constantly unite. Not only do they have commercial and industrial associations in which they all take part, but they also have a thousand other kinds: religious, moral, grave, futile, very general and very particular, immense and very small; Americans use associations to give fêtes, to found seminaries, to build inns, to raise churches, to distribute books, to send missionaries to the antipodes; in this manner they create hospitals, prisons, schools. Finally, if it is a question of bringing to light a truth or developing a sentiment with the support of a great example, they associate. Everywhere that, at the head of a new undertaking, you see the government in France and a great lord in England, count on it that you will perceive an association in the United States."[133]

Alexis de Tocqueville

1. INTRODUCTION – THE DARK SIDE OF RATIONALITY

Imagine you're alive in 333 BC. You're in Issa with the army of Alexander the Great, standing with thousands of other soldiers. You're armed with a long wooden stick with a metal blade and headed south to meet the enemy troops of King Darius of Persia. The situation is serious but not yet desperate. If you stay and fight, there's a big chance that you'll win. The phalanx – a military formation – has proven to be an excellent war strategy. The enemy's cavalry will have their teeth knocked out by the blades of your spears and most of you will survive. But if you decide to run, the enemy's horsemen will catch you and most likely kill you. It seems that the choice is obvious. The right decision for your army is to stay and fight.

It's not that easy, though. I made a mistake in the previous paragraph: I didn't take historical facts into consideration – it was a mistake to suppose that there is such a thing as "us" – a collective will. To think of an army as a deciding unit is a methodological error. The deciding unit is always the individual. I decide for myself whether to stay and fight or run away. The same way, the soldier next to me decides for himself.

If we look at the situation through the lens of methodological individualism or in other words, through the eyes of an individual, we get a different picture. As an individual, I have two options: stay and fight or run. However, I cannot influence the decisions of others. Let's suppose that the others will stay and fight. In that case, we will probably win the battle and most of us will survive. If I also stay and fight, there is a probability that something will happen to me but if I run away, I'm sure that I'll be fine. On top of that, my flight will not even influence the result of the battle. So, it seems that if others stay and fight, it's better for me to run away.

But what if others decide to run away? If I stay, it could be suicide. I could literally be the last one standing. If I choose to run away with others, the enemy might catch and kill most of us. We'll lose the battle either way. But since there is a chance that some of us will manage to escape, it is again better for me to run away. This decision-making process is graphically demonstrated in the table below.

Based on the above-described options, no matter what others do, it's always better for me to run away. And let's also point out that my strategic thinking skills are in no way special. All of my fellow soldiers can do the simple math. As a result, we'll all run away and from the collective point of view, we'll opt for an inefficient strategy despite the fact that all of us will individually make the best decision possible. We acted in our own interest which resulted in a collective tragedy. Ladies and gentleman, meet the dark side of individual rationality.[134]

1.1 SOLDIER'S DILEMMA

	I Stay and fight	I Run away
Others stay and fight	I may die in battle, but most of us will survive	I will be fine; others will probably survive
Others run away	There is a 100% chance that I will die	They will catch and kill almost all of us

Sceptics may object that even though this way of thinking theoretically makes sense, it doesn't describe what we observe in reality. Armies fight and soldiers die more often in battle than on the run. Alexander the Great's army didn't run away either. Despite all that, the problem is real and we have learnt how do tackle it (armies and nations who have not learnt it no longer exist). Have you ever thought why military training is the way it is? Apart from practical things like physical preparation, shooting exercises, or military techniques, it also involves things that may seem strange at first. For instance, long exercises during which soldiers are marching in a unified rhythm while they are singing or saluting together.

It seems that the purpose of such elements of training is to suppress individuality, erase the individual's reflex of an independently deciding person, and replace it with the reflex to automatically obey orders. Also, soldiers don't cut their hair short for hygienic reasons – it's supposed to remove individuality.[135] The objective is to transform individuals into a collective unit. Experiments from the field of evolutionary psychology confirm this too. They show that collective movement and rhythmic chanting improve the cooperation of a group. For a troop, this cooperation means staying and fighting.[136]

This is far from being the only way armies used to deal with this problem in the past. Stalin's order No. 227 from World War II became legendary and known simply as: *"Not one step back!"* (Ни шагу назад! in Russian). He forbade soldiers and military officials to retreat in a battle unless they receive an order from a commanding officer. The so-called blocking detachments were assigned to every front and their role was to shoot at retreating units or individuals on the run. The burning of ships which is said to be ordered by Hernán Cortés in 1519 during his conquest of Mexico, was supposed to serve a similar objective. This way he made it impossible for soldiers to run away and they only had one option left – to stay and fight. There are many more similar stories about big conquerors.

1.2 MARKET FAILURE – PUBLIC GOODS

In economy textbooks, the principle at play in this story is described by what is known as the public goods problem. Instead of an army deserter, there is a so-called free-rider, or an unpaying customer, and the objective is not to win a battle but rather to provide a public good.

This is briefly how the market works when it comes to traditional private goods: although everybody acts in their own interest on the market, the result is a functional chain of productive relationships. Entrepreneurs produce what customers want under competitive pressure. And if customers want it, they must pay for it, which again motivates entrepreneurs to produce more.

With public goods, this chain falls apart. These goods are characterized by one unpleasant feature – it is technically difficult or too costly to exclude free-riders from their consumption.* Consumers may like it at first – it means they can benefit from consuming a good without having to pay for it. But they stop liking it once they think about all the possible consequences. If consumers don't pay, entrepreneurs don't produce. As far as public goods are concerned, watching one's own interest tears apart the chain of productive relationships. The consumer then wonders why they should pay and consequently, the entrepreneur starts wondering why they should produce. At the end of the day, there are some useful services and goods people potentially want, but nobody produces them because it isn't profitable. In other words, there are unrealized gains. There is a market failure.

Today, most of us (hopefully) won't have to face a situation when we have to decide between running away or staying and fighting. More often, we experience a different dilemma – should we financially contribute to the services of national defense? Or, to be more precise, we would have to face such dilemma if the state had not taken the responsibility for the provision of the public good of national defense. Unlike entrepreneurs, the state has one big advantage – it doesn't ask for payments, it simply takes them. It has a legal monopoly for the use of violence. It doesn't have to rely on customer's approval like entrepreneurs. Theoretically, this could be a way to tackle the issue of free-riders. If I wanted to continue with the metaphor from the introduction of this chapter, we could say that the state plays the role of Stalin's blocking detachments. It modifies the calculations of an individual in such way that becoming a free-rider suddenly loses its charm.

---

* In economics textbooks, public goods are connected with another feature: indivisibility. In other words, they aren't subject to the exclusion principle. This feature means that when it comes to the consumption of certain goods, more for you doesn't mean less for me. When my daughter Emily was born, Slovakia gained one new consumer of the public good of national defense, but that doesn't mean that my neighbor, for example, is going to get less. Divisible goods represent the opposite situation. If I buy ice cream for Emily, there may not be enough left for my neighbor's kid. This feature of public goods creates a different type of problem, which economics addresses by the Monopoly Price Theory. It deals with the issue of product pricing on the level of marginal costs as a condition for optimality. I will briefly revisit the problem in the following chapter.

The idea of such market failure and its solution in the form of state intervention isn't a new invention by economists. Famous philosophers also noticed it in the past. David Hume, for example, used the draining of a meadow as an example:

"Two neighbors may agree to drain a meadow, which they possess in common, because 'tis easy for them to know each other's mind; and each must perceive that the immediate consequence of his failing in his part is the abandoning of the whole project. But 'tis very difficult, and indeed impossible, that a thousand persons should agree in any such action... Political society easily remedies ... these inconveniences. Thus, bridges are built; harbors opened; ramparts raised; canals formed; fleets equipped; and armies disciplined everywhere by the care of government."[137]

Adam Smith understood the problem and its solution in a similar way. He said that one of the three functions of the state was building and maintaining such public goods and services that, despite being highly beneficial for society, are of such type that their profit would never cover the costs of an individual and if so, it would be only a small group of individuals.[138]

The problem that lies behind the concept of public goods isn't imaginary. It's this world's sad reality. However, some economists started to draw conclusions that aren't necessarily implied by this problem. Just because it is problematic to exclude free-riders from some public goods, it doesn't automatically mean that it's time for the state and its enforcement to act. Radio and television broadcasts are a typical example. If a station or channel decides to transmit their signal without coding, everybody can access it. Such stations and channels cannot exclude free-riders. Nor do they want to, since apart from entertainment services (with positive costs) they also provide advertisement services (with negative costs). This means that broadcasting commercials brings profit to the station. By connecting these two services and reaching the right balance between them, private entrepreneurs can provide a public good in the form of free radio and television broadcasts. Internet entertainment works on a similar principle.* So, not all public goods have to be provided by the state necessarily.

As will show you later, there are many similar examples and we can find even more of them if we look to the past. Mainstream economists have underestimated people's ability to transform market failures into a profit opportunity for a long time. In addition, they often combined this underestimation of private initiatives with an often uncritical overestimation of the skills of those who stand behind the abstract concept of "the state". They include politicians, officials, lobbyists or voters.

These two tendencies displayed by mainstream economists resulted in misleading claims that students could read in the most popular economic textbooks all over the world. Paul Samuelson taught his students that since the private sector usually doesn't provide public goods to a sufficient extent, the government

---

* There is also ecrypted or cable television and radio broadcast but these forms don't fulfill the characteristics of a public good – namely, the indivisibility principle. Similarly, internet content can also be made accessible only to those who pay for it.

has to do it instead. In his legendary article, he even called his theory of public goods "The Pure Theory of Public Expenditure". By this he clearly indicated the normative impact of his theory. The father of public economics, Richard Musgrave, concluded together with his wife Peggy that if a public good is unrivaled in consumption and the exclusion is not appropriate or possible, market failure arises together with the need of budget financing because some goods that we call public cannot be provided through a market mechanism unlike private goods.*

These are all simplified if not misleading conclusions. And that's the main message of this chapter. First, I will show you that some examples of public goods were at some point provided privately or can be now provided by new technologies like crowdfunding. I will also explain why. In the end of the chapter, I will show you that the concept itself of a public good is not only applicable to the market, but we can also find its principles in the functioning of the state.

2. CROWDFUNDING

Just like sharing economy, crowdfunding is a child of the internet revolution. The very first documented example of a successful crowdfund was an online fundraising campaign for British rock band Marillion.

It was 1997 and the band didn't have enough resources to organize concerts overseas. One of their American fans got the idea of starting a big fundraiser to cover the costs of plane tickets and organization of concerts across the USA. He did so via e-mails and internet fora. The campaign turned out to be a huge success and fans managed to collect $60,000. The band later used crowdfunding to publish their next album.

A few years later, the first specialized crowdfunding platforms started to appear. Their objective was to manage different fundraising campaigns under one roof. ArtistShare started its activities in 2003 and two years later, it was followed by Kiva. But the real breakthrough was brought about by platforms that started at the end of the first decade of the third millennium – at the same time Uber and Airbnb were being created in the minds of entrepreneurs. Namely, these were the still popular Indiegogo (2008) and Kickstarter (2009). What did they bring?

Well, nothing groundbreaking: crowdfunding existed even before internet platforms. What they did bring was a multitude of improvements. Like sharing economy platforms, they enabled people to connect on an unprecedented scale. Crowdfunding platforms connect two kinds of people: those who have a project that needs resources and those who have resources and are looking for a cause to contribute to. The platform enables the former group to create their own subpage

---

* A critical analysis of this approach:[A10]

where they can list more specific information about their project, the amount of financial resources needed for its implementation, photos, promotion videos, and eventual gifts for contributors who are regularly informed about the state of the campaign via the platform. It offers the latter group an opportunity to easily and safely contribute in small amounts while there's a guarantee that they'll get their money back if the conditions of the campaign aren't fulfilled.

Artists were the first ones to use the power of the crowd multiplied by the internet for their creative projects. Later, they were joined by new entrepreneurs and startups with their new product ideas, which is how crowdfunding became quite a powerful "presale" tool. Thanks to crowdfunding, starting entrepreneurs got the possibility to check the consumers' reactions to their products, get feedback, and spread information about their products among masses of people. Especially small, new entrepreneurs used crowdfunding to circumvent traditional funding ways and get the initial capital to start their business. This is how crowdfunding started to be used as a tool for market research, marketing, advertising and funding all in one. After all, even the book you are holding in your hands exists thanks to a crowdfunding campaign by which I tested the potential interest of readers and financed its publishing.

After some time, crowdfunding also started to attract different, more controversial, types of campaigns. For example, on Indiegogo, there was a campaign for collecting money to pay a drug gang from Toronto, which promised that once the reward is collected, they will publish a video showing the local mayor smoking crack. They managed to raise $200 thousand from more than 8000 contributors.[139] Another interesting campaign was that of a young man who accidentally broke his tooth and had neither the insurance nor the sufficient funds for a new one (3600 dollars from 183 people).[140]

New subsections focused on public or community projects started to gradually appear within the existing platforms. Shortly after that, brand new platforms appeared which focused specifically on providing funding for public services. We commonly refer to them as civic crowdfunding platforms. From the economic point of view, they focus on the financing of public goods. Today, they are quite numerous: Ioby, Spacehive, Catarse, Goteo, Tilt (before it was called CrowdTilt), Gofundme, Citizinvestor, Crowdfunder, Razoo, Crowdrise, People's Project (former Narodniy), Voor je Buurt, Co-city, Patronicity, FundRazr, JustGiving, GlobalGiving, Place2Help, Derev, Eppela, or StartSomeGood. Apart from these, I would like to mention Experiment.com and #SciFund Challenge – they focus on providing funding for basic research, which falls under the definition of public goods and is mostly used by ecologists and evolutionary biologists.[141]

Although crowdfunding isn't a huge phenomenon from the overall economics point of view, it is growing exponentially just like most internet technologies. In 2011, the overall amount collected via crowdfunding platforms was more than $1 billion. A year later, it was $2.7 billion, the year after that $6.1 billion and in 2015, this number got to $34.4 billion.[142]

Within the research that I carried out during my PhD studies, I collected data from seven platforms focused on providing funding for public goods campaigns. Throughout their existence, they have collected tens of millions of euros.

Selected crowdfunding campaigns focused on public goods:

Platforms	Total contribution (€)	Number of successful projects	Success rate (%)	Years of data collection (including)
IOBY	5,020,000	1,663	87	2009 – 2017
Spacehive	11,900,000	585	53	2012 – 2018
Goteo	4,765,789	595	75	2011 – 2018
People's Project	3,213,000	105	-	2014 – 2018
Voor je Buurt	3,610,376	695	83	2012 – 2018
StartSomeGood	9,121,819	915	96	2011 – 2018
Patronicity	9,900,000	425	96	2014 – 2018

Source: own processing*

Civic crowdfunding platforms help build numerous community centers, gardens, compost stations, libraries, museums, playgrounds, bike paths; organize events, marches, concerts, fundraising campaigns to help poor children or finance school equipment; renovate parks, sidewalks, squares, statues, historical buildings, waste containers, or playgrounds.

Most people associate these things with the role of state and funding through taxes. How did crowdfunding manage to do the same? How did it convince people to contribute so extensively to public projects everybody benefits from? How did it manage to mitigate the problem of public goods?

How people managed to collect money for public lighting, police, fireworks, statue of Robocop and help Jamaican bobsledders

Crowdfunding platforms are often filled with projects that were created as a response to the state's failure to provide.

The citizens of Delphi, Indiana were facing an increasing rate of criminality in a local park which had been neglected for years. In 2017, two girls were murdered there. The citizens then decided to start a campaign in order to get more public lighting, security cameras, information kiosks, public wi-fi, orientation signs, and reconstruct the entrance to the park. They collected more than $93 thousand (even though their goal was $50

---

* Eva Schwarzová helped me with updates for 2018

thousand) and a public development agency promised to pay another 50 thousand once they completed their objective.[143]

The citizens of Highland Park, Michigan had a different problem. In 2011, two thirds of street lamps stopped working due to the city's financial problems. The city was swimming in debt and decided to take an innovative approach to the question of public lighting: they asked the local citizens to keep their porch lights on during the night. The locals decided to take the matter into their own hands and in 2012, they created a fundraising campaign to buy an LED street lamp with a solar panel. In a few weeks' time they collected $6,250 and within a few months they held a ceremony to turn the light on for the first time. This was followed by another campaign where they collected $13 thousand and gradually built five more lamps. Of course, this wasn't enough to replace the shortage of public lighting, but they managed to light the way in the darkest sections that their porch lights couldn't reach.[144]

Some crowdfunding platforms are specifically focused on a certain type of public service. For example, the platform called Wearebeam specializes in helping the homeless. Every person without a home who joins the platform and expresses the interest to change their life gets their own profile. Since they need money to start the transformation, anybody can choose to contribute. The platform shows you the person's allocated social worker, how much money they need for education/training, transport, or a laptop to search for work, and you can also see how much money they have already collected. Their profile includes a journal where they note what they've already accomplished and which goals they have yet to reach.[145]

Platform called Patreon supports artists – musicians, short story writers, comic books, podcasts, videos, photos, or even research. The contributor can set up a regular monthly contribution to support their favorite artist.

And then there's CrowdJustice – platform focused on financing lawsuits. Not all people can afford to pay a lawyer as well as all the lawsuit-related costs, especially when it comes to the lawsuits where one fights in the name of public interest. To give you an example, the case Aziz vs. Trump was an interesting one. Two young men flew to the U.S. from Yemen, excited to finally live with their dad, a U.S. citizen. Unfortunately, their plane landed a few hours after President Trump signed a new executive order on immigration. Once they arrived, the young men were handcuffed and forced to sign papers they didn't understand. What they signed was their consent to voluntarily give up the statute of legal immigrants. After that, they sent them back on a flight to Ethiopia where they had a connecting flight on their way to the U.S. The aim of the lawsuit was to get the U.S. government to transport the boys back to the U.S. and grant them the status of legal immigrants. The platform collected $37 thousand and the lawsuit was successful – the boys now live with their father.

We can find many similar examples on these platforms. There is a group that fights for electoral rights of US citizens who live in Guam and Puerto Rico; a group that took legal action against the British government for refusing to publish a secret study about the impact of Brexit; there are doctors suing the government for having signed dangerous contracts and you can even find a group that fights for legal protection for the informant from Cambridge Analytica.[146]

Civic crowdfunding isn't always about big, serious things. The citizens of Omaha, for instance, managed to collect money for the Independence Day fireworks display[147] and Robocop fans raised a sum of $67 thousand to build a three-meter-tall bronze statue of their favorite hero in Detroit.[148]

Crowdfunding also enabled the scenario from the film Cool Runnings to take place again. After one decade, the Jamaican bobsleigh team managed to qualify for the winter Olympics (2014 in Sochi) but they didn't have enough financial resources to go there. That was when somebody launched a campaign on CrowdTilt to collect $80 thousand. In a few days' time, the account displayed over $115 thousand. A parallel campaign for the Jamaican bobsleigh team was running on Indiegogo where $40 thousand was collected, so the team could happily participate in the Olympics.

Sport-related funding through crowdfunding is nothing new these days – there are even specialized platforms for it like RallyMe or Pursu.it. Now even porn actors started to turn to crowdfunding since their industry has been strongly affected by streaming services that enable users to get free pornographic content. That's why actors turned to their fans for a direct funding of their production via Patreon or OnlyFans.[149]

Even politicians use crowdfunding now. In 2008, Barack Obama managed to collect $272 million during his pre-electoral campaign from about 2 million of his supporters. Another example is from Malaysia where the state was experiencing a financial collapse under the weight of its public debt. The government decided to launch a crowdfunding campaign in order to lower the public debt and in 24 hours, they collected $1.7 million. The finance minister proudly boasted, saying that "Malaysians have taken their patriotism to a greater height."[150] Few years ago, a group of pranksters in the U.S. attempted to crowdfund the construction of the Great American Wall on the border with Mexico – as a joke.[151] However, it stopped being funny once a Congresswoman proposed a draft of a bill that would enable the government to build the wall and finance it with the resources collected via crowdfunding.[152]

Crowdfunding can sometimes turn against politicians. Let's look at an example from Slovakia. The local crowdfunding platform, LudiaLudom.sk, hosted a campaign aimed at supporting farmers, who in 2018, came from the east of the country to protest in Bratislava, the capital, against the government whom they were accusing of corruption related to allocating subsidies. They managed to collect €27 thousand which they used to cover the costs of fuel and tractor tires necessary for their protest drive.

Crowdfunding was also used as a response to the decision of the Director of the Slovak National Radio and Television Service who cancelled the last remaining investigative program called Reportéri (Reporters). People joined their forces on the Startlab platform and supported the program's continuation outside the public television service. They raised €11,740. As a last example we may state the civic association For Decent Slovakia who needed support to face attacks from the former Prime Minister Robert Fico. People very quickly managed to collect over €80 thousand and the association organized big national protests against the abuse of state power.

3. THERE ARE THREE PROBLEMS WITH PUBLIC GOODS; CROWDFUNDING OFFERS THREE SOLUTIONS

The problematic face of crowdfunding described in the introduction actually consists of three sub-problems:
- the risk of getting the short straw,
- the motivation of a free-rider,
- organization costs.

1) Sometimes you do want to contribute to a public good but you're afraid others won't, and so your contribution goes to waste. Metaphorically speaking, it would be you who would get the short straw. So, you decide not to contribute not because you are mean or selfish, but because you are afraid. You don't want to be the fool who contributed to nothing. That's the first problem – the risk of getting the short straw.

2) Another problem is related to the motivation of a free-rider who happily relies on others and has a reason for it. No matter what they do, they get (or not) what they want – it doesn't matter whether they contribute or not. Because they get no added value by buying a ticket, they happily take a free ride.

3) The last problem consists of the costs of organizing a collective action. In order to be able to provide a public good, a lot of people have to participate in its financing. This is why it's necessary to plan and propose a fundraising project which is later promoted, implemented, and concluded. However, this requires some costs which grow with the number of people that needs to be involved.

In the following three subchapters, I will show you how crowdfunding platforms mitigate these problems. They don't offer a perfect solution, because there is no such thing, yet they do bring handy tools, mechanisms, and institutional settings that help increase the rate of voluntary contributions to public goods.

3.1 ELIMINATING THE SHORT STRAW

Paul Liu lives in Oakland, a port town in California. After the financial crisis, the city suffered big financial problems and among other things, it had to lay off 20% of their local policemen. Even before this happened, Oakland belonged among cities with the highest crime rate.[153] On top of that, in 2013, the local police were under federal supervision for the suspicion of abuse of power.

Paul's house is located in a neighborhood called Rockridge. Two years after the crisis, the robbery rate in Rockridge grew by 50% and burglary rate by almost 40%.[154] Since the inhabitants of the neighborhood couldn't rely on the declining local police, all they could do was take their fate into their own hands. No, they didn't buy guns or establish neighborhood watches – they decided to voluntarily chip in and fund private police.

There were four different scenarios of how their initiative could potentially end up from Paul's point of view (they are basically the same four scenarios from the table in the introduction to this chapter which depicts the soldiers' decision-making process):

1. They manage to get sufficient funds to pay for private police while Paul pretends that the initiative doesn't concern him – he plays the role of a free-rider.
2. They manage to get sufficient means to pay for private police and Paul's contribution is included in it.
3. Nobody contributes. Not even Paul.
4. Paul contributes but others choose to be free-riders and Paul's effort will be in vain.

The scenarios are in no random order. They go from the best (1) to the worst (4) *from the perspective of Paul's decision.* Let's first have a look at the worst scenario (in the table it would be the lower left corner) which could also be expressed by the proverb "no good deed goes unpunished." Paul was willing to help the common cause, but it ended up the worst possible way for him. He voluntarily contributed to a public good, but no public good was realized and, in the end, his contribution was lost. In the initial example with the army, this meant that a soldier stayed and fought but was facing a certain death.

Contributing to public goods does bring certain risks. Namely the risk of losing money for nothing. One doesn't necessarily have to be a greedy egoist in order to become a free-rider. One might just have the justified fear that others won't contribute and he or she will get the short straw.

There is quite a handy solution to this problem. All it takes is to determine in advance how much money needs to be collected in order to finance public good (establishing a financial objective) and then agree that if this threshold isn't reached, all contributions will go back to contributors. In specialized literature, you can find this mechanism under several names: assurance contract, provision point mechanism, or threshold pledge system. On crowdfunding platforms, it is known as "all or nothing". Applying this principle means that if the author of the campaign manages to collect all the necessary means, they are allowed to use them. If they fail to reach the objective, all contributions are returned to contributors.[155]

In case of our soldier, this would mean that if he decides to stay and fight, he can change his decision once he sees the others running away. This is a way to minimize the short straw problem and eliminate one of the motives to become a free-rider. The worst scenario no longer exists – it's impossible for you to get the short straw. In a certain sense, public goods become similar to private goods – even with these it is possible to pay and get nothing.

In the end, Paul and all the other inhabitants of Rockridge were lucky in several ways. Fortunately, they didn't read economy textbooks where they would have learnt that the police are a public good and therefore have to be provided by the government (as Samuelson said), or the need for budget financing will arise (as Musgrave said). Also, the platform CrowdTild (later renamed to simply Tilt), which focuses on public services and projects, was founded at about the same time. This enabled Paul to start a campaign in 2013, which he established with the initial threshold of $8205. In the case of reaching his objective, he was supposed to make sure that citizens have private police at their disposal 12 hours a day five days a week for almost half a year. However, Tilt also makes it possible to set up a second threshold, and reaching it means having the above standard service quality. Paul set it for $20,513 which would mean more policemen and longer duration of the service.

In his campaign, Paul described everything in detail. He wrote about the lack of safety and increasing crime rate in the neighborhood as well as the causes and potential ways to fix the situation. He also picked a specific private agency that was supposed to provide police services, explained why he chose them and listed which services they would provide. Despite this, during the campaign there arose a discussion on the platform as to whether the police will be armed, whether there will be racial discrimination, and whether or not they will disrupt life in the neighborhood. Paul answered all of these questions saying that the policemen won't be armed and their main role will be crime prevention or early capture of criminals. He also added information about the competences and trainings the policemen underwent.

The campaign ended up being so successful that in the following days, it inspired two other neighborhoods who launched similar campaigns with similar objectives. In a couple of days, all of them managed to collect enough resources to reach the first threshold. Two out of the three campaigns even managed to reach their second threshold which meant securing long-term security service.

Rockridge's private police service wasn't just a "blind shot" – it's still there. The locals later established a separate NGO called Safer Rockridge, which became responsible for follow-up activities and further voluntary financing of private police. The organization sends out their own brochures in which they inform the public about news and statistics related to the work of local policemen. The local newspapers also launched a survey among the inhabitants of Rockridge in which 94% participants were satisfied with the police services and 95% did not perceive any negatives connected with their presence; 75% participants felt safer with the new police and 87% wanted them to continue next year.[156]

Apart from being the author of the campaign, Paul is a Google analyst and he wrote a study about the efficiency of private police in his neighborhood. Based on crime data from 2007-2014, he estimated that after the successful campaign, robberies and burglaries decreased by 30%. Also, according to his study, nothing suggested the increase of crime rate in the surrounding neighborhoods.[157]

This is how the inhabitants of Rockridge used crowdfunding to pay for a public service that is usually provided by the state. They managed it thanks to the all-or-nothing mechanism. The question is why this mechanism wasn't used before crowdfunding got popular. I suppose that the answer can be found in high organization costs (we'll talk about them in the third subchapter) – it's quite an arduous task to return every single contribution should a campaign fail.

HOW CROWDFUNDING USES HUMAN NATURE

The neoclassic theory supposes that people decide exclusively to their own benefit and don't take the decisions of others into account. The neoclassic economic theory views an individual as an independently deciding unit. If we wanted to explain how the market works in big anonymous societies, it makes sense to suppose that people primarily take impersonal parameters into account, such as price. However, if we consider the setting of a closer social context, we have to admit that apart from personal gain, people also care about relationships and social status and often find themselves in situations when others are "looking over their shoulder". That's when they behave a lot more altruistically and voluntarily contribute to public goods, contrary to the supposition of some economists.

The endeavor to explain people's willingness to contribute to common goods under certain conditions became one of the liveliest research programs involving various scientific disciplines. Evolutionists have made the biggest progress in this area. Many were inspired by finding an explanation of how the motivation for the common good arose in the environment of natural selection. They came up with various theories, like: kin selection (helping two brothers is like helping yourself),[158] reciprocal altruism (if I help you today, you'll help me tomorrow),[159] cultural and evolutionary reasons (morale, norms, and religion motivate us to cooperate),[160] and group selection (from the evolutionary point of view, a community of altruists stands higher than a community of egoists).[161]

Which psychological adaptations for carrying out good deeds have we inherited? Surely not the willingness to help anybody at any time. If it was so, there would be no public goods problem and nobody would want to be a free-rider. Even market failures wouldn't exist in that case. In reality, what we have inherited is more like "conditioned altruistic reflexes" which trigger the "good deed strategy" only under specific conditions. Economists, psychologists and anthropologists have been experimentally examining them for decades.[162] What have they discovered?

They found out that people really are better (meaning more cooperative) than the homo economicus economic model supposes. In the experiments, people were contributing to the common good, they were happy to share even if they didn't have to and they felt the needed to punish free-riders although it might cost them something. This cooperation may not be perfect, but it would surely surprise several authors of economic textbooks from the first half of the 20th century. The experiments also showed that people's willingness to contribute to public goods is conditioned. Many are willing to contribute, but only if they see others doing it too. Different experiments from various countries reveal that on average, one third of us are free-riders and a half are willing to contribute under specific conditions. The rest are either somewhere in between or not willing to contribute under any conditions.[163]

The research has not only remained in labs. There is a well-known experiment that took place in a school in Zürich, Switzerland where students had the opportunity to contribute to help get poor or foreign students cheap student loans.[164] In another experiment, economists asked tourists to contribute to a new ski slope.[165] What was the result? In both cases individuals contributed more and more frequently once they learned that others contributed too.

Apart from examining human willingness to carry out good deeds, scientists also examined different tools and mechanisms that help increase the rate of contributing. We already know that people are more inclined to contribute to the common good when they communicate amongst each other, when their contributions are publicly visible, when they can choose who they cooperate with, or when they have the possibility to punish free-riders. The crowdfunding all-or-nothing tool is one of the most successful tools to increase contribution rate.

Economists carried out plenty of experiments in which they tested people's willingness to contribute to public goods – with the all-or-nothing tool and without it. The results vary but they are always positive. Some show that the all-or-nothing mechanism doubled the contribution rate. Others say that it practically revealed the preferences of potential free-riders or increased the probability that more people will contribute to its realization, especially if the cost is high and that it works even when participants have limited information.[166] A "meta-study" that assessed such experiments concluded that employing the all-or-nothing mechanism brings big advantages.[167]

There were also field experiments in which the participants had no idea they were participating in an experiment. This enabled economists to assess how people behave in real situations. For example, an economist named Thomas Walker carried out an experiment in Ghana where he tested the willingness of its citizens to contribute to public goods (public toilets, infrastructure). Groups in which he used the all-or-nothing mechanism collected twice or even three times as much money as groups where he did not use it. Another field experiment where people contributed to environmental projects ended up similarly.

It is therefore no wonder that crowdfunding campaigns started to use the all-or-nothing tool massively. They also use other tools which were tested in experiments, for example adding the option of discussing and commenting on a campaign, allowing to post, or publishing information about how many people contributed and how much. It seems that publicly available information motivates those who are willing to contribute when they see that others did too. Now practically every crowdfunding platform includes graphical representations of information about how many people contributed, the sum that has been collected, and how much is still missing. This way all those with conditioned willingness to contribute learn all they need to know.

Crowdfunding platforms learned to use many of our innate mental adaptations to carrying out good deeds circumstantially. People aren't cold-blooded machines that only act in their own interest nor are they enlightened altruists. Our evolutionary past equipped us with a set of social reflexes that are triggered under different conditions and in different situations. The aim of platform architects and campaign authors is to set up projects in a way that makes sure people are most willing to contribute.

Will torrent pirates get a Nobel Prize for economics?

Elinor Ostrom is the only woman who has been awarded Nobel Prize for economics. Her research revealed something which surprised many economists – people are able to voluntarily realize collective projects. Together they can build and maintain an irrigation system, take care of forests and pastures or prevent excessive fishing. Communities all over the world managed to do so by establishing rules and ensuring their compliance together. This is how they were able to punish free-riders and keep continuous, productive cooperation. They have managed to achieve what many economists deemed impossible without the presence of a government.

However, the communities in her research were relatively small homogenous groups. They consisted of tens, maximum one hundred, households that knew one another, already had a long-term cooperation established and came from the same culture. Would it be possible to achieve such a degree of cooperation with thousands or hundred thousand individuals who don't know one another and come from different cultures? And what if they are involved in illegal activities – meaning not only that the state provider of law and order doesn't help them but in addition actively fights against them?

Actually, as Ostrom was carrying out her research, exactly this type of big heterogenous group of anonymous individuals started to form. They were pirates on torrent peer-to-peer (P2P) networks where illegal copies of films, songs, series, or books are shared.

P2P networks work without a central server. Users themselves act as the server and the clients at the same time. The same person can be a provider (seeder) and a consumer (leecher) of media files. Apart from this, there is also a centralized type of illegal sharing. One such example is the Megaupload server, which was shut down by the authorities in 2012 and its founder, Kim Dotcom, was sent to prison. Such a scenario is very unlikely to happen on P2P networks because there is no specific server you can shut down or a specific person that can go to prison. The content is distributed through a huge number of computers.

This advantage also presents a problem – free-riders. P2P networks rely on the willingness of individual users to upload content. But a kind-hearted pirate slows down the speed of their internet connection when their upload is on and increases the risk of having problems with the police without receiving any personal benefits in return. Homo economicus has a clear opinion on that – they will turn downloading fully on and turn off uploading. Actually, the first P2P networks from about 20 years ago (like Gnutella) were filled with free-riders: it is estimated that 70-85% of their members didn't not upload any content, they just downloaded it. Economists predicted their quick decline under the heavy weight of parasitism.[168]

The second generation of P2P networks (BitTorrents) helped to mitigate the problem. Within these networks, it wasn't so easy for pirates to avoid contributing to the common good. The system requires the person downloading to allow uploading as well. The networks even introduced a motivational bonus for those who enabled upload with a big amount of data – they have a better chance to connect and download from someone whom they previously helped by uploading on BitTorrent. Thanks to that, they download faster than their selfish co-pirates who were only uploading when they had to.

However, uploading new content to the network has its risks, mostly when the content is illegal. This turned against a pirate who uploaded the film The Revenant – he was sanctioned to pay a million dollars and was ordered to be on house arrest.[169]

But pirates didn't give up and started to come up with BitTorrent upgrades – the so-called trackers. You can picture them as web pages with detailed information about who uploaded what torrents with files and how many people are currently downloading and uploading them. A tracker serves only as a kind of information center – there are no files uploaded. Trackers can be further divided into public and private. While public trackers are accessible to everybody (The Pirate Bay, 1337x.io), one needs an invitation in order to gain access to private ones (Passthepopcorn, Broadcastthenet and in the past also What.CD), and studies show that they solve the issue of free-riders much more efficiently.[170]

How did they manage it? They all have their own "constitution" where they define the rights and obligations of community members. They are notably similar to those used by the communities from Elinor Ostrom's research. Here are the five basic rules: you shall not create a second account, you shall not share torrents on other trackers, you shall not use anonymization tools, you shall not sell invitations, and you shall regularly contribute with your upload. The last "commandment" is the most important and trackers have many tools to ensure its compliance (they are described in the constitutions which can have more than 20,000 words).

Another important thing is that the access to these platforms is regulated. You only get it if you have an invitation. Invitations are distributed according to the quality of individual members and only experienced members who have reached a certain position in the hierarchy can send them. Some trackers require new members to "undergo an entering test", which tests the speed of their upload or records from other trackers demonstrating their willingness to upload. There is even a tracker where potential new members have to undergo a special interview during which they have to answer a multitude of technical questions and demonstrate knowledge of local rules.[171]

Once a pirate is admitted to a tracker, they begin as a complete greenhorn with the lowest rank. Ascending to higher ranks is connected with fulfilling various requests, such as sufficient uploading, and as a reward they get new privileges.[172] Apart from that, trackers require their users to keep a certain minimum sharing ratio. If members fail to reach the required ratio between downloads and uploads, they lose the acquired ranks and if they don't improve it, they will be deleted. Another set of rules dictates what the name of an uploaded file has to include: size, format, resolution, original source (e.g., 4 GB, MKV, 720p, Blu-ray). One of the tools that ensure the enforcement of keeping a certain level of quality of files is a discussion forum where members assess files and eventual breaches of rules.

With these mechanisms and rules, pirates solved the age-old problem of contributing to a common cause. In addition, they managed to do it in an extremely big, heterogenous and anonymous group. In other words, they successfully instilled law and order in a group that would be typically expected to need some type of central authority.

3.2 BINDING FREE-RIDERS

By the end of the 19th century, Americans received a gift from the French – the Statue of Liberty. The only thing that didn't make it through the Atlantic Ocean was the pedestal. Americans were supposed to build it themselves which turned out to be a problem. The mayor of New York City at the time, who later became a US President, Grover Cleveland, refused to finance the project with public money. Congress didn't help either. $100,000 was needed for the construction of the pedestal (today it would correspond to about $2.3 million) and the situation wasn't looking good. Even the mayors of Boston and Philadelphia offered to build it from public money provided the statue would be built in their city.

Surely everybody knows how the story ended – the Statue of Liberty can be found in New York. But not everybody may know how they managed to build it there. The key character in our story is Joseph Pulitzer – an immigrant from Hungary who is today known for the journalism prize named after him. He decided to get the financing for the pedestal through his paper platform – The New York World newspaper. He organized a big public fundraiser with the aim of reaching many people to contribute with small sums. A paper platform could handle this although it couldn't handle the application of the all-or-nothing mechanism. But Pulitzer came up with another tool: special rewards. Everybody who decided to contribute to this public good found their name with the amount they contributed in one of the issues of the newspaper. In addition, those who contributed one dollar or more got a 6-inch-tall model of the Statue of the Liberty and those who contributed five dollars got one that 1ft tall. That's how Pulitzer managed to collect $102 thousand from 160 thousand people in six months. Among the contributors you could find all age and social groups: small children, pensioners, poor shoe cleaners, or rich factory owners.

Pulitzer's technique was rediscovered by economists in the second half of the 20th century. Namely Mancur Olson in his book called the Logic of Collective Action. He identified rewards for contributors (or punishment for free-riders) to be one of the most important tools of organizing a public action and labelled them selective incentives. Their task is to influence the contributor's decision through extra motivation.

Thanks to selective incentives we no longer rely solely on the kindness of the potential contributor's soul. We can win them over by pointing out the selective benefits available exclusively for contributors or by showing the selective punishments that will be imposed on free-riders. An example of a selective punishment would be Stalin's blocking detachments we mentioned in the introduction. Today there's a tendency towards selective advantages in the form of medals, honors, and granting higher ranks to soldiers for their heroic actions. If selective incentives are set correctly, they can even persuade selfish people to contribute to common well-being and help the community.

It is therefore no surprise that crowdfunding platforms use this tool too. Most of them allow campaign authors to create their own contributors reward structure on their subpage. Anything can be used as a reward, you can find souvenir T-shirts, baseball caps, towels, bags, certificates, or even personal meetings and dinner invitations from campaign authors. On the more unusual side of the spectrum, you can leave a message or carve your name on a board of a wooden bridge or a tile used in the construction of a public swimming pool. The quantity and value of the reward usually corresponds with the amount contributed – the more one contributes to a public good, the bigger reward they get.

Although selective incentives tend to be small things, they can have a big impact on the decision of potential contributors. What's important is that the reward is something you can't get outside the campaign. They have to be somehow exclusive, otherwise free-riders won't bother trying to get them by contributing to a public good. Imagine if Paul from Rockridge, who created the private police fundraising campaign, promised a pound of bananas to every contributor. The prospect of such reward wouldn't motivate them since they can easily get a pound of bananas elsewhere and cheaper. Luckily, Paul was more clever than that – he offered his contributors a special contract with private police which ensured that they would get daily updates about suspicious activities in the neighborhood, a home security alarm connected to the police, bonus patrols when they're on holiday and their house is empty and a direct contact number to the police officer to whom they can report suspicious activities in the area.[173] This offer had the actual potential to convince a potential free-rider that contributing to a public good is worth it.

Another technique of providing public goods privately, which belongs to a category similar to selective incentives, is binding. It's a similar procedure, only we take it from the opposite end: instead of a private bonus to a contribution to a public good, some entrepreneurs bind the purchase of a private good with the financing of a public one. Shopping malls are a typical example of this. In shopping malls, you usually pay for private goods and services (shopping in individual stores) and at the same time you contribute to the provision of public goods: security workers, air conditioning, toilets, cleaning services, parking, etc. Nobody is excluded from the consumption of these public goods (you can use a shopping mall toilet without purchasing anything).

Binding must fulfill certain requirements, though. You can't bind just any two things. There should be a complementary relationship between a private and public good. It doesn't mean that free-riders don't exist. It just means that thanks to the existing complementary relationship, most consumers of public goods end up buying private goods that are bound to them and this includes costs of the public ones.[174]

Slovak rappers are a good example of effective binding – it wasn't easy for them to get rich because everybody just downloads their music or burns CDs, so they've learned that they can make the most money from their music by selling T-shirts, caps, or glasses.

Selective incentives and binding represent two opposite ends of the same institutional tool. When it comes to the former, its primary function is to reward people for their contribution to a public good which motivates free-riders to rethink their attitude. As for the latter, the central idea is a private good bound with a public good which increases its value (imagine a shopping mall without toilets, air conditioning, or parking).

The world is changing and musicians have to adapt to it

Two hundred years ago, the average person had the opportunity to listen to their favorite musical composition once in their lifetime (if they were lucky). Twenty years ago, you could buy a compact disc and listen to the song of your choice whenever you wanted. For the past two years, all we need is the internet. Technology changed the relationship between musicians and listeners. Two centuries ago, physical contact was necessary and you could only access a musical performance if you were invited or if you had paid for it. Free-riders had no chance. Two decades ago, all it took was a business relationship with a publisher as an intermediary. You didn't have to physically meet the musician but you could own a physical product (audio cassette or CD). These days, no connection between the musician and their listeners is needed (apart from the internet one). Music became a public good. The internet gives you the possibility to listen to the album of your favorite artist anywhere and on top of all that, you don't even have to pay for it. Just like free-riders.

We can see that internet technologies don't only help provide public goods, but sometimes they also transform private goods into public ones.

This isn't just some negligible problem; it's a real paradigmatic change in the music industry and nothing demonstrates it better than numbers. In 1996, the revenues of the music industry were $60 billion. Those were the golden years of music publishing companies. But with new technology and the internet, the industry slowly started to decline and in 2014 its revenues went down to $15 billion.[175]

Musicians had two types of reactions to this undeniable fact. Some turned to the state, its laws, and police for help. Others tested new, handy ways of monetizing their music with the use of new technology which was initially the cause of their misfortune.

The ones who turned to the state in Slovakia managed to push forward a new copyright law. Based on the presumption of guilt principle, the "music tax" on various electronic devices that could potentially carry musical records was increased. This includes mobile phones (0.7 % of the price), tablets (0.6%), video cameras (1%), picture cameras (0.35%) or smart TVs (3%). So, if you buy a TV worth 600 euros in Slovakia these days, you will pay another 100 euros on VAT and yet another 18 euros representing the fees for copyright. From the economic point of view, this is nothing but the increase of indirect taxes. Unlike VAT, the taxes don't go to the state budget but to the so-called collective copyright administration organizations (such as our local SOZA – Slovak Performing and Mechanical Rights Society or LITA). These organizations then allocate the collected taxes among their registered authors as the "replacement of authors' reward".

But there are also artists who didn't approach information technology and internet as a threat but rather as an opportunity. The hip-hop community, for instance, also has to deal with the unwillingness of their listeners to buy original records. In addition, because of its explicit nature, hip-hop cannot rely on being played on the radio and thus receiving royalties from SOZA. So, the artists have a good reason to look for alternative solutions to gain profit from their talent and music.

Rappers used the internet and new technologies to their own benefit. They started to sell their merch (original T-shirts, sweatshirts, baseball caps, sunglasses, energy drinks, etc.), referencing the authors themselves (through prints with their names, lyrics or names of songs). This is how they bound the provision of a public service (music) with private ones (merch). Such way of binding works great for two reasons: 1. the value that fans attach to merch is often higher than the marginal costs of its production and 2. unlike music, merch can't be downloaded from the internet for free – it eliminates the problem of free-riders.

They learned how to make money from their music – a public good – even in an environment where copyright becomes an unenforceable relic and where legislation isn't able to ensure their regular income with its laws.*

I'm guessing Pulitzer knew exactly what he was doing when he published the names (sometimes accompanied by a short message) of all those who contributed to the pedestal for the Statue of Liberty. People care about what others think. We can find plenty of evolutionary reasons behind it.[176] It's the part of human nature all social networks are built on. We want to look good in the eyes of others

---

* The problem of piracy has been globally decreasing. The paradox is that this decrease is not due to better laws or stricter punishments for "stealing music and films" but instead it was solved by more comfortable and better quality services of piracy's legal competitors – streaming services such as Spotify (music) or Netflix (films and TV shows) which substantially simplified access to music and films and people are no longer motivated to search, download and wait.

and one of the ways of achieving it is to help in collective action. That's why in some countries, organizations that collect money to help cancer patients hand out small tokens in the form of a daffodil with a pin so that contributors can pin them on their coats. And it is for the same reason that in the past money in churches was collected into a pouch hanging from a long stick so that everybody could see who chipped in and who didn't. Also, crowdfunding campaigns choose rewards people can boast and send out the signal that they've contributed to a good cause and are worthy of being admired.[177]

The power of selective incentives in the form of improving the social image of a contributor has been confirmed by many economic experiments. Voluntary contribution rates to public goods increase once anonymousness is removed and people know who contributed and how much.* Social networks multiply this effect – a lot more people can learn about our good deeds thanks to them and thus they stimulate our motivation to do good things.[178]

Alex Tabarrok proposed an interesting modification to the all-or-nothing mechanism combined with selective incentives.[179] As we've already explained, this mechanism means that a person only pays if the campaign reaches its financial objective. If it fails to do so, contributions are returned. To this Tabarrok added rewards contributors get in case the campaign isn't successful. He decided to reward only those who gave the campaign a chance by contributing and the reward would be given to them by the creator of the campaign. So, why should the creator promise to pay a reward in case their campaign fails? The answer is: in order to attract free-riders who can bet on the failure of the campaign. Not only does a contributor have the certainty that their money will be put to good use if the campaign is successful, they also have the certainty of getting a reward in case it isn't. However, so far, I haven't heard of a platform that would support such mechanism. Nevertheless, it has been tested in experimental conditions and it has been shown that it does increase contribution rate.[180]

The most exciting economic case: lighthouses and new evidence

There are few discussions that make (micro)economists as excited as the one about lighthouses. For a long time, lighthouses used to be the favorite example of a public good that had to be provided by state. The image of a light merchant is ridiculous. Imagine them approaching every ship near the lighthouse and demanding a fee, threatening to turn the light off if the crew doesn't not pay. You can't get much profit from a lighthouse and entrepreneurs don't usually provide unprofitable services. Therefore, economics students are taught in practically all available textbooks that there

---

* Experiments show that the most effective setting is when participants' identities are not made public automatically and they're given the choice to decide. Ioby.org or Goteo.org do it exactly like this.[A11]

wouldn't be any lighthouses without the state. We've already mentioned the most famous of these textbooks – the one written by Paul Samuelson.

This meme lived its own life until 1974, when Ronald Coase decided to get up from his desk and find out the truth (although it probably just meant moving to a different desk in a big London library). He discovered something incredible: a large proportion of lighthouses built in England before 19th century were owned privately. They were built and operated by private entrepreneurs with the objective of generating profit. It was quite an efficient system but then, in the middle of the 19th century, lighthouses were nationalized.

How did the entrepreneurs in the past manage to achieve such a miracle? They connected the financing of lighthouses with fees for anchoring in the port. The purpose of a lighthouse is to help ships navigate dangerous waters near the shore, which makes lighthouse and port services complementary and it's hard to imagine that one service would work without the other. In addition, port fees are unavoidable unlike those for lighthouses. It was enough to bind these two services and the problem was solved. Textbooks could be rewritten. But they weren't – Samuelson didn't use this new knowledge and even in the next editions of his textbooks, he used lighthouses as an example of a public good.

And perhaps it was a good decision because in 1993, an article appeared which took a closer look at how things actually happened back in those days in England.[181] What it revealed about the system of lighthouses at that time was not pretty. Private providers of lighthouse services were sharing the same bed with the king and his agencies. Yes, Coase was right when he said that most lighthouses were built privately. But as for the way this was done, today we would refer to it as Public Private Partnership. When a private merchant requested to build a lighthouse, the king granted him a patent with a monopoly and established fees to be collected by his tax collectors. Later, another public agency squeezed between the king and the merchant: the sailor's guild that later became known as Trinity House and which gradually gained the patent granting monopoly. Élodie Bertrand, a French professor from the National Centre of Scientific Research, followed up on the article and criticized the inefficiency of the whole system.[182] The fees were too high which was profitable to the guild, the kings, and lighthouse operators, but the same could not be said for the sailors.

The lighthouse case froze at this point for several years. In 2018, new evidence appeared and showed that economists weren't doing their job properly. They acted like the character from a short story that lost his keys and searched for them under the street lamp despite having lost them elsewhere. His rationale was that there was light where he was searching.

Lighthouses weren't the only way of sailing safely near the shore. There were also what are known as "sailing lighthouses" – ships with a light on the mast. This idea was born in the heads of entrepreneurial Englishmen in the beginning of the 18th century and their story was recently examined by two young researchers.[183] Unlike lighthouses, ships that provided light operated exclusively on a voluntary basis without consorting with public power. How did they do that? Why didn't Coase and others discover them?

First, the authors of this invention connected the provision of a public good (ship with a light) to a private one (anchoring in the port) similarly to their predecessors. However, unlike them, they had neither the monopoly, nor tax collectors. All they had were advertisements in all inns, cafes, and newspapers. Apart from retrospective money collection, they came up with something like a subscription. That's another way entrepreneurs can exclude those who don't pay from using a public good – by not making it.

Entrepreneurs with lighting ships convinced sailors that their invention can prevent accidents on problematic shores (there are places where it is not possible to build a lighthouse). A ship like that was more flexible than a lighthouse and also less costly – this way entrepreneurs charged less and in order to gain profit, they didn't need to collect as much as lighthouse operators.

On top of that, they applied a handy price discrimination system, which was yet another tool aimed against (potential) free-riders. Big ships that generated more profit had to pay more than smaller, non-commercial ones. The first lighting ship worked so well that entrepreneurs launched collections for the construction of more ships. However, a problem appeared. And it was no textbook problem from a chapter on public goods – it was a problem from a chapter about rent-seeking and about politics.

The accused party in this case was the sailors' guild Trinity House, which gradually got more and more monopoly privileges in the 16th and 17th century. It began with the right to regulate and create orientation marks on sea, which was later followed by the right to license port pilots who helped ships anchor and then they even gained the right to buoys and lighthouses. Trinity House became a key agency which carefully guarded the monopoly to issue permits that they had to lobby so hard for.

Entrepreneurs with light ships were very well aware of this. Back in those days, Trinity House banned many initiatives that tried to circumvent the agency or the king. That's why instead of asking for a lighthouse patent, they requested a regular invention patent where they specified that they wanted to introduce a new type of lighting to the market. In the beginning they managed to escape the radar of Trinity House but their luck only lasted for six months. Then the king withdrew the patent and light ships started to sail in illegal waters and continued to do so for the next two years. In the end, entrepreneurs gave up and used the good old "if we can't beat them, join them" strategy. They decided to pay Trinity House for permission. That's how they gained the monopoly for their operation, which also meant firmly established fees which the king's officials were responsible for collecting.

We can never be 100% sure about the results of a historical analysis. However, this case shows that a purely private provision of lighthouses was most likely possible. It was enough to avoid defining the "navigation market" too narrowly and look beyond the sphere of traditional lighthouses. The remaining question is what other innovative binding ways could entrepreneurs have come up with if Trinity House hadn't monopolized the provision of all complementary and private services such as piloting or loading bottom parts of ships with sacs to improve their maneuvering capabilities. Be it as it may, the history of ship navigation on English shores shows that when interpreting events, apart from market failures we must also take into account the failures of the state. In this case, they played a bigger role than textbook authors supposed.

3.3 ORGANIZATION COSTS AND THE INTERNET

A couple of decades before the French sent the Statue of Liberty to America, Czech patriots launched a fund raiser for the construction of a national theatre. It was a grand project. Unfortunately, they failed to collect sufficient means to build the theatre. So, they conducted a smaller project – a temporary theatre. Among the reasons for the campaign's failure stated by historians, we find the fact that at that time, there were several fund raisers competing with each other simultaneously.[184]

However, economists could definitely add another reason to the list: high organization costs connected with fundraising. The fundraising itself lasted 11 years (from 1851 to 1862). During this time, more than 12 thousand public announcements were published and distributed in the Czech language plus another 8 thousand in German. Also, 2 thousand Czech and 2 thousand bilingual statutes, regulations and guidelines were sent out together with 6 thousand documents including their legal interpretation in German. Only the distribution of these materials alone took six months and it carried high financial, time, and labor costs.[185]

The provision of public goods includes a group of individuals by definition. The bigger it is, the higher the organization costs connected with reaping the benefits of cooperation are. An attentive reader may have noticed the similarity between organization and transaction costs (from the previous chapter). They really are very much alike. The only difference is that transaction costs appear in one-on-one bilateral transactions, while organization costs arise in collective actions in which many people are involved.

Just like sharing economy platforms, crowdfunding platforms can be seen as entrepreneurs who sell the lowering of organization costs. They have to try to create an institutional environment on their platforms that ensures appropriate conditions for carrying out a collective action. Among other things, this means employing the two already described mechanisms: the all-or-nothing principle and selective incentives.

Judging by the present examples, it seems to be working. Or we may at least conclude that platforms are doing much better than their analogue and paper predecessors. It's true that examples of using selective rewards (Pulitzer) or the all-or-nothing mechanism existed before crowdfunding, but they were always very rare because high organization costs prevented their mass proliferation.

In order to better imagine what costs we mean, let's list everything necessary for the preparation, implementation and conclusion of a campaign. First, we need to plan the entire campaign and set up a contribution scheme. We need to decide who will be responsible for transporting the collected money, where they will transport it, and who will supervise it to make sure it isn't misused. Campaign organizers then have to agree on how to inform the public about the progress of the campaign and also on how to create and publish a database of contributors with their corresponding contributions and rewards. Even before all this, they have to make sure that potential contributors know that there's an opportunity to contribute. Organizers have to specify all details, communicate with the public, and answer their questions. In the end, they have to conclude the campaign, inform the public about its success (or failure) and based on that, they either return the contributions or allocate the promised rewards.

All of this represents high fixed costs connected with every effort to finance public goods voluntarily. The higher the costs, the lower the probability of success is. Organization costs can even devour the entire net profit of the collective action and as a result, it is no longer worth it to implement a public good which would otherwise be beneficial.

The organization cost spectre also haunted economists who wrote theoretical essays about how the above-described mechanism could contribute to the solution to the public goods problem. They often reluctantly admitted that their application outside the world of abstract ideas would involve high organization costs which would be an obstacle to their smooth functioning.[186]

Earl Brubaker, one of the first economists who explicitly described the all-or-nothing mechanism, was also familiar with the problem of organization costs. In 1975 he said that he was aware of the "the special difficulties in arranging contracts to which the entire community is a part". That's why, according to him, we need a special intermediary to arrange trade in a collective good and specialize in facilitating the necessary negotiations:

"Their function is to communicate information about the character of collective goods supply to potential purchasers and information about the character of collective-goods demand to potential sellers in order to find a basis for mutually satisfactory exchange. Such intermediation seems a sine qua non for an effective operation of the market for a pure collective good where the number of participants is large."[187]

What Brubaker imagined as a solution to the problem of organization costs is de facto a modern crowdfunding platform which plays the role of a public good intermediary. Crowdfunding enables potential contributors and campaign authors a simple sign-up and information search, which ensures quick, efficient, and cheap communication. Campaign creators can make their own sub-pages on platforms, where they put a detailed description of their project, images, or a short video as well as updated information about the remaining time of the campaign, collected amount, number of contributors, rewards, and latest news regarding the project. The sub-page is also a simple way to share the campaign on social networks and thus get noticed by many people at a minimal cost. In addition, once the platform is built, it can include new platforms at low marginal costs. Not all campaigns have to build their own infrastructure but the platform benefits from the economy of scale.

On top of that, platforms offer fast and simple online payment methods (via a bank card or payment platforms such as PayPal, AmazonPay, WePay) and the contributor decides about the sum they want to contribute. Again, contributors have the guarantee that they´ll get their money back (if the platform fails to reach its objective) since the process is automated and out of the campaign creator's reach. The problem with supervision and enforcement of the agreed rules therefore no longer exists. Also, not everyone is allowed to launch a campaign on a platform which guarantees more safety and trust to contributors.

Implementing all these functions, mechanisms and tools the traditional way – whether via good old-fashioned letters and newspaper or TV and radio – would be practically impossible because the organization costs would be exorbitantly high. So, crowdfunding platforms work on a principle similar to that of sharing economy platforms. Most of them are profitable businesses gaining their profits by selling the lowering of organization costs. They generally charge a small percentage from the total amount of collected contributions and that enables them to finance the whole ecosystem of the provision of public goods.

Platforms keep discovering new settings which increase the voluntary contribution rate to public goods. As we said, there are some platforms which already came up with two thresholds for the collected sum, out of which the first one ensures the basic quality of the service and the second one optimal quality (Tilt). There are also platforms that established a rule saying a project has to get a certain number of fans before the fund raiser is launched (for example Startnext – the biggest German platform).

Apart from the all-or-nothing mechanism, some platforms also offer flexible financing. On some, you can choose to contribute with regular monthly payments (Patreon) and on others you can opt for a non-monetary contribution, like your work or material gifts (Spacehive, Ioby). Several platforms even offer extra help to campaign creators, specifically in the form of different experts who can provide them with personal consulting or webinars (Ioby). Different platform partners (for example, the city of London) are even willing to double the collected amount if the project is successful and fulfills their requirements (Spacehive).

There's no single general recipe for the success of crowdfunding platforms. Different circumstances (e.g., different countries, types of public goods and of contributors) require different rules and settings. We cannot even say if the current platform setting is the best it can be. Maybe there's still another useful tool somewhere out there waiting to be discovered by entrepreneurs.

3.4 CONCLUSION

Looking back, it seems that the arrival and use of crowdfunding is a natural result of the internet revolution and that it couldn't have been any other way. But the creation of platforms required a huge degree of creativity and determination from entrepreneurs. In 2008, there were still no indications that the internet would help radically change the logic of public goods. Yet here I am ten years later writing a book filled with examples of collective action carried out thanks to the internet.

Crowdfunding managed to turn the logic of the public goods problem upside down. Traditional theories say that organization costs and the motivation to get a free ride grow together with the number of people involved in a collective action, which then lowers the chances of the campaign's success. However, in the world of modern crowdfunding, more people mean potentially more contributions (even if they are small) to the financing of the public goods and as well as a higher probability of success.

If David Hume, who wrote about the draining of a meadow, was alive today, he would probably reconsider his conclusion that the cooperation between thousands of people is impossible. In the 18th century it was almost impossible to motivate such a large number of volunteers to participate in a collective action. If the situation described by Hume happened today, somebody would simply launch a crowdfunding campaign and with the help of a thousand of contributors collect the money necessary for drying the pasture.

Crowdfunding helps mitigate all three problems related to public goods: the risk of getting the short straw, the motivation of free-riders and high organization costs. For that it uses three main tools: the all-or-nothing mechanism, selective rewards, and platform communication.

> **Financing army equipment – new challenge for crowdfunding**
>
> In March 2014, pro-Russian separatists in eastern Ukraine began their fight for autonomy. On the 9th of April, Ukrainian minister of the Interior announced that within 48 hours, the fight would be suppressed either by agreement or force. 20 days later, separatist forces started to occupy another region and to this day they control a big part of Donbas. Their ag-

gression not only surprised the Minister of the Interior but also the entire Ukrainian army.

At that time, a big part of their already small defense budget was swallowed by corruption.[188] It was normal for army commanders to ask soldiers to work on the renovation of their own apartments or houses and the Ukrainian army was suffering from a lack of armament, military assets, and equipment. One Ukrainian general of that time said that the army was completely destroyed and demoralized and that 75% of its equipment was obsolete and broken. At the beginning of the conflict, soldiers were sent to fight equipped only with a rifle and it was up to them to get uniforms, bulletproof vests and winter clothing.[189]

But then, five young Ukrainians decided to do something for their country. Instead of enlisting in the army, they founded a crowdfunding platform called The People's Project.com to quickly collect money to pay for new equipment for soldiers on the eastern front. Within a short period of time, many collections were carried out on the platforms, thanks to which ordinary people got to finance anything from new uniforms, bulletproof vests, special glasses, equipment for snipers and special commandos to the armoring of vehicles, bunkers, field hospitals, military drones or healthcare for wounded soldiers. The platform is still active and the contributions oscillate between 1 to 2,000 euros. From the beginning of the conflict until 2018, more than three million euros were collected.

In comparison with the overall budget for the defense of Ukraine (in 2015 it was approximately 2 billion) it may seem like mere pocket money. However, the effectiveness with which this money was used actually helped Ukrainian soldiers on the front. A Ukrainian government-sponsored defense think tank published a study which says that in the beginning, the defense of Ukraine was mostly ensured thanks to voluntary military units and the financial contributions of its inhabitants.[190] Current crowdfunding projects aimed at supporting the Ukrainian army are divided into three big categories: military, health, and social.

The main difference between ordinary platforms and the Ukrainian People's Project platform is the scope of their actions. The aim of The People's Project is to provide public goods for the entire country of 233,062 mi2 with 45.5 million inhabitants. Ordinary platforms tend to target local projects within a town or a region.[191] That's why The People's Project had to face specific challenges that had to be reflected in its activities.

The biggest challenge was to convince people to contribute money to projects that are implemented hundreds or even thousands of miles away from their home, so they never see whether their contributions are used properly with their own eyes. This is why the creators of the platform came up with further tools and rules aimed at building trust and ensuring high transparency in the use of the collected resources.

First of all, the platform does everything possible in order to authentically illustrate how people's contributions help soldiers on the front. It brings regular online updates from the battlefields which display the purchased equipment in action. Contributors can read articles about how their "contributions gave soldiers the chance to walk again" or about how "one of the first patients underwent a biotechnological surgery". They can also read that "Quadrotor PC-1 revealed militants' positions" or be informed about new calls, such as: "Mariupol targeted – soldiers need urgent help."

The platform also provides detailed information about each project before the campaign starts, during it, and once it has been concluded. First, it states reasons why it's necessary to collect money for specific equipment, explains where the money goes and how it will be used, publishes complete lists of purchased equipment with the corresponding price as well as information about how many people contributed and how much. It also keeps a record of all material donations. The available information is updated every 15 minutes. Once sufficient means have been collected, the platform publishes detailed information about how they were used. It informs the users about the state of the order – whether invoices have been paid, whether the goods have been delivered, and which military unit is responsible for its use. Each military equipment delivery has its number and a take-over protocol that has to be signed by the commander of the unit it was delivered to.

Let's take the Defenders of Mariupol campaign as an example. 1,654 people contributed with a total sum of $95,276 (100% of the campaign objective was achieved). By mid-August 2018, 90% of the collected funds were used to purchase equipment for the defenders of Mariupol. Apart from money, people also contributed material donations: night vision Armasight Prime Digital and Sirius IDI MG (6x), riflescope Bushnell ET6245F 6-24x50 FFP 30mm (2 x), tactical backpacks (10 x), terrain vehicle Land Rover Freelander (1 x). The collected money was used to buy a compression generator, tactical glasses, tires, weather station, winter gloves, and laser sights. The majority of the equipment is already being used by units in action.

Last but not least, the platform uses internal and external audits to increase the transparency of its campaigns. For example, in 2015, one of the military volunteers collected detailed information from the battlefield about the use of the equipment the platform provided the soldiers with. One of the results such "audits" lead to was a change in the delivery of equipment: instead of delivering it to specific soldiers, they started delivering it to specific military units. The problem was that soldiers didn't always fill in all the necessary information or they made mistakes in the description of the state of the equipment and because of this, equipment often remained unused or even got lost. The platform couldn't take any legal action in this case: it was difficult to prove retrospectively who got what and in what state the equipment was. Plus, Ukrainian public institutions don't act as promptly as they should. Once the platform started delivering the equipment to military units, the motivation of the recipient changed. Units fulfill their duties more diligently because otherwise they risk not getting any further equipment. Those who don't do things properly lose their reputation and the platform stops cooperating with them. As The People's Project auditor put it: "if the military unit does not follow the delivery procedure, we simply shake hands and say 'thank you'."[192]

In 2016, the platform underwent an external audit carried out by EY (former Ernst & Young). It focused on checking its financial records and tax reports and the result of the auditors' assessment was that The People's Project was the biggest and most transparent organization of its kind in Ukraine. The platform was ranked among organizations that support a transparent and responsible caritative sector in Ukraine in the category of "Army costs in 2015" by the National Assessment of Philanthrophy.

4. STATE FAILURES WHEN SOLVING THE PROBLEM OF PUBLIC GOODS

The previous part described one side of the coin: the (mal)functioning of the market. The conclusion was that new technology helps the public goods market function better than we would have expected. It has never been easier to voluntarily provide a public good for a big group of people than it is today. Because traditional economic textbooks have not yet incorporated this crucial and relevant information about how internet platforms influence the economy, I am perhaps not exaggerating by saying that they underestimate the advantages of the functioning of the market in this respect.

This part will focus on the other side of the coin: the (mal)functioning of the state and the side effects of this often-prescribed medicine to heal the problems of public goods. I venture to say that when it comes to this, economic textbooks offer a distorted view of reality: they undervalue the cost connected with the state as a public provider of public goods. And I'm not the only one who feels that way.

So far, three big analyses of university textbooks of economics and public finances have been published and they all came to similar conclusions: the authors of textbooks write in depth about market failures but when it comes to the failures of politicians, bureaucrats, voters, and the entire public sector, they are a bit too brief. Researchers Fike and Gwartney state that textbook authors dedicate 6x more space to market failures in comparison with state failures. Coyne and Lucas claim that 96% of textbooks mention the free-rider problem in connection with market failure but only 42% mention it in relation with state failures. And finally, Eyzaguirre at al. says that many textbooks give the distorted impression that the state is the automatic solution to market failure, by which they dangerously cross the line between scientific claims and normative conclusions.[193]

This part aims to fix this shortcoming. We will also see that financing public goods with involuntary payments may solve a part of the free-rider problem (taxes are more difficult to avoid than price tags), but it creates further, conceptually identical, problems in the different spheres of public sector. After that I will also show you that the effort to prevent a free-rider from taking a free ride causes many people to pay for a ride they didn't want to take. The presumption of guilt applies: everybody is a potential free-rider even though they don't necessarily have to like travelling.

All of this doesn't only apply to public goods provided by the public sector. An attentive reader has surely noticed that these days, states provide many goods that we would hardly classify as public goods. When it comes to education, healthcare, or culture, it's not difficult to exclude free-riders. All of the problems that I describe below apply to all goods and services provided by the state regardless of whether they are private or not.

4.1 PUBLIC GOOD: A SOLUTION TO THE PUBLIC GOOD PROBLEM

"The typical citizen drops down to a lower level of mental performance as soon as he enters the political field. He argues and analyzes in a way which he would readily recognize as infantile within the sphere of his real interests. He becomes primitive again."

Joseph Schumpeter

Imagine a parallel universe where, for some unknown reason, cultural evolution settled in a social equilibrium without states. In this universe, people live in an anarchistic utopia. It doesn't mean they don't have problems, because there's no such thing as a perfect solution. Plus, people like to grumble about things, so they grumble about anarchy too. Some grumblers even get jobs at universities and start to propose alternative models of social order.

One of these grumblers, let's call him Milton Stateman, gets the idea to create agencies that have a monopoly on violence in certain territories which enables us to solve various problems. To put it simply, they adopt measures that ensure the well-being of everybody. And everybody has to obey the agency since it has a monopoly on violence. But Milton Stateman isn't stupid. He knows that such agency could abuse its power, so he introduces a new rule: people will select the politicians who lead agencies. This way agencies will be "the government of people through people and for people". What could go wrong? We are the state! Vox populi, vox Dei (The voice of the people is the voice of God)!

The idea of "state society" starts to spread uncritically in our anarcho-capitalist utopia throughout universities. But then Paulo Samuelsonos enters the scene with his new theory of public goods and writes and article titled "The Pure Theory of Private Sector". He demonstrates that society with democratic agencies won't work the way Milton Stateman imagines it. Many of society's institutions have the characteristics of public goods and people won't be willing to contribute to them – they would become free-riders instead. According to Samuelsonos, such a society would experience "state failures". He explained his theory using concrete examples in the most popular economics textbook:

Problem of public goods

What would agencies proposed by Stateman look like? Let's look at the incentives that voters who democratically elect their management would have. According to Milton Stateman, it's the voters who have the real power because they get to choose their "rulers". They're there to assure that power isn't abused and public finances aren't wasted.

What Stateman failed to notice was that a well-informed voter has the characteristics of a public good. Why should we expect them to search for information about the decision-making records of individual politicians: whether they tend to keep their promises, abuse their position, or embezzle common resources? The voter will be willing to carry all information costs if they are compensated in the form of certain advantages. But what advantages do they get if their vote is only a grain of sand in the desert of voters? One voter cannot make a difference. The probability of their vote changing the result of the election is close to zero. That's why I say that such a voter will become a free-rider, they won't try to get information about politics, they won't vote for politicians based on their professional qualities and decency. Their choice will be powered by emotions and they will pick their leader based on other unimportant factors, like the shape of their jaw. According to this theory, it's clear that voters will become ignorant. And don't get me wrong – I'm not criticizing voters. It's not their fault. It's a characteristic of the system proposed by Milton Stateman. The result would be the failure of the state caused by the existence of public goods.

Let's come back from the anarcho-capitalist utopia to our world. Today we have vast experience with states where politicians are appointed based on democratic elections. And Paul Samuelsonos' predictions are being fulfilled to the foot of the letter. Ignorance and lack of knowledge of voters is one of the best empirically proven political science facts. And even though the general level of education is higher than ever before, the ignorance of voters hasn't changed. In the U.S., one third of voters think that the Marxist slogan "from each according to his ability, to each according to his needs" is a part of the American constitution and less than a fourth can name at least one U.S. senator.[194]

If American studies didn't convince you, you can test the problem of rational ignorance on yourself. Try to name three most recent bills your local parliament voted on. Are you able to explain how the party that you elected voted and why? What about the particular MPs that you have chosen? Do you know what proportion of public money is allocated to culture, nurseries, and subsidies for farmers or the church? What's the opinion of your political representatives on these expenditures? Are you of the same opinion?

This is basic information voters should know so they can make the right decision on election day. These days it's easy to access it on the internet. However, it doesn't matter how easy it is to access the information – you have not and will not sacrifice your time in order to obtain it. And you have a good reason – it won't help you in any way. Just because politics impacts your life it doesn't mean that you have any impact on politics. Elections will end up the same way every time regardless of how well you are informed.

If a citizenship education teacher, your favorite politician or, a member of the You Are Key initiative (translator's note: Slovak initiative that motivates people to vote) tries to convince you otherwise, you can ask them to perform a short thought experiment: "Imagine a parallel universe in which everything is the same as in our universe, only you didn't vote in the last election." How would that universe have looked like? You don't need supernatural powers to answer that. The answer is: nothing would have changed. The world of politics would be identical in both parallel worlds. This applies to any voter who ever participated or will participate in elections. Voters don't have a good reason to be informed even though the state and democracy would function better if we all were.

Is the ignorance of voters really such a big problem? What does it imply for the functioning of the state? Let's do another thought experiment. Let's imagine democracy in a very strange country. In this country, people never leave their houses, they work from home and their food is delivered by flying drones. Not only do they never leave the house, they don't get any information from the outside world. The only information flow between households and the outside world happens once every four years when drones distribute ballots.

How would democracy work in such world? Probably not very well. Politicians would know that no matter what they do, it won't have an impact on their chance of being (re)elected. They would have a lot of maneuvering space to act in their own interest.

Luckily, we don't live in a country like that. Our problem is that people become voluntarily ignorant. If they do have some information about politics, it's shallow and distorted and they approach voting emotionally. They get carried away by prejudice. This is one of the reasons why people act more like football fans than prudent voters.

And here we get to the core of the problem. Comparing democratic election to ordinary everyday decisions is nonsense. One of the activists from the already mentioned You are Key initiative said he doesn't see why a voter should feel proud or disappointed by the party or politician they chose: "Why should emotions be involved? It's a simple, rational selection from a limited supply. It's just like a stock market or an umbrella store". I agree. Partially.

You can actually be proud of your choice on the stock market or in an umbrella store because there's a direct connection between your decision and what you get as a result (annual return or rain shelter). But there's no such connection when it comes to democratic elections. You will get something out of it, but it's not directly connected to your choice. The difference between a voter and a customer is best described by the following short quotes from two entrepreneurs. The author of the first one is Thomas Bata (1920) whose business motto was: "The customer is our master". The second one is by Jaroslav Hascak (translator's note: Slovak entrepreneur and financier) who summarized business in politics in three words: "Voter means shit".

Voters aren't the only ones who have problems. The problem of public goods and free-riders is present throughout the whole public sector and it concerns everyone who makes decisions regarding the use of public resources and authority. It also concerns politicians, who can choose from two options: they can manage the state in a way that is helpful to everybody, solve public problems, and increase social well-being or they can use their maneuvering space to enrich themselves, their family, and friends.

If you look more closely at both choices, you may notice that the first one possesses features of contributing to public goods from the point of view of a politician (they help everybody around them) and the second one is like purchasing a private good (they help themselves and those close to them). If we want to be consistent in applying the theory of public goods, we can expect politicians to be more interested in the second option and use their state power to help themselves and those around them. This applies to all public sector stakeholders – local politicians, interest groups, policemen, judges, etc. The theory of market failure is to the same extent (at least) the theory of the failure of the state.

These shortcomings of democracy aren't only temporary – they became its systemic characteristics. Let's be honest with ourselves and admit that we have a problem. That's the first step to finding a solution. We know today that democracy, as a decision-making principle, struggles with respecting the rights of minorities. This unpleasant feature of democracy is known as the tyranny of the majority and can be nicely summed up in the following aphorism: two wolves and one sheep cast a vote about what's for dinner. We can fight this shortcoming with constitutional mechanisms and bills of rights that are supposed to make any tendency towards oppression more difficult although they aren't always successful.

What solutions are there to propose knowing voters are irrational and ignorant? The first could be to stop trying to persuade to vote people who either don't want to or are too uninformed to make a decision.* Empirical literature points out that the average citizen's knowledge of politics is a lot more distorted and inaccurate than that of the average voter.[195] So, if everybody decided to vote, we could end up even worse politically. Even though most of this literature comes from the U.S., it's not very different in my country. Campaigns which persuaded the Slovak youth to vote in the 2016 parliamentary elections are a typical example. Post-election analyses revealed that many of the young people voted for a nationalist party lead by Marian Kotleba.[196]

Many use the famous Churchill quote to defend democracy: "Democracy is the worst form of government, except for all the others". But this is a rhetorical trick where a false dilemma is proposed – the choice we have isn't solely binary: between democracy and dictatorship. There's also a third option:free market which is more accessible and efficient than ever before thanks to sharing economy and crowdfunding.

It would also be good to stop thinking in absolute terms and look at the situation from the point of view of marginal decisions. Pointing out the failures of democracy doesn't mean denouncing it in all spheres of life. Nobody wants to establish the rule of the estates or the dictatorship of the proletariat. But if we admit that democracy has its flaws, we can substitute it by the above-mentioned third option in certain areas of life. Something like this already happened multiple times in the past. Today nobody even stops to think about whether we should decide democratically about religion or the rights of minorities. And when we see how public money is being used in healthcare and how voters react to the gravity of problems in education, a legitimate question appears whether it's time to free these sectors from the influence of democratic institutions or not.

Democracy fights back (technical box – to be read at one's own risk)

The theory of rational ignorance has caused some sleepless nights for citizenship education teachers. Suddenly, they could no longer talk about individual failures in democracy that can be fixed by better education. It turns out that ignorance is a systemic feature of democracy.

Just like any (social) theory, this one also had to be challenged. The 1990s saw the birth of many arguments, theories, and hypotheses that were supposed to weaken the cornerstone of the entire theory where voters' ignorance caused the failure of politics. Let's have a look at some of them.

---

* Extract from the You Are Key campaign: "We realize that if those 41% of non-voters become active, they can change Slovakia the way they want to in all key aspects. You Are Key is about you. It is about non-voters who have given up and don't care that they are key. They don't believe that their vote can make a difference. 41% of votes will bring change with 100% certainty. You Are Key is about the 2016 elections because Slovakia without elections is unimaginable. Elections are incomplete without you."

The first attempt to challenge this theory was the theory of big numbers. It says that the ignorance of voters alone doesn't have to be automatically problematic for democracy. It's enough if voters vote randomly as the result of their ignorance (their errors are not correlated). The statistical rule of big numbers ensures that errors mutually eliminate themselves and the informed minority decides the results of the elections (even if they represent only 1% of the total number of voters). A democracy where 99% of voters are ignorant thus resembles a democracy where 100% voters are informed rather than one where 100% of them are uninformed. It isn't a coincidence that this law of statistics also tends to be referred to as the "miracle of aggregation". It may seem like a magical alchemy recipe at first glance: mix 99 units of foolishness with 1 unit of wisdom and you get a compound which is pure wisdom.[197] But this isn't magic. If certain conditions are fulfilled, individual erroneous votes will neutralize and correct themselves and well-informed choices will be decisive.

Another group of theoreticians came up with a theory of information shortcuts. It says that under certain conditions, even uninformed voters can vote as if they were fully informed.[198] This happens when they have access to information shortcuts, such as political brands; recommendations from close people, political commentators, or different organizations. A voter doesn't have to know how states and politics work just like a consumer doesn't need to know how a car works or how a toothbrush is made to drive and brush their teeth.

The most wholesome theory was proposed by Donald Wittman in his book called The Myth of Democratic Failure (1995), where he perfected the analogy between the functioning of the "economic and political market". Wittman has shown that if we consistently apply economic knowledge to politics as a competition of political parties for voters, we see that it yields efficient results. That is – what the people really want.

Bryan Caplan responded to all these theories in his book The Myth of the Rational Voter. On one hand, he accepted many of Wittman's arguments, but on the other hand, he didn't give up the opinion that democracy adopts policies that are inefficient for or detrimental to voters. He tried to soften these two points of view by a claim that doesn't seem very intuitive at first – "democracy is not failing because politicians act systematically against their voters' interests (i.e. voters are not getting what they want) but on the contrary – it fails precisely because voters are getting what they want!"

Caplan used empirical data to show that voters' economic opinions are systematically erroneous: they substantially underestimate the functioning of the market in practice and the benefits of cooperating with strangers. Instead of associating prosperity with higher productivity and effectiveness, they associate it with employment and tend to be pessimistic. In all these areas, voters' opinions are systematically distorted when compared with the consensuses of economists. Caplan didn't stop at the interpretation of empirical observations. He also created a theoretical framework in which he showed that voters' irrationality isn't surprising at all.

Economists generally suppose that the opinions of an individual are merely a means to an end rather than being the objectives themselves. The same supposition has also always applied to voters. However, this view can be challenged by a simple introspection. People often like their own opinions. Being convinced about one's truth often makes one feel good – it's like a consumer good. People don't just want to know the truth; they mostly want to be right. And their preference for their own opinions is the critical point which explains why voters vote irrationally. All they need is a basic economic model – the less costly it is to believe stupid things, the more often people will believe them. But if the costs of sticking to irrational opinions grow, people will become more rational.

Simply put, if you have your own opinion (even an incorrect one) and you're standing on the edge of a chasm, your error (or incorrect belief) may cost you your life. On the other side, believing a false prophet's opinion that the Earth was born 4004 B.C. will probably have zero impact on a "believer's" day (unless they're a staff member at a faculty of geology). So, there are incorrect opinions that we can afford to hold safely and there are also those for which we pay a high price. That's why the amount of consumed irrationality (systematically erroneous opinions) depends on its cost.

However, in democracy, one can afford to consume irrational opinions for almost zero costs since the probability that a person's vote will be decisive approaches zero, the price to pay for his irrational opinions is also practically zero. Therefore, there's a high demand for self-illusion on the side of the voter who believes whatever makes them feel good.

We may say that democracy has an extensive built-in externality. It's like the typical example of a common lake, only in democracy, instead of waste, people throw mental rubbish in. Democracy "isn't working" precisely because people get exactly the politics they ask for.

That's probably the reason why new technologies not only challenged the functioning of democracy but even deepened its problems. With the help of the internet and social networks, everybody can find information that confirms their delusional perception of the world, which polarizes society even further. Modern technologies thus did not lead to voters being more informed and rational – they made their prejudices deepen.

4.2 HOMEBODY TURNS INTO FREE-RIDER

"So far as the economic side of the question is concerned, that is whether the benefits of the proposed activity to the individual citizens would be greater than its cost to them, no one can judge this better than the individuals themselves [...] It would seem to be a blatant injustice if someone should be forced to contribute toward the costs of some activity which does not further his interests or may even be diametrically opposed to them."[199]

Knut Wicksell

Let's suppose we have somehow miraculously resolved all the above-mentioned problems with free-riders in the public sector. Does it mean everything is OK? Not at all. It's not enough to want to solve a problem; you also need to know how. In other words, incentives are not the only problem; there's still the issue of insufficient knowledge.

Forcing free-riders to pay makes no sense if we can't identify who they are, which isn't easy. People are different and the value of things and services is subjective. What one finds to be a useful public good can be an unwanted service to somebody else. And that's precisely the core of the problem of insufficient knowledge. How can a state in the absence of a voluntary contract determine the optimal level of the provision of (public) goods and ensure that only those who should pay will pay and that they will pay exactly how much they are supposed to?

Economists who presented their arguments about market failures in mid-20th century clearly defined conditions for the optimal provision of public goods and at the same time, they explained why the market is unable to fulfill them. But these conditions are independent from an institutional setting, that is, whether a public good should be provided on the market or within the public sector. Samuelsonos' efficiency can be reached when each consumer pays a price that equals his marginal valuation of the public good. For the state as a provider it means it has to implement a system of differentiated taxes derived from the extent the public good is useful for individual tax payers.[200] In case somebody heard or read about a state that has at least attempted to think about this condition (not to mention implement it), please let me know at chovanculiak@gmail.com.

This state would be like a unicorn. Nobody has ever seen it although many have read and wrote about it in books. Samuelson and his successors forged such an argumentation chain that they would have trouble believing it had it come from their opponents. Later, they showed that the market with voluntary payments isn't (even theoretically) able to fulfill the conditions for the optimal quality of public goods because of the free-rider issue. Then they also pointed out that the state doesn't have to rely on voluntary payments (unlike the market), from which they deduced that public goods are the state's domain because it can legally force people to pay (and is therefore at least theoretically capable of making free-riders pay) and fulfill the optimal conditions as a result. Under the words "at least theoretically" when speaking about free-riders, there's a hidden prerequisite related to knowledge. The state really could solve the free-rider problem if it was able to read people's minds and learn what their marginal valuation of different public goods are and tax them accordingly. That is, it would be possible if the state possessed perfect knowledge.

The problem of this argumentation chain is that it proves too much. The reality is that if we temporarily lend the same knowledge prerequisite to the participants of the market, they too will be able to at least theoretically solve the problem of public goods without force. How could something like that be done? Imagine a crowdfunding platform like the ones from the previous part with two modifications:

1. Instead of a financial objective, a campaign creator would first produce a list of the names of all the members of the community who are supposed to contribute derived from their personal evaluation of the public good in question.

2. The campaign would be created with the condition that if even one person refuses to contribute with their part, the campaign will be cancelled and the collected money will be returned to its owners and the public good won't be provided (the free-rider issue is solved).

Contributing to public goods would suddenly become the dominant strategy on such platforms. The free-rider problem would disappear. If somebody doesn't pay, they are automatically excluded from using the public good (together with the rest). Nobody would have a reason to hide their preferences. In this situation, the market offers the optimal level of public goods and no state or taxes are necessary.

A contract as a voluntary solution for the provision of public services was proposed by several economists in the past.[201] However, once they got beyond the theoretical level, they all quickly admitted it won't work in practice. A campaign creator can't read people's minds and isn't able to elaborate a contract where he can establish the price for individual contributors based on their subjective evaluation of a specific public good. Economists realized that the campaign creator would most likely make mistakes and would even include those who aren't interested in the public good in the contract. And that would be the end of it. The contract wouldn't work because one "no" is enough to cancel the whole campaign. Unanimousness is the key condition to removing the motivation to be a free-rider but at the same time, it's a condition which requires a very high level of knowledge.

Being in touch with reality and willing to realize practical problems connected with imperfect knowledge was something we didn't see in many supporters of the "pure theory of public expenditure". They didn't worry too much about whether public officials can ensure the fulfillment of optimal conditions in practice. Nor did they worry whether they make things worse if they impose taxes on people who aren't even interested in public goods in order to make sure free-riders pay. They would transform homebodies into free-riders and create the problem of forced riders. But that means that the original "pure theory of public expenditure" removes its scientific cloak and becomes a mere normative theory representing a philosophy. There's nothing wrong with such convictions, but we cannot present them as positive science. The entire scientific theory was reduced to the moral conviction that some citizens (forced riders) should pay so that the others (public good consumers) can benefit from the provided services. They basically just admitted what Frédéric Bastiat said in his famous quote: "The state is the great fictitious entity by which everyone seeks to live at the expense of everyone else."

But enough with theoretical debates and suppositions. Let's see how the problem of knowledge is approached outside textbooks – in the real world of real politicians.

Some passionate critics of the public sector compare its functioning to socialism. But such comparison is imprecise – at least to the extent to which the public sector functions within the market economy where politicians must take market prices into account. If a state wants to have more teachers or doctors, it has to offer them higher salaries. If it wants to buy school or hospital equipment, it has to do so in the market. When it comes to providing public services, politicians have a fairly good idea of what costs they generate. And not only politicians – the budgets of public administration are publicly available and everybody can take a look at them. You can find how much the services of police, firemen, public television, the anti-monopoly body, or the academy of sciences cost.

Cost calculation isn't a problem for the state. Problems arise once we ask if these costs were worth spending – whether they brought sufficient added value in order to be justified. On the market, this information is expressed by the consumers' willingness to pay. The fact that consumers are willing to pay to cover entrepreneurs' costs (plus their profit margin) gives their services a seal of social validation. Thanks to this, we know that entrepreneurs create an appropriate combination of production factors and increase the well-being in society with their activities. The public sector is financed by involuntary taxes. There is no seal of social approval. We don't know if politicians spent money on something that was really necessary or if they just wasted precious resources that could have been used elsewhere.

When I say wasting resources, I don't mean spending money on obvious nonsense or corruption. I assume that all stakeholders act with the best intentions. I assume that politicians do care about the well-being of society. But they have a knowledge problem. They face a dilemma: should they spend the last collected euro to improve the hospital in the capital, a school in the north of a country, the national theatre, or a football stadium? This euro would be helpful in all of these examples – some would get better healthcare, some better education, and some better entertainment. Teachers try to convince them that educated citizens are the best investment, doctors say that the country cannot move forward without healthy citizens, actors say that culture is the basis of developed society, and sports coaches point out the importance of sports in the healthy development of the youth. How should these kind-hearted politicians decide? Whom should they trust? Plus, let's not forget another important stakeholder – the tax payer. They convince politicians that they should let them keep the last euro because they know how to use it best.

When a private entrepreneur spends too many resources on a particular service, they get immediate feedback – consumers won't be willing to pay for it and they experience losses. Next time, they'll think twice before spending excessively. It also works the other way around – if they are too frugal, their product won't sell well and they experience losses again. But what feedback do politicians have? None. Their income doesn't come from consumers but rather from tax payers. And nobody asks their opinion – they simply have to pay taxes.

> **What is the value for money of value for money? (Technical box – to be read at one's own risk)**
>
> More technocratically oriented people say that even though democracy has its flaws, the public sector needs a group of analysts who calculate how to optimally provide public goods. In other words, "How to get the best possible value from every last dollar?" We basically need the highest value for money possible. This expression has frequently been used in many contexts in my country over the last few years. Everybody keeps using it – from the prime minister to analysts from the office located on Na vrsku 12 (where my colleagues and I sit). Applying value for money evokes in some (mostly journalists) a universal cure. Only politicians don't feel like swallowing the pill.
>
> There are actually two components to the value for money: the trivial one and the unrealistic one. The trivial one consists of simple recommendations: if we want to do something, we should first establish our objectives, list the ways to achieve them and finally select the one that helps us reach our goals at the lowest possible cost. Everybody who has so much as planned a family vacation is familiar with this procedure. The reasons why politicians use it are listed in the previous part dedicated to twisted motivations.
>
> However, the second component of the value for money points to an important problem caused by lack of knowledge. It focuses on evaluating the costs and benefits of different uses of public money. Its objective is to solve the problem of the absence of knowledge about customers' willingness to pay. It tries to do so by using special economic methods – contingent valuation methods or CVM. They are something like sophisticated questionnaires that collect information about how people value different things – mostly those the value of which is unknown on the market, for example, public goods. However, CVM methods are considered contro-

versial in economics. In fact, there's one big Methodenstreit (German for conflict concerning the right method) in which even many Nobel laureates are involved.

The conflict is framed by two big oil disasters: the shipwreck of oil tanker Exxon Valdes by the Alaskan shore in 1989 and the accident involving BP's oil rig Deepwater Horizon in the Gulf of Mexico over 20 years later. The disasters caused the demand for methods of evaluating damage to the environment and at the same time, opened the debate about their validity. There are two ways of testing the exactness of these methods: the internal and the external test.

The internal test consists of testing the consistency of CVM results with the predictions of neoclassic economy. The sensibility of consumers and their willingness to pay for the change of the amount or scope of a good were the most frequently tested aspects. However, this test brings unclear results. CVM critics point out experiments in which participants rated the cleaning of one lake the same way as the cleaning of five lakes. But the method's defenders have their own experiments in which this problem isn't so apparent. A critic called Hausman asks them to apply an addition test; participants are divided into three groups: the first one evaluates public good X, the second one public good Y, and the third one public goods X and Y together. In order for the CVM method to pass the internal test, the evaluation of the third group minus the evaluation of the second group should equal the evaluation of the first group.

But CVM's supporters are a lot more worried about the external test. Testing via criterial validity means comparing CVM results (results of a hypothetical survey) with the evaluation of people in real conditions, which includes actual payments. An example of this is comparing the value people assign to a piece of art when asked about it in a questionnaire and when they actually have to pay for it. In specialized literature, you often find that this validity test is key. At the same time, it points to the biggest weakness of CVM: the presence of something known as hypothetical bias. This term describes the difference between the declared value under hypothetical conditions and the demonstrated value in real conditions. The evidence about the presence of hypothetical bias in CVM is quite clear and this distortion is often positive – participants inflate the value in their answers.

Research shows that the "value for money" project has a problem and we can find it already in its first word – it's not possible to exactly determine the value that public goods financed from taxes really bring. This means that it's not possible to realize a complete and fully-fledged costs and benefits analysis. But that doesn't mean that the existence of the project can't improve the functioning of the state. It can make obvious theft and waste in the system visible. It also helps solve the problem of twisted motivation. But this isn't that easy either. As a matter of principle, politicians don't seek measures that bring maximum value for money but rather the maximum number of votes for money.

If you had been paying attention during citizenship studies, you may have objected that even though politicians don't get feedback in the form of loss and profit, they have another form of feedback: democratic elections. If they make bad decisions, voters react and they will be replaced by somebody who will do it better. This objection is justified. Democracy really is a system where some feedback is present (at least more than in other forms of government like dictatorship or monarchy). But this doesn't mean that this feedback is sensitive enough to discover nuances such as the efficiency of the last spent euro. We can best understand the shortcomings of democratic feedback when we compare it with market feedback.

The first difference is in the way competition works. On the market, there is parallel competition – there are many entrepreneurs at the same time and consumers can choose from them. They can see what services they provide, for which prices and of what quality and they choose the one who best fulfills their conditions. This is different in politics – here we have serial competition. This means that at one specific moment we have one ruling party or coalition. Voters aren't able to compare the quality and price of the services provided by different politicians (but they can compare their promises). All they see is how politicians and their promises alternate – in series: one after another. This places an intellectual demand on voters because they have to get into complicated contrafactual contemplations and try to estimate how political programs of different parties work in practice. In the end they only see one alternative – the winner of the elections. And they are the official elected choice for everybody. In politics, only one solution can win and losers cannot do anything.

This isn't true for the market. On the market, different people with different preferences can get diverse services and goods. That's its great advantage. Imagine what "democratic cars" would be like. More specifically, if we left democratic mechanisms take care of automotive production. Different groups of people would have different preferences, be it a small city car, bigger terrain vehicles, economical vehicles, or high-performance vehicles. But in democracy, only one solution wins so there is always a part of voters who aren't content. It doesn't matter what you choose, what matters is the choice of the majority.

And it's not only that your choice couldn't matter; in reality, you are supposed to vote about cars, education, healthcare, pensions, and even about whether it should be allowed to smoke certain plants, all at once. In democratic elections, all topics are tied into one single moment which is casting the ballot into the urn. "It's like asking: 'Do you like gnocchi and sex with animals? '", complained a Slovak MP when he was asked to vote in a connected vote about the approval of the Eurobond and expressing a vote of confidence to the government. What should a voter who has to express their views on hundreds of topics with one ballot do? Imagine how the market would work if the consumers had to buy a house, cellphone, toothpaste, internet connection, toilet paper, dinner, furniture, and a holiday under one contract by one single company. On top of that, they would only be allowed to change the company once every four years.

Not to mention that on the market, you buy goods and services while with politics you only choose promises for the future. Voters don't have any certainty as to whether politicians will keep all their promises. Voting is the purest form of speculation. Also, voters have no feedback about whether their decision was right. Their choice has no impact on the result, so they have no way of knowing if they choose wisely. When I buy toilet paper from a bad brand or go to a bad restaurant, I realize quite quickly that I made a mistake. Voters can get burned in elections even several times without feeling any pain – they have no feedback.

This was a brief outline of how democratic mechanisms function. As a result, there are fewer interactions, less competition, and feedback in democracy and therefore also less knowledge generated by a learning process. This is why all the industries of the public sector stagnate, and the reason why the biggest innovation in education over the last century was to swap blackboards and white chalk for whiteboards and black markers. Politicians and voters simply cannot replace entrepreneurs and customers.

4.3 CONCLUSION

The theory of comparative advantage is basic study material in economics classes. It brings the counter-intuitive claim that international trade is beneficial for all countries regardless of what they're good at. So, even a country that isn't good at any kind of production can get involved in international trade with a country that is, on the contrary, outstanding at everything. This helps both of these countries because thanks to cooperation, they produce more than they could produce on their own. It's interesting that economists have been unable to generalize this principle and apply it to other contexts for so many years. Apply it to market failures, for example.

The fact itself that the market isn't capable of ensuring the optimal amount of public goods (in absolute terms) doesn't automatically imply that it also has a comparative disadvantage in this area and that the state should take over. It's like saying that a country cannot produce socks only because we have information about its disadvantage. Many economists would teach the theory of comparative advantage during one class and then a few classes later, they would calmly lecture about market failures being the sufficient prerequisite for state interventions. They would do so without asking themselves whether or not the state generates more problems than the failing market.*

---

* This problem mostly concerns economists from the first half of the 20th century. For instance, Adam Smith was well aware of it. Right after the quote from the introduction of the chapter where

The first half of this chapter was aimed at showing that the internet has improved the comparative advantage of the voluntary provision of public goods. The question that yet has to be answered is how it changed the functioning of the public sector. It seems that if the internet and social networks have had any impact on democracy and its mechanisms, it is more negative than positive. On one hand, there are suspicions from manipulated election results and ongoing information wars involving professional social network trolls. On the other hand, people spontaneously create their own bubbles themselves like echo chambers where they mutually confirm one another's opinions which widens the gap of opinions between different groups. Not to mention spreading fake news. All of these factors impact political competition which has brought many unexpected and troubling results for some.

If the definitions and theories from economics textbooks are correct, under the present conditions we should witness a gradual retreat of the public sector and its substitution by the private sector. It's not that simple, though. It seems that politicians don't consider textbook conclusions about comparative (dis)advantages and they don't want to give up their position of power. Crowdfunding is replacing the public sector in two ways and neither of them are the result of self-reflection of politicians but rather of its absence or their mistakes.

The first category includes campaigns which are complementary to public services and finance what politicians forgot about or didn't even think of, such as different community centers, communal gardens, events, etc. The second category consists of declining public libraries, neglected parks, broken public lighting, dysfunctional police, or underfinanced armies.

Economists in the first half of the 20th century used to say that public provision is a reaction to market failure. Today I venture to say that providing public goods via crowdfunding is a reaction to state failure. Crowdfunding, just like sharing economy, therefore functions as a litmus test for political incompetence and corruption when it comes to using public finances.

Crowdfunding platforms have to face one more problem I haven't mentioned yet. Economists call it the crowding out effect. It tends to be quoted in the sphere of investment – when public investments crowd out private investments. However, it's also applicable within the sphere of public goods because private initiatives face unfair competition. Their competitors have the opportunity to get their resources through forced payments and sell their services for free. That's hard to compete with. Private initiatives have to not only deal with the free-rider problem but also convince customers to pay twice – once through taxes and then

---

he talks about the need of financing public projects by the state, he warns that sometimes a bridge of public finances is thrown "over a river at a place where nobody passes or merely to embellish the view from the windows of a neighboring palace." With this he identified two problems that we described earlier: the problem of knowledge (bridge that will end up being useless because somebody did not assess the situation correctly) and the problem of incentives (it embellishes the view from the palace and was built because its owner acted in his own interest).

again through the initiative. This big issue can be overcome when the quality of public services becomes unbearable. On one hand, this is good news for ordinary people – when things are bad, they have an alternative. On the other hand, the crowding out effect prevents the provision of many private of public goods through crowdfunding from happening.

What should politicians do who have the public's interests at heart and want to approach crowdfunding head on instead of running away from it? The first step would be not to ban it, although this isn't such an issue when it comes to crowdfunding. Crowdfunding platforms don't have to face the attacks of narrow interest groups like sharing economy platforms. Despite that, there are analysts who consider financing through crowdfunding to be an undemocratic privatization of public services.[202] It was most directly expressed by Emma Hofman in her article called "Crowdfunding for the Public Good is Evil". She doesn't like it when people take things into their own hands when the state lacks resources or fails to provide quality service. I will let you, readers, judge this attitude.

So, what should a politician do apart from not imposing bans? First of all, they should let people have the opportunity to provide public goods privately and lower their tax burden accordingly. This is how they could reduce the problem of crowding-out. In other words, this would allow people to disconnect themselves from public services.

But it's not that easy. The problem lies within the expression "lower their tax burden accordingly." Since taxes are paid involuntarily without being tied to a countervalue, we cannot say how much of it goes to public lighting, police or park maintenance. It's therefore difficult to determine how much less the people who chose the private option should pay into the tax system. But if we want the beneficial power of competition to work in the area of public services, we must prevent double charging.

As an economist I could go on forever generating arguments why the private alternative has better incentives and feedback mechanisms than politicians in the public sector. I can use the example of Rockridge's private police who can't abuse their position and slack off like their colleagues from the public sector. Voluntary payers would respond to it immediately by refusing to prolong their subscription. At least this is what economic theory predicts. A true answer to who should provide what will only be given by competition. But in order for competition to work, implicit subsidies for public services have to be cancelled. So, if a group of citizens decides to disconnect from public services and starts using a private alternative, their tax burden has to be proportionately lowered.

How does cooperation work if you let everybody do their bit? Case study: Wikipedia

Imagine if somebody in the early 90s came up with the idea to create a free internet encyclopedia. A part of their business plan would be to delegate the creation and editing of content to its users instead of employing staff. One of the project's key performance indicators (KPI) would be that in 30 years' time, this project will turn into the biggest encyclopedia in the world which would be vastly more extensive than the Encyclopedia Britannica. If this business plan got in the hands of the economists of that era, they would happily use it as a didactic tool during their lectures. The first exercise would be: identify all "market failures" that will make the project fail.

With the already mentioned torrent P2P networks, contributing to public goods had quite a simple form – you just had to leave the uploading on. It's different in case of an internet encyclopedia. Contributing to it requires significant intellectual effort, time and regular attention. Of course, today we know that this plan has been a success. This encyclopedia exists, its name is Wikipedia and it did reach its KPIs. But what you may not know is how it managed to achieve it.

Wikipedia's founder, Jimmy Wales, was aware of all the problems the idea of an encyclopedia without encyclopedists had. The fact, that he first established Nupedia – Wikipedia's older sister that you may not have heard about – proves it. Nupedia's objective was also to provide free content, but it was supposed to be created by professionals with relevant formal education and skills. Even more importantly, all content was supposed to be reviewed and edited by other professionals and editors. Nupedia's reviewing process consisted of seven steps that were supposed to ensure that only good quality content enters the encyclopedia. In its first year of existence, 21 articles were approved and published on Nupedia.

Wales realized that this way he would not reach his objective, so he created an alternative: Wikipedia. Unlike the centralized Nupedia, it started to work as an open, decentralized system in which basically anybody could add, edit and supervise articles. After one month, 200 articles were published on Wikipedia and after the first year the number went up to 18,000. It's no wonder that Nupedia was disconnected from live support within three years. It was its freer sister who survived. This brings me back to the question: how come?

We can find two factors behind Wikipedia's surprising ability to produce public goods in the form of freely available information: the size of Wikipedia's community (1) and the character of the good it provides (2).

(1) The vast majority of Wikipedia users are free-riders. According to a public survey, two thirds of its users consider themselves as readers only,

23% as occasional contributors, and only 7% as regular contributors. We have to realize that Wikipedia is the 7th most frequently visited website on the internet with more than 77 million registered users. So, even though only a small proportion of them regularly contribute, it's enough to keep the production high. Altogether they have created over 2.5 billion edits – changes in articles. According to a user survey, they are mostly motivated by their desire to share knowledge and correct mistakes. It's also interesting, that 90% of contributors are men.[203] We may therefore assume that adding an article to Wikipedia is like catching a mammoth in the past – a sign of social status.

Apart from that, Wikipedia's passionate contributors also have traditional types of motivation, like improving their reputation and social standing within the community. If a user regularly contributes with good quality contributions and edits, they can get different rewards in the form of a medal or special honors such as the Slovak "Order of the Friendly Wikipedia Contributor ".[204] Also, a user can go up within the hierarchy and become a local administrator or "bureaucrat". Administrators have more control over articles – they can limit others' possibilities to contribute and edit articles or change their titles; they can block naughty contributors. Each user can send an application to an administrator and the community of "bureaucrats" will judge their work and decide by a consensus whether they will be accepted. Naturally, all functions and posts on Wikipedia are unpaid.[205]

(2) Wikipedia produces public goods in the form of information, which has several great features. First of all, if somebody creates a piece of information, it can be consumed by a practically unlimited number of people without spending it. More for you doesn'tt mean less for me. Economists call such goods non-rival goods. Also, an informative article can be the result of an extensive work from one person but also of a compilation of small contributions by millions of cooperating users. Everybody can therefore make a difference on Wikipedia or reach great things together with others. This is possible via a handy web app through which several users can simultaneously edit one document. The nature of information together with the size of the Wikipedia community are behind its immense success.[206]

Despite all that, contributing alone isn't enough. Each society needs law and order that ensure its peaceful coexistence and productive cooperation. Similarly to P2P torrents networks, Wikipedia also has its constitution. It's composed of five basic pillars:

1. Wikipedia is an encyclopedia (not a dictionary, blog or a specialized journal)
2. Wikipedia is impartial (written from a neutral point of view)

3. Wikipedia is free content (that anybody can use, edit and distribute)*
4. Wikipedia's editors should treat each other with respect and civility
5. Wikipedia has no firm rules

Wikipedia has policies and guidelines but their principles and spirit matter more than literal wording – if you want to start to edit articles, you don't have to read them and it's mostly enough to use common sense.

However, it's not enough to list the rules and guidelines on paper or the web. Mechanisms that ensure their compliance, monitor and punish those who break them, or resolve conflicts are necessary too. In its beginnings, Wikipedia was basically an open virtual space without a fence and guard dog. Gradually, different restrictions that created at least a thin line between "us" and "others" started to appear. In the beginning, everybody could create and delete articles. This is now reserved mostly to registered users. Unregistered users can also edit articles, but such edits are suspicious and they get very quickly into the hands of local editors.

On the 13th of September at 12.08 PM, I tried as an unregistered user to edit an article about Ľuboš Blaha – an open communist and Slovak MP. I created a new subsection titled "*Ľuboš Blaha and the internet*" and I wrote a provocative paragraph about how he embarrassed himself several times on the internet.

Although the article about Ľuboš Blaha is relatively marginal on Wikipedia, an admin called Jetam2 deleted my trolling contribution in exactly 8 minutes. There is a record about my action and Jetam2's reaction in the history of reviews and anyone can look it up.[207] Each Wikipedia article has an internal journal where you can find all edits made on it, so it's easy to track who made what changes and assess whether the edit is worth keeping or deleting. Editors can also turn on notifications to articles and when somebody tries to add open lies, an editor can delete all changes and the troll's effort will be in vain.

Plus, every change can provoke a behind the scenes discussion within which a consensus on sensitive matters is sought. It isn't always found. Sometimes, conflicts result in editing wars in which users get back at each other by adding their own changes and refuse to keep the other party's changes. In such situations, administrators put an article into a "demilitarized zone" within which it can only be edited three times by one user in 24 hours (three-revert rule – 3RR). In case the topic is controversial, an article can be put into confinement and edits by unregistered users are turned off.

---

* Everybody has free access to Wikipedia. In order for things to remain this way, its content is protected from the automatic application of copyright and the paradox is that it's done through copyright. A license called Creative Commons Attribution-Share Alike 3.0 ensures that the burden of intellectual property cannot be applied to any Wikipedia articles or works created from them.

Wikipedia's Arbitration Committee is its "Supreme Court". It consists of 12 administrators who are elected within the community and named by Jimmy Wales himself. So far, the committee has issued a decision on almost 400 cases. When it comes to the resolution of disputes, rather than the content of an article, the Committee takes into account the behavior of users involved in the conflict.[208] The Committee also has the right to veto Jimmy Wales's decisions – this way he gave up a part of his power over Wikipedia. This is why Wales says he's more like a British queen rather than an American president.

The functioning of Wikipedia is best seen when it comes to current events. For example, when in 2011 a tsunami wave caused a meltdown of a nuclear reactor, one could watch a Wikipedia article being created before their own eyes. In a couple of days, one single sentence with a grammar mistake grew into an extensive text with detailed information about submarine earthquakes, tsunami waves, the Japanese nuclear plant, possible causes and results of the disaster and the overall course of events. The first bit of information appeared on Wikipedia 32 minutes after the accident and today the article is 46 pages long and includes almost 400 links to sources and literature.[209] Collective intelligence connected to the internet was thus in real time creating something that would take analogue encyclopedists several years or decades to write.

LAW AND ORDER IN INTERNET ANARCHY

"It is high time to shift out of the pragmatic mind-set that has been our national characteristic. The grand alternatives for social organization must be reconsidered. The loss of faith in the socialist dream has not, and probably will not, restore faith in laissez-faire. But what are the effective alternatives? Does anarchism deserve a hearing, and, if so, what sort of anarchism?"

James M. Buchanan,
Nobel laureate in economics (1986)[210]

1. INTRODUCTION – PRISONER'S DILEMMA

"The economics of governance is an unfinished project whose time has come."[211]

Oliver E. Williamson, Nobel laureate in economics (2009).

Imagine you are watching a TV show and in the beginning, the police catch the main character – Jack. Jack is innocent, but only the TV spectators know that. He's later sentenced to 15 years in prison. In the scene where he says goodbye to his family, we see a relative secretly give him a carton of cigarettes. Jack manages to smuggle it into prison where cigarettes are the local currency. In episode two, Jack ventures out to the prison courtyard for the first time where the other inmates are already standing around. Jack doesn't know anybody and doesn't know what to do. All he can rely on is the carton of cigarettes hidden in his mattress.

Although prisons are one of the most strictly guarded places on our planet, from the prisoners' point of view, they're like bubbles of anarchy. Prisoners cannot rely on guards to physically protect them – their resources are limited and they can never ensure 100% security. Not to mention some of them are corrupt. Guards don't resolve prisoners' commercial disputes over their contraband items. You cannot simply go ahead and complain that your inmate didn't deliver you the cellphone you paid for with cigarettes. Phones aren't allowed and neither is keeping cigarette cartons.

Later, the rumor that a bald guy with a cobra tattoo on the back of his neck sells cellphones reaches Jack. The price of a Nokia 3310 in good condition is one carton of cigarettes. That's exactly how much Jack has in his mattress – hooray! Every good microeconomist can smell the potential benefits of a voluntary exchange in the air. A political economist might sense a problem. Jack and the bald guy with the cobra tattoo can indeed carry out a mutually beneficial exchange, but they live in an institutional vacuum. There's no such thing as the Commercial Code in prison and prisoners cannot call the police if somebody steals from them. They don't even have access to fair trial where the court could settle their disputes. They live in society without law and order – they live in anarchy.

Life in anarchy brings its problems. Thomas Hobbes, one of the most famous political philosophers, described it as a lonely, poor, brutal, and short life where everybody is at constant war with everybody.

Why was he so skeptical? Both, Jack and the bald guy, can potentially improve their situation if they exchange the cellphone for cigarettes. The problem is that each of them can improve their own situation even a bit more if they don't stick to their part of the agreement; the bald guy kicks Jack's ass instead of giving him the phone or Jack runs away instead of handing him the cigarettes. They don't need to attend Game Theory 101 in order to think two steps in advance and realize that their business partner has the same motivation to cheat as themselves. He may promise that he's not like that and that he'll stick to his word but, as Hobbes said: "Covenants, without the sword, are but words and of no strength to secure a man at all." In the end there will be no exchange and Hobbes's predictions about a lonely and poor life will become reality.

Productive cooperation amongst people isn't a guarantee. It requires certain institutions and rules to govern in society. We know it even from our childhood days when the basic exchange institution was the "from hand-to-hand" rule. It created trust between the parties involved in the exchange and ensured smooth cooperation. The simultaneous transfer of a toy car from Johnny's hand to Tom's and the crayon from Tom's hand to Johnny's hand eliminated the option of cheating. However, adult society and the world of more complex exchanges somehow require more sophisticated solutions.

Hobbes came up with one of them and named his legendary book after it: Leviathan. He proposed the establishment of a special organization to which we would give the authorization to legally use violence in order to enforce law and order, to create laws, hire policemen, and establish courts. We basically create a state that provides law and order services on a certain territory. This idea has remained present in political philosophy in the following centuries. The state has become a generally accepted tool to bring us from the world of barbarians and step into the world of civilized society. Nobody in their right mind would choose to live in a "natural state" – a stateless state. In common language, anarchy has become a synonym for chaos and the state has become a synonym for order and securities.

1.1 SMALL-SCALE INFORMAL ANARCHY

"A dealer is afraid of losing his character, and is scrupulous in observing every engagement. When a person makes perhaps twenty contracts in a day, he cannot gain so much by endeavouring to impose on his neighbors, as the very appearance of a cheat would make him lose. Where people seldom deal with one another, we find that they are somewhat disposed to cheat, because they can gain more by a smart trick than they can lose by the injury which it does their character."[212]

Adam Smith

We already know that Hobbes was overly skeptical about anarchy. For most of human history, people lived in more or less egalitarian social groups without a ruler who had a monopoly on violence.[213] We also know that post-indigenous peoples now live in the original way – in groups without state rules.[214] Those of you who want a taste of life in anarchy can read about Eskimo tribes in arctic

America, Pigmy people from Zaire, Yurok tribe in North America, Ifugaos in the Phillipines, South American Kuikurus, or Indonesian Massimos.²¹⁵

In order to reject Hobbes, it isn't enough to point out societies that lived or have lived in the "natural" stateless state, yet their life wasn't a constant war of everybody against everybody. Hobbes backed up his conclusion with good analytic arguments that are these days usually presented in an abstract form – through the prisoner's dilemma game. It is basically a formalized version of Jack's story.

Prisoner's dilemma takes place at a police station where two suspects are being individually interrogated. Each of them has two options: either cooperate with their accomplice (refuse to testify) or betray (testify). From both suspects' points of views, it's better to remain silent. This way, the policemen won't get any evidence and they'll be conditionally released. It's definitely better than incriminating each other and both ending up in prison for five years. The problem is that everybody has their selfish motivation to betray their accomplice (testify against them).

Such a game results in an unpleasant dog-eat-dog balance. Everybody cheats everybody and there's zero cooperation. But there's a catch – the one-off nature of the situation is the common denominator of the prisoner's dilemma, Hobbes's book, and Jack's story. All it takes is to stop seeing life as a one-round game and the pessimistic prognoses about (non)cooperation fades away.

If people are exposed to repeated interaction, cheating stops being a rational strategy. Repetition creates an opportunity to punish a cheater by refusing to cooperate further with them. At the same time, it creates a positive motivation for being honest because it brings the benefits of long-term cooperation. The rational calculation in the prisoner's dilemma shifts. To cheat once may lead to a short-term gain, but it deprives us of future gains. The continuation of a (business) relationship becomes a valuable asset that can be lost. So, if the future matters to someone, the absence of cheating is a rational strategy for them.²¹⁶

In my country, people often say that repetition is the mother of wisdom. However, it seems that this mother had at least two children because repetition is also the mother of cooperation. It's the repeated opportunity to do business that stimulates willingness to cooperate and suppresses opportunism and cheating. Adam Smith also noticed it, hence his quote in the introduction. People don't need the sword of Damocles in the form of a state enforcement apparatus hanging over them in order to be honest and cooperate. All it takes is potential future cooperation – this way it becomes self-enforcing.

The power of repetition brings cooperation even to areas where one would least expect it. For example, to a battlefield on the western front of WWI where the soldiers of the Triple Alliance were standing (or more likely sitting) in trenches facing the soldiers of the Central Powers. The nature of trench warfare created the environment of repetition that resulted in some unexpected actions. Many books have been written about this subject and it was also captured by the film Joyeux Noël (2005). The film was based on a real event that took place on Christmas Eve in 1914 on the French-German border. Soldiers from both armies left the trenches unarmed, shook their hands and played a football match together. But that's not all. Their private journals contained records that testify how German soldiers walked around the front within shooting range of the enemy who wasn't paying attention and shouted apologies when their artillery launched an unannounced bombardment. An unexpected symbiosis in line with the "live and let live" motto arose between the soldiers.[217]

What does this imply for Jack from our introduction story? In order for him to initiate cooperation in the jungle of prison, he has to create an environment of repeated interaction. For example, he can open the carton of cigarettes and offer one to the bald guy, provided he lets him make a phone call. The bald guy can act greedily and take the cigarette without letting Jack make his phone call, but this way he says goodbye to any future cooperation. There won't be any more cigarettes from Jack. If he cares at least a little bit about what happens in the future, it's better if he sticks to his part of the deal. The same goes for Jack who doesn't have any good reason to be opportunistic either. This way, a peaceful, voluntary and mutually beneficial cooperation is established even in a world where the state doesn't possess a monopoly on law and order. Repetition really is the mother of cooperation.

However, such bilateral communication has its limitations. It may be effective, but it's not the most efficient. The world in which you do business only with those with whom you are planning a long-term cooperation is a small world indeed. But there is at least a partial solution – let's add communication to all this. In bilateral cooperation, the punishment for not keeping the deal is a one-person boycott by the cheated party. If this happens within a community, club, guild, or another social group, rumors and communication make sure that multiple people boycott cheaters. So, it becomes beneficial not to cheat against your business partner even if you aren't planning to see them ever again. Cheating could cost you something precious – the way others see you, your reputation.

This is how the power of repetition multiplies. Instead of putting off one person from cooperation, cheating puts off others as well. If the bald guy decides to trick Jack, not only will it cost him a future income of cigarettes but also future cooperation with other prisoners. The functioning of this mechanism isn't as simple and direct as it is with bilateral communication. It requires the fulfillment of additional information requirements.[218]

It is no longer enough to know your partner's face, you also need to know their name which is soaked with their reputation – information about their past behavior towards others. Reputation is a substitute for personal experience. A good name is a valuable asset that opens doors to future business deals. In order for reputation to fulfill its function, we need to assure an undisturbed information flow. Members of society must have an information channel through which they learn if somebody has cheated in the past. From the historical perspective, this channel has always been fueled by the desire of people to gossip and talk behind others' backs and it played the role of a decentralized immune system that protected them from tricksters.* This task was later performed by blacklists, lists of fraudsters, and walls of shame.

Historical and analytical research carried out by economists has revealed many examples of societies with functioning anarchy.[219] Prisons are like a modern lab where a decentralized way of ensuring law and order grew organically. Instead of chaos, they're ruled by organized anarchy. Ever since scientists have started exploring social life in prisons, they keep coming across a specific set of norms that arose independently and determine what's forbidden – for example, ratting out others to guards, being noisy, stealing, not paying one's debts, meddling in others' business, complaining about somebody, or physically attacking somebody for no reason. The norms are known under the name of the Convict Code and they exist despite there being no official record, approval, and enforcement by the police. The Convict Code is an unintended result of many repeated interactions between inmates and its compliance is enforced in a decentralized manner – by gossip, insults, beatings, or exclusion from social life and business activities.[220]

1.2 LIMITED ANARCHY

Luckily, ensuring law and order in anarchy doesn't only depend on slow evolutionary forces which form norms and decentralized enforcement. There is also a consciously created alternative. It includes different associations, communities, and guilds with their founders and rule-makers who consciously created formal ways of providing law and order. I'll call them clubs. They were labelled as such by Nobel laureate James M. Buchanan when in his article titled "*An Economic Theory of Clubs*"[221], he explained that goods and services aren't only private or public but there's also something in-between these two categories: club goods and services. He also further described what interest private entrepreneurs have in providing goods and services in clubs. An example of this is a disco club which, apart from alcohol (private goods), offers music, cleanliness, and safety (club goods).

Historically, clubs didn't only serve entertainment purposes. They are behind the birth of a comprehensive phenomenon known as the first financial stock exchange. Imagine you're in Amsterdam, it's 1614 and another commercial expedition to India is about to take place. Dutch company *United East India* that's behind this expedition is reaching unexpectedly high profits. You decide to invest and buy its shares. Stock brokers offer you various tools: direct purchase of shares, forward contract, options, or short selling. You're willing to buy, others to

---

* Anthropologists say that a group of approx. 150 persons is capable of functioning without any more complex, formal structure. This number is called Dunbar's number and represents the limit for individuals to create and maintain relationships in a group. If the size of the group goes above this number, direct social contact will begin to disappear together with informal trust.

sell. But who's going to ensure that you'll get your profit and that the shares are really yours if the expedition is a success? What if somebody tricks you? After all, it's quite a long-term investment with people you don't know.

Turning to the state would be a mistake. Not only because the state doesn't work the way it should, it also consciously and systemically tries to prevent this type of business because it considers it hazardous. Luckily for the first brokers, investors, and company owners, they didn't read Hobbes's Leviathan (it hadn't been written yet). Instead of indulging in philosophical discussions, they figured out how to instill law and order in the world of financial transactions. They created a club with entering conditions, a code of conduct, and punishments for non-compliance. They created the first stock exchange in Amsterdam. Businessmen from Amsterdam were followed by businessmen from London in the 18th century who would meet informally and do their business in cafés. Later, one of these cafés – the already mentioned *Jonathan's Coffee-House* – turned into the famous London Stock Exchange. The café worked like an investment club with many rules. For example, if somebody refused to pay what they were supposed to or otherwise tricked his business partner, they were labelled lame duck and their name was published on a wall of shame. Not only did they lose good reputation in the eyes of their business partners, the other businessmen, investors, and brokers weren't willing to cooperate with them either.

As time went on, the clubs established more detailed entry requirements and ethical rules. For instance, the New York Stock Exchange forbade the use of swear words (punishable by one-week suspension of activities), sanctioned smoking in meeting rooms and halls ($5) and standing on top of chairs ($1). Private stock exchange clubs came with strict rules for companies hoping to enter the market. They required transparency, logging, and the publishing of requested data.[222]

The story of New York's diamond dealers is no less intriguing. Despite (or due to) trading goods of extremely high value, they gave up the option of publicly provided law and order and opted for private alternatives. Their main private alternative consisted in creating a specialized club called The New York Diamond Dealers Club. Only verified members had access to it and one of the entry requirements was to belong to the Orthodox Jewish community, which created such strong trust among diamond dealers, that they were able to trade without big formalities.* In case of conflicts, instead of turning to the police, they turned to the private club with its own special problem-solving authorities.[223]

Economic research of anarchy has made a significant progress in the last few decades.[224] Amongst other things, there is some interesting research about how the pirates of the Caribbean discovered the benefits of constitutional democracy in the 18th century – even before the Founding Fathers of the USA.

---

* Before somebody starts thinking: "Of course the Jews chose the most lucrative business again", it has to be said that the causality relationship is the other way around – the unique requirements for trade with diamonds "chose" Jewish communities because they were able to conduct this type of trade thanks to their high rate of trust, closeness and strong social, religious and family pressure.

As a society of sea wolves, pirates also needed to maintain law and order on board. They needed rules that would prevent stealing, fights and conflicts and enable fast coordination on board – mostly during "working hours" which, in this case, meant robbing and persecuting. They obviously couldn't rely on the public authorities whose ships they were attacking. That's why they created their own constitution, rules for electing commanders, and limitations to power – their own system of checks and balances. It not only enabled them to successfully cooperate outside the reach of the law, but it also made life on anarchistic ships more pleasant than on ships sailing under the Royal Navy flag.[225]

The research also examined trade in different medieval guilds and traders' associations in the Mediterranean that even created international commercial law, lex mercatoria.[226] Private trade flourished in China[227] as well as in Mexico, California[228], and Africa.[229] The inhabitants of the American Wild West, who at that time, were out of reach of the state's visible hand, created private property clubs, associations of cattle breeders, and material extractions groups to provide law and order services.[230] Cattle breeders in Shasta, California have been ignoring public institutions to this day and they have their own rules for the resolution of disputes.[231]

This way of privately providing law and order generally only works in small homogenous clubs with regular interactions and easily accessible information about the members and their past behavior. The above-mentioned associations would start (and some of them even started) to experience problems if their activities were to be conducted on a larger scale in an anonymous and heterogenous society constantly joined by new members. You would hardly find associations or clubs that reached the size of entire cities or countries.

The reason is that with the growing size of the club, the aspect of repetition is lost (the mother of cooperation slowly disappears), the network of interactions gets thinner, social relations get looser, and the costs of information infrastructure grow rapidly. It becomes increasingly difficult to find out in advance if somebody is to be trusted and if they're a club member and also to inform others about one's experience or somebody's departure from the club. The entire mechanism that used to help keep law and order collapses. In anonymous society, fraudsters have no pressure to keep a good reputation, which decreases the individual members' trust in cooperation with a random person. Most economists who admit and explain the functioning of law and order without the state agree with this conclusion. The bigger a group gets, the lower the effectiveness of privately provided law and order is.[232]

Jewish diamond dealers also felt the consequences. A lot has changed since the original study was carried out in 1992.[233] The end of the second millennium brought globalization and more and more Indian dealers became involved in diamond trade. With the growing number of the members of the traders' community and the increasing heterogeneity, the mechanisms that kept law and order among Jewish traders for over a millennium started to weaken.[234]

1.3 WAS HOBBES RIGHT AFTER ALL?

"... return on opportunism, cheating, and shirking rise in complex socities. A coercive third party is essential."[235]

Douglass North, Nobel laureate in economics (1993)

The functioning of private law and order in big societies is problematic which is a serious issue. The key factor behind the growth of people's wealth is the extension of the division of labour to bigger units. It enables a more intensive specialization connected with increasing productivity. Was Hobbes right after all? The developments in American prisons in the second half of the 20th century, where the Convict Code used to work successfully, will get us closer to obtaining the answer.

The idylic prison life as it is portrayed in Shawshank Redemption started to fall apart in the 1960s due to a rapid increase in the number of prisoners. In California, it grew almost four fold between 1945 and 1970. Today, the USA is a country with the highest number of prisoners in the world. The structure of prison population changed due to the influx of convicts from different minorities and of various ethnicities and races. While in 1951, there were two white convicts for each minority convict, in 2011 there were three minority convicts for each white convict. Their average age has also decreased. All of this together caused the decentralized system of convict conduct to stop working.[236]

We already know what happened next from TV shows and films. The decentralized system of norms was replaced by centralized prison gangs that are now depicted as a source of violence and fear. But, as it tends to be, public perception of the world lags behind the reality. It's true that when the Convict Code fell apart, there was a period of increased violence in prisons. However, with the formation of gangs, the trend started to turn. Prison gangs now work as law and order providers and as they grew in the 70s, the rate of violence in prisons started to decrease. The number of riots decreased eight fold and the number of murders went down by 94% and it is even lower than in the general population outside prisons.[237]

This was achieved thanks to an institutional tool that managed to overcome the information problems of the Convict Code in a big anonymous society. It's referred to as the system of community responsibility.

A prison gang is not a golf club. It's basically an involuntary club based on racial segregation where strict rules apply. One of these rules says that everybody is responsible for everybody's actions in relation to other gangs. This means that if a member of the Nazi Low Riders gang owes money to a member of Nuestra Familia and decides not to pay, every member of Nazi Low Riders is responsible for his debt. In such a situation, two things happen:

1. The members of Nazi Low Riders will collect money to pay off the debt of their member to the member of Nuestra Familia because they want

to protect their gang's reputation, since it's important for their business activities.

2. They will impose an exemplary punishment on their own member who didn't pay his debt because nobody likes to pay for other people's debts.

This mechanism helped restore order in prisons and renew the contraband trade that flourishes in North American prisons. Prisoners trade cigarettes, drugs, steroids, stamps (they are used as a means of payment), tattoos, cellphones, computers, SIM cards. Estimates now indicate there's one cellphone per one prisoner.[238]

Prison gangs as communitites of shared responsibility lowered the information problems of reputation and enabled the discipline of repeated interactions to do its job on a higher level – instead of the individual level, we are talking about the level of gangs.

However, prisoners weren't the first to come up with this mechanism. European traders used a similar system when they wanted to revive commerce between the 11th and 14th century. They also had to deal with the problems of cooperation in a big anonymous society. If they wanted to establish a one-off business interaction with somebody coming from far away, they were facing three challenges: 1. they could not expect future cooperation; 2. they did not know whether the person was trustworthy and how they behaved in the past; and 3. there was no way of damaging their reputation in case they wronged them. One could not expect cooperation to flourish under such circumstances.

Profesor Avner Greif showed in his books and articles that traders solved the problem precisely through a system of community responsibility. A trader didn't have to know the reputation of another trader – it was enough for him to know that they were a member of some community (town, guild, society) that was accountable for their potential mistakes and that this community had a good reputation. Such a system lowered the demanding information requirements of reputation mechanisms in a relatively big and anonymous society.[239]

Nevertheless, the system of community responsibility had its limitations and it became the victim of its own soccess, as it is emphasised by Greif. With the expansion of trade across Europe, individual communities grew in sizes and numbers and it became increasingly difficult to determine who belonged where. It was also easy to abandon a community once you have commited fraud. According to Greif, these were the factors that undermined the functioning of the system of community responsibility in medieval trade.[240] When identifying their business partner, traders couldn't rely on skin colour or tattoos like prison gangs do nowadays. These "brands" cannot be falsified or ereased and in prisons, they constitute a trustworthy identification method to identify a member of a gang.

So, what replaced the system of community responsibility according to Greif? States as we know them today: as territorial monopoly for the provision of law and order. It made sense from the point of view of expanding cooperation and decreasing information demands. As a territorial monopoly, the state lowers information costs both inwards (1) and outwards (2):*

(1) When enforcing compliance, states don't rely on the loss of reputation of individual parties of trade. The punishment doesn't come in the form of a collective boycott or ostracization because that would require a complex information infrastructure. Instead, it comes from an independent third party – courts, police, prison guards. It is no longer important to find out about the reputation of a future business partner just like it no longer matters if we can damage their reputation in case they trick us. If somebody commits fraud, it is enough to report it to relevant authorities and the punishment will come in the form of a fine or imprisonment. The transfer of information within a club isn't necessary. The threat of a punishment from a "third party" creates pressure to behave well. This system significantly lowered inward information costs.

(2) We no longer need to find out who belongs to which community, club, or association. The state works on a territorial basis, so you can be sure that its rules apply to everybody who lives within this territory. This radically lowers information costs of the provision of law and order. Everybody can be sure that the person they enter into cooperation with has to obey the same rules and that in case of a conflict, they can turn to courts and police. So, there's no such thing as faking one's identity. Costs of the acceptance of members disappear too – every born individual is automatically a member of the state and it isn't necessary to verify or assess their qualities and consequently inform other members whether they actually became a member. The costs of informing other members about the change in rules (not knowing the law will not excuse you) or training new members on existing laws decrease too. The state can also accept members of different states provided they respect the rules of the territory they are currently operating in (perhaps with the exception of diplomats).

Friedrich Hayek also noticed the advantages of the state as a territorial monopoly for the provision of law and order:

"I believe there is one convincing argument why you can't leave even the law to voluntary evolution: the great society depends on your being able to expect that any stranger you encounter in a given territory will obey the same system of rules of law. Otherwise you would be confined to people whom you know. And the conception of some of our modern anarchists that you can have one club which agrees on one law, another club agrees on another law, would make it just impossible to deal with any

---

* In the following lines, I will not take state failures into consideration and I will suppose that the state can fulfill its functions. My aim is to analytically isolate the potential advantages of the state under certain technological conditions and consequently compare these advantages once technological conditions change.

stranger. So in a sense you have, at least for a given territory, a uniform law, and that can only exist if it's enforced by government."[241]

On the one hand, it's true that creating the state apparatus involves high fixed costs (certainly higher than in the case of private alternatives, whether they are spontaneous norms with decentralized enforcement or information clubs). On the other hand, the marginal costs of other people involved in cooperation significantly decrease, which is important precisely when it comes to big anonymous societies.*

Territorial monopoly tackles all types of cooperation or inappropriate behavior within cooperation and that brings significant bulk savings. Society with a territorial monopoly doesn't need creators of rules (politicians), enforcement apparatus (policemen) and conflict mediators (courts) for every single area of the economy separately. Everything is subordinate to one provider – the state.

Arguments in favor of law and order providers with a territorial as opposed to private alternatives don't mean that somebody started to establish states as we know them and with good intentions. What I'm describing here is just one of the adaptation advantages of territorial monopoly in the world of cultural evolution. The whole concept of nationalism with its quasi-religious symbols and rituals can therefore be an ad hoc rationalization of the benefits of economic cooperation within larger territories. So, if somebody managed to accidentally (or with predatory intentions) form a state, they were able to create unified rules with a single provider of law and order which brought (perhaps unintentionally) the extension of cooperation as a consequence. In the same way nobody had to consciously discover private property or democracy which are, under certain technological and social conditions, useful cultural artefacts.

Because technological and social conditions keep changing, the adaptational advantage of individual institutions changes as well. The internet has been the biggest source of changes in recent years. It completely transformed the way information is stored, copied, and transferred, which is very important precisely from the point of view of the provision of law and order.

---

* That doesn't mean that the state could extend its territorial monopoly to the entire world. We can see that there's no such thing as global government and there are reasons for it: such a state would have extremely high organization costs of its administration and also external costs (inhabitants' disapproval with the policy that imposes costs on them) and at the same time, it wouldn't bring remarkable benefits from additional trade – international trade has existed between many different states.

2. INFORMATION EVOLUTION IN BRIEF

"Cyberspace is no different than real space... To this extent activity in cyberspace is functionally identical to transnational activity mediated by other means, such as mail or telephone or smoke signal."

Jack Goldsmith, 1998

In the first chapter, we talked about how new technologies and the internet influenced transaction costs when they tried to solve the issue of information asymmetry. The second chapter showed us how they influenced organization costs and the problem of public goods. This chapter shall explore the evolution of storing, copying, and transferring information in general and what role the internet played in this area.

Language can be seen as the first step in the evolution of information within the history of humanity. It served as a means to improve cooperation and coordination between people when hunting, collecting food, defending themselves, or attacking an enemy group. You can do all of this without using language, but it goes much smoother when you do use it. Apart from creating more complex sentences, nothing of great significance happened in the next tens of thousands of years in terms of the evolution of information. It was an era of great information poverty. Storing information was left to the human memory through oral transmission and its transfer depended on the physical closeness of people and their willingness to talk and listen.

The next evolutionary step which took place was approximately 3000 BC with the discovery of writing. Sumerians developed the first written language and it was mostly used for economic and record-keeping purposes. Writing enabled people to store information outside their heads; this also made it easier to be copied because it no longer required oral transmission – a written record was enough. Just like with language, the discovery of writing lead to a period of technical refinement of writing itself (from pictograms to logosyllabic script) and also its carrier (from clay, stone, skin and finally paper).

Although writing improved the precision of recording and storing information, it was still costly to copy and transfer it. There were even special professions that consisted in copying information but it was a slow and expensive process. This changed after the discovery of printing – first, in China in the 11th century and later in Europe in the 15th century, when Gutenberg printed his famous 42-line Bible. Printing press radically decreased the costs of copying which brought information to wide masses of people for the first time in history. It was the first step out of information poverty and it fundamentally changed the political and religious landscape of Europe.

So, it became possible to easily store and copy information, but transferring it was still slow. Information was still bound to the physical world and its transfer was limited by the existing means of transport. Since the fastest and the most reliable of these was the horse, information could travel at a maximum speed of 43.5 miles per day – just like people and goods. People used pigeons for the transfer of simpler information but their reliability and flight range were somehow limited, not to mention the information capacity.

The invention of the telegraph in the beginning of the 19th century was the first significant innovation in the field of information transfer. The telegraph enabled a fast transfer of information over long distances. Its coding was slow and accessibility was not ideal either – it required one's physical presence in a central office where information was decoded. This limitation was mitigated by the first telephones at the end of the 19th century that required neither coding nor anybody's physical presence.

The absolute revolution in information access was brought about by the new information technology of the most recent decades and it completely transformed all the three above-mentioned aspects: storage (hard disk drives and cloud), copying (easy and with practically zero marginal costs) but mostly information transfer. The internet freed information from the physical world and during its transfer the limitations of space and time lost their importance from both the technical and the economic points of view. The costs of internet connection and downloading content keep decreasing.[242]

Some people may argue that such speed of information was there during the entire 20th century in the form of radio and TV broadcast thanks to which masses of people from all continents could easily and quickly get lots of information. Yes, it's true that radio and television made low-cost information transfer possible. However, it was centralized and it only went one way. One point of transmission reached millions of spectators and auditors. Plus, this 20th century technology not only brought entertainment but also state propaganda in the socialist Soviet Union and equally socialist Nazi Germany.

Picture: TV and radio information transmission scheme

There was also technology that transferred information in both ways in the 20th century – telegraphs and telephones. Still, they were far from enabling the scaling of communication between big groups and creating a distributed network where everybody could be connected with everybody at once. Telephones and text messages generally made it possible to connect two people only.

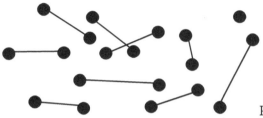

Picture: Telephone and telegraph information transmission scheme

The internet combines the best of television and telephone. For the first time in human history, we have a communication tool that is massive and two-directional. People transmit and receive and at the same time and are a part of an extensive distributed network that allows everybody to communicate with everybody. If it doesn't seem like such a big step to you, try to imagine how to build Facebook or Twitter with the help of SMS or Instagram via MMS. Analogue infrastructure was simply not enough to build a distributed network.

Picture: Internet network information transmission scheme

In addition, in the last decade, we have been able to fit the whole distributed internet network into our pockets. These technologies profoundly changed the way information is stored, copied, and transferred. For the first time in history, we experience a surplus of information – we are no longer limited by the accessibility of information but by the willingness to consume it. What does it imply for society from the point of view of providing law and order?

3. GLOBAL INTERNET CLUBS WITH SUPER-MEMBERSHIP

In the introduction to this part, I have explained how private provision of law and order works in smaller communities and the related problems with information costs that arise at the level of a big anonymous society. The state "cleverly" resolved information demands because it doesn't have to worry about the information required to discover a person's reputation since it punishes fraudsters with its monopoly on violence. It also doesn't have to worry about the identification of its members because its law and order are applied to all the inhabitants of its territory.

The arrival of information technology gave private clubs which provide law and order a strong dose of doping. It gave rise to internet clubs with reputations and "super-membership cards on steroids".

3.1 REPUTATION ON INTERNET STEROIDS

"We're trying to design a system that instills trust within the marketplace, not one that is in place because of a US law."

Brian Burke, Director of Global Feedback Policy, eBay

Thanks to the internet, we can now find global internet clubs of unlimited size. This was impossible with traditional clubs. The internet has turned the theory of optimum size upside-down. The definition by James M. Buchanan which says that the creation of a club has to balance on the edge between earnings (membership fees) and costs (they arise when the club is too full) related to every new member is no longer true. On the internet, a much simpler math applies: the more, the better. It doesn't mean that new members don't generate new costs for internet clubs. Some clubs even struggled with the initial influx of new members and their customer lines, servers or complaint-handling departments fell to their knees with exhaustion. However, it's just a question of fixed investments that don't pose a problem of principle when scaling the size of the club. As a matter of principle, there's no reason why there shouldn't be an internet club that includes all the inhabitants of our planet as members. Facebook got closest to this – it's approaching the limit of 2.7 billion users.

In this book, I'm not going to describe just any internet clubs. I'm going to focus on those that provide law and order services. Just like with traditional clubs, the main tools of internet clubs are reputation systems. In this part, we'll look at the options clubs have when designing them. Specifically, there are three sets of parameters that internet clubs can set and adapt to their conditions:

- they determine how users express the evaluation of their experience with other users;

- they determine how obtained data is analyzed, processed and aggregated;
- they determine the form in which the reputation of users is published and spread amongst the members of the club.

The correct setting of all three parameters creates a functional reputation system even in a big anonymous society. It's important to optimally design the management of information flow between users and potential users who are interested in cooperation so that everyone is motivated to cooperate peacefully and avoid cheating.

FIRST SET OF PARAMETERS: FROM QUALITY TO QUANTITY

Information about somebody's evaluation of their experience with another person is of a qualitative nature. Since experience is subjective, a reputation system designer has to propose a way to objectivize it – a system able to transform quality into further processable quantity. The father of internet reputation, auction portal eBay*, proposed a rating where users can mark their experience as positive, neutral, or negative. Originally, sellers were also allowed to rate buyers. Users could also provide written feedback with a short message for future buyers or sellers.

An author of a reputation system also needs to think about whom they will authorize to rate others and under which conditions. In the past, even eBay users who hadn't carried out any business transactions were allowed to post ratings. Everybody could rate everybody. Nevertheless, it was tempting to cheat in such an open system – worsening the reputation of competitors and improving your own. So, eBay changed the settings so that users can only rate those with whom they were involved in business interactions.** It didn't entirely remove the problem of revenge, though. It used to be common for sellers to wait with their rating until buyers post theirs so that they can return the favor in case it was negative. Since buyers sensed the possibility of revenge, they didn't post bad ratings and as a result, there was a distortion in the process of transforming qualitative experience into quantifiable data.

Airbnb had the same problem and their solution was to give users a two-week window to post simultaneous evaluations. eBay chose a different way: sellers can no longer post negative rating about buyers, which takes away their leverage for revenge.*** Buyers were left only with the option to report fraudsters. eBay also limited laxly given negative ratings from buyers who purchased items from rep-

---

* Platform eBay was the first internet club to start providing law and order.
** Some internet services don't limit those who can post ratings (Tripadvisor, Yelp). It results in significant problems with false ratings and buying good reputation.
*** Despite that, they did not manage to remove the problem of revenge completely. One of the reasons may be the fact that sellers can always turn to a court and demand to be paid damages for having their good name tarnished by bad rating. They usually don't win the dispute but the fact that you, as a customer, can be sued for posting a bad rating is unpleasant. This happened, for instance,

utable and reliable sellers. If a buyer wants to post a negative rating about a seller, they first need to wait for seven days until emotions wear off. In addition, they must first answer questions like: "Did you discuss the problem with the seller?", or: "Did you give them enough time?", in order to make the rating as relevant as possible and avoid rash negative ratings.

In 2007, eBay extended the possibilities of expressing (dis)satisfaction. It added a detailed seller rating within which buyers can award them with one to five stars in different categories (complete description, communication or how quickly the goods were sent). It's not only more precise but also anonymous unlike the previous system – it should motivate buyers to post more accurate and honest ratings. Anonymous ratings reveal hidden problems that may not appear in public rating.

SECOND SET OF PARAMETERS: FROM RAW DATA TO APPLICABLE STATISTICS

The above-mentioned mechanisms are supposed to get the maximum amount of quantifiable data out of subjective experience. But internet clubs cannot serve their users raw data. They first need to analyze, process, and aggregate it in order to obtain the maximum information value.

Let's again begin with eBay. First, eBay assigns values of +1, 0, or -1 to ratings in the form of positive, neutral, and negative and then makes a simple calculation so that the user gets one number in its absolute value which cumulatively captures the experience others have with them. The longer and more actively the user has participated in the given internet club, the higher it is.

Another way eBay processes raw data is to divide the total of positive ratings by the total of both positive and negative ratings which results in a percentage of positive transactions of a given club member. This indicator tells us more about the user's quality and not only about how long they have been in the club and how active they have been. Still, some economists point out that this number can be distorted. Empirical research shows that users with positive experience tend to provide feedback more often than those with negative experiences.[243] Basically, people don't like to give negative feedback and that distorts the percentage upwards. So, economists suggested a different calculation. According to them, the numerator should contain positive ratings of the given club member, and the denominator should consist of the total number of their transactions. Such way of aggregation would relatively worsen the reputation of users who have a lot of transactions and few ratings. In other words, those with whom others have worse experience and decided not to rate them.

Economists also tested this way of calculating reputation in an experiment. They found out that buyers who had the possibility of the improved version of the rating system were more likely to return to eBay and purchase items again than the control group that only experienced traditional rating. Their conclusion

---

to Michael Steadman when he gave a negative rating to a watch seller because the goods he received by mail were dysfunctional.[A12]

was that this way of data aggregation better captures how buyers are treated.[244] eBay has not applied their proposed upgrade so far.

Of course, there are many ways of processing and aggregating raw data. If an internet club enables its members to give star ratings, it can be advantageous to aggregate data by simple distribution – you will see how many one-star, two-star, three-star, etc. ratings a user got. Amazon does it like this. If stars are awarded for different parameters, the club shows its members the average number of stars for each of them. This is how it's done on eBay and Airbnb. The internet club Taobao (Chinese version of eBay) even employs an algorithm to add ratings. If a seller rates a buyer positively, but the buyer doesn't respond, the algorithm will automatically award positive rating to the seller on the grounds of the saying "silence gives consent".[245]

Another important parameter when processing raw data is the depth of history – how far in the past the reputation system goes. The absolute number rating on eBay includes all ratings no matter how old they are but when calculating percentage, only ratings awarded in the last twelve months are taken into account. You can check a seller's profile and look up comments and ratings for any period of time (last month, year, their entire history). Reputation systems critics point out that sellers can first build a good reputation and stoop to fraud. However, this strategy can only work if a seller's overall reputation doesn't get worse. Since club members can look up their reputation in the recent past, the scope for monetizing reputation for fraud disappears.

In analysis and aggregation, clubs don't have to exclusively rely on explicit ratings. They can also use indirectly obtained ratings because they are aware of practically every single click from their users. They use big data analysis and learning machines to get further interesting information and connect it with an explicitly awarded reputation. They analyze the messages members exchange and use NLP tools to get a lot of useful information for law and order provision purposes.[246] The remaining question is to what extent the mechanisms for processing and aggregating ratings should be published. On the one hand, transparency increases trust in the club but on the other hand, it creates space for manipulation. If users know how their overall reputation is built and what is taken into consideration by the club, they can learn how to abuse the system more easily.

THIRD SET OF PARAMETERS: FROM OPERATIONAL STATISTICS TO THEIR CORRECT INTERPRETATION

The aim of the third set of parameters is to present processed data in a manner that appeals to club members and prevents their misinterpretation. Finding good quality data and processing it correctly is not enough; setting the correct format for its presentation is just as important.

eBay uses the total of ratings in its absolute value according to which it allocates colored stars. For 10-49 points, a user is awarded a yellow star, for 5000-

9999 a green star, and for 500K-999K green with a tail. The colored stars chart allows a fast comparison of how long members have been in the club. eBay also introduced badges that are awarded to their best sellers ("eBay Top Rated Seller"). If a seller fulfills the established requirements (at least 98% positive ratings, 4.5 stars in detailed rating, 100 carried out transactions in the amount of at least €3,000 during the last year and a low conflict rate), their profile picture is marked with a badge that increases their trustworthiness. Also, eBay guarantees them lower fees. The third set of parameters also includes the order in which sellers appear in a search. Internet clubs prioritize sellers with good reputation or those who possess badges.

Segmentation of club members according to different features can also make the correct interpretation of rating information easier. Different people value different things, so one may find more added value in the ratings of people they identify with. The segmentation tool is used, for instance, by Airbnb whose search takes into consideration whether you are traveling on holiday or business. Amazon displays ratings from family accounts and students separately.

Implementing the "rating of ratings" also ensures the quality of ratings and their better interpretation. Current reputation systems already contain millions of feedback inputs and it can be difficult to select those with high information value. This is why, for instance, Amazon allows users to rate ratings and the best-rated ones (positive and negative) are the most visible.

3.2 SUPER-MEMBERSHIP CARDS ON INTERNET STEROIDS

A well-designed reputation system on internet steroids is able to capture, process, and distribute a lot of information about many people, in other words: to scale the information up to a big anonymous society. Internet trade became popular also thanks to this.

However, if internet clubs had stuck to providing law and order only from behind the keyboard, there would have been no big revolution. Buying and selling things represents only a small part of services that we use in or daily lives. Most interactions take place outside of our living rooms. People travel, work, eat, and sleep away from home while physically meeting other people. In order for privately provided law and order within internet clubs to be relevant, it has to step out of our homes and begin to form interactions outside. The internet alone wasn't enough for that to happen – it required the fundamental innovation in the form of pocket internet.

A combination of plastic, glass, and aluminium in the shape of handy phones connected with GPS navigation and mobile internet brought internet law and order services into the real world. This important step is closely connected with the arrival of iPhone smartphones in 2007. It was no coincidence that only a few years after that, we started to see the first extenstions of internet clubs into the real world of human interactions in the form of the most popular sharing economy platforms: Uber and Airbnb.

Did Uber and Airbnb take a swim in the waters of anarchy?

Although sharing economy platforms managed to solve the problem of information asymmetry by private regulation, most people would not list them among the examples of internet clubs that provide law and order services. Primarily, these platforms have never operated in the environment of anarchy and their owners themselves did everything that was possible in order to function within the legal framework even though they were not always successful.

Despite that, I think that they did step into the murky waters of anarchy with at least one foot. First of all, their presence was illegal in certain places and at certain times. If you are involved in illegal activities, you cannot rely on the help of public law and order providers. Although they were at the edge of legality, the platforms never had problems with internal cooperation. Law and order have always been kept there – customers pay what they are supposed to pay and drivers get what they earn. This may seem like a matter-of-course to us, but functioning law and order is not automatic, just like Hobbes warned in the introduction.

Apart from keeping good internal cooperation, platforms also protect their members from external threats. Uber paid their drivers' fines at airports, Airbnb stood behind their accused host in New York and helped him win a lawsuit.[247]

Uber even created special software called Greyball aimed at protecting their members from public inspections. First, the software identified a potential threat – a public inspector whose credit card matched with other credit cards used by public authorities or the software noticed that the user always logged in and out near public offices or used a phone purchased by public authorities. Inspectors could also be revealed through social networks accounts. When the software noticed that a suspicious person wanted to order a service, it launched a fake version of the mobile app of Uber including a map with non-existent drivers. Such person's order was always cancelled after some time. That's how Uber protected its drivers from the "attacks" of the public sector.[248]

Platforms also experienced some attacks from the inside. For example, one driver in China changed his profile photo to a picture of a zombie by which he wanted to "motivate" riders to cancel their order before his arrival so that he can earn the cancellation fee. In some cities, drivers coordinated themeselves to log out of the application to create a fake lack of drivers and thus increase travel fares. Drivers in Nigeria hacked Uber and installed a special application that manipulated GPS navigation and charged their customers several-times the correct amount. There were also some sneaky users amongst customers; they tried to circumvent increased travel fares by moving to the other corner of the street where the higher price no longer applied. Platforms needed to fight these practices in order to ensure their internet club functioned properly. [249]

So how did smartphones with mobile internet manage to break the wall between the virtual and physical world? They turned into something like "super membership cards". When you are sitting at home shopping via eBay, you can be sure that both you and the seller are members of the same internet club and the same rules apply to both of you. Thanks to pocket internet, you can experience this feeling also in real interactions in the outside world. A smartphone with an active mobile app is your super membership card that helps you prove that you belong to the same internet club as somebody with whom you are about to cooperate in the real world; be it to get a ride, sleep at their place, bring them lunch or provide some kind of service to them. Such super membership card has several super features.

Most importantly, they are super-transparent. Everybody can see who is or isn't a member of a club at extremely low costs. For instance, thanks to being an Uber member, I can travel from Bratislava to New York City and once there, I can sit in a complete stranger's car and rest assured that we're both members of the same club and the same rules apply to both of us. The same goes for Airbnb accommodation or jobs through TaskRabbit or the new sub application UberWorks.[250]

Also, it's impossible that within an internet club, I cooperate with somebody who isn't a member because one can only enter after completing entry requirements and respecting the rules. Clubs have their tools to verify if somebody is using a super membership card that doesn't belong to them or if they want to sign back up after they were expelled. Other members can learn very quickly about somebody's expulsion – they simply no longer see them in the app.

To a large extent, this removes Hayek's concerns that if law and order is not provided by a territorial monopoly, people will clash and everybody would have different ideas about what rules of cooperation apply, who enforces them, and who settles disputes. Thanks to mobile internet, you can now cooperate with people with whom you share a club membership. So, you can have several providers of law and order services in the same territory. We no longer need to rely exclusively on a territorially-defined provider (state); we have the alternative of a functionally-defined provider (clubs specializing in different areas: transport, accommodation, work, etc.).

Once information was liberated from the physical world, the potential for a paradigm shift in the way law and order services are provided appeared as well – services are no longer bound to a territory, which enables the rise of non-territorial providers.* Why should we be happy about it? Well, there are at least two reasons: more intensive competition and customers' consensus.

3.3 TWO BIG ADVANTAGES OF NON-TERRITORIAL PROVISION OF LAW AND ORDER SERVICES

MORE INTENSIVE COMPETITION

"It is flexibility of voluntary rules which in the field of morals makes gradual evolution and spontaneous growth possible, which allows further experience... the existence of individuals and groups simultaneously observing partially different rules provides the opportunity for the selection of the effective ones."[251]

Friedrich Hayek

Even law and order providers with a territorial monopoly face competition. They may have the monopoly for services within their territory, but they cannot avoid competition from other territories. If such a provider messes thing up, people pack their suitcases and leave. Comrades from the ex-soviet bloc were a bright example. There's no better evidence of their incompetence and bad services than the fact that they had to put sharp wire around their territory and hand out guns to border patrols.

Charles Tiebout was the first economist to point out the (potentially) important role of territorial competition. This type of competition even bears his name – Tiebout competition. In his article titled *"A Pure Theory of Local Expenditures"*, he responded to Paul Samuelson regarding the problem of public goods. He showed that public goods can be provided efficiently if we start to look at them from a different angle – the local one.

When people act like free-riders and have a problem voting with their wallets (to pay for public goods), they may start to vote with their feet (move away for public goods). If the mountain won't come to Muhammad, then Muhammad must go to the mountain. Instead of local governments trying to provide public goods that would satisfy the inhabitants, the inhabitants start to choose among local governments according to the sort of public goods they provide. Territorial competition together with "foot voting", under specific conditions, leads to an optimal local public good providers. People get the public goods they want in return for their taxes.

---

* Card companies are the closest historical equivalent to today's internet clubs. They work as intermediaries between many anonymous people while they protect them from fraud and solve disputes. But they could not be used to rent houses, travel by car or get a job which is now possible via Airbnb, Uber, or TaskRabbit.

The problem lies within the phrase "under specific conditions". Apart from traditional prerequisites, Tiebout included the following conditions in his model:
- perfect mobility of people (zero costs of moving);
- people don't work and live from dividends (nothing keeps them at one place);
- big number of territorial providers (people have a choice);
- absence of externalities between territories (one territory doesn't contaminate the air in another territory).

These unrealistic prerequisites immediately attracted numerous critics.[252] The first one is their most frequent target. Mobility of people is far from being cost-free and people don't move so easily. Also, when choosing their target territory, they not only decide according to the local public goods, they consider things like the distance from their family, friends, work, etc., which casts a shadow over the second prerequisite. In addition, if you want to move, you cannot transport everything with you. Some things and their value are bound to a specific territory.

The number of territorial providers isn't ideal either. First of all, you cannot just establish a "local state" wherever you please. In the European context, we saw such attempt in 2015 when Vít Jedlička, a Czech politician, established a new country called Liberland on the western bank of the Danube between Serbia and Croatia on a territory of 2,7 mi2. According to him, this territory was terra nullius – no man's land. The establishment of a new country in Europe has raised a lot of global interest. Things like that don't happen every day. Others attempted the same thing at sea – like Milton Friedman's grandson, Patri Friedman, and his sea institute Seasteading.

To sum up and underscore it – all of these real world's complications cause that Tiebout's competition between territories doesn't function optimally.*

When he was writing his article, Tiebout had no idea that his model would be better applicable to technology that was to be invented half a century later. His theory can be much better applied to internet clubs than to territorial governments. Instead of voting with their feet, people vote by downloading an application. When it comes to internet clubs, the moving costs are practically zero. You don't like your law and order provider in the services of accommodation, transport or work? You're only two clicks away from deleting their application. Actually, you can have several applications installed on your phone and switch between them according to your current needs. So, the transition from one provider to another doesn't require you to sell your house or say goodbye to your friends.

---

* Although it doesn't work optimally, it still has some influence and puts pressure on states to act more responsibly. This type of competition can be also found among private clubs, hotels, shopping malls or condominiums.[A13]

Internet clubs are like floating societies – they can overlap on one territory. At the same time, new ones just keep appearing – they don't need to ask for permission and their number is practically unlimited.* New applications appear every day. All you need now is a group of programmers and subscription on a cloud hosting and tomorrow you can start your own internet club. The costs are incomparably lower than the costs of establishing a new country.

All of this means that the potential for competition is much bigger for non-territorial law and order providers. The cumbersome competition between territories has been replaced by intensive competition within the same territory. It results in many benefits: constant pressure on experimenting and innovation, feedback in the form of loss and gain, the opportunity to compare quality simultaneously in the same place but also with a higher degree of specialization. Individual clubs can specialize in different areas of law and order and provide top professional services in the areas of transport, retail, cleaning, microwork, etc., unlike states that may specialize in one territory but provide law and order in all areas from labor law and commercial disputes to finance market transactions.** Internet clubs enable both, traditional territorial decentralization (states, regions, cities, neighborhoods) and functional decentralization – the disintegration of a tied package of services provided by the state into individual services.

In this chapter, I have practically focused my attention on how internet clubs and platforms maintain order among their members – how they punish them for bad behavior and reward their positive actions. But the same issue has to be tackled when it comes to internet clubs and platforms themselves – how do we prevent them from abusing their position? Let's first take a look at how this is solved in the context of traditional law and order providers – states.

First and foremost, there are mechanisms like democratic elections, separation of powers, constitutional limitations and transparency. Try to imagine a law and order provider who ignores all of this – leaders are elected non-democratically, they have absolute power to change rules, watch their own interests, and the government process is not transparent – the public is only informed about final decisions. Political science textbooks call such entities dictatorships and, in the column marked examples they put North Korea. It's interesting that all of this also applies to another type of entity: an entity which provides us with good quality services and minimal abuse of power. In an economics textbook you'll find it under the notion of company and the examples column would state Apple, for instance. When electing the CEO of Apple, nobody asks customers or employees their opinion and the CEO doesn't ask for it either when implementing changes.

---

* It's not that easy when it comes to a complete absence of asking for permission since mobile applications usually have to ask for it from app stores (Apple Store, Google Play). Both these stores are internet clubs without a territory themselves and the analysis from this subchapter applies to them as well. I would like to thank Juraj Bednár for pointing this out to me.
** Vast empirical literature shows that private arbitral tribunals are more efficient, faster and precise at resolving specialized commercial disputes. That's why so many international companies have included a clause about private arbitration in their contracts.[A14]

The CEO is acting in their own interest and the entire decision-making process is nontransparent.

So, what's the difference between North Korea and Apple? It is the (im)possibility of consumers to say "no, thank you." There's a difference between deciding not to buy an iPhone and crossing the border between North and South Korea. The sovereignty of consumers is the strongest mechanism keep any entity in check and the best protection from the abuse of power. People don't always realize that. They tend to highly overestimate democratic control and the extent to which the freedom of choice lets them check politicians. At the same time, they highly underestimate the extent to which being able to say "no, thank you" puts pressure on an entity to provide good quality services and stay away from abuse of power. They don't realize that they have much more power and opportunities to defend themselves against a supermarket than against their local tax office. They can complain about both, but they can only say "no, thank you" to the supermarket.

In the book Machinery of Freedom, David Friedman, Milton Friedman's son, asks the reader to imagine the following:

"Consider our world as it would be if the cost of moving from one country to another were zero. Everyone lives in a housetrailer and speaks the same language. One day, the president of France announces that because of troubles with neighboring countries, new military taxes are being levied and conscription will begin shortly. The next morning the president of France finds himself ruling a peaceful but empty landscape, the population having been reduced to himself, three generals, and twenty-seven war correspondents."[253]

The strongest weapon in the hands of members that can be used against internet club owners is the opportunity to uninstall the club app from their smartphones. There's no such opportunity with territorial monopoly and if there is, it's quite expensive, which is one of the reasons why states have problems to provide good quality services and why they abuse their power and competences.

Critics may object that despite the low costs for the departure of customers and the entry of competitors, the competition between platforms is not that significant. This is because established platforms have some advantages over their starting competitors in the form of a network effect.

Cemeteries are filled with dead platforms. Let's not only look at winners.

The success of certain internet clubs makes some people paranoid. They're afraid that today's successful platforms are destined to be successful forever, and that once they've crushed their competitors, their customers will suffer. They'll raise their prices and we'll all miss good old analogue services. How can they achieve that? The answer is: the network effect.

The value of a platform increases with every new member because they increase its interaction scope. I'm on Facebook because Tom is there. Mike is creating an account at this very moment because I'm there and Mike's wife will create her account tomorrow to be able to watch her husband's activities. Even an anti-hair loss shampoo producer would pay for their own Facebook if one of us suffers from hair loss. The platform that manages to get the wheels of network effect turning wins and the winner takes all.

However, this is a very simplified way of looking at life (and death) of platforms. Even if they make the network effect work, they cannot afford to rest on their laurels because the cemetery is filled with platforms who did. Many have already forgotten about them. What the display doesn't show, the mind doesn't remember. It may even be worth it to introduce an all e-Saints' Day so we can annually commemorate all the deleted programs and applications. Everybody is talking about Facebook today but before it, there was Friendster, some ex-college students may even remember Unister, and MySpace was supposed to have promising futures too. Before Spotify we had iTunes, before Chrome we had Explorer, before Google we had WebCrawler, Yahoo!, or AltaVista. Do you remember ICQ or discussion forums? Your father may have had an account on AOL – the giant of the first years of the internet.

The spiral of getting new people and increasing value is two-directional. The higher it increases, the deeper it falls. All the above-listed giants experienced it. Each of them provided a lot of internet services (from blogs, electronic mail, maps or fun via chat apps and video sharing) and at a specific point of time, they were on the top. Before someone better appeared. And this is how it has been going on until today. 15 years ago, everybody thought eBay was some kind of an undefeatable golem but today its revenues represent 7% of the revenues of Amazon. Until very recently, everybody thought that Facebook was the last internet hegemon with its rapid growth and incredible size. However, people spend less and less time on it. Since 2013, the time spent on this social network has gone down by 54% and it's mostly losing the attention of young people. According to the most recent survey, 44% of people aged 18-29 deleted the Facebook app from their phones. In 2012, 68% of teenagers considered Facebook to be their main network and in 2018 it was 15%. Young people prefer Instagram (owned by Facebook), YouTube, Twitch, Snapchat, Reddit, or the newest youth network – TikTok which in 2018 grew faster than Instagram and has already a billion downloads. Social networks competition also comes in the form of games, such as Fortnite, where entire communities of young people are born and "live".

In addition, competition not only works in series but also in parallel. There's no point in classifying platforms because they all compete with one another. Google couldn't have known that its biggest competitor in search would be Amazon, where more than a half of product searches take place these days. Most platforms are in reality competitors and they compete for one of the most precious commodities of the present era – your attention. Their added value works on a simple principle: advertisers value more the possibility to show people their products than customers are willing to pay in order to avoid their ads. What's the best way to lower people's willingness to avoid advertisement? Offer interesting content. YouTube, Facebook, WhatsApp, Snapchat, Twitter, Google, LinkedIn, Reddit – they all want your attention.

Even if a platform wins the battle for attention in one category (e.g., photos, mini videos, social networks, microblogging, etc.), it still has to continue fighting for attention using all other possible attention catchers. Their actual victory consists in providing free quality content to customers. In order to monetize their attention, the platform needs advertisement, so it has to fight on another new front: for the attention of attention shoppers – advertisers. And that's not easy. For instance, Twitter with over 330 million users was the monthly winner in the microblogging category, but it was only after 12 years of its existence that it managed to sufficiently monetize the attention it had and gained profit for the first time. Competition amongst platforms is therefore a lot more intense than it may seem at first. In reality, everybody competes with everybody on several different fronts.

Another competition-strengthening factor is the digital character of platforms. For traditional network monopoly, the entry into the industry is very demanding in terms of capital, and competing with them means building huge factories and installing wires, piping, and loops. This is connected with high costs of switching to the competition even on the side of the customer. Digital platforms don't have to do any of that – they get to their customers via the internet and thanks to cloud technologies they don't even need much capital. A good idea and a couple of programmers is all it takes to launch competition. Every startup that's now worth billions started this way. Switching to the competition has significantly decreased and leaving a platform is easy. This is precisely what creates the biggest pressure and forces companies to keep on innovating and adapting themselves to their customers. If you don't want to adapt to your customers, you have to make sure they have no possibility to leave. But unlike states, platforms can't force anybody to stay.

There are currently many alternatives to each dominant platform and they're only waiting for the big player to stumble or hesitate with innovation. This claim represents the core of the theory of contestable market, which is expected to bring a Nobel Prize to its author, William J. Baumol. According to Baumol, the beneficial effects of competition lie within the threat of potential competitors. The mere idea of competitors entering the market makes entrepreneurs behave as if they were already there. Let's take the example of Uber: it has to fear Lyft, which in 2017 grew faster than Uber and it took Uber's share on the shared transport market by 14 percentage points in the U.S.. Lyft's share grew from 4% in 2015 to 20% in 2017 and reached 39% in 2019 and in San Francisco, Uber's home town, it already has 41%. Uber itself experienced a fall in the market after the #DeleteUber campaign in 2017 when it lost over 200 thousand customers in the course of a few days. [254]

Nobody can deny that Uber still possesses a big part of the market, but it may just be a matter of time. Its competitive advantage is not so much its international size but rather its local accessibility. As a customer, I'm interested in how many drivers Uber has in Bratislava rather than its share in the New York City. So, Uber has to fight numerous local battles. In Bratislava specifically, it's a fight against Bolt, whose strategy is no secret: it waits until Uber wins the fight with local regulators and uses the saved resources to propose lower fares.[255] Customers travel cheaper and drivers earn more. Bolt also brought its own innovation such as paying with phone credit. Uber, Lyft and Bolt aren't the only competitors – there are many other similar apps: Curb, Carma, Didi Chuxing, Grab, Ola, Easy Taxi, Gett, or Flywheel.

There is also a new project by Google called Ware Ride that uses an elaborate network of transport information maps and connects people who commute to work daily. This is sharing in the true sense of the word and the project's objective is to decrease the number of cars on the roads and save people money. Taxi drivers haven't given up either. Autocab, the biggest manufacturer of taxi equipment in Great Britain, is working on a taxi app that should work on similar principles as Uber. Another company is developing an app called iGo Everywhere that connects local taxi applications so customers can order taxis from different companies and in different cities with one single application.

We can see that lack of competition isn't a problem when it comes to shared transport platforms. There are plenty of alternatives and it's starting to be quite difficult to keep track of them. That's precisely why new apps like RideGuru or GoA2B were invented; they specialize in comparing prices and showing the current availability of drivers from different platforms – we could say they're platforms of platforms.

Another sharing economy icon, Airbnb, is experiencing a similar situation with competition. Airbnb may be the biggest accommodation platform, but it still has many competitors who enter its comfort zone. If we look at shares in the overall accommodation market, Airbnb has 15%, the second biggest platform Expedia (HomeAway platform) has 12%, and Priceline (Booking.com platform) has 9%.[256] Apart from that, Airbnb also has competitors who focus on various small segments: MisterBandB (misterb&b) and Gay HomeStays specialize in providing accommodation for homosexuals; Onefinestay in luxurious houses and flats; Oasis Collection in business trips and high standard; HomeExchange in exchange stays for families, teachers, pensioners, etc. Like Uber, Airbnb must also fight for local markets. Its biggest competitor in Western Europe is the German platform Windu and in Eastern Asia the Japanese Zizaike. The platform Tuija has even beaten Airbnb in China.

Of course, this development doesn't mean that every successful platform will fail in a few years' time and be replaced by a new one. It doesn't even mean that competition in the platform market is perfect. It just means that arguments about the network effect and the amount of data as an insurmountable barrier are exaggerated. Every currently dominant platform had to beat the network effect of its predecessor in the past and there are many competitors who are ready to beat it.

The best argument against the logic of network effect are older economics textbooks with their specific examples. For example, Voigt in Institutional Economics from 2000 mentions the consolidation of the VHS video cassette standard as opposed to the competition formats Betamax and Video 2000 as an example of the network effect. Back then, nobody could imagine that competition would come in the form of CD, USB, DVD, mobile HDD, and not to mention the internet or Cloud. New battles for attention keep on appearing. As I'm writing this book, a war for customers' living rooms is starting. Big companies like Apple, Amazon, Google, or Facebook are developing home assistants that are supposed to form a part of smart homes.

Companies that currently have the network effect advantage can't be sure of anything. In capitalism, entrepreneurs have only one certainty: uncertainty. The current balance of network effect will remain in equilibrium until it's disrupted by another equilibrium. It's a very unstable equilibrium and the theory of network effect can only explain the time of stability.

However, even a temporary monopoly is a monopoly which brings along all its negative points. Economists don't like monopolies because they cause two socially harmful phenomena: they increase prices and decrease production volume on purpose. We usually don't see these harmful phenomena in connection with internet giants. On the contrary, they often provide their customers with free services and don't limit the supply in any way. Also, monopolies tend to rest on their laurels – they stop innovating and lose interest in their customers. This is again not true in case of internet companies that currently belong among the most innovative companies in the world.*

---

* There's a certain stop for innovativeness. It comes in the form of patents. Today's biggest companies try to get a patent for everything to ensure the biggest number of patent monopolies for themselves. Professor Alex Tabarrok refers to this as modern feudalism. Big players prevent small ones from entering the market. If somebody wanted to start a new Google in his garage, lawyers from other companies would "dismantle" it in a couple of days. Patenting the one-click buying for

If you had described today's world of internet platforms as a futuristic vision to somebody back in 1989, they would've laughed at you. Such enormous amount of information, comfort, efficiency and fun accessible by the tip of your finger and even for free? No one would have believed you.*

CUSTOMERS' CONSENSUS

"I believe that conceptual agreement among individuals provides the only benchmark against which to evaluate observed rules and actions within those rules..."[257]

James M. Buchanan

Territorial law and order providers have a very specific recruitment policy: once you are born on their territory, you are their citizen whether you like it or not. For the vast majority of citizens, this membership is something like the original sin for which no consent is required.

This obvious involuntariness has been troubling to many philosophers, economists, political scientists, and authors of citizenship education textbooks. They all believed that the status quo was legitimate – that the state's role in society was important. They were also aware that state uses violence without asking for from anybody. It's difficult to defend the morality or efficiency of social institutions in the absence of consent. So, people with rich imaginations came up with the concept of the "social contract". In their theories, the state had the role of a voluntary club which we entered based on our consent with the social contract. Of course, this very simplified version is far from bulletproof. Try to remember if a government office ever sent you a letter including a complete contract with the rights and obligations of both parties – the citizen and the state. We have certainly never received anything like that. So, theoreticians came up with more sophisticated versions of the social contract story.

---

20 years by Amazon is a typical example. The patent expired on the 11th of September 2017. Until then, other traders, webs, and platforms simply couldn't use it.

* Some of you may object by saying that Google provides us with Gmail, Google maps, Google drive, the Office package, and other services but they aren't for free. Instead of paying with our money we pay with our data and privacy. It's true yet it seems that people are fine with it. Economist Caleb Fuller tried to measure how much people are willing to pay to increase their privacy level on the internet (using a Google browser which doesn't collect their data). His study revealed that 86 % of people aren't willing to pay anything (they prefer paying with their privacy) and the remaining 14% would be willing to pay only a minimal amount (16 cents per day). So, even though people like to emphasize how much they care about privacy, it's a mere declaration of their preferences. When it comes to real actions and demonstrating their preferences, they opt for a free alternative which collects their data. We can therefore say that the current state of internet companies who offer free services in an exchange for privacy merely reflects people's preferences.[A15]

One of the earliest versions included the argument that the social contract was signed in the distant past. States came into existence with the consent of their inhabitants; it's just that there are no written records about it. The most famous representative of this interpretation was John Locke who used the examples of Ancient Rome and Venice that were opened after a conclusion of a social contract.[258] Even if we admitted that the signing of a social contract is something that actually happened sometime in history, the remaining question is why we should feel bound by it today. Locke had an answer to that question too. According to him, the social contract included an easement according to which it was established that the contract would apply to everybody who would ever live on the given territory.

Later, philosophers and economists stopped coming up with nonexistent historical events and started to develop more abstract social contract theories. One of them is the theory of implicit social contract. It says that although we have never explicitly signed any document with the state, we implicitly give our consent to its conditions, for example, by using its services (roads, sidewalks, parks) or by simply not moving behind its borders.

The theory of the hypothetical social contract is even more sophisticated.[259] Those who support it say that even though people have never actually signed a contract with the state, they would do so if they had the chance. Different philosophers with different suppositions about human nature and conditions for the signing of the contract came to various conclusions about what "the right" social contract should look like.

A similar approach is represented by the theory of conceptual social contract which says that we can analyze the current form of state as if the constitution was the result of the consent of citizens.[260] Unfortunately (what I really mean is fortunately), I don't have enough space here to dedicate further attention to grown-up fairytales that try to justify the legitimacy of the state recruitment policy. In case you are interested, I recommend the works of my favorite political philosopher Michael Humeur. He provides the best overview of theories together with some objective criticism in his book titled The Problem of Political Authority.

The aim of this philosophical/historical detour wasn't to make you fall asleep but rather to show you the argumentative somersaults that were invented in effort to connect the currently most wide-spread law and order provider with the consent of its customers. And perhaps also to show you how important it is that after long centuries we can now enter internet clubs and platforms that provide law and order services only with our explicit, non-hypothetical, voluntary, and revocable consent. Downloading an app and creating an account in an internet club is actually nothing else than the signing of a social contract in which the customer agrees to the entire package of services and rules. James M. Buchanan refers to it as a constitutional choice. People not only choose the product (transport, accommodation, etc.) but also a set of rules and institutions that form a part of the internet club. Since everybody who joins the club has to agree with them first, the membership is completely voluntary which brings many positives.

If the service provider cannot rely on automatic recruitment of members and needs their explicit consent, they need to try much harder. They have to offer the right price-quality ratio because otherwise their customers will turn around and switch to the competition. For internet clubs it means that they need to provide fair and reasonable laws, impartial and fast courts, and reliable protection from fraud and fraudsters.

If law and order services are provided with the consumer's consent, we find all the advantages we mentioned when comparing private and public regulations. Internet club owners have to plan things in the long-run and it's in their own interest to provide good quality services. On the contrary, democratic politicians limit their planning scope by the electoral term and it's in their own interest to help narrow interest groups.

3.4 FORGOTTEN IDEA — PANARCHY

I have this rule. If I think of a new idea, I can be sure that somebody already thought about it before me and has written an entire book on the subject. The rule confirmed itself when I was working on this book. I came across the term panarchy.

It was Paul Émile de Puydt from Belgium who at the end of the 19th century came up with the concept. He was a botanist and economics was his hobby. In an article titled *"The Great Political Thought Experiment"*, he leads a fictional dialogue in which he asks why we can't choose which form of government we want to live under the same way we choose many other services. It would be enough to stop binding state services with a specific territory and to give people the option to "unsubscribe" from their current government and sing up with another. Why shouldn't people choose if they want to live in a monarchy, republic, social democracy, or socialism without having to move? According to Puydt, in such a world it would be enough to:

"Go to the Bureau for Political Membership, take off your hat in regognition of the head of the committee, and ask politely for your name to be sratched off one list where it was written and transfer it to any list you please. The head of the committee will put on glasses, open the register, enter your decision, and give you a receipt. You take your leaver, and the revolution is accomplished without spilling any more than a drop of ink."[261]

Of course, in the 19th century, Puydt couldn't have imagined that one day we would have cellphones in our pockets that would include apps and interconnect all of us via the internet. He was working with the technology of the given era: clerks, paper, ink, receipts. But he did realize many advantages of this meta-philosophy; specifically, the force of intensive competition and voluntary consent in the area of state-provided services which would make states more efficient and customer friendly.

Neither Puydt nor other defenders of panarchy side with a specific form of government or political philosophy in their works. People are different and their preferences vary. Panarchy gives us the opportunity to live in the state of our preference. The defenders of this concept consider panarchy to be a meta-framework with an ongoing competitive process to find the perfect form of government. It is a free market with states. And it doesn't take much to implement the concept in practice: it would be enough to add the right of disassociation to the existing right of association. Panarchy is the opportunity to carry out one-person revolutions.[262]

When critics asked panarchists how they imagine the functioning of such non-territorial states based on voluntary entry, they most frequently answered with an analogy to religion. Religion and faith used to be bound to a specific territory and nobody was asked what they wanted to believe in. There could only be one provider of the facilitation of contact between the believers and a god. This is no longer true and we don't find it strange at all. Quite the contrary, it would be strange if somebody wanted to go backwards and connect a territory with one single religion. But the reality of a medieval villain was completely different – if someone had told him that one day people of several religions would share the same territory and that faith would only be a matter of a free decision, he would have been very surprised.

I'm not able to say whether a similar fate awaits the present-day states and whether in 500 years people will find it strange that state services should be provided on a territorial basis and without the explicit consent of the inhabitants. But I am convinced that new technologies make this scenario more realistic than in the past. We already have some tangible proof – internet clubs that provide law and order services. They may operate in economies which are de jure in the arms of territorial providers who don't ask for consent, but they had to overcome problems that were so specific that they de facto could not rely on them. They were halfway to anarchy. Despite that (or because of that) they were able to ensure the functioning of services that we currently associate exclusively with the state: protection from fraudsters and thieves, dispute resolution, and creation of laws.

3.5 HALFWAY TO ANARCHY: LACK OF POLICEMEN

People generally don't distinguish between "the state should do X and Y" and "the state is capable of doing X and Y". They automatically suppose that the first claim implies the second. However, the state doesn't often work as many wish it would when they're looking for solutions to problems in society. As I've said in previous chapters, politicians and bureaucrats may not always have the purest of intentions. Even if they do, they may not have sufficient knowledge for the creation of laws and rules, and even if they do, they may not be able to implement it in the real world.

Some may simply accept this imperfect situation and others may embark on a long journey of influencing public affairs directly through politics.

Then there are those who cannot afford to do either. Their livelihood depends directly on the functioning of services that are usually provided by the state, such as police investigation or punishing perpetrators. Internet entrepreneurs from the beginnings of the internet belonged to this group of people. The founders of PayPal are a nice example:

The aim of PayPal was to enable people to transfer money quickly and simply via the internet. After one month of operation, it had one thousand members, after three months 100 thousand and one million at the beginning of 2000. Unfortunately, fraud and its level of sophistication increased together with revenues and the number of members. In 2001, the company's monthly incomes were $1.7 million while the monthly costs on fraud reduction reached 10 million. This business model was unsustainable. In the context of PayPal, fraud meant the use of stolen credit cards, stealing passwords and accounts or hackers programming (ro)bots to gain money by transferring small amounts.[263]

PayPal tried to turn to public authorities with their traditional methods. The state approaches fraud ex post – starts to investigate it after it has happened. If somebody breaks the law and carries out many small purchases via a stolen account, it is expected that the victim contacts the police who later launch an investigation and search for the culprit. If they find them, they send them to the court which decides their guilt or innocence and a punishment. If everything goes smoothly, the culprit ends up in prison.

This approach failed in the case of PayPal and similar companies. At that time, states didn't have the necessary equipment, human capital, resources, or motivation to solve such a high rate of internet fraud. In his study, economist Edward Stringham interviewed one of the founders of internet pay systems who became a victim of internet fraud in the late 90s. He described his experience with the police.[264] He called them, they came to his house and he started to explain what happened:

"Someone broke into my computer."

"Where did they break in from?" asked the officer as he looked at the room's windows and doors.

"From the Internet."

"What's the Internet?"

Peter Thiel, the co-founder of PayPal, had a similar experience when he found out that the FBI doesn't have an e-mail address to which he wanted to send them information about the perpetrator who attacked their server. When the agents arrived, they didn't know what an internet advertisement was. Although these days (hopefully) most policemen know what the internet is and how e-mail addresses work, it's still very likely that they aren't technologically literate enough to deal with modern internet crimes.

Policemen aren't only powerless in cases where multiple small crimes are involved. One Friday evening in 2016, hackers sent a branch of the Federal Reserve System (FED) in New York 35 requests for the transfer of the total of $951 million to private accounts in the Philippines and Sri Lanka. They were pretending to be Bengali officials from the Central Bank of Bangladesh. Because in Bangladesh it was already weekend, it went unnoticed at first. When FED officials sent $110 million, they realized they sent them to a private account, which roused suspicion. That's why they didn't send the remaining $841 million. Before the money ended up on private accounts, it passed through a German bank which noticed that the hackers made a mistake when copying the beneficiary's name. They entered "Shalike Fandation" instead of "Shalika Foundation". The bank froze the transaction, but the perpetrators still managed to get $58 million and spend it on online casinos which made it untraceable. The case has never been solved and the money hasn't been returned. The governments of the biggest states in the world weren't able to catch and punish the perpetrators.[265]

Sufficient human capital isn't the only problem of public providers of law and order. It is even more problematic that internet fraud is often international. Which state and policemen should act when the perpetrator comes from Kenya and the service is provided by an American payment system? Another problem is that internet fraud often consists of a multitude of small frauds that police don't want to investigate. A survey among the top hundred financial companies on the London Stock Exchange has shown that British police refuse to investigate financial fraud unless the damage exceeds £100,000. In addition, companies complain that they have to get the evidence themselves because the police refuse to launch their own investigation without it.[266] It's hardly surprising; the ex post approach to crime – investigation, collecting evidence, issuing accusations, and judicial verdicts – is extremely expensive and it's impossible to deal with every single fraud.

Imagine how PayPal and other companies must have felt when they turned to the state to help them with the influx of $100 crimes from all around the world. I think defenseless is the right word. They simply couldn't rely on the state. What were they supposed to do? It wouldn't have helped to venture into academic debates about the function of the state, just like they didn't have time to enter politics to change it and help solve their problems. Instead, they decided to take matters in their own hands and create their own protection system against fraud. It was the only way they could fulfill their function – to gain profit.

Unlike states which generally understand fraud as a problem to be solved ex post, PayPal started to look at fraud as a crisis management matter and looked for ways to prevent it. According to Thiel: "The goverment approach assumes that you can solve everything after a problem occurs. It might have worked in a small-town settting where everyone knows everyone else, but it clearly doesn't work in the current world."²⁶⁷ For PayPal, fraud became a cost just like any other costs they have to minimize when providing services.

This is why PayPal and other companies started to develop sophisticated anti-fraud systems on the basis of human and artificial intelligence. The systems constantly monitor the activities on all accounts via data mining; geographical indicators, and order history mark suspicious transactions which require additional verification. Based on a multitude of parameters, they created blacklists with profiles that are blocked, whitelists with profiles that are authorized to send money automatically, and greylists with suspicious profiles. The latter are verified by their own "investigators" who have the power to stop transactions, freeze accounts and expel members. PayPal employs a special kind of detectives who investigate crimes before they take place. Their task is to investigate transactions when money from several accounts is transferred to a single one, when the activity on otherwise passive accounts suddenly increases, or when unusually high sums of money are sent to unusual parts of the world. Given this extensive security policy, PayPal is according to its co-founder, Max Levchin, actually more like a security agency that pretends to be a provider of financial services.

PayPal developed many new fraud prevention and monitoring systems that supervise millions of transactions in real time. Systems not only search for already identified patterns but also actively learn to search and predict new patterns that can lead to fraud. Paypal implemented a lot of innovation that is considered standard these days. An example of this is the Gausebeck-Levchin test and one of its first commercial applications – the CAPTCHA test. You know it from websites where you need to copy a distorted text to prove you aren't a robot. Another example is the system of account verification when PayPal transfers a couple of cents to a user's account and asks them to verify the sum. PayPal is currently used by 170 million people and the value of its yearly transactions carried is $200 million. Fraud rate dropped from two-digit numbers to 0.5%.²⁶⁸

Companies like PayPal now offer several different services: they assess fraud risk in different types of transactions, price it as estimated costs, take active steps to lower them, and often provide insurance against these risks. Their clients (e-shops) thus don't have to deal with fraudulent activities as a legal problem. Fraud prevention became a regular cost just like paying the rent.

When creating their own systems, companies have to constantly try to avoid two types of mistakes. If the rules and algorithms they create are too lax, they'll fail to detect many fraudulent transactions and have high costs related to fraud as a result. If, on the contrary, they push too hard and adopt rules that are too strict, together with many fraudulent transactions they'll also stop many legitimate ones that would otherwise bring them higher profit.

It's easy to mistakenly believe that a trader wants to reduce fraud to minimum. It isn't wise to have a 0% fraud rate if it means that 50% of legitimate transactions are rejected too. In that case, the best way to prevent fraud is to stop trading completely. An efficient security system therefore requires a comparison of the costs of accepting fraudulent orders with the costs of rejecting legitimate ones.

This is the basic problem that has to be dealt with not only by private law and order providers but also by public providers (in the form of state laws and enforcement). If we want to draw a comparison, the logic similar to comparing public and private regulations applies. Private law and order providers have a big motivation (gain profit and avoid failure) and fast feedback (angry customers and high losses), which helps them set the system as efficiently as possible. Public providers are short of these advantages. The livelihoods of politicians and policemen aren't directly affected by adopting the correct rules and ways of their enforcement. Sometimes the contrary is true. A policeman who doesn't investigate the right people or investigates the wrong people is rewarded.

Politicians and regulators create rules for the entire economy and don't have access to direct feedback about whether the rules they selected are too strict or stifle too much economic activity compared to the advantages they bring. In politics, the discussion tends to turn into a false binary choice between preventing evil or not. The problem with wanting to prevent all evil is that we may end up preventing a lot of good too. It can then easily happen that overall, we make the world a worse place instead of a better one.

3.6 HALFWAY TO ANARCHY: ABSENCE OF THE JUDICIARY

"We should be wary of wholesale rejection of ODR (online dispute resolution). Claims of inaccess to justice, it transpires, are often smoke screens for self-preservation on the part of lawyers (consciously or unconsciously). Nostalgically, they hanker after the Rolls Royce service that today's finest court systems can doubtless deliver. But that is a service that is now affordable only for a very few, and everyone else is left to walk. We need an accessible and reasonably priced system for all, and I have found a no more promising option for that future than that offered by various types of ODR."[269]

Professor Richard Susskind, President of the Society for
Computers and Law

Real world dysfunctional police aren't the only problem internet clubs face. It's not enough to catch and punish perpetrators and sometimes it isn't even clear who the victim is. This is where courts come in. In Slovakia, we tend to complain about our judicial system and our subjective feelings are backed up by objective statistics. According to OECD's Doing Business ranking, the average resolution of a court dispute which goes through the lowest to the Supreme Court lasts on average 550 days in Slovakia. That's nothing when compared with how courts work in developing countries.

In India, for instance, they stopped counting it in days. An average dispute that goes through multiple court levels lasts more than 10 years. India has 13 judges per one million inhabitants. Slovakia has over 250. If all Indian judges stopped sleeping, eating, and taking breaks and they would resolve 100 disputes per hour, it would take the next 35 years to resolve all the accumulated disputes. China also has problems in the justice sector, namely the independence of the courts, their reliability and predictability. Corruption flourishes here and ideology and political party affiliation also heavily influence verdicts.[270]

Internet platforms therefore cannot rely on a functional public justice system in developing countries. However, conflicts and disputes arise there just like they do in western countries where the judiciary is (more or less) functional. So, they again took matters in their own hands and came up with a private alternative.

Taobao (means treasure hunt) is currently China's biggest internet platform and it's owned by Alibaba. It's a Chinese version of eBay, with about half a billion users and is bigger than eBay and Amazon combined.* Taobao uses complex reputation systems to enforce its rules and it also has its own fraud risk management systems (just like PayPal, for example). Because both tools are integrated under one roof, Taobao utilizes a bigger amount of paired data and is able to operate a more elaborate system of big data analyses and predictions.[271]

Apart from that, Taobao has one more tool which isn't very common for the western world's platforms. In 2012, it launched its own User Dispute Resolution Center. Yes, eBay** and Airbnb have something similar, but in Taobao's Center it's not trained personnel or hired judges who are responsible for issuing verdicts but the platform users themselves. It's a new case of extensive crowdsourcing of justice services to ordinary users – peer-to-peer judiciary. Taobao has currently two million free-time judges who resolved over three million disputes. Together with an automated system, the center can resolve 99% of disputes before they even get to Taobao's employees.[272]

How does it work? Let say, that Li-Chi Liu, a young Chinese woman orders a summer dress from Taobao. But what she receives looks more like a parody of the dress. I'm sure you're familiar with this scenario: washed out colors, threads sticking out and most importantly – it's two sizes smaller than what you ordered. So, she asks the vendor for a refund. This normally works but, in this case, he decides to stand behind the quality of his goods and accuse Li-Chi Liu of being a speculator who wants to abuse the system and a dispute arises. It's Li-Chi Liu's turn. If she insists on having been tricked, she can choose between two courts of justice: she either turns to the platform's employees or opts for the Centre with free-time judges. Let's say she selects the second option.

---

* In 2016, the gross merchandize value (GMV) was $136 billion for Amazon and $547 billion for Alibaba.

** Ebay alone solves the unbelievable number of 60 million disputes yearly between vendors and customers. If we considered them as judicial disputes, eBay would be the biggest court of justice in the world. Many of the cases are resolved by an algorithm during the first phase. First, the disputing parties are asked to fill in information and provide details about the conflict. This information is then processed and assessed together with other parameters (users' reputation, how regularly they shop, how often they returned goods and complained).[A16]

The second step involves filling a complaint form and enclosing evidence in the form of photos of the summer dress. Li-Chi Liu has three days to do that. Then the platform randomly selects from two million judges a jury composed of 13 judges (in the past they selected 31). The appointed judges don't know each other and they can't communicate. The only information they get is related to the dispute. They each have 48 hours to upload their ruling with eventual comments into the system. It's decided by a simple majority.

Imagine that Li-Chi Liu manages to convince seven judges and the verdict is that the vendor has to give her the money back. What happens if the vendor decides to ignore it? They're only free-time judges after all. What can they do to about it? Taobao doesn't have police stations or prison cells and can't send a commando to detain them. Still, it can do many other things. It can damage their reputation, freeze their account, take the money they owe from other transactions (AliPay is a part of the platform), lower their position in the search engine, or cancel their access to the platform. Taobao doesn't need batons to enforce its rulings.

On average 2000 judicial disputes take place on Taobao every day and one free-time judge can be involved in several at once. Not all judges are the same; Taobao rates their competence and experience and allocates cases to judges according to their complexity. The judges are also classified according to their specialization: some specialize in mobile phones, others in the quality of textiles and others in identifying counterfeit goods. The most interesting thing is that they aren't paid for their work. Their reward is a better reputation on the platform and bonus credits they can use to support a charity organization of their choice.

Taobao's free-time judges not only make rulings on disputes between its members but also between the members and the platform itself. For example, when vendors feel they were unfairly punished or when they broke a rule that they consider silly under the given circumstances. This not only ensures legal redress and satisfaction but also the improvement of laws on the platform. Verdicts can become a binding precedent that changes the members' rights and obligations. Thanks to this judicial feedback, over 140 rules that regulate how vendors operate their business have been modified.[273] Taobao's law and order system is therefore experiencing a gradual bottom-up revolution, just like in the Anglo-American common law system where judges contributed to its creation.

The platform's whole system of privately provided law and order services is fast, simple and efficient. The authors of a study on Taobao say that it isn't "simply an exchange platform, but one in the process of developing a modern legal system that enforces contracts, resolves disputes and prevents fraud. As a private supplier of market legal infrastructure when formal institutions are lacking, Taobao essentially provides a means for creating law."[274] We could hardly expect this type of innovation to come from students and researchers of faculties of philosophy or law. It was brought about by institutional entrepreneurs who scaled their business model to a big anonymous society; in Taobao's case, half a billion people. The number of disputes grew gradually with the increasing membership and trade volume. The fact that platforms account for 90% of China's e-commerce volume and 10% are independent e-shops indirectly indicates that it's working. It's the other way around in the U.S.; internet platforms represent 24% and e-shops which can rely on relatively better functioning public law and order services represent the remaining 76%.[275]

Similar to other platforms, Taobao not only sticks to internet trade but also transmits its infrastructure into the real world. In remote places in China where people don't have internet access or reliable post service connection, Taobao opened over 30 thousand first contact points where its managers help people who don't have the internet or bank accounts buy and sell via Taobao.

It's therefore obvious that where there's a will (or no choice), there's a way and a private platform can provide services related to the resolution of disputes. However, it doesn't mean that Taobao is some kind of a peaceful oasis for China's inhabitants and that the government won't start to use it for its own purposes. Towards the end of 2016, the Chinese government decided to adopt some private laws and rules created by Taobao as a part of official legislation for e-commerce. This can create obstacles for Taobao's competitors who are interested in entering the industry and at the same time, it's an indication of close relationships between the platform and the government. These have resulted in public subsidies for Taobao and in the future they may result in data sharing within the massive Chinese reputation system the government has created in order to rate the "obedience of citizens." Taobao can therefore play an important role in the centralization of power and information owned by the Chinese government.

3.7 HALFWAY TO ANARCHY: WHEN LAWS ARE WRITTEN BY ENTREPRENEURS

"We're promised instant catalog shopping — just point and click for great deals. We'll order airline tickets over the network, make restaurant reservations and negotiate sales contracts. Stores will become obsolete. So how come my local mall does more business in an afternoon than the entire internet handles in a month? Even if there were a trustworthy way to send money over the internet — which there isn't — the network is missing a most essential ingredient of capitalism: Salespeople."[276]

Clifford Stoll, 1995

At this stage of the book, nobody will be surprised that entrepreneurs can write laws. All platforms have their own game rules, be it YouTube, Facebook, or Amazon. It wasn't always this way. The institutional environment of first internet clubs looked more like an ancient bazar, where spontaneous interactions gave rise to sales practices first, then later a parliamentary democracy where politicians make the laws.

eBay is a perfect example. When Pierre Omidyar started it in 1995, he didn't have a lot of experience with commercial law, establishing and setting institutions and neither did he study what laws and regulations applied for auction houses. He was a programmer after all. He put up the following five commandments on the gates to his club to assure smooth cooperation between people:

eBay is a community where we encourage open and honest communication between all of our members. We believe in the following five basic values.
- *We believe people are basically good.*
- *We believe everyone has something to contribute.*
- *We believe that an honest, open environment can bring out the best in people.*
- *We recognise and respect everyone as a unique individual.*
- *We encourage you to treat others the way that you want to be treated.*

He left the detailed rules of individual stores up to the community itself and to spontaneous development. Soon, generally accepted norms of behavior, communication between members, closing deals and negotiating conditions arose. They were divided according to type of business; there were different principles applying to trading sports collectors' cards, coins, antiques, or dolls. The public forums together with comments were the virtual space where informal norms were honed. It was a space to discuss the details of the functioning of the community and where their first spontaneous leaders were formed. They gradually gained the reputation of experienced members to whom the competence to see to the correct interpretation of the existing norms, conflict resolution, and punishing fraudsters was entrusted. One such group of six experts got the nickname The Posse and they were something between local tribe chieftains and a neighborhood watch.[277]

eBay encouraged active community life, but the number of members, stores, and level of anonymousness increased with the growing community. The small village with the community spirit transformed itself into a busy metropolis. Soon they let go of the informal approach and replaced it with formal legislation and explicit rules.[278] The next step was the creation of a central reputation system and official ways of conflict resolution.

Nowadays, eBay laws now cover practically all aspects of life within the internet club: information about what goods and services can be sold under which conditions (for example, relics from WW2 with Nazi themes), precise rules concerning lists of proposed items, feedback policy, and cases of extortion or manipulation with reputation. They also cover the protection of vendors against speculators who unrightfully ask for a refund or return the goods damaged.

These rules aren't the exclusive result of a centralized decision-making process of owners and top management. Although eBay is not a democracy, it has to reflect vox populi – what customers want. 1997 brought bigger changes: modification of categories, website layout, and fees for adding items into auction. The changes provoked a wave of negative reactions and the management received a lot of angry e-mails as a result of which they adapted some changes and completely revoked others. In order to prevent such a situation from being repeated, eBay established a supervisory board from selected members with whom it consults planned changes. Other platforms have similar boards.

Taobao even experimented with creating a house of representatives composed of experienced members who help create internal laws. When Taobao wants to adopt a change of rules, they pass the draft of the bill to the house of representatives where members can comment on it and vote. Taobao publishes their comments together with the result of the vote and adapts the bill accordingly. Between June 2015 and February 2017, they voted this way on 42 different rules and more than 10 thousand voters participated in each vote.[279]

Enough of standing on the edge of anarchy, let's dive headfirst into the dark waters of the internet.

4. DIGITAL CRYPTO ANARCHY ON THE DARKNET

"Life in cyberspace seems to be shaping up exactly like Thomas Jefferson would have wanted: founded on the primacy of individual liberty and a commitment to pluralism, diversity, and community."[280]

Mitch Kapor

When social scientists want to empirically examine life in an anarchy (meaning outside of stately-provided services), sooner or later they get to examine criminals. They cannot, by definition, rely on public institutions but they have to co-operate among themselves. So, they need to find alternative ways of securing law and order. The economic analysis of life in anarchy now represents a progressive research program.[281]

In this subchapter, I'll talk about internet criminals. They have some things in common with their "analogue" colleagues. First of all, they must know how to avoid public institutions and police investigation. That implies that they have to work secretly and anonymously. They also have to build parallel institutions in order to ensure trust that enables them to cooperate with their customers but also amongst themselves.

As for analogue criminals, we all have some idea of how they solve this problem. We know from films that when trading, they meet in abandoned warehouses or dark alleys. We also know that they love cash. Cash enables a secret and anonymous exchange of values. They don't need a third party (bank or notary) and there's no physical or electronic trace left after the transaction.

How do internet criminals ensure secrecy and anonymousness? Hiding in warehouses and dark alleys and using cash won't help in their case. Internet criminals minimize their contact with the physical world. It was always problematic to keep your identity hidden on the internet, but the following two technologies from the first decade of the 21st century helped solve it: anonymity networks and cryptocurrencies. Anonymity networks are the new dark alleys and cryptocurrency replaces cash. I'll talk specifically about the two most widespread applications: Tor and Bitcoin.

Before we continue, I would like to highlight that what follows is an economic analysis. I will try to avoid moral and ethical conclusions and remain focused on the technical aspect of the subject. The objective is to understand whether or not and how non-state organizations can provide law and order in the environment of anarchy. Whether you approve or condemn the use and sale of drugs, it's your value principle. I will use the word "criminal" in its technical sense – to denote a person who breaks applicable laws even though some might consider that these laws are amoral and represent the punishing of innocent people for victimless crimes.

4.1 TOR – THE INTERNET'S DARK ALLEY

"You should be treating your anonymity like your teenage daughters virginity."
DarkWebNews

The most important task of every internet criminal is to remain anonymous – to disable public authorities from tracing the connection between their internet activities and themselves. There are three popular services that anonymize one's moves on the internet and one of them is especially popular: Tor.*

Tor is the acronym of The Onion Router and it serves three purposes: secret and anonymous moves on the internet, secret and anonymous server hosting, and circumventing censorship and other internet obstacles. The Tor software was developed by a group of people who originally worked for a Naval Research Laboratory in the U.S. – for the U.S. government. These days it is administrated and further developed by an NGO in cooperation with universities and it is open and free for all. All you need to do is download it from www.torproject.org.

---

* Two other anonymity services are: I2P (Invisible Internet Project) and Freenet, an internet P2P network where once something is uploaded, it cannot be deleted by anyone. But they are both smaller than Tor and they get a lot less financial and research attention. Tor currently has the biggest number of nodes and therefore the biggest network effect.

I'm not going to pretend that I know how the encryption technology via Tor works. Wikipedia says that it's a layered encryption (hence the onion in the name and logo) which takes place through a multitude of random servers. The technical aspect isn't that important for our purposes; what is important is that it works quite reliably.

An important function of the Tor application is the possibility to create "internet within the internet" via the Tor hidden service. This hidden internet tends to be called the darknet. It includes all websites with servers created via the Tor network and their domain is .onion. A server created this way cannot be identified nor can its location be traced. Not even Tor developers themselves can do it. If you want to access a darknet website, you need a special Tor explorer. It looks like your typical Firefox browser, the only difference being that it opens the door to the world of the darknet and when using it, your IP address is anonymized so that nobody can reveal who you are and where you connect from. The downside of the darknet is a user-unfriendly search; it reminds one of the 90s. The two attempts at creating darknet search engines are called Torch and Gram. The Hidden Wiki catalogue serves as a list of Tor links to many darknet webs.

This is what a typical darknet address looks like: http://6khhxwj7viwe5xjm.onion/?ai=552713. It's the address of the currently most popular e-shop on the darknet, where you can find everything including drugs and falsified documents. Tor is not only used by criminals; it's also used by ordinary people who care about not being watched by state authorities with every click they make on the internet. This has been becoming more and more important since the scandal of massive public tracing by the National Security Agency.*

Apart from these people, Tor is also used by those who hide from totalitarian regimes, fight against the breach of human rights, informants who want to blow the whistle on government scandals and are afraid for their lives, or journalists who work on dangerous cases. They use Tor services like SecureDrop or GlobaLeaks through which they can upload incriminating documents without having to be afraid of being traced. This technique is also used by the New Yorker, The Guardian, or Forbes and the WikiLeaks organization also has a similar service. Among other things, Tor is also an excellent tool for organizing civil movements against dictatorships and enables access to information censored by such regimes. It serves, for instance, to overcome the great Chinese firewall or censored Wikipedia in Turkey.

All of this contributed to Tor's application developers winning the prize of the Free Software Foundation in 2011 for a project with social contribution. The justification said that Tor enabled almost 36 million people around the world to experience free access and liberty of speech on the internet while ensuring their privacy and anonymity. This network played a key role in the communication

---

* It is clear from the documents published by the U.S. informant, Edward Snowden, that NSA has a long-term problem with deanonymizing Tor. An NSA analyst, placed an image titled "Tor Stinks" into their internal presentation.

of dissident movements in Iran and recently also in Egypt. Electronic Frontier Foundation recognized Tor as an important tool in the area of human rights and the Foreign Policy magazine placed Tor's authors amongst the world's top hundred thinkers for creating a safe anonymous network for informers.[282]

For those who enter the darknet, anonymity and privacy come first. Tor network technology is relatively safe, but one can commit many errors when using it and pay for these mistakes. One manual for the correct usage of Tor strongly recommends not changing the explorer window size because a combination of various parameters (log-in and log-out time, individual window size settings or other traditional web habits) can lead to successfully connecting an internet identity with a real one.[283] Later, we'll see how one tiny internet mistake cost someone their anonymity and also their freedom.

Asymmetric encryption – one of the most important inventions the government wanted to ban

Despite all that we have said earlier, not even the darknet can assure a 100% guarantee of safety and anonymity. Even Tor experienced attacks that revealed its weak points inspite of the efforts of numerous security experts and universities to ensure its safety. Plus, there are the previously mentioned errors that take place between the keyboard and the chair which, on multiple ocasions, lead to revealing and confiscating Tor servers together with the communication of its users by state authorities. I'm talking about communication that didn't happen through assymetric encryption. Users who used this technology had nothing to worry about. So, what is assymetric encryption and how does it work?

The story of assymetric encryption began in the 1970s at a scientific conference, when a professor from Standford University presented new research in the area of encryption. It wasn't his own research – it was carried out by his two students who were quietly sitting in the audience. They weren't sitting there because the professor wanted to steal their fame, but because he wanted to protect them from government agents. A couple of weeks before the conference, the faculty received a letter from a federal agency warning them that if their students presented the research, they would consider it treason. The university lawyers assured the faculty management that if agents did try to sue them, the school could easily win the dispute on the grounds of the first ammendment of the constitution which protects freedom of speech. However, the faculty could only cover the costs of a dispute concerning its member, not its students. Hence it was the professor who presented the research.

What was so dangerous as to warrant federal agents and accusations of treason? It was a new way of message encryption. Traditional encryption looks something like this: first, you code a message into mathematic signs, then you apply various complex mathematical operations. If somebody wants to read it, they use the same procedure, only the other way around. It's like locking a message and handing someone the same key you have so they can unlock it and read it. Such encryption is called symmetric encryption.[284]

The academics from our story were working on a new encryption – assymetric encryption. They noticed that some mathematical opperations can be done a lot more easily in one direction than in the other. We can best understand it with an example: let's say we select two random prime (numbers that are only divisible by 1 or the number itself) numbers – 17 and 31 – and your task is to multiply them. If you have primary education or can use a calculator, you can tell me the result very quickly: 527. Now let's go from the opposite end – I'll tell you a number which is the product of two prime numbers (a semi-prime number) and your task is to find out which prime numbers I used. This task is incomparably harder than the first one. Try it: the number is 5963; which two prime numbers do you have to multiply in order to get this number? You will find the correct answer in the footnote.*

Assymetric encryption uses similar mathematical principles. PGP (Pretty Good Privacy) is a well-known app that uses two keys instead of just one. The first key (the public key) enables the encryption but not the decryption of the message. For that there's the private key. In practice it looks like this: you publish your public key so that people can send you encrypted messages, but you keep your private key so that you're the only one who can decrypt them. It's like handing out small open treasure chests to people around the world without giving them keys; they can insert and lock a message inside but once it has been closed, it can only be opened by someone who has the (private) key. Such encryption is very practical. Unlike symmetric encryption, you don't need to send the decryption key to the recipients of the message. Somebody can intercept it, get your key and read your communication. In assymetric encryption, the public key is given to everybody and the private one stays in the hands of the recipient. It enables you to encrypt your communication without having to send the decryption manual to anybody. If you use such encryption on Tor severs and an unauthorised person happens to physically get to your communication, they won't be able to read it because they don't have the private key.

A similar type of encryption is not only used on the darknet. Its most widespread application is the RSA encryption invented by researchers from the Massachussets Institute of Technology (MIT), and now it's practically used all over the internet: social networks, electronic mail, e-shops,

---

* Correct answer: 89 and 67. A simple true-false test is an important part of asymmetric encryption.

or internetbanking. You also use it every day: all it takes a visit to a website beginning with "https". Without assymetric encryption, anybody could read your e-mails, log-in details, paswords, and bank card numbers anytime they want. The internet wouldn't work without assymetric encryption.

The onion principle of Tor network
(technical contribution from Pavel Lupták)

Let's say that you want anonymous access to the website www.iness.sk. You download the Tor explorer and enter the address: www.iness.sk. The Tor client contacts one of the Tor directory servers from the list of Tor's directory servers, the addresses of which are saved in your Tor client and administered by the community of Tor developers (in some countries like China, these servers are forbidden, so you need to get access through the Tor relay servers). The Tor directory server allocates you three random nodes from the Tor network – Tor entry node, Tor middle node, and Tor exit node – and their public keys and addresses. Your Tor client creates an anonymous Tor circuit as follows:

It takes the corresponding HTTP request (for example: GET/POST request to www.iness.sk) together with the address iness.sk and it encrypts it with the public key of the Tor exit node. It adds the address of the Tor exit node and encrypts the whole thing with the public key of the Tor middle node. To that it adds the address of the Tor middle node and encrypts the entire thing with the public key of the Tor entry node. This is how we get the Tor onion which has been encrypted three times in a row – the topmost layer by the public key of the entry node and the bottommost one by the public key of the end node.

In order to completely decrypt the Tor onion (and get the HTTP request for www.iness.sk), we need three private keys which are possessed only by the three Tor nodes themselves (entry, middle, and end) while asymmetric encryption makes it impossible for one to read all their three addresses at once but only the immediate one where you want to send the onion once you have opened the given layer.

Once you have created the multi-layered onion and you finally open www.iness.sk, you take the onion and send it to Tor entry node which decrypts it using its private key. When this is done, it gets the address of the middle node and a partially open onion. Then you send it to the Tor middle node which decrypts it with its private key. Once it's done, it gets the address of the Tor exit node and a more open onion. You forward it to the Tor exit node and all it can do is decrypt it with its private key. After this, it gets the address www.iness.sk and the HTTP request itself.

Tor exit node then connects to the address www.iness.sk and sends the HTTP request there. And, of course, it sends back a reply which gradually goes through the individual nodes until finally reaching the client. This means the following:

The Tor exit node can already see inside of the resulting message you want to send to www.iness.sk. So, if you want to avoid interception on the Tor exit node, you need to use an encrypted https connection (end-to-end encryption). Each Tor node knows from whom it got the message, it can decrypt it with its private key and get the address of the next immediate node where it's supposed to send it, but that's it. It doesn't know who the original sender and final recipient are because it doesn't have the private keys of the other nodes which are essential for the decryption of all the layers of the onion.

A Tor connection regularly falls apart (for example each 10 minutes) and a new one with new entry, middle, and exit Tor nodes are created. In the Tor client settings, entry and exit nodes can be specified, which can lower the safety of the Tor network, but you can enter the internet from the IP address of any country.

4.2 BITCOIN – THE DIGITAL CASH

"The one thing that's missing, but that will soon be developed, is a reliable e-cash."[285]

Milton Friedman, 1999

The second problem criminals have to deal with is the way of exchanging values anonymously and without intermediaries. "Analogue" criminals use cash. Public institutions know this, so they limit cash transactions. For instance, they set the maximum amount of a commercial transaction in cash: in Italy it's €3000, in France €1000 and in Slovakia €5000. The European Central Bank (ECB) decided to stop printing €500 notes for the same reason.*

What makes cash attractive for criminals? On the microlevel, the current form of cash has several attractive features inherited from the original form of money – gold. Most importantly, cash enables the anonymous and final exchange of values where no third party is needed and there's no trace of the transaction. This also applied to gold. However, on the macrolevel, we can find a significant difference between gold and today's cash. With gold, there was no authority with a monetary policy monopoly that could arbitrarily manipulate its parameters, which cannot be said for today's cash. But criminals don't have to worry about it

---

* Some macroeconomists see a different motivation behind it. The transition from cash to electronic money would give central banks new, more powerful tools for intervening in the functioning of the economy.[A17]

unless extraordinary circumstances occur (e.g., the collapse of money's purchasing power). I won't go further into those.*

So why didn't criminals start to use internet banking or PayPal just like the rest of the world? Internet money has several advantages compared to gold or physical cash. First of all, it can be easily transferred. All you need instead of suitcases full of money is a couple of clicks. From the criminals' point of view, these benefits are insufficient and they hardly compensate for the main disadvantage of internet money – the fact that it's actually not money but something economists call a money substitute. It's a type of sub-money which has an administrator on whom they fully depend. Most often this is a financial institution, e.g., a bank, or an internet company, such as PayPal.

In order for you to use this kind of the electronic money, you must first fulfill the requirements for registration which include proving your identity. All transactions are then approved and registered by the intermediary. Without this intermediary, "your" electronic money has no value, it literally does not exist. It's the administrator of electronic services who has the key and you have to trust that they mean well, that they won't cheat you, that they won't make a mistake and that the information about your transactions won't get into the hands of an unauthorized person.

Of course, this won't do for criminals. They want cash, which is final means of settlement. You don't have to register anywhere, trust anybody or ask for permission to transfer values. What you have in your hands in cash is itself a representation of a value that can be immediately exchanged for something else.

As Miltron Friedman predicted in his quote, the challenge for the 21st century was to create digital cash that would represent the best of both worlds: fast and simple transaction typical for internet money plus the anonymousness and absence of intermediaries typical for cash. What was the problem then?

In the digital world, it's very difficult to fulfill one requirement related to money: scarcity. The information revolution has brought a cost-free transfer, safekeeping, and copying of information and it was this last characteristic that represented the biggest problem for the creation of digital cash. If you can copy money easily and if it can be done by anyone, it quickly collapses into a spiral of hyperinflation. Gold could fulfill the function of money only because alchemists never managed to synthetize it. And internet money works only because it has administrators who swore not to create new money as they please and see to it that others within the system won't do so either.** They make sure nobody can pay two people at once with one bit of electronic money. The problem of this

---

* If you are interested in this subject, I recommend you read *Bad Money* by my colleague, Juraj Karpiš, which was already mentioned in this book.

** Actually, banks do kind of create new money out of thin air, but they do it in accordance with the administrator of all administrators – the central bank, which keeps the creation of money in check with the aim of achieving macroeconomic objectives.

solution is that although it's digital, it no longer has the properties of cash. And therefore, all the above-mentioned benefits disappear.

Milton Friedman's prophecy about cash and digital money was fulfilled in 2008 when an article titled "Bitcoin: A Peer-to-Peer Electronic Cash System" started to circulate on the internet.* Its author (or team of authors) signed as Satoshi Nakamoto. He didn't find a way of creating the digital equivalent of gold – scarcity in the internet space –, but he proposed an elegant solution to circumvent the problem.

Instead of scarcity, Nakamoto proposed the creation of a transparent database in which everybody is authorized to look into at any time and make sure nobody tried to pay twice with one bit of electronic money. As he put it: "The only way to confirm the absence of a transaction is to be aware of all transactions."[286] In order for the database to be safe and not require an intermediary, he suggested its decentralization – transferring the responsibility of its maintenance and updating to the users themselves. This solution created many new technical complications, the removal of which, done through cryptography and economic motivations, got the name of blockchain.

I'm not going to pretend that I fully understand all the technical details of the functioning of Bitcoin and blockchain. It isn't essential to understanding the social impact of this technology. However, it is useful to understand at least the basic logic of the individual technical complications and the solutions that Nakamoto proposed. If not for anything else, then at least to make sure nobody fools you by saying that blockchain can be used for something that's contrary to its own logic.

HOW BLOCKCHAIN WORKS

Everybody knows that blockchain is a database. But it isn't just any database. Its structure reminds one more of a ledger than of Excel. Changes in the database don't happen by rewriting the existing records but by adding new ones. So, when one bitcoin is transferred from Susan to Veronica, the existing numbers in the database aren't rewritten but new information about the change is added. A new page of the ledger then contains the following information: "Susan: minus 1 bitcoin" and "Veronica: plus 1 bitcoin". I'll call such a change a transaction; one page of the ledger will be referred to as *block*; and the whole ledger as *blockchain*.

This ledger has one more special feature: its full contents are distributed in many computers around the world. I say "feature" instead of "benefit" on purpose. Such distribution of a database has its pluses and minuses and we'll talk

---

* Already back in the 1990s there were some projects that aimed at creating digital cash. In 1994 it was Magic Money and one year later Digicash which offered the so-called cyberbucks. But all these projects failed and had problems with intermediaries or with ensuring scarcity.[A18]

about them later. However, the two main advantages of blockchain when compared to a traditional ledger are: the unchangeability of history and a decentralized consensus on the truth.

The first advantage can be explained easily: if a traditional ledger is kept, for instance, at an accountant's home, they can treat it like Excel – they can decide to rewrite a past entry. But this is dangerous because it can lead to Susan's losing her property or accidentally "acquiring" some more. A ledger administrator can always lose our trust. Blockchain tackles this issue through a hash function that lets you "stamp" individual pages of the ledger (blocks) so that they cannot be modified as one pleases. And if somebody tried to do that, they would be discovered immediately. Under specific conditions, the history on blockchain is unchangeable.

Explaining the second advantage is more difficult. How do you reach a decentralized consensus about what is the truth on blockchain without somebody punching the desk saying "this is the truth"?

It's most important to understand how new transactions are created in the database. In other words, how new blocks full of legitimate transactions are added to blockchain and which mechanisms will prevent somebody from smuggling in an illegitimate transaction. An illegitimate transaction is a transaction by which somebody tries to break the principle of the scarcity of money and wants to use the same bitcoin to pay twice. How come all of this happens at decentralized accountants' at the same time and in the same way? How do you get a decentralized consensus on the truth? In the case of centralized databases, this isn't a problem – there is one authority responsible for adding and monitoring new transactions. Blockchain is different.

A good way to demonstrate how something functions is by showing what prevents it from functioning. There are two possible types of fraud on blockchain. The first one goes as follows: Susan owns one bitcoin and decides to send Veronica 2 bitcoins. On blockchain, every transaction starts by being "shared with the world". Susan sends the information about her transaction to other participants of the network so that they can note it in their blockchains. At this point she already has a problem. The protocol itself (communication tool) will reveal an illegitimate transaction – somebody wants to send more than they have written in their ledger. All decentralized accountants immediately reveal and refuse this attempt thanks to their complete ledgers.

The second type of fraud is more sophisticated. Let's say that Susan has one bitcoin and she tells Veronica that she is sending it to her, but she doesn't tell anybody else about it. She pretends it still belongs to her. In order to prevent this, it's necessary for the decentralized network of accountants to agree on where the truth is – which blocks (ledger pages) with transactions are to be trusted and copied in their own blockchains (ledgers). The proof of work by computing power substitutes the need to trust the main accountant. But what's "the proof of work" and why should it contain the truth?

First, we need to understand at least superficially what the already-mentioned hash function does. It not only works as a stamp; it has another important function. We can imagine hashing as a process that can transform a bit of information (e.g., listed transactions on one page of a ledger) into a code consisting of 64 characters – numbers and letters. This code is called hash and it looks like a random sequence of characters. But in reality, it's not random; it's unique for the original hashed message. If you try to hash the title of this book (through SHA 256) you resulting hash would look like this:*

0A31DC4F6CA37BBA59758AC035C7513B00304D4A231B3E9314B38D670CEA5698

One important feature of hashing is that even the slightest modification of the original information (e.g., you add a full stop at the end of the book title or you write 2btc instead of 1btc in a transaction), the resulting hash changes completely. This is the hash for the book title with a full stop in the end:

0C3DBEA8A5A62D6EC4F73F5029239D32BFA2E3ECC71549A66D0C382F9CE09F0D

Plus, the whole hashing process goes one way only. If I hadn't told you the original text hidden behind the two previous hashes, you would have a problem figuring it out. Actually, you would probably never manage to do so. Otherwise, the entire internet, which is built on hashing, would have a problem. If you don't believe me, try to deduce what I hid in the following hash:

C6D928C4F82D9364EE748238C2FE57FFEBBEBAFA693BB657BF04083F353AD5C1

Now that we know how hashing works, imagine somebody announces the following competition:

Attention, everybody! I solemnly declare a competition for finding the number which, when entered at the end of a ledger page (block) and consequently hashed, will produce a hash that begins with twenty zeros.

Since nobody has invented a way to get the original message from a hash, the participants can only guess. They have to try and add random numbers to the end of the ledger page and hash the whole page in order to check whether the final hash happens to begin with 20 zeros. Such guessing involves a lot of computing power. A participant has to try billions of numbers before finding the right one. In blockchain, this process is called mining.**

If somebody finds the number that has to be added at the end of a page (block), it's easy to verify if it really is correct. It's enough to write it at the end of the page, hash the whole thing and verify if there really are twenty zeros in the beginning of the hash. Everybody can do this – miners or decentralized accountants. It's an easy way to verify if somebody really did a lot of (calculating) work without hav-

---

* I recommend you try it. It's the best way to understand and remember it. Google knows many webpages that can generate hash, for instance: https://www.xorbin.com/tools/sha256-hash-calc0ulator

** The difficulty of this process is automatically modified according to the number of people who participate in the competition. If there are many miners, the number of zeros of the final hash increases to thirty, for example. If there are few of them, it may decrease to 10.

ing to do it again. This is the above-mentioned proof of work. Also, it's important that all this work is unchangeably connected with the list of transactions on the page of the ledger. If somebody changes as little as a decimal point, the entire final hash changes – it no longer begins with twenty zeros.[287]

Now you may feel like asking a good question: "What is all this good for?". Let's go back to the example with the second type of fraud. Susan sent Veronica 1 bitcoin and kept it from everybody else. In order for Veronica to accept Susan's bitcoin, the transaction would have to be included in a ledger page (block) which is stamped by a hash. This means that there's proof about carried out work on the given page (block). So, Susan, a potential fraudster, actually had to carry out computing work in order to find a special number for her fake ledger page containing a fraudulent transaction. Veronica accepts this page (it has a stamp) and puts it in her own ledger (blockchain).

But suddenly, Veronica starts getting stamped pages from other network members that have a completely different hash. The reason is that they don't include the transaction Susan concealed. At first, Veronica is confused and doesn't know who is lying. But soon she sees that more stamped pages keep coming from the network and they differ substantially from Susan's version.

If Susan wanted to continue lying to Veronica, she would have to keep on adding new stamped pages (blocks) of her fake version of the ledger and she would need to be faster than the rest of the network.* She would need to provide more proof of work. To be able to do so, she would need to have higher computing performance than everybody else. This is hard to imagine with Bitcoin. Unlike other cryptocurrencies, its distribution over the world is so broad that controlling it would require the involvement and work of an unimaginably high number of the best performing computers. All this in order for someone to devalue the cryptocurrency they wanted to take over.**

There is a simple rule that applies on blockchain: the truth is in that version of the ledger that is backed up by the biggest amount of proof of work. The ledger considered to be true by the members of the network is the one with the biggest number of stamped pages. On blockchain, size matters. So, Veronica in the end decides to believe the rest of the network and the whole fake branch of Susan's ledger (blockchain) which includes the fraudulent transaction, will cease to exist. Susan was wasting her electricity on producing the proof of work and all that remains after her attempt at fraud is the hot air around her graphic card. Veronica will figure out that Susan hasn't sent her any bitcoins. The truth wins in the end

---

* Each new page (block) also contains the hash of the previous page in its header – this is how individual blocks are tied and create blockchain. When one block is changed in the history, all the other blocks change with it. This makes them incompatible with another version of blockchain where one older block contains one different transaction.

** In January 2017, the computing power of the Bitcoin network equaled two billion ordinary portable computers. That is approximately 200 thousand times more than the performance of the 500 world's top performing computers. It really is difficult to take over 51% of Bitcoin's computing power.

even though it can take some time. This is why people tend to wait for several minutes until most of the network confirms the validity of the version of the ledger – next to each other, you will see a couple of newly added pages with valid stamps (blocks and hashes).

Now you know how the truth is found behind the proof of work. And although there's no central authority on blockchain and every decentralized accountant owns and manages only their own copy of the ledger, everybody can agree on what is true. That's how a decentralized consensus is born.*

The last remaining question is how to motivate *"participants"* to carry out proof of work. Because we are talking about the solution of a complex task that requires high-performing processors and electric energy – which isn't free –, motivation is necessary. Here we have to mention another one of Nakamoto's genius steps: blockchain is designed so that each successfully approved block also generates a certain amount of local currency for the successful seeker (originally this was 50 bitcoins but this amount is reduced by half every four years). The circle is complete and the entire ecosystem is stable: in itself it defines and generates an asset responsible for motivating miners who keep it functional in return. Discovering and verifying the truth became a profitable business and fraud is quickly uncovered and punished by sank costs. As we said earlier, this process is called mining.

Mining exists on blockchain not because it's difficult to copy a new bitcoin but because it's on the contrary, very easy. Mining protects the network from fraudsters who want to copy new bitcoins without work. A critic concerned about the environment may ask why mining has to be so energetically demanding. Why don't we rely on a simple consensus with democratic voting where every decentralized accountant has one vote and everything that gets 51% and more is the truth? Because such a network would be very vulnerable. It would be enough to create a lot of new accounts and outvote the existing ones. Computing power isn't that easy to create and copy. Hardware is expensive and so is electricity. That's what guarantees the safety of the network; voting through computing power may not be democratic, but it's definitely safer.**

It's difficult to sufficiently appreciate the innovation Nakamoto came up with in his article from 2008. He managed to uniquely combine the then existing technology and knowledge. I'm not only talking about cryptographic technologies, distributed peer-to-peer database, hashing, digital signature, or the proof

---

* Some crypto-enthusiasts started to overestimate the reach of the truth generated on blockchain. This truth remains the truth only within the borders of Bitcoin. It's the truth about the inner state of the blockchain network and doesn't tell us anything about the physical world outside blockchain.
A19

** In 2018, some developers of the Ethereum cryptocurrency were working on a new way of ensuring consensus. It was supposed to be called the proof of stake and it should not be so energetically demanding. Instead of providing proof of work, randomly chosen members would have to prove the amounts of owned cryptocurrencies and the length of their possession.

of work. The start of Bitcoin also required knowledge from other scientific disciplines: Game theory, microeconomics, macroeconomics, and political economics. He needed to combine everything and translate it into specific functional parameters of a big ecosystem full of diverse agents. The rules of the system had to be matched with the agents' motivation, competence, and sometimes conflicting interests. These agents were main developers, miners, clients, infrastructure creators, creators of user applications, or users themselves. Not only did Nakamoto's article create digital cash, it also created a completely new scientific discipline called cryptoeconomics, which connects all the above-mentioned technologies and knowledge.

HOW BLOCKCHAIN DOESN'T WORK

As Bitcoin's popularity and value rose, an entire new industry started to grow around it. Hundreds of clones of cryptocurrencies which addressed Bitcoin's weaker points (anonymousness, verification speed, block size or transaction fees) appeared together with numerous advisors and futurists who turned their noses up at Bitcoin and proclaimed blockchain itself the technology of the future.

Blockchain fans started to ignore and even refuse the importance of mining the internally generated cryptocurrency and emphasize the importance of blockchain as an open, unchangeable database. But this is a misunderstanding of how the entire ecosystem functions as a whole. It isn't possible to remove blockchain from Bitcoin and start to use it for other purposes – not if we want it to maintain all its important characteristics, such as safety, decentralization, and trustworthiness.

In order for blockchain to really be a safe, unchangeable and trustworthy network, it has to be sufficiently distributed. This implies many independent miners and even more people who supervise them and approve their hashed blocks. For that it is, naturally, necessary to have an internally generated currency which motivates decentralized miners to continue mining. If you operate a blockchain where decentralized people aren't motivated to mine its internal currency or their rewards are paid outside of the system (e.g., by a third party), the entire consensus will be centralized and determining the truth will depend on few selected players (who verify transactions or pay miners).

It was the concerns about the centralization of Bitcoin that lead to extensive discussions about increasing the capacity of one block. In Bitcoin, one block has the size of 1 MB. That's quite little and it limits the overall number of transactions to several hundreds of thousands per day. But thanks to blocks being so small, the whole blockchain can be kept by ordinary users and the entire network is significantly decentralized. If the block capacity is multiplied, the size of the entire blockchain would grow substantially and the number of users would decrease together with the decentralization of Bitcoin. Bitcoin would become more centralized.

Successfully decentralized blockchain can't create databases with big capacities and in addition, blockchain itself is also a very inefficient and costly database. If somebody created a traditional central database with the same volume of transactions which is currently processed by Bitcoin, it would only require trivial performance. A standard portable computer that can perform 14 thousand transactions per second would be able to process all transactions carried out on Bitcoin's blockchain per day in 20 seconds and the processing of annual transactions would take only two hours. Just to compare, MasterCard and Visa carry out approximately two thousand transactions per second, while Bitcoin can manage only 4.[288]

Bitcoin uses such slow, inefficient technology for one reason: to remove the need of a central authority – somebody who administers the database and acts as an intermediary in transactions. The question is why should intermediaries (banks, states, big companies) use such slow and inefficient technology that aims to substitute them.[289] Why should it be used by the state which acts as the final arbiter and maintains its "trustworthiness" via a violent apparatus? If a database or transactions have a final arbiter, there's no need to create blockchain. In this case, the truth won't be the result of a decentralized consensus but of the decision of a politician or official who is backed up by policemen holding their batons.

BITCOIN IS NOT ONLY FOR CRIMINALS

This subchapter partially explores internet technology from the point of view of digital criminals which can give the wrong impression that Bitcoin is predominantly used by criminals – it's not. Just like Tor, Bitcoin is used by many people and criminals represent only a small, gradually decreasing part of them. While in 2012, 30% of all Bitcoin transactions came from the darknet, where people mostly trade illegal goods and services, today it's only 1%.[290] The reason why Bitcoin's popularity with criminals is decreasing is its pseudo-anonymity. Bitcoin is a public ledger and anybody can read it whenever they wish to see all transactions that look something like this:

Address: 1BoatSRRHtKNngktXEeobR76b53LETtpyT

Sent: 0,0012 btc

To address: 3E93XjqK4Cxt71BGeP2VrpcotM8LZ853C8

This transaction is absolutely anonymous until somebody manages to make a connection between the Bitcoin address and the person's identity. This can happen at two points: either upon entering the system when you decide to buy bitcoins, for instance, on the stock market, and you identify yourself with an ID or upon leaving the system when you decide to use your Bitcoins to buy something and you share your name and address with the seller. In these situations, Bitcoin ceases to be anonymous not only from that point onward but also retrospectively. So, anybody in the world can see what you bought and for how much. This is off-putting for criminals, so they start to use alternative, more anonymous cryptocurrencies, like Monero or Zcash.

As Bitcoin loses its popularity with criminals, the number of its legitimate users who use it as a means of exchange keeps growing. Thousands of traders all over the world accept this currency these days. In Slovakia, for instance, there are over 100 places where you can use it. You can buy a musical instrument, a circular saw or the best hotdog in town at a street food stand. You can find Bitcoin ATMs outside the capital as well. This expansion is also to the credit of entrepreneurs who started to build the necessary infrastructure. In Slovakia, brothers Peter and Martin Bešina founded a successful company called CryptoDiggers. The company develops payment gateway for e-shops which accept cryptocurrencies and even operates ATMs. But Bitcoin is also used by big global companies, such as Microsoft, Dell, or Subway. In one Swiss canton you can even pay taxes with it.

If you now decided to start using only Bitcoin in your everyday life, you wouldn't be the first. Kashmir Hill, a reporter from Forbes, tried it for a week and wrote a book about it. A young married couple, the Craigs, decided to live exclusively on Bitcoin for one hundred days and filmed a documentary about it. These attempts took place in 2013 and 2014 which is like medieval times from the point of view of crypto technology. In Prague, one of the main world centers of crypto currencies, life like this wouldn't be a problem at all. I happen to know some people who do all they can to avoid state money and who rebuilt their lives in order to maximize their contact with cryptocurrencies.[291]

But Bitcoin brings the biggest value in places where people are exposed to non-functional public institutions, discrimination or persecution. Imagine you are a woman living in Afghanistan. If you want to be involved in the division of labor and gain independence, you have a problem. In Afghanistan, women are not full citizens with rights. They aren't expected to participate in life outside of their households, not to mention entrepreneurship or owning a bank account. There are two Afghan women who, despite facing this challenge, became successful entrepreneurs and Bitcoin played a significant part in their success stories.

One of them is Roya Mahboob who founded a successful IT company in which she employs Afghan women.[292] From the very beginning, she had problems with accepting payments from abroad and with paying her employees because they didn't have access to a bank account and paying their salaries in cash was dangerous. So, Roya decided to switch to Bitcoin. This is how her employees gained economic independence for the first time in their lives in the strongly patriarchal Afghan society.

The second entrepreneur is Fereshteh Forough, the founder of an NGO called Code to Inspire which teaches Afghan women programming and how to work as freelancers.[293] Forough was born as a refugee in Iran, she didn't have papers and couldn't open a bank account. So, she switched to Bitcoin just like Roya and she teaches her trainees how it works.

This problem is not only faced by the people of Afghanistan. According to the World Bank, there are two billion people in the world who don't have the possibility to use a bank account. The vast majority of them come from developing countries where on average only 18% of people have a bank account in comparison with the almost 90% in developed countries. Some people may trivialize this problem: why would people in the African savanna need a bank account given they don't expect to get any international contracts? Well, actually this is a big problem which amounts to almost $600 billion per year – it's the amount of yearly remittances that migrants from developing countries send back home to help their families survive difficult times. Two thirds of their recipients are women.[294]

Sending money through various countries is more difficult than one would imagine even in today's online world. A significant proportion of money is eaten up by high fees for intermediaries, the entire process takes numerous days and requires various actions from senders and recipients, not to mention the related risks – take, for instance, an old woman in Nigeria who has to personally come to the branch of a financial intermediary in the neighboring village and then return home safely with pockets full of cash her son sent her. Given all these obstacles, Bitcoin transactions are faster, cheaper, simpler but mostly safer for people in the developing world.*

The proof that these aren't just wild ideas of an analysts but rather practical solutions to real people's problems is in the existence of crypto banking apps like Abra, BitPesa, Bitso, Nebeus, Rebit, Toas, MicroMoney, or Coins.ph, which are already used by hundreds of thousands of people from the poorest parts of the world to send money home to their relatives. This way they don't need bank accounts and they can circumvent multiple intermediaries. All they need is a phone worth 30 dollars[295] and an internet connection in a local café or community center. These may not be a-matter-of-course in the developing world but they're definitely more accessible than a bank account (more than half of people from the developing world use the internet these days).[296] These apps gradually substitute other services typically provided by banks, such as investments or microloans.

Bitcoin and cryptocurrencies can also help in the area of humanitarian aid. Governments and politicians in the developing world are often corrupt and when humanitarian aid passes through their hands, a big part of it tends to get lost or allocated to the wrong people. These apps enable humanitarian organizations to circumvent governments and intermediaries and send the aid directly to people in need. For example, the UN used the Ethereum cryptocurrency within the World Food Program to help refugees who often don't have a bank account but possess a mobile phone with applications.[297]

---

* Just for comparison: by the end of 2018, a Bitcoin transaction in the amount of approximately $185 million took place. The transaction costs were 17 cents and it was confirmed in a matter of tens of minutes. Try to imagine how long it would take traditional banks, how much it would cost and if it would even be allowed.[A20]

Bitcoin and cryptocurrencies also made life significantly easier for those who escape from criminal regimes. They can sell all their property, convert it to bitcoins, and "pack" into 25 English words (the so-called seed). It's enough to remember them and they can cross the borders with all their property without risking someone confiscating it. Once they get to a safe zone, all they need to do is type the words into the app and simply renew the property.

Bitcoin saves lives

"We can already see a parallel world growing in front of us – a world with interesting, positive characteristics. I believe that the result will be also interesting and will solve many problems our society faces so that mankind can move forward." Juraj Bednár

The inhabitants of Venezuela are going through a socialist hell. Store shelves are empty and people starve. Some time ago, the news spread across the globe that Venezuelans broke into a ZOO to find something to eat. If you are amongst the socially vulnerable in Venezuela, the state sends you a check for $9 per month.

An economy won't collapse itself – politicians have to contribute to that. Venezuelan politicians have implemented almost everything against which basic definitions from economics textbooks warn. They tried to support the economy by fighting against entrepreneurs, imposing price regulations, and printing money. As a result, they lack everything from toilet paper and food to electronic appliances. The Venezuelan bolivar collapsed. In 2017, you could buy coffee for two thousand bolivars but a year later it cost two million.[298] In November 2018, the inflation rate exceeded million percent. This puts Venezuela in a situation similar to Zimbabwe and Germany in their "best years". Venezuelans became hostages of their currency's hyperinflation which destroyed savings at the speed of light.

But people are resourceful. The most resourceful Venezuelans managed to turn socialism against itself. They transformed price regulation into their advantage. The state regulates the prices for electric energy which is practically a free good in Venezuela. Everybody can get as much as they want unless there is a blackout – planned or unplanned. It's precisely the accessibility of electric energy that Venezuelan bitcoin miners use. They became entrepreneurs who buy an undervalued commodity (electric energy) and transform it into a more highly valued commodity (bitcoin).

Bitcoin mining on unspecialized hardware isn't an economic jackpot but the Venezuelans are content with it. It allows them to buy basic food, medicines, soap, or electronic appliances to make their lives at least a bit more bearable. Bitcoin allows them to shop outside their country where, for a long time, there hasn't been much to buy. Their favorite e-shop is American Amazon which doesn't accept bitcoins, but they can buy Amazon gift cards with them on the eGifter web portal.

Venezuelans see another advantage in Bitcoin – they don't have to physically possess it. That's very important in a country with a rapidly increasing crime rate and curfew after 8PM. Thieves who focused on piles of banknotes stand no chance against Bitcoin.

There are special exchanges which serve to transfer the "mined production" from cyberspace to the physical world. One of them is the Venezuelan SurBitcoin exchange where you can exchange bitcoins for bolivars and bolivars for dollars. Venezuela currently has the second biggest sales volume globally on LocalBitcoins.com, where people buy bitcoins in the value of million dollars daily.[299] That's decent for a country marked by an economic collapse.

However, it isn't all that pretty. Actions cause reactions and the Venezuelan government's interventions against miners are getting more and more strict. The police arrested an employee of the above-mentioned stock exchange and accused him of money laundering and tax fraud.

Even in Venezuela, cryptocurrencies gradually move from the "criminal" category to the "ordinary business" category. Dash is another cryptocurrency that's getting more popular. Unlike Bitcoin, we know who the authors are and they founded the Dash Merchant Venezuela organization which aims to convince and teach local merchants to use cryptocurrencies. By the end of 2018, they were used by almost 2500 stores. Small family enterprises were gradually joined by bigger companies, such as Subway or the local business chains. When I was writing this book, even KFC was considering whether they would accept Dash or not.[300] The main advantage of Dash is that people don't need an internet connection or smartphones. Dash offers the Dash Text service – something like an SMS wallet with which you can pay from a simple mobile phone without an internet connection.[301]

Apart from Latin America (Venezuela and Argentina), cryptocurrencies are becoming more popular in Zimbabwe and other African countries which face high inflation and where holding the local currency is not financially safe for the locals.* Bitcoin is also gaining popularity in Iran, where the currency is more stable but financially isolated from the outside world for political reasons.

---

* A critic may object that Bitcoin also went through quite high inflation in 2018, when its value dropped in a relatively short time from almost 20 thousand dollars to 4 thousand. But for Venezuelans who had been using it for several years it was but a short episode which first inflated and then deflated the value of their property. From a more long-term point of view, bitcoin was experiencing a slow deflation. On the other hand, we must admit that the problem of volatility is still relevant when it comes to cryptocurrencies, but it can be resolved as I will show you later.

In the western world people started to use Bitcoin mostly for ideological reasons or out of curiosity while people in developing countries switch to Bitcoin and other cryptocurrencies out of necessity. They need to protect themselves from their country's collapsing currency, save up money for the future, mine money to buy medicine or to send home from abroad. Today cryptocurrencies actually help hundreds of thousands of people globally.

5. CRYPTO MARKETS OF THE INTERNET'S "WILD WEST"

"I came across this website called SilkRoad. Its a Tor hidden service that claims to allow you to buy and sell anything online anonymously... Let me know what you think..."[302]

January 28, 2011, a post on Shroomery.org from a user named Altoid.

This was Altoid's first and last post on the Shroomery forum. Later he published a couple of similar posts on Silk Road and other, mostly Bitcoin, forums. Within three weeks, Silk Road had 151 registered users, 38 store items and carried out 28 successful transactions. What was Silk Road? It was the "eBay of the darknet for goods that were regulated or banned by the state and it used Tor and Bitcoin. While eBay's first sold item was a broken laser pointer, Silk Road's was a package of marijuana.[303]

The story of the Silk Road marketplace began in the summer of 2011 when it had approximately a thousand of registered users and a journalist from Gawker wrote an article about it. After its publication, the number of registered users grew to 10 thousand and apart from consumers, Silk Road got noticed by American senators and DEA agents.

All the sudden attention shocked Silk Road's hidden servers so much that they crashed. After the technical break, Silk Road returned stronger and with a new function. It implemented dynamic pricing of goods which made transactions with the volatile bitcoin easier and it also gave the opportunity of insurance against its fluctuations (hedging). That brought stability and security into the business. At that same time, Silk Road started to employ new people. They posted a job ad on Bitcointalk.org where they looked for a lead developer; the wage was in bitcoins and ownership shares in the company. The ad was signed by Altoid. Remember it – this ad will play an important role.

Another milestone in the life of Silk Road was the arrival of the "DPR". After about a year in his function, the admin announced that from that moment on, he would act under the name of Dread Pirate Roberts (DPR), who was the main character in the movie Princess Bride (1987). This character was interesting because it was actually not one specific person but an identity that was assumed by several people. Once a pirate with the DPR identity stole enough wealth, he revealed his secret to his successor and handed him his identity which could uninterruptedly continue doing its pirate job. When DPR appeared on Silk Road, questions arose as to whether the original founder handed the dangerous business over to their successor.

The business was indeed dangerous but also highly profitable. It's is estimated that at its peak, Silk Road had monthly sales volumes of millions of dollars and a part of it went to the owner of the crypto market in the form of fees. The estimates say that almost 10 million bitcoins passed through Silk Road during the two years of its existence.[304] Most sales involved drugs, but mostly soft ones or less dangerous ones. Although the darknet is a place of anarchy out of the state's reach, it doesn't mean people could do whatever they pleased on Silk Road. Anarchy is a state without rulers not without rules. For example, Silk Road strictly forbade selling stolen credit cards, guns, poisons, or child pornography.*

Thomas Hobbes would turn in his grave if he heard about Silk Road's commercial success in an anarchist space. How did Dread Pirate Roberts succeed?** How did he build a successful "eBay" in conditions where he couldn't rely on public authorities but actually had to defend himself against them? How did he manage to create a relatively safe space for sellers and buyers who don't know each other, are spread across the whole world, come from different cultures, and use anonymizing tools while their objective is to hide their real identity and substitute it with an internet one? An identity, which doesn't point to any real person and which can be easily thrown away at practically zero costs to create a new one. This is more difficult with a real identity and that's exactly the problem. If you do business with an anonymous person and they trick you, you cannot complain and you'll never know who actually tricked you. Providing law and order services in such an environment meant being exposed to the most difficult conditions political philosophers and political economists can imagine.

---

* But there are also darknet crypto markets which opted for a more "progressive" attitude and enabled, for instance, also selling child pornography, but the community despised them, they never reached commercial success and were subject to hackers' attacks.

** People used the internet to buy and sell illegal goods and services even before Silk Road and DPR, but it was generally done through smaller websites or forums focused on one geographical area or community, they were not freely accessible to everyone and they didn't display their range of goods publicly. The internet served as a communication tool but the business itself was done personally.

5.1 DREAD PIRATE ROBERTS VS. THOMAS HOBBES

On the one hand, internet anonymization helped to avoid the state and its sanctions but on the other hand, it created identity problems. But they aren't unsolvable: the fact that identity is anonymous doesn't have to mean that it cannot be unique. Anonymity means that it's impossible to connect a real person with their internet account. But an anonymous user can have their own digital identity with the corresponding reputation. You need to find a way to ensure the authenticity of identity to make sure that the person hiding behind an anonymous identity with whom you communicate today is the same person with whom you communicated yesterday and the same person with whom your friend will communicate tomorrow. Asymmetric encryption makes this possible using private and public keys.

When encrypting a message, you use somebody's public key to encrypt a message that can only be read by somebody who has a private key. When they want to reply to you, they use your public key to encrypt the message and you're the only one who can read it with your private key. All it takes is to turn this procedure around and you get a perfect identity authenticity verification tool. If I use my private key to encrypt a digital message, its authenticity can be verified by anybody who has my public key. This way I create a digital signature. The message will no longer be secret, but a new function is added – authenticity verification. The point is that I'm the only one who can encrypt a message with my private key, others only have access to my public key.

By combining these two procedures (encryption and digital signature), you can communicate with anybody and be sure of two things: your communication is private and you're really communicating with the person who has access to the private key corresponding to the given identity. This is crucial for the functioning of anarchy on the darknet. It makes the existence of authentic anonymous identities with their corresponding reputation possible.

Just like all the platforms, clubs, and webs that we mentioned, Silk Road enabled its users to rate satisfaction and leave feedback. The pressure of reputation on good behavior worked just like it did everywhere else. People not only used star ratings but also verbal ratings. Once an identity built a good reputation, it was easier for them to do business, they had more orders and could afford to charge more.[305] For a person with such an identity, bad ratings are just as bad as for somebody who received the rating for their real identity, for instance, on Airbnb or eBay. A tarnished reputation limits the possibilities of further business transactions.

The specific aspects of reputation on the anonymous darknet are visible especially in the beginnings of a newly-created identity. In the beginning, when a reputation is zero, one has nothing to lose by cheating. Also, creating a new darknet identity is very simple and practically cost-free. This cannot be said for Airbnb and eBay. This is why law and order providers on the darknet had to primarily focus on the initial phase of a new crypto market or on newly-registered customers or sellers. This is when the reputation pressure doesn't work yet and there is zero trust.

The first rule on the darknet and crypto markets is : start small. If you have just created an account on a crypto market, you have zero reputation and decide to order a large package of drugs, you probably won't succeed. No dealer would take the risk. Even Silk Road itself recommended its users to start with small orders. That's how they can find a seller willing to sell them something. The same goes for beginner sellers who can choose from several strategies of signalizing their trustworthiness and willingness to operate long-term on the darknet: they can offer free samples, free shipping, refund in case their package is confiscated, or various initial discounts. A professional character of their internet profile can also be a good signal – they should put some effort into their business name, logo, etc. – because sellers who are planning to stay in business long-term are more likely to bear such costs.

There are also more sophisticated ways of signalizing quality. A seller can offer a discount to a customer if they provide feedback (positive or negative). It may look like bribery at first, but this is actually a strategy that's only chosen by sellers who possess good quality goods, have just started their business and have not yet built their reputation – at least according to an empirical analysis on Taobao, where this possibility was introduced.[306]

Crypto markets also try to prevent obvious fraudsters from trading. Silk Road didn't let everybody trade on their platform either. A seller had to first auction their place in it which not only brought profits for the market itself, but also helped to separate wheat from the tares. A seller who has a long-term cheating strategy would probably not invest into a license. They might be able to trick their first few customers before their bad reputation catches up with them, but resources obtained this way may not be sufficient to cover the costs of the license given that customers are only willing to get involved with new sellers for smaller transactions.

Nevertheless, none of the above has prevented certain sellers from monetizing their good reputation. If a seller lost their supplier, suspected that they were being watched by the police or decided to stop their illegal business, they had two ways of ending their presence on the darknet. They could announce to their customers that they would soon end their activities and request them to finalize their orders or continue to accept orders, collect money, and quietly disappear. The second option represented a temptation several darknet sellers couldn't resist. There are several legends circulating around crypto markets about top vendors with top reputations who disappeared out of the blue together with the money for their last orders that were never delivered.

This brought popularity to the infamous *Tony76*. He appeared on the Silk Road crypto market about a year after it was launched and very quickly became one of the most reliable vendors with an excellent reputation. The 20th of April is the biggest sales day on the darknet; something like Black Friday in traditional shops.* On this day, *Tony76* offered a good discount, received money for a multitude of orders and then disappeared into thin air.³⁰⁷ He earned more than $100 thousand in two days.** Instead of the promised ecstasy, many of his customers experienced depression.

However, there is smart protection against this type of fraud too. Darknet platforms often offer the escrow service. Silk Road offered it too and it regularly reminded their customers to use it when trading. If a customer decides to use it, when purchasing drugs, he doesn't send bitcoins directly to the seller's account but sends it to an intermediate account controlled by the crypto market. It pays the money to the seller only once the customer has confirmed that they got the goods. Silk Road used to charge a fee of 6.23% for this service. The higher the value of the order, the lower the fee.

As a part of this service, Silkroad also provided conflict resolution services. If the business wasn't going as planned and one of the parties felt cheated, they could click on the "conflict resolution" button. A website administrator would then listen to both parties and decide who was right – decide whether they would return secured bitcoins to the buyer or forward them to the seller. Practically all disappearances of vendors who cheated their customers happened when the customer didn't use the escrow service but trusted the seller and sent them bitcoins right before obtaining their goods.

The problem of building initial reputation was not only an issue for customers and vendors, but also for crypto markets themselves. Their creators can close the business at any time and disappear for good together with bitcoins stored on their local accounts or within the escrow service. This is why it was important that they convince users that they can trust their beginning crypto market and safely open an account to transfer cryptocurrencies.

They took similar steps to beginner sellers in order to build trust. They also began small and, in the beginning, they were selling their own drugs on the crypto market themselves. They too used costly quality signals, for instance, they invested in a good-quality logo, detailed information, and website design. The programming language complexity also played an important role. If a creator used a simple, less-sophisticated language, not only was his website an easier target for hackers, it also signaled that they weren't willing to invest sufficient resources (time and money) and there's therefore a bigger chance that they're a fraudster with dishonest intentions. The correlation between the complexity of the chosen programming language and the longevity of crypto markets has also been empirically proven.³⁰⁸

The willingness of the creators to integrate the possibility of paying with several cryptocurrencies (not only Bitcoin) into the ecosystem can serve as another

---

* The 20th of April – 4/20 or 4-20 – was chosen because 4:20 is the international smoking time.
** But there are also traders who ended honestly and announced that they had earned enough and don't want to take any further risks. They asked their customers to finish their last orders, completed the orders and closed their business. This was the case of *JesusOfRave* from Silk Road.^A21

costly signal of quality. The new Nightmare Market crypto market which was established in the end of 2018, integrated seven different cryptocurrencies together with the most recent cryptographic procedures that ensure the platform's safety. Another trust-building strategy is to limit the entry of users to those who are invited or recommended. It sends a signal that creators don't just want as many members and shops as possible, but instead they are interested in the long-term building of a community of verified users.

But not even expensive trust signals always guaranteed that the creators of a crypto market wouldn't just take the deposited bitcoins and perform an exit scam. According to Europol's statistics, 31 out of the examined 89 crypto markets ended in a fraudulent manner. Another 24 ended honestly – they announced the end and enabled the users to withdraw their deposited bitcoins. The rest ended either because they were discovered by the police or attacked by hackers. However, there are also crypto markets with long-term excellent reputations which have been working for about 6 years now (Valhalla or Dream Market).[309]

Fortunately, there is a protection against this type of exit scam. Today it is used by several modern crypto markets that don't have dishonest intentions. It's called Multisig and it's something like a contract which involves several signatures. This type of contract can be concluded with Bitcoin technology; the buyer doesn't send bitcoins directly to the seller or deposit them to an escrow account on the crypto market, but rather sends them to a special Bitcoin address.

You can picture it as a money box for bitcoins which can be opened only when two out of three persons use their keys. In case of crypto markets, these three persons are the buyer, the seller, and the crypto market. If everything goes smoothly and the buyer gets his goods, they use their key, the seller does the same and the bitcoins are released. If things don't go smoothly and a conflict arises between the buyer and the seller, it's the admin who decides about bitcoins (just like in the case of escrow). If the crypto market admin wanted to commit an exit scam, they don't have automatically granted access to the bitcoins deposited in the Bitcoin money box. The buyer and the seller can agree without the crypto market and use their two keys to unblock bitcoins and this doesn't require the involvement of an administrator. Exit scams make no sense under such circumstances.*

5.2 DRUGS: QUALITY AND SAFETY

I personally don't approve of drugs. I practically don't drink alcohol, smoke, I avoid simple carbs, and I have uninstalled the Facebook app from my phone.

---

* This solution isn't perfect either. There's still the theoretical possibility that the crypto market creator and the seller is the same person or they are future accomplices. In such case, not even the Multisig contract can help because the fraudster would possess two out of three keys. However, this scenario is currently very unlikely to happen since there are thousands of traders who operate in crypto markets and a conspiracy involving such a high number of people is improbable.

Drugs are dangerous toys. But, just like everything else, you can choose a better or worse way to use drugs. A typical problem for recreational drug users is that the people they need to deal with may be dangerous and the goods they purchase may be of poor quality. Silk road brought improvements in both these aspects.

Buying drugs in the physical world isn't easy. Since it's illegal, people involved in this activity are more willing to take risks and face violence or even initiate it. It's not always pleasant to meet them. The manufacture of drugs is illegal too – before a drug gets to the final user, it goes through many intermediaries that may dilute it and as a result it's more dangerous and can lead to overdose or unexpected reactions.

Silk Road solved both problems to a high extent not only thanks to reputation mechanisms but also thanks to different rules typical for crypto markets. An entire organic "customer protection" system grew on Silk Road. For example, there was this popular user group called The Avengers which provided the services of independent LSD testers. They tested drugs both on themselves and in labs and they submitted reports and chemical analyses. They also rated packaging, speed of delivery, and sellers' communication. First, they would buy the drugs themselves, but later vendors started to send them for free in order to show off their quality goods.[310]

Even doctors and drug specialists were involved in Silk Road. One of them called himself DoctorX, which was not merely a pseudonym – he officially identified himself as doctor Fernando Caudevilla, a Spanish doctor with years of experience in the field of drug addictions and mitigation of adverse effects of drug use. He established his own "office" on the forum where he advised people on problems of this kind. His forum belonged amongst the most frequently visited ones on Silk Road and admins pinned it to the top of the website to make it visible to everyone who enters for the first time. Users would bombard him with questions related to drug use or the effort to quit them and he became a star.*

But it's not only users themselves and positive feedback that testify about the quality and safety of drugs on Silk Road and other crypto markets. Academics who dedicate their professional lives to drug use research came to the same conclusions.** Tests of drugs ordered directly from Silk Road or other crypto markets showed that there is a 90% chance that customers will get the substance they ordered in the quality they selected.[311] Crypto market drugs were also tested in a Spanish laboratory where it was confirmed that 90% of samples had the same contents sellers stated.[312] Those who mistrust academics and independent labo-

---

* He even saved the life of a man from Eastern Europe when he helped him distinguish withdrawal symptoms from a serious disease the symptoms of which he experienced as he was gradually quitting heroin. The man complained that other doctors (in the physical world) refused to treat him when they learned he was a drug addict.[A22]

** Doctor Monica Barratt from Australia conducted research in the National Drug and Alcohol Research Centre where she wrote a dissertation thesis on the subject of drugs on the internet.[A23]

ratories can read the following report by FBI agents who ordered drugs and had them tested:

"Since November of 2011, law enforcement agents participating in this investigation have made over 70 individual purchases of controlled substances from various vendors on the Silk Road Underground Website. The substances purchased have been various Schedule I and II drugs, including ecstasy, cocaine, heroin, LSD, and others. As of April 2013, at least 56 samples of these purchases have been laboratory-tested, and, of these, 54 have shown high purity levels of the drug the item was advertised to be on Silk Road."[313]

It wasn't only about the quality of the drug itself but also about the safety of its purchase. Instead of heading into a dark alley to meet a stranger, it was suddenly enough to make a couple of clicks. Today's war against drugs which takes place in many states has turned the drug industry into an extremely violent one, not to mention the other costs of this war: financial, moral, and people wasting their lives in prison. Silk Road proposed an alternative world where drug trade can be done at minimal social costs.

5.3 PROTECTION AGAINST PUBLIC ORDER PROTECTORS

"Disruptive innovation does not take root through a direct attack on the existing system. Instead, it must go around and underneath the system."[314]

Clayton Christensen

Innovation happens constantly on crypto markets, just like on any other market, and their creators try to make trading as simple as possible for their sellers. They basically do the same thing as eBay, Airbnb, or Uber – they gain profit by selling a reduction in transaction costs. They also provide law and order services but with one difference: their customers are not only afraid of being tricked by their business partner but also of being attacked from the outside by S.W.A.T. teams that kick doors down. This is why crypto markets compete in providing innovation in the area of safety and protection from "external aggressors" and they constantly integrate applications into their systems and tools aimed at protecting identity and keeping the anonymity of the user.

For example, crypto markets ensure payment anonymization. As I have said, Bitcoin is pseudo anonymous, which means that if somebody can pair a Bitcoin address with a real person, they have the opportunity to track all their past and future transactions. To solve this problem, there are special Bitcoin "washing machines" and "blenders". They take a bunch of bitcoins, put them in a dark room, mix them thoroughly and once they are newly divided, it is very difficult to find out who paid for what and whether they traded on crypto markets at all.

In addition, crypto markets have started to switch to alternative cryptocurrencies like Monero or Zcash that have a higher anonymity rate. They have also switched to two-factor identification for signing in or they require a PIN code for any manipulation with the account, which increases security. When I was writing this book, Nightmare was the most progressive crypto market in this respect – it allows users to hide their login and create a publicly visible pseudonym. The aim is to increase protection against brute force attacks (guessing log-in details).

At the same time, crypto markets try to improve user interface for traders. Their functions and possibilities start to look like those of professional platforms like eBay or Amazon. Nightmare, for example, offers many options for the editing of a subpage of shops with the opportunity to "employ" sales assistants. Crypto markets also start to use elements of machine learning and big data analysis. They mark suspicious trade which goes beyond a certain limit or frequency and dedicate special attention and protection to these cases.

Traders also contribute to security. In "darknet commercials" they compete in how little data they keep about their customers, what safety elements they use in communication and how their processes are secured so that there is no leak of information about their customers in case they get arrested. Elaborate ways of disguising drugs in the packaging are another big competitive advantage. From the customers' point of view, this is the most vulnerable point where the digital world of the darknet meets the physical world. If the vendor sends only a little bit of powder or strip of paper (LSD), they most often pack the drugs into a vacuum sachet and send it in an envelope together with several letters so that no one could tell it apart from other envelopes. If they send pills or a bigger amount of powder, they need to get creative. Obviously, we won't get to know what the best tricks are, but there are cases when they were sent in various cheap plastic toys, ballpoint pens, batteries, thick catalogues with a cut-out hole for drugs, a sealed shampoo sample that came as a supplement to a women's magazine, a carboard box with double bottom, or in bubble foil. The drugs were sometimes hidden so well that not even customers themselves could find them at first and they thought they had been tricked by the seller.[315]

For their own safety, customers must carefully think about their delivery address. The smarter ones select various delivery points, abandoned houses or external mailboxes. Although sending drugs via mail and delivery services may seem dangerous, it's actually not so much the case. Even if the police manage to intercept a package with contraband goods that was heading to your home, it isn't that simple to prove you also ordered it. Anybody can send you anything. Plus, the number of packages and letters that goes through postal services is very big and post offices don't tend to have the necessary technical equipment for intercepting drugs. The situation gets a little more complicated when the contraband crosses borders but even in this situation they don't monitor all mail; they only intercept what is suspicious. On top of that, public authorities have limited resources and launching a police action isn't free, so the heads of police departments don't usually approve costs to catch small fish.[316] One Canadian LSD dealer from Silk Road estimated that less than 1% of packages failed to make it to his customers. That also includes scams from the side of customers when they falsely reported a missing package in order to get a refund.[317]

5.4 EVEN AN EXPERT MAKES MISTAKES

On the 3rd of October 2013, 29-year-old Ross Ulbricht entered a library in Glen Park in San Francisco. He went up to the first floor, sat behind a desk, opened his laptop and started surfing on the internet. Suddenly, someone in the room shouted: "I´ve had enough of you!", and a police officer stormed into the room, pushing Ross away from his computer. He didn't have time to sign out from the websites or lock his computer with a security code.

This is how FBI agents got the evidence that Ross was signed-in at Silk Road as DPR. They also found other evidence which was suspicious. One wouldn't expect that it would be left by a person who managed to build a darknet imperium worth billions. According to the agents, Ross kept an uncoded personal journal where he documented all his activities on Silk Road including an alleged order for a murder. He also supposedly kept unsecured communication with colleagues and was logged-in in all forums to which he posted in the past under several pseudonyms.

Ross Ulbricht was accused of several crimes connected with operating the Silk Road black market: from money laundering and smuggling to drug sale and hacker activities. In the beginning, the prosecution even mentioned accusations from planning and ordering a murder which was the main argument why Ross couldn't get out of prison on bail. But this accusation didn't make it into the indictment and was officially withdrawn.

However, the label of a dangerous man stuck with Ross. That may explain the extremely strict punishment he got in the end: double life sentence plus 40 years in prison and a fine in the amount of $183 million. Ross's family didn't give up the fight. Up to this day they speak publicly about the case, contact journalists, politicians, and activists and keep on appealing. In one of the appeals, judges weaved in the entire tragedy of the case into its dismissal:

"*Reasonable people may and do disagree about the social utility of harsh sentences for the distribution of controlled substances, or even of criminal prohibition of their sale and use at all. It is very possible that, at some future point, we will come to regard these policies as tragic mistakes and adopt less punitive and more effective methods of reducing the incidence and costs of drug use.*

At this point in our history, however, the democratically-elected representatives of the people have opted for a policy of prohibition, backed by severe punishment."[318]

This needs no further comment.

You may be asking how the agents even managed to find Ross despite all the praised anonymizing and privacy tools. As in majority of similar cases, here the mistake also happened somewhere between the keyboard and the chair. Policemen and agents can make millions of mistakes during investigation, but it's enough for an internet "criminal" to make one and they're done. Do you remember the job advert at Bitcointalk.org in which Altoid looked for a lead developer for Silk Road? He included the e-mail address where candidates can send their CVs: rossulbricht at gmail dot com. He left this trace in the very beginning. It was the human factor that failed and that can be found behind the vast majority of other cases of arrested crypto market traders. It's not the decryption of Tor or asymmetric encryption but a human error or naivety.

A similar case involved an Australian trader who created a new account on Silk Road under the nickname of Shadh1 in 2012. There was no way to connect him with this nickname except for the license plate of his BMW. Shadh1 ordered drugs from the Netherlands and sold them in Australia. When asked to enter the order delivery address, he didn't think of anything better than entering his own name and home address. When he failed to receive 12 orders in a row, he didn't even stop to think why and kept on ordering. But his 12 orders were at that time examined by the customs and drug enforcement agents were preparing a raid on his house. When they got into his house, they found an unlocked computer with all trading records.

I don't need to go very far from home to find an example of arrested crypto market traders or admins. Our neighbors, the Czechs, have their own "crypto criminal". His name is Tomáš Jiřikovský and he was the operator of a crypto market called Sheep Marketplace which was in operation around the same time as Silk Road, but it ended for different reasons. Several months after the end of Silk Road, Jiřikovský pulled an "exit scam". He disconnected the server and took all bitcoins users deposited as a trading guarantee. Then he tried to launder it with the help of his wife and that's how he failed. When he was buying a new residence worth almost 9 million Czech crowns, the bank reported a suspicious transaction and Jiřikovský and his wife were detained by the police in 2015. Two years later, he was sentenced to nine years in prison. In Slovakia, we have so far "only" had one case of an arrested crypto market seller.[319]

5.5 CRYPTOHYDRA

"Silk road is not one man. Silk road is an idea......"

DPR, Silk Road 2.0

In Greek mythology, the Hydra is a monster with the body of a snake and nine dragon heads. It has a super power – American writer Nassim Taleb would call it "antifragility".³²⁰ If you cut off one of Hydra's heads you only make it stronger – two new heads grow back. Crypto markets are the Hydras of the darknet. Authorities have managed to find and close several of them, but the result was the opposite of what they expected – the rise of even bigger and safer crypto markets. When they closed the original Silk Road in 2013, Silk Road 2.0. was created within 35 days. After some time, they managed to discover and stop this version as well, but it took Dread Pirate Roberts only 35 days to come up with a new, better version: Silk Road 3.0. At the time of writing this book there's also version 3.1.

But Silk Road has never been the only crypto market. It already had several competitors during its existence: Sheep Marketplace, Black Market Reloaded and Atlantis. Atlantis was a bold project that aimed at getting crypto markets into the mainstream. In comparison with Silk Road, it offered a better user interface and apart from bitcoins it also accepted litecoins. It focused its adverising on "surface web" – its founders gave interviews for newspapers and TV shows and paid for Youtube adverts and tutorials. They automatically offered the position of trusted vendors on Atlantis to vendors who already had a good reputation on other crypto markets. Thanks to public key authorization tools, they could be sure that these are indeed the invited vendors and not just somebody who stole their identity. Despite all that, consumers turned out to be quite conservative and Atlantis took a lot of time to develop until the creators finally decided to close it and ran away with the deposited crypto money.

The outlook for crypto markets was pessimistic towards the end of 2013. Silk Road was closed by the police and other crypto markets were also shut down one by one, whether it was because of a hackers'attack or because the creators ran away with bitcoins. However, in the shadows of these dying giants, their younger siblings were growing, waiting for their opportunity. Twenty new crypto markets were created in the following months. Most of them didn't even make it to the end of the following year, but the genie was out of the bottle and it was impossible to get it back in.

Darknet trade was abundant between 2015 and 2017. Fraudsters, of course, took advantage of this situation and some crypto markets pulled unexpected and painful exit scams. Evolution and Outlaw are the most popular examples where creators escaped with property worth millions of bitcoins. At the same time, frauds like this helped launch reliable and trustworthy crypto markets, such as AlphaBay which became the biggest crypto market of its generation. At its peak, it had about 400 thousand users and its daily trade amounted to $ 600-800 thousand.*

Good times ended halfway through 2017 when agents of the international operation "Bayonet" in Canada and Thailand closed AlphaBay's servers and arrested its owner, a 26 -year-old Alexander Cazes, a Canadian living in Bangkok. The

---

* This footnote was supposed to contain a link to an educational webpage called DarkWebNews, but agents closed it halfway through 2019 despite no trade taking place on the website. It served merely to publish information about the functioning of crypto markets.

end of this story is especially unfortunate given that Cazes committed suicide in a Thai prison several days after his arrest.

After AlphaBay, it was Silk Road 3.1. and Dream Market that took the lead. Dream Market started in 2013 and together with Valhalla they are the two longest existing crypto markets. Apart from them, there are several other active crypto markets and new ones keep appearing. The overall volumes of transactions on crypto markets has multiplied since the end of the original Silk Road and it's estimated that in the EU alone, the monthly trade volume amounts to €10-18 million.[321]

These are small numbers from the point of view of the overall amount of money involved in the drug trade but if we look at it from the perspective of the eight years of crypto markets' development, we see a clear sign that anarchy can survive on the internet. Public authorities admit it too; in its report on drugs, the Europol says that: "It is possible that darknet markets will disrupt traditional drug markets in the same way as has been seen in some areas for legitimate commodities", and at the same time admits that: "Law enforcement interventions in the form of darknet market takedowns disrupt darknet markets, although the overall ecosystem appears to be fairly resilient with new markets quickly becoming established. Cybercrime and online criminality are evolving rapidly, at a scale and speed never before seen, making it difficult for law enforcement and prosecutors to keep pace."[322]

5.6 CONCLUSION – THOMAS HOBBES MUST BE TURNING IN HIS GRAVE

"Anonymity makes it technically impossible to centrally enforce rules or laws in crypto anarchy; all relationships must be either contractually established or voluntarily accepted."

Pavol Lupták[323]

Tor and Bitcoin have changed the world. The Pandora's box is now open and these two technologies allow the existence of a parallel society where state enforced rules don't apply and every single interaction between people takes place in an anarchical environment. It's like the Wild West of the internet and just like the actual American wild west, it isn't ruled by chaos, injustice and constant fighting where everyone is against everyone, as people often assume.

Despite the lack of public regulation on the darknet, the products sold there are very close to what manufacturers and sellers promise. Despite nobody having the legal competence to collect taxes on the darknet, public services that we typically associated with the state are provided there. On the darknet, there are private providers of law and order whose aim is not only smooth trade among the members but also the protection against the external enemy – public authorities. All of this happens under conditions which are extremely unfavorable from the point of view of voluntary cooperation: people come from different cultures, they don't know each other, they're anonymous, they can delete their identity at any time and create a new one.

Not everybody necessarily likes what is sold on the darknet. People may be opposed to somebody selling drugs and guns. It's interesting that these people often don't agree on which of the two should be forbidden. Some call for the legalization of drugs but are against legal guns, others want legal guns but wants drugs to remain illegal. However, this is a book about economics and I'm trying to avoid moral judgements here.

After all, the darknet and cryptocurrencies are only means which can be used to good or bad purposes. Just like you can use your knife to slice an avocado but also to silence your neighbor, you can use the darknet and cryptocurrencies to escape dictators but also to escape justice. If you are outraged that criminals use encryption and anonymizing technologies, it's like being outraged that they use the telephone for communication and cars for transport.

6. DECENTRALIZED CRYPTO MARKET

"We tend to forget that there is such a thing as technological progress in contracts. People discover new ways of making agreements, and over a period of time we obtain considerable benefit from this sort of technological progress"[324]

Gordon Tullock

Despite all the previously-described mechanisms and tricks, crypto markets had one weak spot – they were centralized platforms which had their owner and servers. A single error in the website code or an admin's lack of attention while logging in would be enough to trace and arrest the owners or hack and switch off the servers. Another problem was that even though they used a payment system which worked even without an intermediary, people were still trading through an intermediary (crypto market or another type of platform). These intermediaries could betray your trust – they could embezzle bitcoins that you deposited on their platform, misuse the information you chose to disclose, or at least charge you for their services or censor and regulate commercial transactions.

In 2014, a British hacker and activist, Amir Taaki, decided to change this. Together with his colleagues he participated in the Hackathon competition in Toronto where they programmed a prototype of the first decentralized peer-to-peer marketplace. It was a marketplace that doesn't have its own owner or servers, doesn't collect information about anybody, doesn't charge any fees, and – most importantly – cannot be switched-off like traditional crypto markets. Amir Taaki won the competition and earned $20,000. Soon after that he was contacted by several developers who wanted to continue with his project. This continuation got the name of OpenBazaar and the first functional version appeared in 2016. A year later, OpenBazaar 2.0. was launched and it has been working successfully ever since.

6.1 WHAT DOESN'T KILL YOU MAKES YOU STRONGER – OPENBAZAAR

"A specter is haunting the modern world, the specter of crypto anarchy. Computer technology is on the verge of providing the ability for individuals and groups to communicate and interact with each other in a totally anonymous manner... These developments will completely alter the nature of government regulation, the ability to tax and control economic interactions, the ability to keep information secret, and will even alter the nature of trust and reputation... Just as the technology of printing altered and reduced the power of medieval guilds and the social power structure, so too will cryptologic methods fundamentally alter the nature of corporations and of government interference in economic transactions."[325]

Timothy May, 1992

Amir Taaki got the idea of creating a decentralized crypto market after the original Silk Road was shut down. This wasn't the first nor the last time such a thing happened in the world of digital criminals. The first big clash between digital criminals and brick-and-mortar laws is represented by the case of Napster, a pirate network.

Napster was the first widely spread platform for pirate file sharing, mostly of mp3 music. It was founded in 1999 by a 19-year-old student, Shawn Fanning. Napster worked as an intermediary for copying mp3 files among computers. Its main function was the administration of the list of all files included in the network and a comfortable interconnection of those who offered them with those who requested them. The service quickly got 80 million users and its popularity increased fast. However, its end came equally fast.

In 2000, mp3 records of the band Metallica appeared on Napster before they were supposed to be officially published. It infuriated the members of the band and they sued Napster. They were backed up by rapper Dr. Dre and other artists who created an association called Artists Against Piracy. The structure of the platform ended up being its Achilles heel. Napster had its own server and owners who operated its services. In other words, it was centralized. The service was switched off in 2011 and the creators had to face court disputes.

The internet learns fast. The second generation of file sharing services didn't make the same mistake. After Napster came Gnutella, which delegated the services of list administration and connecting users to the users themselves. So, there was no longer a centralized database or a node that connected all users. These functions were decentralized and a P2P network was all that remained. Intermediaries ceased to exist and users (supplying or demanding) connected directly. Gnutella couldn't be switched off like Napster and the situation became more complicated from the judicial point of view as well. Instead of a single creator that all lawyers of big publishers and producers could point a finger at, they were suddenly faced with an anonymous crowd of ordinary people who shared files on the internet.

Amir Taaki's genius idea was based on using this technology to create a decentralized marketplace. The OpenBazaar app's entire database and function is "chopped" into small pieces and distributed within the network of users – just like a film that you download via torrents. OpenBazaar has no central server, so it cannot be switched off. Plus, it's open software which means that all the work its programmers and developers did is freely accessible. So, if somebody arrested or otherwise removed the people responsible for its development, it wouldn't change anything; the app would keep on working and anybody could work on its further development.

OpenBazaar became the first functional decentralized marketplace where sellers meet buyers directly without having to pay any charges and where nobody checks or authorizes their activities, collects information about them, or censors their trade. OpenBazaar is like a shipping center with unlocked doors that floats in the air, knows no state borders, where nobody is the boss and no trade inspection can close it.

An attentive reader surely feels like asking: if OpenBazaar is decentralized, who can guarantee that trade goes smoothly without fraud and if fraud takes place, are fraudsters punished? As we said in our earlier examples, in the case of sharing economy platforms (Uber, Airbnb), internet clubs (eBay, Taobao) or crypto markets (Silk Road, Dream Market), this was always the role of a central owner. They had the motivation and knowledge to set the rules correctly, enforce their compliance or resolve disputes – they provided law and order services.

OpenBazaar approached this challenge in two ways: it partly automated and partly outsourced law and order services. Thanks to this, their provision doesn't require the active participation of a central owner. The backbone of the institutional infrastructure is created by two tools: reputation systems and Bitcoin's Multisig contract. OpenBazaar's developers designed the former to work automatically without requiring the active participation of an arbiter. With the latter, they transferred conflict resolution services from a third party to a secondary market. Let's illustrate it with examples. This is how trade on OpenBazaar works:

Mathew, a fan of cryptocurrencies, finds the Parallel Polis store on OpenBazaar where they sell T-shirts with their logo. Mathew can see that Parallel Polis has several good ratings, so he orders two L-sized T-shirts without any worries. Polis gets an order notification and waits for another one which confirms that Mathew deposited the necessary amount of bitcoins to an account secured by a Multisig contract. After this, Polis sends two T-shirts to Mathew. Once he physically gets them, he enters his private key to the Multisig contract by which he confirms that the transaction was complete. Polis confirms the transaction and bitcoins are released from a secured account directly Parallel Polis' wallet. Finally, Mathew can post a review about Parallel Polis. The transaction is smooth, automatic, and without any required intervention from OpenBazaar.

But life isn't always that easy. What if Polis sends the wrong size and refuses to exchange the T-shirt or doesn't send anything? If Mathew relied on OpenBazaar, he would return to a centralized world where everything stands and falls at one single point. For these cases, OpenBazaar's developers enabled the outsourcing of conflict resolution services. They created an open market with mediators whom OpenBazaar has no control over and who compete amongst themselves in the effort to gain customers' trust. Such a system offers Mathew and Parallel Polis the opportunity to agree in advance how to resolve a potential dispute – they choose a mediator.

This is how it works in practice: before the transaction starts, Parallel Polis selects several acceptable mediators from whom Mathew selects the one he trusts. The selected mediator automatically gets the third Multisig contract key and should a conflict arise, he decides whether the Bitcoins should be returned to Mathew, sent to Parallel Polis or be split in half. This way OpenBazaar develops an open market of conflict resolution services that doesn't dependent on a central intermediary. Mediators compete with each other in several areas:

- Expertise: They specialize in different types of transactions: T-shirts, collectors' items, services…Some mediators refuse to get involved in some types of trade (e.g., with illicit substances or guns).
- Price: they may charge per unit or a percentage of the value of the order and their rates vary.
- Reputation: how many cases they resolved, clients' satisfaction, and the trust they gained.
- Licenses and diplomas: there are also mediators who act under their real name on OpenBazaar and list their real address and information about their practice in mediation.
- Rules: mediators establish rules before a contract is signed and they require compliance from both parties. The objective is a smooth transaction and to easily find out who was wrong if there's a dispute (for instance they want the seller to use shipment services with delivery tracking). They also compete in rules they apply for conflict resolution (how they assess evidence, how much time they give to respond, and what type of evidence they require).

OpenBazaar currently has a lot of mediators. One of them is Jacob Long, a lawyer from Florida, who offers expedited mediation in three cases: first, when the delivery is marked as delivered by the shipment service and the buyer doesn't confirm the delivery via the Multisig contract; second, if they don't confirm it within 10 days (20 days for international shipments) or in the case of a delivery without shipment tracking and third; if the seller doesn't mark the order as dispatched within one day from the moment when the buyer deposited bitcoins to a secured account. If rules are broken, he contacts the guilty party and if they fail to provide an explanation, the mediator will side with the second party. For other cases, Long gives the accused party 10 days to explain the problem from their perspective. During dispute resolution, he goes by the principle of prevailing evidence.

The combination of the Multisig contract with mediators significantly limits the fraudsters' opportunities to systematically steal from their partners, but this system also has its weak spots. It happened several times on OpenBazaar that there was a secret agreement between the seller and the selected mediator or when sellers even created a fake identity and acted as an independent mediator for themselves. This made them easily win any dispute (and sign two out of three Multisig contract keys).

The effort to solve this problem made developers launch the service of verified mediators. They use the verification application Keybase which maps social network accounts and can anonymously match the identity of the social network account's owner with that of a mediator on OpenBazaar. To become a verified mediator, one needs to prove that they have owned the existing accounts on social networks long enough. The aim is to put off quick new mediators from cheating. Verified mediators get a special badge and they can also back up their trustworthiness with a guarantee in the form of "drowned bitcoins" that are released in case they trick somebody.[326] Developers have also been working on a reputation system for mediators aimed at evaluating the speed, precision and fairness of their verdicts to replace external forums and discussions.[327]

OpenBazaar already has been functioning successfully for two years thanks to these tools. In this time, it has attracted 100 thousand users from more than 150 countries who act as "mini servers" and ensure the operation of the entire network. Although OpenBazaar is a non-censored market place with integrated Tor function, you won't find many illicit products there, such as drugs or guns (apart from air rifles or pen guns). The most frequently purchased items include: books, comic books, cigarettes, plant seeds, subscription to various internet services, posters, statues, or old video games.[328] You can also find more unconventional items such as unpasteurized goat's milk or collectors' items from the Nazi and North Korean army that are forbidden in some countries.

Open Bazaar can become an important tool for people from the developing world who live in dysfunctional state regimes with dysfunctional law and order services. Up to this day, most inhabitants of this planet have belonged to that group. No matter where they live, what language they speak, and what their social class is, OpenBazaar enables them to buy and sell anything without the involvement of a third party – e.g., a corrupt government eager to get its share.

OpenBazaar is the perfect example of progress without permission; progress that brings free market and good quality law and order services to places where people have to wait to see political reform. It's a smart tool for exporting quality institutions without the involvement of soldiers or bombers. You can live in a country where the judicial system doesn't work and the police are puppets in the hands of corrupt politicians and still get involved in the world's free market without having to pay any fees, fill in any forms, have to have a bank account or an ID. You just need to know basic math and have an internet connection.

OpenBazaar is a functional combination of various technologies: BitTorrent, the anonymizing Tor service, asymmetric encryption through the Bitcoin payment system and the related Multisig contract service as well as individual applications, such as Keybase. The result is a marketplace where no central authority is needed to operate the server, keep a trade database, resolve disputes, transfer money or regulate. It doesn't even require anybody to know the real identity of traders and buyers. All of this is either done by the user network or is no longer necessary. However, the merciless power of competition applies to this area too and we have yet to see if somebody comes up with a better combination of available technologies. The Particl.io. project is currently trying to do just that.

6.2 THE FUTURE OF TRADING – SMART CONTRACTS?

"Glassblowers will starve."

Stella Zázvorková

This quote comes from the iconic Czech film Pelíšky in a scene when a passionate communist, Bohuš Šebek (Miroslav Donutil) presents his family with a set of unbreakable plastic cups invented by a group of smart minds in the Polish People's Republic and his mother reacts by saying the above. Some believe that law and order providers will share the fate of glassblowers – judges and policeman will "starve". Only they won't be replaced by "smart minds from the Polish People's Republic" but by smart contracts.

If I wanted to sell smart contracts in a teleshopping program, I would name them Will Remover 2000. The aim of a smart contract is to remove the possibility for people to change their minds or consciously cheat during an agreed commercial transaction. Where people cannot cheat, no judges or policemen are needed. They are replaced by software capable of removing the will of the contractual parties. It automatically carries out the steps agreed in the contract without the need for a third person to step in. It works on the principle of an algorithm: "if X happens, Y follows". The best comparison (also used by Nick Szabo, the author of the idea of smart contracts) is to a vending machine.[329] You just need to insert coins, press the button corresponding to your desired product, and the machine carries out the operation automatically to give you a cup of hot coffee or a chilled soda can.*

The advantages of a smart contract can be best seen in a comparison with a traditional contract.

A couple of years ago, I became a huge fan of MMA. It's the first sport I enjoy watching without actively doing it. Once I bet with a friend on the legendary match between Khabib Nurmagomedov and Conor McGregor. I said McGregor would win with his left-hand shot and my friend bet on Nurmagomedov's skills to wrestle on the ground. We each bet €50 and we set the betting odds to 1:1. The question was how to seal the deal so that neither of us would withdraw after the match. Before smart contracts came, we had three options:

First, there was informal trust. We're good friends who trust each other. We know that the other one won't change his mind once he finds out his favorite didn't win. And if he did, we could spread unpleasant information about him among our common friends.

The second option was a formal contract. We could have written up an official contract, have it confirmed by a notary and if the other party wanted to withdraw, we could have simply turned to police and courts.

Finding an intermediary was the third option. We could have tried to find a platform that facilitates bets among friends. If it exists, we could have entered the details of our agreement and the amount of money we wanted to bet. Once the match was over, the platform would have decided who won and who gets the money. **

Smart contracts promise to be the fourth option. We enter our deal into a program without having to rely on trust, a formal contract, or an intermediary. One day after the match, the program checks the results on the internet and automatically sends money to the winner of the bet. Smart contracts are supposed to enable people to irrevocably commit to sticking to the deal they made with their business partner. The algorithm doesn't give them a choice. From the moment of signing the contract, everything should be automated and self-enforceable. Although intelligent contracts are an interesting idea, they haven't found a widespread practical application so far. There are two reasons for this: the robustness of blockchain and the code of a smart contract itself and the contact with the outside world.

---

* In reality Smart contracts are more automatic than vending machines. You can break a vending machine and steal its contents and they're often dependent on electricity from the nearest building. It isn't that easy with smart contracts, or at least it's their purpose to make it more difficult.

** In the case of the bet with my friend, I would use the first option, but I'm going to continue my search for the solution to the problem of cooperation between complete strangers in anonymous society; this is where smart contracts compete with the second and third option.

PROBLEM NUMBER 1: WHEN IS BLOCKCHAIN ROBUST ENOUGH?

People talk a lot about blockchain. But there's blockchain and then there's blockchain – blockchain alone as a technology isn't safe. It becomes safe when controlling it requires more and more "proof of work" and when the computing power that carries it out is distributed all over the world. To put it simply, the safety of a specific blockchain grows with its increasing decentralization. Today, the original blockchain (Bitcoin) is considered the safest.

Bitcoin is the oldest cryptocurrency and it is secured by the biggest amount of computing power. Each bitcoin transaction represents a perfect smart contract in the form of "Susan sent 1 bitcoin to Veronica." It's fully automated, verified by the user network, and self-enforceable. No police are needed for transferring bitcoins. This is why we can say that smart contracts that take place on the network really are safe – there's nobody who could cheat the network.

However, Bitcoin smart contracts have limitations related to their capacity and programming. Bitcoin has a limited script language which means the developers are restricted when writing their own programs and contracts on the network. Bitcoin smart contracts are generally very simple: they can be a transfer of bitcoins from one person to another or the already-mentioned Multisig contract which creates a secured account with three keys.

Canadian programmer Vitalik Buterin didn't like these limitations; he believed that Bitcoin technology has the potential to be friendlier to programmers and smart contract creators. So, in 2013, he composed a theoretical draft about how to improve Bitcoin and named it Ethereum. In 2014, he convinced investors and together with his team managed to collect $ 18 million in bitcoins.[330] He used the money to develop Ethereum and in 2015, a new blockchain was born. Unlike Bitcoin which was designed as a payment system, Ethereum aimed to be a network without a specific use. It offers broader possibilities and enables programmers and smart contract creators to apply more complex conditions and new functions.[331]

You can picture Ethereum as a big computer with parts scattered around the whole world that protects the network from "free-will" but comes at certain costs. The decentralized Ethereum computer is extremely slow; its overall computing power equals to that of the first smartphones from the 1990s.[332] This lack of speed buys us the security of decentralization. Just like in the case of Bitcoin, all Ethereum's transactions are announced to the entire user network that adds them to their own version of Ethereum. They're rewarded with ether – the local currency which serves as remuneration for carried out work and fuels the global computer. Rather than becoming a payment tool, ether's ambition is to become the fuel that enables the implementation of smart contracts. At the same time, it represents a share of the global computer network.*

---

* Two Slovaks who live in Switzerland launched a similar blockchain project called Decent. In 2016, they collected 5881 bitcoins through crowdfunding. Decent doesn't have the ambition to

What has Ethereum managed to do so far? Well, despite its advanced technology, not much. So far, we don't have any examples of commercially successful applications used by the masses that would do something completely new or at least overcome the way things have been done until now. In the abstract of his white paper, Buterin drafted several applications with the potential to work on the decentralized basis of smart contracts. There's the possibility to create a database which would capture the ownership of digital assets and financial tools (tokens), the ownership of some types of physical devices (smart property), or a possibility to carry out equity crowdfunding (ICO – Initial coin offering) or even manage an entire company (DAO).

The first attempt to apply DAO received a lot of attention and basically connected several applications into one (tokens, smart contracts, ICO). However, the name of this experiment wasn't very original – the authors named it after the concept itself: DAO – Decentralized autonomous organization, which would be like naming your company 'Company'. Perhaps this is why the first phase consisting in getting investors through ICO was very successful. Ethereum users invested \$120 million[333] into the network and received tokens which are like company shares.

The difference between DAO and a traditional holding company is that instead of a founders' agreement, DAO has a programmed code and supplier-consumer relationships are replaced with smart contracts. All company assets can be found on the Ethereum blockchain address. The result is an "idiot-proof" decentralized and autonomous company. If a client wants to approach DAO, they submit a proposal then token owners study it and vote on it. If they accept it, the conditions agreed upon with customers or suppliers are programmed into a smart contract that defines who is responsible for what and what their competences are. If several successful business transactions take place, the company gains profit which is divided between token owners according to their shares.

Things would have been great if DAO hadn't been attacked by hackers one month after it started operating and if they hadn't taken approximately \$50 million. When I say hacking, don't think of it as an attack on a server (Ethereum has no server); hackers merely found an error in the code of the smart contract which was behind the birth of DAO and, in accordance with the rules of blockchain, stole the tokens of DAO owners. It triggered a public discussion about whether Ethereum should agree that the attack didn't actually happen, which would mean taking the stolen tokens from the thieves and returning them to their original owners. In other words, the discussion was about something that most "blockchain advisors" deem impossible: changing the history of blockchain and consciously modifying it according to what seems to be 'more fair'.

This solution was implemented to a certain extent although a smaller section of the network refused it and created a 'branch' of the original blockchain and named it Ethereum Classic. The rest returned to their blockchain at the time

---

become a new currency but wants to provide innovative database services.

before the attack and continued as if nothing had happened. As I'm writing this, the current price of Ethereum is about 110 USD and 4 USD of Ethereum Classic. Based on that it's clear whose opinion was more important in the network. At the beginning of 2019, Ethereum Classic received another blow: it became the victim of "double payment". Somebody managed to take over more than 50% of the network's performance and spend one "ether classic" twice. This way the attackers earned $500 thousand.

The events really prove that not all blockchain is the same. Despite the fact that Ethereum is the second most valuable cryptocurrency (after Bitcoin), the network users managed to coordinate amongst themselves and change the history.

However, if blockchain manages to reach a high rate of decentralization and becomes difficult to control, smart contracts become really smart in comparison with their traditional alternatives. To illustrate it, let's compare the Multisig contract both on and off blockchain.

The Multisig contract outside blockchain is nothing new and many institutions offer it today – banks, financial houses, and notaries. The procedure is simple: you approach a trustworthy service provider with your business partner and an intermediary; you explain the terms of your contract to them and they give each one of you one key. The provider's role is to make sure that the contract is honored, so anytime two out of three parties turn up, they provide them with the contents of the secured account. Nevertheless, this service provider is only human. They may make mistakes (fail to notice that somebody gave them a falsified key) or intentionally cheat (steal the contents of the secured account without fulfilling the "2 out of 3 condition").

A contract on blockchain is etched in stone. Whatever happens, you only have access to a secured account if you have two out of three keys. Blockchain isn't a person like a banker or notary; it's a network of economically motivated users bound by cryptography, which ensures an automatic, safe, and self-enforceable contract implementation. In blockchain, no single person has privileged access and therefore nobody can deceive you or lie.

PROBLEM NUMBER 2: CONTACT WITH THE OUTSIDE WORLD

A smart contract is like a production line with robots. Everything is automated and secured (blockchain serves this purpose) except for one thing: somebody has to fill the dispensers with the material that circulates on the assembly lines. Blockchain alone can't do this. A smart contract requires knowledge about what's going on in the outside world. It needs to know who won – McGregor or Khabib? The information has to get to blockchain and if this is taken care of by a specific person or institution, the smart contract will no longer be so smart because its trustworthiness depends on the trustworthiness of the person responsible for uploading information to blockchain.

Some developers tried to address this problem by creating Oracle applications. In antiquity, oracles were places of prophetic predictions, interpretation of dreams, and revealing the will of gods. In the world of smart contracts, Oracle denotes applications capable of extracting information from the outside world and incorporating it into blockchain without the involvement of a specific person or institution. They employ decentralization and peer-to-peer technologies.

Oracle is an application that enables people to comment on real world phenomena. For instance, on who won the MMA match from the 6th of October. The objective of Oracle developers was to set up the application protocol in a way that even a group of egoists, fraudsters, or complete strangers could agree on the truth in the end. They set the voting rules in order to motivate people to tell the truth and prevent them from lying. Their recipe for success can be illustrated by the words of Nobel Laureate Thomas Shelling who in 1960 proposed a thought experiment in his famous book titled The Strategy of Conflict*:

"You are to meet somebody in New York City. You have not been instructed where to meet; you have no prior understanding with the person on where to meet; and you cannot communicate with each other. You are simply told that you will have to guess where to meet and that he is being told the same thing and that you will just have to try to make your guesses coincide"[334]

The point of the game is to find the place you expect others to expect that you expect that they expect you to come. For New York City, most people would agree that this place is Grand Central Station in Manhattan. The fact that most New Yorkers would agree on this place isn't the result of an objective truth etched in stone but rather the result of motivational settings and communication protocol. In a situation where people can't communicate and are supposed to agree on something, they look for an intuitive and obvious answer. Schelling referred to this as the focal point and later it became known as the Schelling point.

It was Shelling's focal point idea that Buterin used in the development of the first Oracle app called Schelling Coin. Later, other applications followed, such as TruthCoin or WITNET. How did they manage to ensure that people dispersed across the globe vote for the truth on blockchain and avoid lies? From a meta-perspective, the Oracle app has no way of finding out and verifying what the truth is. So, it considers what most decentralized voters (oracles) agree on to be the truth.

Now imagine you're an oracle in the TruthCoin app and you are supposed to vote on who won the MMA match on the 6th of October. If you vote the same way as the crowd, you get a financial reward. If you vote against the crowd, you face financial sanctions. What would you do? The safest way is to go with the crowd and vote for the truth because at this point, the truth represents a Shelling point just like in the example of Grand Central Station in Manhattan. This way

---

* Prize motivation: "for having enhanced our understanding of conflict and cooperation through game-theory analysis."

the circle is complete and allows external truth to enter the world of blockchain without the need for an intermediary.

Of course, a system set up like this immediately attracts fraudsters that attempt to cheat it. The easiest way of doing so is by creating a coalition of fraudsters and manipulating the vote on the truth. The best defense is having plenty of decentralized oracles across the globe; it makes it more difficult to coordinate fraud. Another mechanism that can make fraudsters' lives more complicated is a secret vote. Although a fraud coordinator can get many supporters and even bribe them, it's impossible for them to verify if they really voted as promised. They may promise to lie but, in the end, do what's most convenient – stick with the crowd and tell the truth. This way they benefit from the bribe as well as the reward for telling the truth – they become double agents.

Still, there are also charming fraudsters who do manage to get more and more supporters to cheat the application in a joint effort. This may trigger another protective mechanism: TruthCoin automatically modifies rewards and punishments according to how close the vote was. For instance, if 90% voted that Khabib won the MMA match (true), neither the financial reward nor the punishment would be of great significance. However, if a fan of McGregor attempts to bribe oracles into lying during the vote, the growing coalition of liars would also mean the increase of both: rewards for telling the truth and punishments for lying. If 40% of coordinated liars voted for McGregor, it would cost them quite a lot and the algorithm of TruthCoin would generously reward those who voted truthfully. This automatically creates a pressure that suppresses every attempt for coordinated fraud.

This is how Oracle apps can be used (and are used) to verify freely available information from the outside world for which a Shelling point can be easily found. Examples include sports results, election results, weather forecast, and other commonly known events and phenomena. For instance, betting agencies or prediction markets find it very useful when creating their smart contracts. However, Oracle app is hardly of any help in case of contracts where the required information from the external world is of a private nature and cannot be looked up on the internet.

Getting information from the outside world isn't the only problem – composing a smart contract can be a problem in itself. Its main advantage is supposed to be that it's written in the form of an explicit code: if A happens, B follows. Still, in the real world we're unable to capture all possible A scenarios in advance. Real world contracts are incomplete. It took economists almost two centuries to realize it and when they finally did in 2016, they were rewarded with a Nobel Prize for Economics (Oliver Hart and Bengt Holmström).*

The existence of companies, vertical integration, or employment relationships are the specific consequences of the world's complexity – it's impossible to cap-

---

* They got the Nobel Prize for creating new theoretical tools valuable to the understanding of real-life contracts and institutions, as well as potential pitfalls in contract design.

ture all its nuances in a natural language in which contracts are written. All of these institutions exist because we're unable to specify all possible future eventualities in contracts. Sometimes they're even impossible to describe in advance. Commercial law is full of principles, exemptions and mitigating circumstances that take this uncertainty and incompleteness into account and they cannot be easily programmed into a code. It requires a subjective assessment within each specific context. You cannot always program clarity into a business relationship; sometimes it's good to use good old common sense.

A smart contract between me and myself or how entrepreneurs do business thanks to our laziness

There aren't many economic jokes. Let me tell you one of the few that exist: two economists enter into a showroom with luxurious cars. When they stop by a red Ferrari, one of them says: "I want a car like this", and the other one replies: "Apparently you don't." Now you understand why there are so few economic jokes. The point of the joke lies within one basic economic concept – demonstrated preference.

Economists say that people's preferences are revealed by their actions and real decisions. If you want to know what people really want, look at what they buy or do instead of listening to what they say. People often claim they want something but do something else. They often say they want to eat a healthy diet, exercise regularly, and get rid of bad habits. But when things get real, they overindulge in bread, their only physical activity is avoiding the gym, and their only regular training is in chain-smoking.

As it tends to be, each problem creates a business opportunity. This is the origin of business ideas that help you bind your future "bad me" and let your present "determined me" decide. Thanks to such "self-binding" we can now enjoy reading The Hunchback of Notre-Dame because its author, Victor Hugo, was one of those who suffered from a very common condition: he did everything except for what he was supposed to do. His solution was to buy huge supplies of ink, change into his nightgown and get rid of all his other clothes. He had no other option but to write daily and as a result he wrote a 500 page-long book in a couple of months and even managed to meet the deadline for handing over the manuscript.

Speaking in today's terms, Victor Hugo concluded a smart contract with himself. In time t=0 he concluded a contract with Victor Hugo in time t=1. Several apps now exist that enable you to conclude a similar contract without having to get rid of your clothes or locking yourself at home.

The app Beeminder records and makes statistics of your progress in several areas (weight loss, exercise, work, studying, spending time on social media) and motivates you financially to complete your objectives. If you fail to do so, it costs you money you deposited as guarantee. The app can be connected with an automatic assessment device and the achieved result can be verified via GPS, smart watch, or apps (RunKeeper, MapMyFitness). In case of food, it uses photos with time and date. Another such platform is Stickk where you can choose an arbiter to check on how you progress with your objectives. On FatBet you can make a bet with your friends as to how much weight you'll lose. Wake N Shake only allows you to switch of your alarm in the morning once you have shaken the phone long enough. Pavlok, the smart bracelet, even sends an electric shock to your body in case you fail to complete your objective.

Entrepreneurs thus try to remove lifestyle problems that are becoming the subject of paternalistic state policies more and more. The above-mentioned apps are only used by a fraction of the population, but they would surely be more popular if the state implemented variable health insurance charges – people who lead a healthy lifestyle would pay less than those who don't exercise, make bad nutrition choices, and practice bad habits.

6.3 KLEROS: TWO HEADS ARE BETTER THAN ONE

Kleros is an application that attempts to shift the current way of writing and enforcing contracts as well as conflict resolution towards more decentralized alternatives.

Kleros is named after kleroterion – a randomizing device from Ancient Greece used to select citizens to court juries. In blockchain, Kleros is an app that selects and motivates anonymous free-time judges to analyze evidence and issue verdicts in the field of smart contracts. Selection and motivation are the two key concepts for Kleros. To fulfill them, Kleros was inspired by a judicial system that worked in Athens 2,500 years ago.

Judges were selected based on three principles: candidates had to apply voluntarily, their selection was random and they received a reward for their service. Kleroterion looked like a big stone machine that was fed special dice and its task was to randomly select jurors. Today we can carry out a randomized selection without major problems but this can't be said about motivating judges to issue fair verdicts, which is what the developers of Kleros decided to focus on.

Let me illustrate it with a practical example: Martin from Slovakia orders web design and development from Kai-Mook from Thailand and they draw up a smart contract on the Ethereum blockchain. They use a template for contracts concerning web design to which they insert specific information about the design and contents of the website as well as the deadline for its creation.* At the same time they use the Multisig service, choose Kleros as their mediator, and specify the details of mediation (the Kleros department will deal with any potential conflict, how many jurors they're willing to pay, and who will pay them – whoever loses the dispute or they split the costs).

When a conflict arises, three other characters enter the scene: Oxana from Ukraine, Habibuna from Kenya, and Dida from Brazil. They all have several things in common: they have signed up on Kleros at the department of Website Development; they have experience with HTML, CSS and JavaScript; and can spare several hours per week to earn some extra money. All three of them were selected randomly by the system when they activated the Kleros tokens. When resolving the conflict between Martin and Kai-Mook, they work individually because none of them knows who the other jurors are. Their work starts after receiving a message which goes something like this:

You were selected a juror for conflict resolution in the domain of website development. Click here to read the statements of both parties and here to download evidence. You have three days to study the case and issue your verdict.

When Oxana, Habibuna, and Dida start to analyze evidence, they can be sure that they'll be paid for their services in the form of fees that Martin and Kai-Mook committed themselves to paying upon signing their smart contract on Ethereum. They can be a little less sure when it comes to the special tokens of Kleros. They needed to activate them to apply for the resolution of the particular dispute. A potential judge first decides how many tokens they activate – the more tokens are activated, the higher the possibility of being selected. Once they've been selected by the randomizing system, their activated tokens are frozen until all jurors issue their verdict.

Oxana, Habibuna, and Dida have to decide whether Martin is telling the truth and Ki-Mook didn't deliver the website they agreed on or whether he's just refusing to pay for a job well-done.** Let's say that in the end it turned out that Martin was too critical and Kai-Mook did everything they agreed on. All three jurors supported the position of the supplier and the money is released from a secured account. Martin can still appeal and when he does, the conflict resolution will involve twice as many jurors + 1 (to make it an odd number). If Martin wants to appeal, he needs to be aware that Kleros will randomly select seven jurors each of whom have to be paid.

What happens to the frozen tokens of the three Kleros judges? They are released once the verdict is issued and judges either get them back or lose them – it all depends on whether they voted for the truth. Which verdict represents the

---

* Various companies now offer the services of creating templates for various types of smart contracts, eg., Aragon, OpenZeppelin or OpenLaw.
** There's also a third way the dispute can end: the jurors give the supplier one extra week to work on the website and decide afterwards.

truth? The one the majority votes for.* Just like the Oracle application, Kleros also uses a Shelling point. In their case, it's to ensure a fair verdict. If all jurors see the same statements and evidence and are equally interested in finding out the truth, they should all come to the same conclusion. The more jurors are involved in the resolution of a dispute, the higher the probability that the verdict will be truly fair.

This system, of course, doesn't ensure flawless justice. There's probably no judicial system in the world that can do that. Still, it ensures that jurors who don't study evidence properly, aren't experienced enough or don't care for justice are eventually penalized by gradually losing their tokens. On the contrary, those who do their job properly gradually gain new tokens which not only bring them financial rewards (tokens are an asset with a certain value and can be bought or sold) but also the possibility to participate in more disputes.

Another advantage of Kleros, in comparison with traditional courts, is the absence of communication. If jurors can communicate, they can also influence each other. The protocol of Kleros excludes this possibility, which results in a better use of the "crowd wisdom" and higher convergence to the truth.**

Kleros lets you set practically all parameters according to the type, complexity, and importance of the dispute. Individual parties can use a smart contract to agree in advance on the rules applicable to a potential dispute such as which department will be responsible for its resolution, what fees they're willing to pay, who will pay them, what the minimum number of jurors should be, what number of activated tokens will be required (the higher it is, the more experienced the jurors are), how much time jurors have to resolve the dispute, etc. There's a difference between solving a dispute about a badly programmed website and a dispute related to a trade worth millions that contains complex contracts. The fees depend on supply and demand. If the resolution of a conflict doesn't require significant expertise and there are enough jurors who could do it, the fees are low. In more sophisticated disputes, they can climb up to very high numbers.

Stable cryptocurrencies

There's is one main obstacle that keeps cryptocurrencies from spreading more widely: volatility. Cryptocurrencies change their value quite quickly and unpredictably; definitely faster than world currencies like the dollar or euro. This cannot be said for cryptocurrencies but a smart solution has been discovered for this problem. It's called stablecoin – a stable cryptocurrency.

---

* In case of non-binary disputes, the true value is within a certain range from the median.

** In old Jewish courts, jurors presented their verdicts and opinions consecutively, from the youngest and least experienced ones to those who had the most authority. It was supposed to prevent more experienced judges from influencing others.[A24]

There are two ways of creating stablecoin. The first one requires the establishment of a company which issues "crypto-meal vouchers". Traditional meal vouchers display the nominal value in euros and can be used in specific businesses while you can be sure that the value of a €4 meal voucher is for euros. The company Tether attempted to do something similar in the crypto world: create a crypto voucher with a fixed value against the dollar. You can exchange one tether for one dollar. How is it possible? The company committed itself to hold one USD on its bank account for each tether it issues and gets profit from fees only (like companies which issue traditional meal vouchers).

They say that there's beauty in simplicity but, in this case, simplicity also contains a certain risk. Although Tether has been here for quite a long time (in the crypto world context) – since 2014 –, there are quite serious concerns whether the company really has $2.5 billion on its account. This sum represents the value of Tether's currently circulating crypto vouchers. This solution may have reduced volatility but it also limited decentralization. This way of creating stablecoin erases the main advantage of cryptocurrencies – the absence of an intermediary you have to trust.

Then there's the second way of creating stablecoin where a centralized issuer of crypto vouchers no longer plays the main role – it's played by a decentralized network of "pawn shops" connected to the Ethereum blockchain and smart contracts. MakerDAO, one of the oldest Ethereum network companies, is behind the creation of this stablecoin.

In December 2017, MakerDAO launched a new cryptocurrency called DAI the value of which was firmly tied to the dollar. The DAI stablecoin is a perfect example of crypto economics. Its authors used a lot of cryptographic knowledge combined with economic knowledge and created a stable ecosystem where everybody is motivated to contribute so that the value of one DAI approaches the value of one dollar as closely as possible.

How does DAI work? As I said, it's a system of something like decentralized pawn shops where you can deposit ether and pawn it with the help of smart contracts. Just like in traditional pawn shops, you get a loan for your collateral but instead of dollars, they pay you in the DAI cryptocurrency. Why would somebody do that?

Imagine that you own 20 coins of ether with a total value of $3000. It's time for you to declare your taxes and you realize that you have to pay an unexpectedly high tax to the state. Unfortunately, you don't have enough cash because you invested all your money into your business. At the same time, you don't want to sell your ether because you believe that its value will increase. Thanks to DAI, this isn't a problem. You can take your 20 ether coins and lock them in a decentralized pawn shop within the Ethereum network where you take a loan in the DAI cryptocurrency. You can pay your taxes with it because it's de facto dollars. If your financial administration doesn't accept cryptocurrencies, you can simply exchange DAI for dollars at a safe rate with a value of 1:1.* Once your cash-flow increases and you manage to save some money, you can use it to buy DAI again at the rate of 1:1 and use it to pay off your loan in the decentralized pawn shop which will give you your 20 ether coins back.

You can use DAI not only to pay your taxes but for everything else you can do with euros or dollars – send it to somebody, lend it, pay for services, buy food, invest, or buy other cryptocurrencies. DAI looks like dollars, has the same value, and can be used for the same purposes. Thanks to DAI, the American FED felt what it is like to have a competitor in issuing dollars for the first time.

How come DAI steadily maintains its value against the dollar in the absence of a central manager who guarantees or balances its value? Instead of such a person, DAI relies on people who want to earn easy money. When the value of DAI drops below one dollar, it's very easy to bring DAI into a decentralized pawn shop and pay off the debt with a discount, which gets you your guarantee back in the form of ether. What discount are we talking about? Let's say you deposit ether in the value of $1,500 in such a pawn shop and you take a loan of 1,500 DAI which allows you to pay your taxes. If, after certain time, the value of one DAI goes below $0.9 you can buy 1,500 DAI for $1,350 and then exchange it for your ether in the original value of $1,500. You earn $150 (minus interest charged by the pawn shop). At the same time, DAI gets out of the system, supply decreases and this gradually leads to the increase of their price against the dollar until the price of one DAI approaches one dollar again.

The same principle (only the other way around) also works when the price of DAI gets over the limit of one dollar. In that case, it's profitable to deposit your ether in a pawn shop, withdraw DAI and exchange them for dollars at a good price. This increases the supply of DAI which pushes the price down.

It's quite easy to balance deviations in the prices of DAI against the dollar and the related self-regulating mechanisms work well. The problem gets more complicated when changes occur in the price of the guarantee in the pawn shop – the price of ether. While it goes up, everything is fine; from the point of view of the decentralized pawn shop, your guarantee is safer and it enables you to borrow even more DAI. The problem appears when the prices of ether start to decrease. That's when your debt ratio in the pawn shop increases. If there's a more significant drop, the value of ether in the pawn shop can get lower than the borrowed DAI itself. In such a situation, the debtor can be tempted to forfeit the pawned ether and never pay off their loan. That's why the protocol motivates people not to borrow 100% of the value from the pawn shop but rather just a smaller

---

* The exchange rate at the time of writing this book: 1 DAI = 0,989726 USD.

percentage depending on how big of a risk they're willing to take. They risk losing their pawned ether.

The smart contract of decentralized pawn shops is set so that when the value of ether drops and approaches the limit when the pawned ether should have the same value as the value of the loan, an opportunity opens for others to buy the pawned ether. Those who buy it earn money and those who have deposited it there and failed to pay off their debt lose money and the decentralized pawn shop gets rid of the risk. The risk of buying off is the reason why the debt ratio against pawned ether varies in the ecosystem, however, it generally moves around 60% of the dollar value of ether. It means that if you deposit ether in the value of $1,000, on average you can borrow approximately 600 DAI. This is because you want to have some time to "come" to the pawn shop and pay off your debt in case the value of ether decreases without giving others the chance to buy off your pawned asset.

A system set this way is quite resistant against the drop in the value of ether. Unless we talk about extreme conditions (e.g., the value of ether decreases by 50% in 10 seconds), everything should run smoothly. The recent past has proven this well: from the end of 2018 **until now** the price of ether dropped from $1,400 to $130 yet the value of DAI has remained close to 1 dollar.

This way of creating stablecoin has way more potential than the first one. It doesn't require maintaining trust towards the issuer of crypto vouchers and monitoring if they have sufficient money on their account. On the contrary, the DAI stablecoin is a part of blockchain with all the advantages of decentralization. In addition, new stablecoin systems are currently being developed and they'll make it possible to deposit various cryptocurrencies in a pawn shop and connect the value of stablecoin to other popular currencies like the euro or Swiss franc.

6.4 CONCLUSION – ARE YOU AGAINST US IF YOU DON'T DECENTRALIZE?

"We reject: kings, presidents, and voting. We believe in: rough consensus and running code."

MIT professor Dave Clark, one of the many fathers of the internet, 1992

Some may have at least subconsciously substituted the descriptive terms "decentralization" and "centralization" with the prescriptive terms "good" and "evil". However, this is far from being black and white. Decentralization also has its disadvantages and centralization can be the optimal solution in some situations.

You don't always want a service without an owner or a boss – for instance, when the service is only in its developmental stage and you need to quickly react to a fast-changing environment or make a lot of executive decisions.

We shouldn't forget that decentralization also comes at certain costs. If you want a decentralized solution, it's important to set the service as correctly as possible in the first step because any further changes in the rules and parameters are difficult to make. It's sensible to accept these as well as other costs of decentralization only under specific conditions – mostly when the costs of centralized solutions increase. This can happen for several reasons.

I wrote about one of them in the first chapter. Progress without permission can trigger strong resistance from those who issue permission. Sharing economy platforms (Uber, Airbnb, PayPal, eBay) already went through it and social networks are going through it now (Facebook, Twitter) as they are considered to be the causes of problems faced by democracy and in the future it may concern other platforms and internet clubs. In such cases, the presence of a center is problematic because it gives state authorities a specific person to interrogate, accuse and arrest. This doesn't apply for decentralized solutions which are the better option in such cases.

Nowadays, basically all centralized internet services or apps have their decentralized version or one that is being developed:

Instead of Facebook there's DiasporaFoundation or Sapien.network.

Instead of Twitter there's Mastodon.social or the undeletable memo.cash.

Instead of YouTube there's D.tube.

Instead of Wikipedia there's Everipedia.

Instead of Amazon and eBay there's OpenBazaar.

Instead of Chrome there's Brave.

Instead of iTunes and Spotify there's LBRY.

Instead of Uber there's SnagRide or Arcade City.

Instead of Airbnb there's CryptoCribs Bee Token or PopulStay.

Instead of Medium and different blogs there's BlockPress or Honest.cash.

Instead of betting offices there are decentralized prediction markets Augur, Gnosis or Stox.

Instead of centralized pawn shops there are their decentralized versions Bisq and Hodl Hodl.

Instead of traditional insurance companies there's Etherisc.

Instead of cloud services there are Siacoin, Filecoin or Storj.

Despite the numerous decentralized alternatives and solutions, I don't think that we'll witness a big decline for their centralized competitors anytime soon. Centralization has its advantages when it comes to management and so far, nothing has indicated that states are preparing for draconian repressions or that an Orwellian revolution is taking place on the internet. Still, I think it's excellent that decentralized alternatives exist, that somebody is working on their improvement, and that they're ready just in case politicians go crazy. They constitute an important back-up plan if things go wrong and also lower the probability that they would go bad at all. Politicians now have to count with the possibility that a "new world" is ready and people can move there if they please. This world has more and more functional elements that create its functional institutional infrastructure. Imagine a combination of OpenBazaar, Kleros, and Bitcoin. This is how we get a decentralized service of conflict resolution on a decentralized marketplace that uses a decentralized currency and payment system.

The last long-term vulnerable spot is in package delivery – a point where the digital world meets the physical one. But they say that there's a solution to this as well although it remains only theoretical for now.

A group of university scientists from Ontario and Quebec designed an anonymizing system for delivery services called Lelantos that uses the principles of Tor for the anonymization of package delivery. In this proposal, delivery takes place through a network of shipment companies while each of them knows only two bits of information about the delivery: whether it was delivered or sent further. Nobody in the delivery network has complete information about the route and the number of nodes the package will go through on its journey. Asymmetric encryption and smart contracts are used in communication and commands. Theoretically, the system enables anonymous delivery where it's practically impossible to match the buyer with the vendor. Breaking the anonymous delivery would require the coordination of all members of the delivery chain who would have to meet and put their partial information together.[335] By members of the delivery chain I not only mean drivers in vans full of packages who circle around neighborhood streets but also drones which deliver packages from above the rooftops.

Are dead drops the future of the black market?

Some darknet trade analysts say that crypto markets (centralized and decentralized) aren't necessarily the best way of doing trade on the internet. They argue that "one on one" trade is beginning to spread. Dedicated platforms with publicly displayed goods aren't the place of first contact. Instead, this takes place in a secret forum or discussion room where vendors and buyers meet and exchange their contact details. They initiate their conversation with an encrypted chat application (like Signal or Telegram).

This way a seller doesn't have to worry about somebody hacking the crypto market, losing their e-shop, or that the police will discover the server and they might lose their freedom. Also, it's no longer an issue if the crypto market operators pull an exit scam. Customers also see advantages in it: they don't have to install Tor and take into consideration a multitude of security measures. On the downside, there's no objective way of knowing the reputation of both parties and using escrow services isn't easy either.

This kind of "one on one" trade often uses the so-called dead drop delivery. Wikipedia defines it as a "method used to pass items or information between two individuals using any hidden location, such as a loose brick in a wall, a (cut-out) library book, or a hole in a tree, although a cut-out device is often used."[336] This method is starting to be used in one-on-one trade. The main advantage is that the customer doesn't have to provide their address or name. They only receive instructions about the hiding place of their purchased goods and vendors don't need to go to the post office or get in touch with shipment companies. They hide the packages in several locations and send their customers information about their whereabouts. This speeds up the entire process and customers don't have to wait for the delivery. However, the trade must take place within the same city or region.

Dead drops turn entire public areas into a delivery system, the functioning of which requires less information and fewer meetings and with that it also brings lower risk. This area is also subject to innovation and today dead drops can contain mini Bluetooth transmitters that make their location easier to find. Customers need a special app that picks up the signal and once the user has signed-up they enter a code that leads them to their package.[337]

CONCLUSION — REFLECTIONS

"Technologies lead, politicians just follow."

F. Braun

CONCLUSION – REFLECTIONS

WHAT THIS BOOK WASN'T ABOUT

In one of the introductory quotes to this book, Milton Friedman says that the internet is going to be one of the major forces for reducing the role of government. I'm not that optimistic. I don't know how it will all turn out. Internet technologies certainly have the potential to bring competition to areas which were monopolized by the state, but they can also become a tool the state can use to monitor its citizens – we're seeing the first signs of this in China and other countries. Not to mention that internet content requires physical – offline – infrastructure for its functioning. The state can reach this physical infrastructure with armed police and monitor its use.

These are two dystopian scenarios, but I mention them because I don't want anybody to interpret this book as futuristic. I'm not announcing the arrival of society which is free thanks to the internet. I don't know how big the role of the state will be in the future. This book merely highlights one important fact: the internet has made many of the arguments in favor of state intervention less relevant. It doesn't mean there will be a free society. It just means that it's more possible than it used to be.

This book isn't a crystal ball – it's a hammer. You can use it to crush arguments of those who are in favor of expanding the role of the state in society. If somebody brings up information asymmetry, public goods, or other market failures in a discussion, you can ask them whether they have heard about sharing economy, crowdfunding, cryptocurrency, or internet clubs. There is no need to question their ethical, political, or philosophical beliefs. No matter what their idea of the correct ratio between state and market is, internet technologies should shift it towards the market because internet technologies make it work better than they thought (no matter what they thought).

This text can also help with interpreting the future. If we experience an increase in the influence of the state in society, we can be almost sure that it wouldn't be because of market failures that noble politicians are trying to fix but rather as a result of the state's failure because somebody used it to increase their wealth or political power.

If I really had to guess what the future will bring, I would be carefully optimistic. The internet has, to a large extent, been the space of progress without permission. If it stays this way, we can expect to see new areas where internet entrepreneurs replace failing politicians.

One of these areas could be providing law and order services beyond the scope of business relationships. We didn't mention criminal law in the third chapter. In this area of law, we talk about the investigation and punishment of crimes where there's no consensual relationship established in advance, which is why it leaves a big space for innovation through internet technologies. I'm not aware of any widespread applications, platforms or internet clubs that directly tackle crime in the physical world. As an exception I could state a Slovak application called HAKA, which helps identify and report stolen cars.*

IF YOU DON'T LIKE IT, MOVE TO SOMALIA!

"We will create a civilization of the mind in cyberspace. May it be more humane and fair than the world your governments have made before."[338]

Perry Barlow

Critics ask those who call for freer society where the state plays a minimum or zero role to move to Somalia. They say they'll find their promised land with an absent state there.** Who knows if Piere Omidyar (founder of eBay), Peter Thiel (co-founder of PayPal), Travis Kalanick (co-founder of Uber), Satoshi Nakamoto (Bitcoin creator), or Amir Taaki (author of the idea of OpenBazaar) had to listen similar "recommendations". All these gentlemen claim to be libertarians or at least it can be inferred from their written works. In their endeavor to live a freer life they didn't decide to move to Somalia. Unlike 16th century settlers, they didn't have to cross the ocean and look for a new world to escape an old, institutionally rigid Europe either.

These modern adventurers discovered and settled a completely new world – the digital world of the internet which represented a green pasture without institutions where they could organize their lives according to their own principles and establish their own game rules and regulations. New digital companies were established with the explicit consent and in direct competition with other adventurers. It was a place of progress without permission, without bosses or censorship.

Modern adventurers didn't mind that offline society got stuck and is balancing on the edge. There are countries where nothing changes (better scenario) or where populists come to power (worse scenario). In 2019, Andrej Danko, who was then the Speaker of the National Council of Slovakia, said: "Democracy is

---

* The topic of criminal law is one of the most difficult ones in economic and political literature that analyzes the possibilities of stateless societies. The ways of privately provided law and order services in criminal law are mentioned by several authors but these are mostly just hypothetical constructs.[A25]

** Critics argue that society without state is poor and life in it is dangerous. By using Somalia as an example, they achieve the opposite. Comparing the wealth and safety of the western world with Somalia is intellectually imprecise. If we want to isolate (at least to certain extent) the influence of the absence of state on Somalian society, we need to compare it with other similar African societies where it is present. Several academics did just that and they reached a conclusion that surprised critics: the absence of state in Somalia brought improvements in many well-being indicators and its people are doing better than their neighbors.[A26]

CONCLUSION — REFLECTIONS

good but at the end of the day somebody has to say who has to obey and who has to work… I would like to see the state govern with a firmer hand."

We are much better off in the online world. It may not be a perfect place, but it has one big advantage: you're free to say: "No, thank you". You're free to choose between various providers of different regulations, public goods, and law and order services that exist in digital communities where hundreds of millions of people use the internet to find accommodation, shop, travel, work and cooperate. This institutional infrastructure required no legislative intentions, no votes of the parliament and no signature from a president. It was progress without permission.

In this sense, a parallel can be drawn between the arrival of the internet and the rise of dissident movements in the former socialist Czechoslovakia. In 1978, Václav Benda described the rise of this parallel society in his legendary essay. He explained that the aim of dissidents shouldn't be to get involved in cosmetic modifications of socialism nor openly try for a radical revolution.* He proposed a third way: he suggested that people combine their efforts and gradually create parallel structures capable of performing the essential duties and functions that the state fails to provide or at least supplement the functions that are being partially provided by the state and humanize them.

Benda called for the creation of a parallel society that offered a parallel culture, education, information, economy, and civic institutions in socialist Czechoslovakia where the state had a monopoly on all these areas.

The internet appeared 40 years later and with it came the parallel structures in all the above-stated areas. It's an interesting coincidence that Benda graduated from theoretical cybernetics at Charles University which was a discipline that stood behind the arrival of the internet.

Václav Benda's message is now spread through an association called Parallel Polis. You can find its branches in Prague and Bratislava. Parallel Polis claims that it doesn't enter into direct conflict with state power, it does everything it is required to do but also tries to organize itself according to its own rules, examine new possibilities of social order and parallel financial, education, and communication systems. You no longer need to move to Somalia; Parallel Polis will do just fine.

---

* This dilemma appears in practically every movement which aims to bring a social change. Should we try for a radical change or take gradual steps that require compromise?

CONCLUSION – REFLECTIONS

TUTORIAL FOR A BENEVOLENT RULER

"The argument for liberty is [...] an argument against all exclusive, privileged, monopolistic organizations, against the use of coercion to prevent others from trying to do better."[339]

Friedrich Hayek

If somebody gets to the steering wheel of the state and wants to help the companies, technologies, applications, and adventurers this book talks about, what should they do? The answer is: not much, it will suffice not to ban them. They don't need any special care, subsidies, or support. On the contrary, it could paradoxically harm them. All they need is an opportunity to compete with other players on the market including the state itself. If there's such a thing as good state, it's a state you aren't afraid to compete with.

When people get used to smart regulations on Airbnb or Uber, when they get used to addressing the need of local public goods through crowdfunding, and when they get used to conflicts on eBay or Taobao being resolved fairly within a couple of days, it will, after all, also help the state and its public services.

Most politicians will probably refuse this positive influence of competition at first and find millions of arguments why they should have no competition. It isn't surprising. A local baker would be of the same opinion thinking they should be the only one who produces bread on their street. They've been here for many generations, using the same recipe and people have always liked their bread. But a system as a whole needs competition. Competition motivates better performance and enables us to discover how we can improve things. Both the baker and the state need competition.

Today it seems unimaginable that the state would give up the monopoly in some areas and enable competition. Just like 500 years ago, Queen Elisabeth couldn't imagine that people in England could belong to various churches, not go to church every week, and pray from anything other than the Bible selected by the state. This is why she adopted the Act of Uniformity in 1558, in which she banned all of that. A few decades ago, it seemed impossible that somebody would systematically produce their own regulations impacting millions of people from different countries and continents who don't know one another. It was also difficult to imagine that people could collect money themselves and use it for public projects and it seemed extremely unlikely that there would one day be private platforms with their own detective offices that resolve tens of millions of disputes yearly and provide law and order services. Today it's all happening and nobody knows what the role of the state will be in 500 years' time.

CONCLUSION – REFLECTIONS

IF I HAD TO...

When one of my friends heard about the arguments used in this book, he asked me several excellent questions:

"But surely there are some good state regulations that the private sector can't provide?"

If I had to state one state regulation that is necessary, it would be the regulation of politicians and officials. A strict regulation of their rights, capabilities and decision-making is essential. It's the pillar of freedom in society. Luckily for us, such regulations are in place today (to certain extent). They include the constitution, which limits the power of the state, and the principle that public officials cannot do anything which isn't explicitly permitted in their job. It seems to me that lately less and less attention has been paid the topic of public sector regulations even though failure in the form of information asymmetry is ever present and obvious in the public sector. Let's forget about the regulation of entrepreneurs for a while at least and let's talk about how to better regulate politicians, officials, and the entire public sector.

"In your opinion, which are the public goods people don't contribute to enough?"

If I had to name one public good we definitely need more of, it would be the willingness to fight for freedom. All it takes is to make your voice heard and object if a politician decides to usurp a part of people's private lives and toss it into the political arena. No state can provide this public good which is logical because it stands on the other side of the barricade. Nevertheless, it's a very important public good because if people aren't willing to provide it their society will sooner or later experience problems.

"Isn't the state the most successful provider of law and order in the history of mankind after all?"

If I had to name the most successful provider of law and order, I would say it's God. He adopted the ten commandments Moses brought from Mount Sinai. It contained ten basic rules that most people live by these days. In order to enforce them, God employed a lot of policemen and jurors with supernatural powers who see to their compliance and punish those who break them. This law and order provider lasted longer than any other and nobody managed to conquer his kingdom. You say you don't believe in the existence of God who sent two stone plates to Moses and that we would know that we shouldn't kill and steal even without him? Well, I don't believe the fairytale that without the state we wouldn't have law and order services or that society wouldn't exist without the state.

CONCLUSION – REFLECTIONS

REFERENCE

SHARING ECONOMY AND INFORMATION ASYMMETRY

1. Mesoudi, A. et al. (2013) The Cultural Evolution of Technology and Science, Cultural Evolution https://www.researchgate.net/publication/300606222_The_Cultural_Evolution_of_Technology_and_Science , Nelson, R.R. (1994) The Co-evolution of Technology, Industrial Structure, and Supporting Institutions, Industrial and Corporate Change, Volume 3, Issue 1, 1 January 1994, Pages 47–63, https://academic.oup.com/icc/article-abstract/3/1/47/741092

2. Anderson, D. (2013) The Short, Contentious History of the Gurney Cab Company in San Francisco, FoundSF http://www.foundsf.org/index.php?title=The_Short,_Contentious_History_of_the_Gurney_Cab_Company_in_San_Francisco

3. Carriage Men Protest (1890) San Francisco Morning Call newspaper, Vol 80, No. 110, 18. September 1890, Page 3, available online at California Digital Newspaper Collection https://cdnc.ucr.edu/cgi-bin/cdnc

4. Akerlof, G. A. (1970), The Market for" Lemons": Quality Uncertainty and the Market Mechanism, The Quarterly Journal of Economics, Vol. 84, No. 3, August 1970, Pages 488-500, https://www2.bc.edu/thomas-chemmanur/phdfincorp/MF891%20papers/Ackerlof%201970.pdf

5. Stiglitz, J.E. (1997) Information and the Change in the Paradigm in Economics, Nobel Lecture, ONLINE: https://www.nobelprize.org/uploads/2018/06/stiglitz-lecture.pdf

   Wright, J. D. (2012) "The Antitrust/Consumer Protection Paradox: Two Policies at War with Each Other," Yale Law Journal 121, no. 8 (2012): n20

6. McLaughlin, P. a Sherouse, O. (2017) Regulatory Accumulation since 1970 https://www.mercatus.org/publications/regulation/regulatory-accumulation-1970

7. Niskanen, JR. (2017) Bureaucracy and Representative Government. New York: Routledge, pp. 251, ISBN 9781351530415, ONLINE: https://www.taylorfrancis.com/books/9781351530415

8. Arrow, K. (1974) The limits of organization, W. W. Norton & Company; 1st edition

9. LYTTON, D. T. (2013) Kosher Certification as a Model of Private Regulation: Regulation 27, pp. 24-27, ONLINE: https://object.cato.org/sites/cato.org/files/serials/files/regulation/2013/9/regv36n3-4n.pdf

   LYTTON, D. T. (2013) Kosher: Private Regulation in the Age of Industrial Food. Massachusetts: Harvard University Press, pp. 240, ISBN 9780674072930, ONLINE: https://www.amazon.com/Kosher-Private-Regulation-Industrial-Food/dp/0674072936

10. Caplan, B. (2018) The cast against education. New Jersey: Princeton University Press, pp. 416, ISBN 9780691174655

11. Hodges, G. R. G. (2008) Taxi! A Social History of the New York City Cabdriver. Baltimore: The Johns Hopkins University Press, pp. 225, ISBN 9780801885549

CONCLUSION – REFLECTIONS

Schneider, H. (2017) Creative Destruction and the Sharing Economy:Uber as Disrtuptive Innovation. Cheltenham: Edward Elgar Pub, pp. 160, ISBN 9781786433428

12   Rasmussen, W. D. a kol. (1976) A SHORT HISTORY OF AGRICULTURAL ADJUSTMENT: Agriculture Information Bulletin NO. 391, pp. 21, ONLINE: http://naldc.nal.usda.gov/download/CAT87210025/PDF

13   Gelder, L. (1996) Medallion Limits Stem From the 30's: The New York Times May 11, 1996, pp. 1001023, ONLINE: http://www.nytimes.com/1996/05/11/nyregion/medallion-limits-stem-from-the-30-s.html

14   NYCITYCAB.COM, (2018) ONLINE: https://nycitycab.com/Business/TaxiMedallionList.aspx

15   Taxi Services Regulation and Competition (2007) OECD: Policy Roundtables, pp. 251, ONLINE: https://www.oecd.org/regreform/sectors/41472612.pdf

16   Zuylen-Wood, S. (2015) The Struggles of New York City's Taxi King: Bloomberg Businessweek August 27, 2015, ONLINE: https://www.bloomberg.com/features/2015-taxi-medallion-king/

17   Hernandez, R. a Choi, D. (2018) The rise and fall of New York City's „Taxi King" who reportedly agreed to cooperate with the government as a potential witness against longtime business partner Michael Cohen: Business Insider, May 23, 2018, ONLINE: http://www.businessinsider.com/nyc-taxi-king-rise-fall-2017-8/#medallion-prices-skyrocket-for-a-time-3

18   Norenzayan, A. (2014) Big gods: How Religion Transformed Cooperation and Conflict. New Jersey: Princeton University Press, pp. 264, ISBN 978-0691151212, ONLINE: https://www.amazon.com/Big-Gods-Religion-Transformed-Cooperation/dp/B00K56U0Z4

19   Ensminger, J. (1997) Transaction Costs and Islam: Explaining Conversion in Africa, Vol. 153, No. 1, The New Institutional Economics Religion and Economics (March 1997), pp. 4-29 ONLINE: https://www.jstor.org/stable/40752982?seq=1#page_scan_tab_contents

20   Greif, A. (2004) Contract Enfoceability and Economic Institutions in Early Trade: The Maghribi Traders' Coalition. The American Economic Review, Vol. 83, No. 3, pp. 525 – 548, ONLINE: https://web.stanford.edu/~avner/Greif_Papers/1993%20Greif%20AER%201993.pdf

21   Munger, M. C. (2018) Tomorrow 3.0: Transaction Costs and the Sharing Economy (Cambridge Studies in Economics, Choice, and Society). Cambridge: Cambridge University Press, pp. 190, ISBN 978-1108447348

22   Munger, M. C. (2018) Tomorrow 3.0: Transaction Costs and the Sharing Economy (Cambridge Studies in Economics, Choice, and Society). Cambridge: Cambridge University Press, pp. 190, ISBN 978-1108447348

23   Heller, N. (2017) Is the gig economy working? The New Yorker, May 15, 2017, ONLINE: https://www.newyorker.com/magazine/2017/05/15/is-the-gig-economy-working

24   Nevarez, G. (2016) Immigrant Families Benefiting from Home-Sharing Economy, Study Finds: NBCNEWS, ONLINE: https://www.nbcnews.com/news/latino/immigrant-families-benefiting-home-sharing-economy-study-finds-n692836

Ghosh, S. (2017) Uber in London has become a war between white working-class cabbies and non-white immigrants: Business Insider, Jul 4, 2017, ONLINE: http://uk.businessinsider.com/uber-london-war-immigration-2017-7

25 Murillo, D. (2017) When the sharing economy becomes neoliberalism on steroids: Unravelling the controversies: Technological Forecasting and Social Change, Volume 125, pp. 66-76, ONLINE: https://www.sciencedirect.com/science/article/pii/S0040162517307072

26 Eckhardt, G. M. (2015) The Sharing Economy Isn't About Sharing at All: Hardward Business Review, January 28, 2015, ONLINE: https://hbr.org/2015/01/the-sharing-economy-isnt-about-sharing-at-all

27 Yan, J. (2017) China's Booming Sharing Economy: Foreign Affairs, November 9, 2017, ONLINE: https://www.foreignaffairs.com/articles/china/2017-11-09/chinas-booming-sharing-economy

O'Marah, K. (2017) WeWork and Meetup: Uberization For Demand Sensing: Forbes, November 30, 2017, ONLINE: https://www.forbes.com/sites/kevinomarah/2017/11/30/wework-and-meetup-uberization-for-demand-sensing/#5d5ca55a7945

28 Murillo, D. (2017) When the sharing economy becomes neoliberalism on steroids: Unravelling the controversies: Technological Forecasting and Social Change, Volume 125, pp. 66-76, ONLINE: https://www.sciencedirect.com/science/article/pii/S0040162517307072

29 Munger, M. C. (2018) Tomorrow 3.0: Transaction Costs and the Sharing Economy (Cambridge Studies in Economics, Choice, and Society). Cambridge: Cambridge University Press, pp. 190, ISBN 978 -1108447348

30 Sahlins, M. (1972) Stone Age Economics. Chicago: Aldine Atherton, pp. 348, ISBN 0-202-01098-8, ONLINE: https://libcom.org/files/Sahlins%20-%20Stone%20Age%20Economics.pdf

31 Cook, C. a kol. (2019) The Gender Earnings Gap in the Gig Economy: Evidence from over a Million Rideshare Drivers, pp. 62, ONLINE: https://web.stanford.edu/~diamondr/UberPayGap.pdf

32 Hall, J. (2016) The Effects of Uber's Surge Pricing: A Case Study, ONLINE: http://1g1uem2nc-4jy1gzhn943ro0gz50.wpengine.netdna-cdn.com/wp-content/uploads/2016/01/effects_of_ubers_surge_pricing.pdf

33 Brodeur, A. a Nield, K. (2016) Has Uber Made It Easier to Get a Ride in the Rain?: IZA No. 9986, pp. 28, ONLINE: http://ftp.iza.org/dp9986.pdf

34 Tanz, J. (2014) How Airbnb and Lyft Finally Got Americans to Trust Each Other," Wired, April 23, 2014, http://www.wired.com/2014/04/trust-in-the-share-economy/

35 Horton, J. J. (2017) Labor Market Equilibration: Evidence from Uber, ONLINE: https://www.semanticscholar.org/paper/Labor-Market-Equilibration-%3A-Evidence-from-Uber-Horton/2e668481068d50e22181ba8226ca586aa7fae2f6

36 Tabarrok, A. a Cowen, T. (2015) The End of Asymmetric Information, Cato-unbound, ONLINE: https://www.cato-unbound.org/2015/04/06/alex-tabarrok-tyler-cowen/end-asymmetric-information

37 Demsetz, Harold (1969) "Information and Efficiency: Another Viewpoint," Journal of Law and Economics: Vol. 12 : No. 1 , Article 2.

38 Mises, L. (1979) Economic Policy: Thoughts for Today and Tomorrow. Chicago: Regnery/Gateway, pp. 108, ISBN 978-1-933550-01-5, ONLINE: https://mises.org/library/economic-policy-thoughts-today-and-tomorrow

39 Olson, M. (2008) Vzestup a pád národů (The Rise and Decline of Nations): Ekonomický růst, stagflace a společenská rigidita.Nové Město: Liberální institut, pp. 251, ISBN 8086389516

Buchanan, J. M. (2003) Public Choice: Politics Without Romance: Policy, Spring 2003, ONLINE: http://www.montana.edu/hfretwell/documents/332/buchananpublicchoice.pdf

CONCLUSION – REFLECTIONS

40   Stigler, G. J. (1971) The Theory of Economic Regulation: The Bell Journal of Economics and Management Science, Vol.2, No. 1, pp. 3-21, ONLINE: https://www.jstor.org/stable/3003160

41   Wyman, K. M. (2013) Problematic Private Property: The Case of New York Taxicab Medallions, Yale Journal on Regulation, Volume 30, Article 4, ONLINE: http://digitalcommons.law.yale.edu/cgi/viewcontent.cgi?article=1367&context=yjreg

42   Horwitz, J. a Cumming, C. (2012) Taken for a Ride: Slate, JUNE 06, 2012, ONLINE: http://www.slate.com/articles/business/moneybox/2012/06/taxi_medallions_how_new_york_s_terrible_taxi_system_makes_fares_higher_and_drivers_poorer_.html

43   Perry, M. (2012) Taken for a Ride by the NYC Taxi Cartel: Carpe Diem, June 12, 2012, ONLINE: http://www.aei.org/publication/taken-for-a-ride-by-the-nyc-taxi-cartel/

44   Tepper, F. (2015) Uber Releases Hourly Ride Numbers In New York City To Fight De Blasio, ONLINE: https://techcrunch.com/2015/07/22/uber-releases-hourly-ride-numbers-in-new-york-city-to-fight-de-blasio/

Griswold, A. (2015) So What if New York Has More Ubers Than Taxis?: Slate, March 25, 2015, ONLINE: http://www.slate.com/articles/technology/technology/2015/03/more_ubers_than_taxis_in_new_york_actually_that_doesn_t_mean_much.html

45   https://www.authbridge.com/news/sos-button-in-uber-ola-apps-for-passenger-safety/

46   https://www.uber.com/blog/boston/now-it-only-takes-one-touch-to-say-im-on-my-way/

47   Gallagher, L. (2017) The Airbnb Story: How Three Ordinary Guys Disrupted an Industry, Made Billions...and Created Plenty of Controversy. Boston: Houghton Mifflin Harcourt, pp. 256, ISBN: 978-0544952669

Stone, B. (2017) The Upstarts: How Uber, Airbnb, and the Killer Companies of the New Silicon Valley Are Changing the World. Boston: Little, Brown and Company, pp. 145, ISBN: 978-0316388399

48   Gannes, L. (2013) After Home-Trashing Incident, Airbnb Builds an In-House Enforcer Team. July 16, 2013, ONLINE: http://allthingsd.com/20130716/after-home-trashing-incident-airbnb-builds-an-in-house-enforcer-team/

49   Hayek, F. A., (1945) Využití znalostí ve společnosti (Using Kowledge in Society). ONLINE: http://www.monumenttotransformation.org/atlas-transformace/html/v/vedeni/vyuziti-znalosti-ve-spolecnosti.html?fbclid=IwAR3AmMSraJcFWLN45Lu-eu6g7FMco8Ek8J6292l6Zo3H9le-bI1MQ00MijF8

50   Kleiner, M. M. a Krueger, A. B. (2008) The Prevalence and Effects of Occupational Licensing: NBER Working paper series, pp. 15, ONLINE: http://www.nber.org/papers/w14308.pdf

51   Adam B. Summers, "Occupational Licensing: Ranking the States and Exploring Alternatives," Reason Foundation Policy Study, no. 361, July 2007, ONLINE: http://reason.org/news/show/occupational-licensing-ranking.

52   Morris M. Kleiner (2006) Licensing Occupations: Ensuring Quality or Restricting Competition? (Kalamazoo, MI: W.E. Upjohn Institute, 2006), 56

53   Department of the Treasury (2015) Council of Economic Advisers, and US Department of Labor, Occupational Licensing: A Framework, July 2015, 13.

54   Carroll, S. L. a Gaston, R. J. (1981) "Occupational Restrictions and the Quality of Service Received: Some Evidence," Southern Economic Journal 47

CONCLUSION – REFLECTIONS

55 Kleiner, M. M. a Krueger, A. B. (2013) "Analyzing the Extent and Influence of Occupational Licensing," Journal of Labor Economics 31, no. 2, pt. 2 (2013), pp. 173–202

Kleiner, M. M. a Krueger, A. B. (2008) "The Prevalence and Effects of Occupational Licensing" (NBER Working Paper No. 14308, National Bureau of Economic Research, Cambridge, MA, September, 2008), 2

Kleiner, M. M. (2015) "Reforming Occupational Licensing Policies," Brookings Institution, Hamilton Project Discussion Paper 2015-01, January 2015, ONLINE: http://www.brookings.edu/~/media/research/files/papers/2015/01/28%20reforming%20occupational%20licensing%20kleiner/reform_occupatio

Federman, M. N. a kol. (2006) "The Impact of State Licensing Regulations on Low-Skilled Immigrants: The Case of Vietnamese Manicurists," American Economic Review 96, no. 2 (2006), pp. 237–41.

Patrick McLaughlin, Jerry Ellig, and Dima Yazji Shamoun, "Regulatory Reform in Florida: An Opportunity for Greater Competitiveness and Economic Efficiency," Florida State University Business Review 13, no. 1 (Spring 2014): 95–130

56 Denmon, C. (2014) Ride Sharing vs. Traditional Taxis: How do Injury Insurance Claims Compare? July 5, ONLINE: https://www.huffingtonpost.com/christian-denmon/ride-sharing-vs-tradition_b_5273964.html

57 Morris, D. Z. (2017) Lyft Could Have One-Third of the U. S. Rideshare Market by Christmas: Fortune, November 12, ONLINE: http://fortune.com/2017/11/12/lyft-us-rideshare-market-report/

JC (2018) 2017 Rideshare Infogrpahic: Lyft Makes Record Gains on Uber, November 2018, ONLINE: https://www.ridester.com/2017-rideshare-infographic/

Lyft, Vehicle inspection, ONLINE:https://www.pdf-archive.com/2017/03/14/lyft-inspection-feb-2017/lyft-inspection-feb-2017.pdf

New driver welcome kit (2018)
ONLINE: https://help.lyft.com/hc/en-us/articles/115013082088-New-driver-welcome-kit

58 Liang, S. a kol. (2017) Be a "Superhost": The Importance of Badge Systems for Peer-to-peer Rental Accommodations, ONLINE: https://www.researchgate.net/publication/313860092_Be_a_Superhost_The_Importance_of_Badge_Systems_for_Peer-to-peer_Rental_Accommodations

Teubner a kol. (2016) It's only pixels, badges, and stars: On the economic value of reputation on Airbnb, https://www.researchgate.net/publication/309204371_It's_only_pixels_badges_and_stars_On_the_economic_value_of_reputation_on_Airbnb

59 Burns, J. (2018) Uber Riders Report High Fees From „Vomit Fraud" And Ghost Trips: Forbes, Jul 24, ONLINE: https://www.forbes.com/sites/janetwburns/2018/07/24/uber-riders-are-seeing-high-fees-from-ghost-trips-and-vomit-fraud/#669d1fa5a545

60 Petri, A. E. (2018) How this Innovative App Became Africa's Uber: National Geographic, February 15, ONLINE: https://www.nationalgeographic.com/photography/proof/2018/february/safemotos-kigali-rwanda-africa-tech/

61 Uber Under the Hood (2016) Welcome all bug bounty hunters, March 22, ONLINE:https://medium.com/uber-under-the-hood/welcome-all-bug-bounty-hunters-597a40c423f7

CONCLUSION – REFLECTIONS

62 Ross, B. (2014) It's Time to Let the Governemnt Drive: Uber.gov, December 3, ONLINE: https://medium.com/@blakeross/uber-gov-29db5fdff372

63 CBS News (2017) TSA screenings fail to spot weapons most of the time, agency says, November 9, ONLINE: https://www.cbsnews.com/news/tsa-screenings-fail-to-detect-explosives-guns-knives-70-percent/

64 Skarbek, D. (2014) The Social Order of the Underworld: How Prison Gangs Govern the American Penal System. Oxford: Oxford University Press, pp. 240, ISBN 978-0199328505

65 Slováček, P. (2017) Přechody pro chodce: Absolutní přednost není, ale...(Pedestrian Crossings: There is no such thing as absolute priority but...), ONLINE: http://www.auto.cz/prechody-pro-chodce-absolutni-prednost-neni-ale-109749

66 Zervas, G. a kol. (2015) A First Look at Online Reputation on Airbnb, Where Every Stay is Above Average, April 12, ONLINE: http://www-bcf.usc.edu/~proserpi/papers/airbnbreputation.pdf

Slee, T. (2017) What's Yours Is Mine: Against the Sharing Economy. New York: OR Books, pp. 240, ISBN 978-1944869373

67 Cook, J. (2015) Uber's internal charts show how its driver-rating system actually works: Business Insider, February 11, ONLINE: http://uk.businessinsider.com/leaked-charts-show-how-ubers-driver-rating-system-works-2015-2

68 Teubner, T. a kol. (2017) Price Determinants on Airbnb: How Reputation Pays Off in the Sharing Economy, ONLINE: https://www.researchgate.net/publication/315838775_Price_Determinants_on_Airbnb_How_Reputation_Pays_Off_in_the_Sharing_Economy

Gutt, D., a Herrmann, P. 2015. "Sharing Means Caring? Hosts' Price Reaction to Rating Visibility," in ECIS 2015 Proceedings, pp. 1–13, ONLINE:

https://medium.com/airbnb-engineering/building-for-trust-503e9872bbbb

Lampinen, A. (2015) Monetizing Network Hospitality: Hospitality and Sociability in the Context of Airbnb, February, ONLINE: https://www.researchgate.net/publication/275522360_Monetizing_Network_Hospitality_Hospitality_and_Sociability_in_the_Context_of_Airbnb

Resnick, P. a kol. (2006) The value of reputation on eBay: A controlled experiment: Experimental Economics, Volume 9, Issue 2, pp. 79-101, ONLINE: https://link.springer.com/article/10.1007/s10683-006-4309-2

Gürtler, O. a Grund, C. (2006) The Effect of Reputation on Selling Prices in Auctions: Discussion Paper Series of SFB/TR 15 Governance and the Efiiciency of Economic Systems, ONLINE: https://ideas.repec.org/p/trf/wpaper/114.html

Resnick, P. a Zeckhauser, R. (2002) Trust among strangers in internet transactions: Empirical analysis of eBay's reputation system: The Economics of the Internet and E-commerce, pp. 127-157, ONLINE: https://www.emeraldinsight.com/doi/abs/10.1016/S0278-0984%2802%2911030-3

Abrahao, B. a kol. (2017) Reputation offsets trust judgments based on social biases among Airbnb users, July 20, ONLINE: http://www.pnas.org/content/early/2017/08/22/1604234114.full

69 Newman, R. a Antin, J. (2016) Building for Trust: Insights from our efforts to distill the fuel for the sharing economy, ONLINE: https://medium.com/airbnb-engineering/building-for-trust-503e9872bbbb

CONCLUSION – REFLECTIONS

70   O'Dell, C. (2016) How Airbnb Builds Trust, Engagement, and Community Through Peer-to-Peer Ratings, ONLINE: https://www.apqc.org/blog/how-airbnb-builds-trust-engagement-and-community-through-peer-peer-ratings

71   Fradkin, A. a kol. (2018) The Determinants of Online Review Informativeness: Evidence from Field Experiments on Airbnb, April 20, ONLINE: http://andreyfradkin.com/assets/reviews_paper.pdf

72   Masterov, D. V. a kol. (2015) Canary in the e-Commerce Coal Mine: Detecting and Predicting Poor Experiences Using Buyer-to-Seller Messages, ONLINE: https://www.gsb.stanford.edu/sites/gsb/files/ec091.pdf

Chew, J. (2017) Improving Airbnb Yield Prediction with Text Mining, October 20, ONLINE: https://towardsdatascience.com/improving-airbnb-yield-prediction-with-text-mining-9472c0181731

73   Airbnb Policy Tool Chest (2016), ONLINE: https://www.airbnbcitizen.com/wp-content/uploads/2016/12/National_PublicPolicyTool-ChestReport-v3.pdf

74   Brynjolfsson, E. (2017) Machine, Platform, Crowd: Harnessing Our Digital Future. Brilliance Audio; Unabridged edition, pp. 408, ISBN 978-1543615791

75   Campbell, H. (2018) 11 Common Reasons You Can get Deactivated as an Uber Driver, ONLINE: https://therideshareguy.com/10-things-that-can-get-you-deactivated-as-an-uber-driver/

Weber, M. T. (2018) How Not To End Up On The Uber „No Ride" List, January 16, ONLINE: https://www.forbes.com/sites/marcwebertobias/2018/01/16/how-not-to-end-up-on-the-uber-no-ride-list/#5ff179f2f0da

Carey, J a kol. (2016) Uber Driver Attacked in Arlington After He Asks Passengers to Stop Drinking in Car, February 22, ONLINE: https://www.nbcwashington.com/news/local/Uber-Driver-Attacked-in-Arlington-After-He-Asks-Passengers-to-Stop-Drinking-in-Car-369739571.html?_osource=SocialFlowFB_DCBrand

Lilico, A. and Sinclair, M. (2016) The Cost of Non-Europe in the Sharing Economy. Annex I of Goudin, P., The Cost of Non-Europe in the Sharing Economy: Economic, Social and Legal Challenges and Opportunities. Brussels: European Parliamentary Research Service.

76   Hannagan, C. (2015) By the numbers: Taxi driver is the job with the No. 1 murder rate, January 29, ONLINE: http://www.syracuse.com/opinion/index.ssf/2015/01/by_the_numbers_job_with_the_number_1_murder_rate_taxi_drivers.html

Newall, S. (2015) Where are all the female cab drivers? December 17, ONLINE: https://www.independent.co.uk/news/uk/mad-friday-the-imbalance-between-male-and-female-cab-drivers-a6777566.html

Cook,C. a kol. (2019) The Gender Earnings Gap in the Gig Economy: Evidence from over a Million Rideshare Drivers, March 8, ONLINE: https://web.stanford.edu/~diamondr/UberPayGap.pdf

Forbes Woman Africa (2017) The Sharing Economy: 400,000 Guests At Home, October 6, ONLINE: https://www.forbesafrica.com/woman/2017/10/06/sharing-economy-400000-guests-home/

77   Saner, E. (2017) Will the end of Uber in London make women more or less safe? September 25, ONLINE: https://www.theguardian.com/lifeandstyle/2017/sep/25/will-the-end-of-uber-in-london-make-women-more-or-less-safe

	Zuluaga, D. (2017) Taxi and private hire vehicle regulation: A Briefing. Institute of Economic Affairs, ONLINE: https://iea.org.uk/wp-content/uploads/2017/12/Taxi-and-Private-Hire-paper.pdf
78	Uber Under the Hood (2016) Safety at Uber, March 6, ONLINE: https://medium.com/uber-under-the-hood/safety-at-uber-6e638616bd4a
	National Geographic (2005) Flash Facts About Lightning, ONLINE: https://news.nationalgeographic.com/news/2004/06/0623_040623_lightningfacts.html The odds of becoming a lightning victim in the U.S. in any one year is 1 in 700.000.
	B. R. (2015) A crash course in probability, January 29, ONLINE: https://www.economist.com/blogs/gulliver/2015/01/air-safety one in 5.4 million
	Shapiro, N. (2017) Perfect Strangers: How Airbnb is building trust between hosts and guests, December 1, ONLINE: https://www.airbnbcitizen.com/perfect-strangers-how-airbnb-is-building-trust-between-hosts-and-guests/
79	Davies, R. (2015) Uber says five-minute delay for minicabs „huge mistake" for London, ONLINE: https://www.theguardian.com/technology/2015/nov/03/uber-five-minute-delay-minicabs-mistake-london-tfl
	Dillet, R. (2014) Uber, LeCab And Others Now Have To Wait 15 Minutes Before Picking You Up In France, ONLINE: https://techcrunch.com/2013/12/28/uber-lecab-and-others-now-have-to-wait-15-minutes-before-picking-you-up-in-france/
80	Eldon, E. (2012) DC City Council „Uber Amendment" Would Force Sedans To Charge 5x Minimum Taxi Prices (Kill UberX), ONLINE: https://techcrunch.com/2012/07/09/dc-city-councils-uber-amendment-would-force-sedans-to-charge-5x-taxi-prices-and-kill-uberx/
81	UNWTO: World Tourism Organization (2018) 2017 International Tourism Results: the highest in seven years, ONLINE: http://media.unwto.org/press-release/2018-01-15/2017-international-tourism-results-highest-seven-years
82	Elliott, S. (2016) Airbnb Japan May Be Shut Down By Insanely Strict Laws: Sharing Economy Battle Rages On, ONLINE: https://www.inquisitr.com/2811400/airbnb-japan-may-be-shut-down-by-insanely-strict-laws-sharing-economy-battle-rages-on/#5Bc8wX8sDSz9VTp1.99
83	Nakamura, Y. a Takahashi, M. (2016) Airbnb Faces Major Threat in Japan, Its Fastest-Growing Market, ONLINE: https://www.bloomberg.com/news/articles/2016-02-18/fastest-growing-airbnb-market-under-threat-as-japan-cracks-down
84	Griswold, A. (2017) New York City is using sheriffs and obscure building code violations to crack down on Airbnb, ONLINE: https://qz.com/1084108/1084108/
85	Airbnb Citizen (2017) Airbnb: Fighting hotel price-gouging saving millions for consumers, ONLINE: https://www.airbnbcitizen.com/airbnb-fighting-hotel-price-gouging-saving-millions-consumers/
86	Benner, K. (2017) Inside the Hotel Industry's Plan to Combat Airbnb: The New York Times, ONLINE: https://www.nytimes.com/2017/04/16/technology/inside-the-hotel-industrys-plan-to-combat-airbnb.html
87	Hunter, B. (2017) The Hotel Industry's Sneaky Plot to Take Down Airbnb, ONLINE: https://fee.org/articles/the-hotel-industry-s-plot-to-take-down-airbnb-using-state-power/

88 Leyonhjelm, D. (2017) What if politicians used the sharing economy for work travel? The Sydney Morning Herald, October 2, ONLINE: https://www.smh.com.au/opinion/what-if-politicians-used-the-sharing-economy-for-work-travel-20170928-gyqat5.html

89 Palagashvili, L. (2015) Lessons from the Uber-De Blasio Showdown, ONLINE: https://www.mercatus.org/expert_commentary/lessons-uber-de-blasio-showdown

90 Nguyen, T. (2015) Uber takes its war on New York City to another level, ONLINE: https://www.vanityfair.com/news/2015/07/uber-takes-on-nyc-deblasio-over-proposed-driver-cap

Smith, C. (2015) Battlin' Bill de Blasio's Uber Fight, ONLINE: http://nymag.com/daily/intelligencer/2015/07/battlin-bill-de-blasios-uber-fight.html

Helderman, R. (2014) Uber pressures regulators by mobilizing riders and hiring vast lobbying network,: The Washington Post, December 13, ONLINE: https://www.washingtonpost.com/politics/uber-pressures-regulators-by-mobilizing-riders-and-hiring-vast-lobbying-network/2014/12/13/3f4395c6-7f2a-11e4-9f38-95a187e4c1f7_story.html?utm_term=.304aa25874cb

Shiryaevskaya, A. (2017) Uber tops 500 000 signatures on petition to halt London ban, ONLINE: https://www.fin24.com/Tech/Companies/uber-tops-500-000-signatures-on-petition-to-halt-london-ban-20170926

91 Coz, E. (2015) Company claimed that city's proposed regulations would have ended local service, ONLINE: http://www.heraldtribune.com/news/20150908/sarasota-opts-to-deregulate-uber---and-taxis

92 Somerville, H. (2015) Airbnb to create 100 clubs to advocate for home-sharing, ONLINE: https://www.reuters.com/article/us-airbnb-sanfrancisco/airbnb-to-create-100-clubs-to-advocate-for-home-sharing-idUSKCN0ST2RL20151105

93 Hafner, K. (2006) How ebay makes regulations disappear – Technology – International Herald Tribune: The New York Times, June 4, ONLINE: http://www.nytimes.com/2006/06/04/technology/04iht-web.0604ebay.1883719.html

94 Heller, J. (2017) Útoky taxikářů mají opačný účinek. Uberu přihrály nové zákazníky i řidiče,(Attacks by Taxi Drivers Have the Opposite Intended Effect- They Got Uber New Customers) ONLINE: https://zpravy.idnes.cz/spor-taxi-uber-novi-zakaznici-ridici-dvb-/domaci.aspx?c=A170928_071825_domaci_hell

95 Moore, A. a Balaker, T. (2006) Do economists reach a conclusion?: Econ Journal Watch, Volume 3, Number 1, January 2006, pp. 109-132, ONLINE: https://econjwatch.org/file_download/104/ejw_ab_jan06_moorebalaker.pdf

96 Dills, A. a Mulholland, S. E. (2018) Ride-Sharing, Fatal Crashes, and Crime, ONLINE: https://www.researchgate.net/publication/322664017_Ride-Sharing_Fatal_Crashes_and_Crime

Grenwood, B. a Wattal, S. (2015) Show Me the Way to Go Home: An Empirical Investigation of Ride Sharing and Alcohol Related Motor Vehicle Homicide

97 Verger, R. (2017) Uber can actually help prevent drunk driving accidents – in some cities, ONLINE: https://www.popsci.com/uber-drunk-driving#page-3

98 Moskatel, L. a Slusky, D. J. G. (2017) Did UberX Reduce Ambulance Volume? October 24, ONLINE: http://www2.ku.edu/~kuwpaper/2017Papers/201708.pdf

CONCLUSION – REFLECTIONS

99 Jiang, M. (2015) How the company changing the way we travel can change the way we save lives, March 17, ONLINE: https://medium.com/invisible-balloons/uber-911-5d28d7428de6

100 Wallsten, S. (2015) The Competitive Effects of the Sharing Economy: How is Uber Changing Taxis?: Technology Policy Institute, pp. 21

101 Airbnb blog: The Environmental Impacts of Home Sharing in Cities Around the World, ONLINE:https://blog.atairbnb.com/wp-content/uploads/EnvironmentalImpact-Blog-MP-01.jpg

102 Airbnb citizen (2016) Airbnb Policy Tool Chest, ONLINE: https://www.airbnbcitizen.com/wp-content/uploads/2016/12/National_PublicPolicyTool-ChestReport-v3.pdf

103 Samuelson, P. Public Goods and Subscription TV: Correction of the Record. Massachusetts Institute of Technology, pp. 81-83, ONLINE: https://econ.ucsb.edu/~tedb/Courses/UCSBpf/readings/SamPayTV.pdf

104 Stone, B. (2017) The Upstarts: How Uber, Airbnb and the Killer Companies of the New Silicon Valley Are Changing the World. Boston: Little, Brown and Company, pp. 384, ISBN 978-0316388399

105 Varga, P. (2017) Má UBER právo nerešpektovať právo? (Does Uber have the right to not respect the law?): Právne noviny, ONLINE: https://www.pravnenoviny.sk/ma-uber-pravo-nerespektovat-pravo

106 Pollman, E. a Barry, J. M. (2017) Regulatory Entrepreneurship, Loyola Law School, Los Angeles Legal Studies Research Paper No. 2017-29, ONLINE: https://papers.ssrn.com/sol3/papers.cfm?abstract_id=2741987   Elert, N. a Henrekson, M. (2016) Evasive entrepreneurship: Small Business Economics, June 2016, Volume 47, Issue 1, pp. 95-113, ONLINE: https://link.springer.com/article/10.1007/s11187-016-9725-x

107 Munger, M. (2017) Michael Munger on Permissionless Innovation: The Library of Economics and Libery, ONLINE: http://www.econtalk.org/archives/2017/10/michael_munger_4.html

108 Smith, A. (2017) Bohatství národů(The wealth of nations). Praha: Grada, pp. 904, ISBN 9788086389608

109 CNN Money (2005) Ohio law would regulate eBay sellers, March 7, 2005, ONLINE: http://money.cnn.com/2005/03/07/technology/ohio_ebay/index.htm

110 Burleson, D. (2015) eBay fights States who enforce auctioneer license requirements, ONLINE: http://www.dba-oracle.com/t_ebay_auctioneer_license.htm

111 Jackson, E. (2012) The PayPal Wars: Battles with eBay, the Media, the Mafia, and the Rest of Planet Earth, WND Books; 1 edition (May 31, 2012)

112 Cnet (2002) eBay's Billpoint draws states' attention, May 1, 2002, ONLINE: https://www.cnet.com/news/ebays-billpoint-draws-states-attention/

113 Cnet (2002) Feds: Paypal not a bank, May 1, 2002, ONLINE: https://www.cnet.com/news/feds-paypal-not-a-bank/

114 Legal Information Institute (1979) 39 CFR § 320.6 – Suspension for extremely urgent letters, ONLINE: https://www.law.cornell.edu/cfr/text/39/320.6

115 A. J. Smith (1999) Privatized infrastructure: the role of government. London: Thomas Telford Publishing, pp. 241, ISBN: 978-0727727121, ONLINE: https://books.google.sk/books?id=IpRBuPlQ65YC&pg=PA36&redir_esc=y#v=onepage&q&f=false

CONCLUSION – REFLECTIONS

116 Ladd, B. (2008) Love and hate in the automotive age. Chicago: University of Chicago Press, pp. 236, ONLINE: http://press.uchicago.edu/ucp/books/book/chicago/A/bo5775730.html

117 Marsden, R. (2015) Rhodri Marsden's interesting objects: Lord Winchelsea's red flag, Independent, July 4, 2015, ONLINE: https://www.independent.co.uk/life-style/motoring/features/rhodri-marsdens-interesting-objects-lord-winchelseas-red-flag-10358534.html

Munger, M. C. (2018) Tomorrow 3.0: Transaction Costs and the Sharing Economy. Cambridge: Cambridge University Press, pp. 190, ISBN 978-1108447348, v knihe je citovaný: (Karelovitz, 1968, p. 122)

118 Lambert, F. (2017) Tesla is leading a new charge to allow direct sales in Texas with a pure free market approach, ONLINE: https://electrek.co/2017/03/12/tesla-direct-sales-texas/

119 Crane, D. A. (2014) Tesla and the Car Dealers' Lobby: Regulation 37, no. 2 (2014): 10-4, ONLINE: https://repository.law.umich.edu/cgi/viewcontent.cgi?referer=https://www.google.sk/&httpsredir=1&article=2319&context=article

120 Bort, J. (2012) Elon Musk: Tesla Is Not Breaking The Law, Business Insider, October 22, 2012, ONLINE: http://www.businessinsider.com/elon-musk-tesla-is-not-breaking-the-law-2012-10

121 Lambert, F. (2018) Tesla is currently fighting for the right to sell its cars directly in 8 states, ONLINE: https://electrek.co/2018/02/14/tesla-pushing-right-to-sell-cars-directly-states/

122 Juma, C. (2016) Innovation and Its Enemies: Why People Resist New Technologies. Oxford: Oxford University Press, pp. 432, ISBN 978-0190467036

123 Stringham, E. (2015) Private Governance: Creating Order in Economic and Social Life. Oxford: Oxford University Press, pp. 296, ISBN 978-0199365166

124 Harford, T. (2017) Fifty Things that Made the Modern Economy. Little, Brown Book Group, pp. 352

125 Fitzsimmons, E. G. (2016) Uber Not to Blame for Rise in Manhattan Traffic Congestion, Report Says: The New York Times, January 15, 2016, ONLINE: https://www.nytimes.com/2016/01/16/nyregion/uber-not-to-blame-for-rise-in-manhattan-traffic-congestion-report-says.html

126 Fitzsimmons, E. G. (2016) Uber Not to Blame for Rise in Manhattan Traffic Congestion, Report Says: The New York Times, January 15, 2016, ONLINE: https://www.nytimes.com/2016/01/16/nyregion/uber-not-to-blame-for-rise-in-manhattan-traffic-congestion-report-says.html

127 Hook, L. (2017) How Uber and Lyft are reinventing the bus: Financial Times Magazine, ONLINE: https://www.ft.com/content/733e4108-a88c-11e7-ab55-27219df83c97.

Woodman, S.: Welcome to Uberville: Uber wants to take over public transit, one small town at a time, ONLINE: https://www.theverge.com/2016/9/1/12735666/uber-altamonte-springs-fl-public-transportation-taxi-system

128 Hawkins, A. J. (2018) Uber Express Pool offers the cheapest fares yet in exchange for a little walking, ONLINE: https://www.theverge.com/2018/2/21/17020484/uber-express-pool-launch-cities

129 Li, Z. a kol. (2017) Do On-demand Ride-sharing Services Affect Traffic Congestion? Evidence from Uber Entry, ONLINE: <https://papers.ssrn.com/sol3/papers.cfm?abstract_id=2838043

130 Cramer, J. a Krueger, A. B. (2016) Disruptive Change in the Taxi Business? The Case of Uber, NBER Working Paper No. 22083, March 2016, ONLINE: http://www.nber.org/papers/w22083

131 Rayle, L. a kol. (2014) App-Based, On-Demand Ride Services: Comparing Taxi and Ridesourcing Trips and User Characteristics in San Francisco: University of California Transportation Center

Working Paper, ONLINE: <https://www.its.dot.gov/itspac/dec2014/ridesourcingwhitepaper_nov2014.pdf>.

132 Steele, J. (2018) Ace Parking says Uber, Lyft have cut parking business up to 50% in some venues: The San Diego Union-Tribune, February 22, ONLINE: http://www.sandiegouniontribune.com/business/growth-development/sd-fi-ace-parking-uber-lyft-competition-20180222-story.html

CROWDFUNDING AND PUBLIC GOODS

133 Tocqueville, A. (2000) Democracy in America, George Lawrence, trans.; J. P. Mayer, ed.; New York: Perennial Classics

134 Friedman, D. (1986) PRICE THEORY: AN INTERMEDIATE TEXT. South-Western Pub. Co, pp. 560, ISBN 978-0538080507

135 Komárek, S. (2012) Muž jako evoluční inovace? (Man as evolutionary innovation?), Academia, EAN: 9788020020864

136 Cross, L. a kol. (2016) How Moving Together Brings Us Together: When Coordinated Rhytmic Movement Affects Cooperation, ONLINE: https://www.ncbi.nlm.nih.gov/pmc/articles/PMC5177969/

137 Hume, D. (1960) , An Enquiry Concerning the Principles of Morals s. 538-539

138 Smith, A. (2017) Bohatství národů. Praha: Grada, pp. 904, ISBN 9788086389608

139 Cook, J. (2013) Rob Ford Crackstarter, ONLINE: https://www.indiegogo.com/projects/rob-ford-crackstarter#/

140 Self, J. (2011) Fundraiser Closed! Tooth goal has been REACHED!!! ONLINE: https://www.indiegogo.com/projects/fundraiser-closed-tooth-goal-has-been-reached#/

141 Wheat, R. E. a kol. (2013) Trends in Ecology & Evolution: Cell Press, Volume 28, Issue 2, February 2013, Pages 71-72, ONLINE: https://www.sciencedirect.com/science/article/pii/S0169534712002984 Byrnes, J. E. K. a kol. (2014) To Crowdfund Research, Scientists Must Build an Audience for Their Work, ONLINE: https://www.ncbi.nlm.nih.gov/pmc/articles/PMC4262210/

142 The Statistics Portal (2018) Crowdfunding, ONLINE: https://www.statista.com/topics/1283/crowdfunding/

Crowdexpert (2018) http://crowdexpert.com/crowdfunding-industry-statistics/

143 Delphi Historic Trails Safety and Security, ONLINE: https://www.patronicity.com/project/delphi_historic_trails_safety_and_security#!/

144 IOBY (2019) ONLINE: https://www.ioby.org/project/soulardarity https://www.ioby.org/project/parker-village-shines

Oneil, A. Soulardarity Streetlight Campaign: Bold Beginnings, ONLINE: https://www.indiegogo.com/projects/soulardarity-streetlight-campaign-bold-beginnings

Jackson K. (2014) Soulardarity, ONLINE: https://www.ioby.org/project/soulardarity

Jackson K. (2017) Parker Village Shines, ONLINE: https://www.ioby.org/project/parker-village-shines

CONCLUSION – REFLECTIONS

145 Beam Campaign, Jamal, ONLINE: https://beam.org/campaigns/jamal-electrician-training

146 Legal Aid Justice Center (2017) Aziz v. Trump, ONLINE: https://www.crowdjustice.com/case/dullesdetainees/?referer=stories

We the People Project (2017) US Denies Veterans Voting Rights, ONLINE: https://www.crowdjustice.com/case/righttovote/?referer=stories

Good Law Project Limited (2017) The Government's secret Brexit studies, ONLINE: https://www.crowdjustice.com/case/secretbrexitstudies/

Justice for Health (2016) Justice for Health: NHS Judicial Review, ONLINE: https://www.crowdjustice.com/case/nhs/?referer=stories

Wylie, C. (2019) Join the fight: defend the Cambridge Analytica whistleblower, ONLINE: https://www.crowdjustice.com/case/cambridge-analytica-whistleblower/

147 Bryan, M. (2018) 2018 July 5th Midtown Fireworks, ONLINE: https://www.ioby.org/project/2018-july-5th-midtown-fireworks

148 Imagination Station Detroit (2018) RoboCop To Find His Home At The Michigan Science Center! ONLINE: https://www.kickstarter.com/projects/imaginationstation/detroit-needs-a-statue-of-robocop/posts/2177272

149 Alptraum, L. (2019) Porn companies are embracing crowdfunding. ONLINE: https://www.theverge.com/2019/4/3/18283012/porn-pornography-companies-crowdfunding-indiegogo-patreon-vod-free-pink-white-productions?fbclid=IwAR0iKJ2bOmZetHYoPCNtVQ5MxLV7n-wVEcw4uiqFEt_7O4UZIy6w9D0BynyA

150 Metro Plus (2018) Malaysia raises money from citizens to pay off $251bn national debt, June 1, ONLINE: https://punchng.com/malaysia-raises-money-from-citizens-to-pay-off-251bn-national-debt/

151 America First Us (2018) ONLINE: http://www.americafirstus.org/campaigns/

152 Bonazzo, J. (2018) Criticized Over Plan to Crowdfund Trump's Border Wall, Observer 05/22/18, ONLINE: https://observer.com/2018/05/border-wall-crowdfunding-diane-black/

153 Lo, P. (2014), 'In Gentrifying Neighborhoods, Residents Say Private Patrols Keep Them Safe', Al Jazeera America, ONLINE: http://america.aljazeera.com/articles/2014/5/30/oakland-private-securitypatrols.html (retrieved 8 January 2017).

154 Kane, W. (2013), 'More in Oakland relying on private security', SFGATE, ONLINE: http://www.sfgate.com/crime/article/More-in-Oakland-relying-on-private-security-4815336.php#page-1 (retrieved 8 January 2017).

155 Friedman, D. D. (1989) Machinery of freedom.Open Court, pp. 267, ISBN 978-0812690699;

Brubaker, E. R. (1975) Free Ride, Free Revelation or Golden Rule?: Journal of Law and Economics, 1975, vol. 18, issue 1, pp. 147-61;

Schmidtz, D. (1990) The Limits Of Government: An Essay On The Public Goods Argument. Westview, pp. 197, ISBN 978-0813308715;

156 Safer Rockridge (2016), 'Security Patrols to Continue in 2016', Rockridge News, 31(2): pp. 5, 13.

157 Liu, P. and Fabbri, M. (2016), 'Perceptual Deterrence: The Effects of Unarmed Private Patrols on Crime', RILE-BACT Working Paper Series 2016/03.

158   Dawkins, Richard C. (1976) The Selfish Gene, Oxford University Press

Hamilton, W. (1964). "The genetical evolution of social behaviour. I". Journal of Theoretical Biology. 7 (1): 1–16.

159   Axelrod, R. (2006) The Evolution of Cooperation. Basic Books; Revised edition ISBN-10: 0465005640

Ridley, M. (1997) The Origins of Virtue. Penguin; New Ed edition, pp. 304, ISBN 978-0140244045

Taylor, M. (1987) The Possibility of Cooperation (Studies in Rationality and Social Change). Cambridge: Cambridge University Press, pp. 220, ISBN 978-0521339902

160   Henrich, J. (2015) The secret of Our Success: How Culture Is Driving Human Evolution, Domesticating Our Species, and Making Us Smarter. New Jersey: Princeton University Press, pp. 464, ISBN 978-0691166858

Bowles, S. (2013) A Cooperative Species: Human Reciprocity and Its Evolution. New Jersey: Princeton University Press, pp. 280, ISBN 978-0691158167

Wilsons, D. S. (2016) Does altruism exist?: Culture, Genes, and the Welfare of Others (Foundational Questions in Science). Yale University Press, pp. 192, ISBN 978-0300219883

161   Bowles, S. (2013) A Cooperative Species: Human Reciprocity and Its Evolution. New Jersey: Princeton University Press, pp. 280, ISBN 978-0691158167

Wilsons, D. S. (2016) Does altruism exist?: Culture, Genes, and the Welfare of Others (Foundational Questions in Science). Yale University Press, pp. 192, ISBN 978-0300219883

Boyd, R. (2016) How humans became outliers in the natural world: Lectures

Nowak, M. a Highfield, R. (2011) Super Cooperators. Canongate Books, pp. 288, ISBN 978-1847673367

162   Ensminger, J. a Henrich, J. (2014) Experimenting with Social Norms: Fairness and Punishment in Cross-Cultural Perspective (Russell Sage Foundation Series on Trust). Russeell Sage Foundation, pp. 492, ISBN 978-0871545008

163   Gächter, S. (2006) Conditional cooperation: Behavioral regularities from the lab and the field and their policy implications, Discussion Paper No. 2006-03 .

164   Frey, B. S. a Meier, S. (2004) Social Comparisons and Pro-social Behavior: Testing „Conditional Cooperation" in a Field Experiment. The American Economic Review 94

165   Heldt, R. (2005) Conditional Cooperation in the Field: Cross-Country Skiers' Behavior in Sweden, ONLINE: http://users.du.se/~the/Heldt_Cooperation_infield.pdf

166   ISAAC, R., D. et al. (1989) The assurance problem in a laboratory market. Public Choice, Vol. 62, pp. 217-236.

RONDEAU, D., et. al. (1999) Voluntary revelation of the demand for public goods using a provision point mechanism. Journal of Public Economics, 72, 455-470.

Cadsby, Ch. and Maynes, E. (1999) Voluntary provision of threshold public goods with continuous contributions: experimental evidence. Journal of Public Economics, 71, 53-73

Marks, M. B. a Croson, R. T. (1999) The effect of incomplete information in a threshold public goods experiment, Volume 99, pp. 103-118, ONLINE: https://link.springer.com/article/10.1023/A:1018316500800

167   RONDEAU, D., et. al. (2005) VCM or PPM? A comparison of the performance of two voluntary public goods mechanisms. Journal of Public Economics, 81, 1581–1592

168   Eytan, A. a Bernadro, H. (2000) Free Riding on Gnutella. ONLINE: https://www.hpl.hp.com/research/idl/papers/gnutella/gnutella.pdf

Hughes, D., Coulson, G. a Walkerdine, J. (2005) Free Riding on Gnutella Revisited: The Bell Tolls? ONLINE https://ieeexplore.ieee.org/abstract/document/1471660

169   Cullins, A. (2016) The Revenant' Pirate Avoids Prison, Fined $1M , ONLINE: https://www.hollywoodreporter.com/thr-esq/revenant-pirate-avoids-prison-fined-933620

170   Meulpolder, M., a kol. (2010) Public and Private BitTorrent Communities: A Measurement Study. ONLINE: https://www.usenix.org/legacy/event/iptps10/tech/full_papers/Meulpolder.pdf

Chen, X., X. Chu, a J. Liu (2012) Unveiling Popularity of BitTorrent Darknets. ONLINE: https://www.researchgate.net/publication/221289585_Unveiling_Popularity_of_BitTorrent_Darknets

171   Harris, C. (2017) Institutional Solutions to Free-Riding in Peer-to-Peer Networks: A Case Study of Online 'Pirate' Communities, ONLINE: https://www.cambridge.org/core/journals/journal-of-institutional-economics/article/institutional-solutions-to-freeriding-in-peertopeer-networks-a-case-study-of-online-pirate-communities/2F379FE0CB50DF502F0075119FD3E060

172   Harris, C. (2017) Institutional Solutions to Free-Riding in Peer-to-Peer Networks: A Case Study of Online 'Pirate' Communities, ONLINE: https://www.cambridge.org/core/journals/journal-of-institutional-economics/article/institutional-solutions-to-freeriding-in-peertopeer-networks-a-case-study-of-online-pirate-communities/2F379FE0CB50DF502F0075119FD3E060

173   Rockridge, S. (2016), 'Security Patrols to Continue in 2016', Rockridge News, 31(2): pp. 5, 13.

Safer Rockridge (n.d.), 'FAQS', ONLINE: http://saferrockridge.org/faqs#accordion-3 (retrieved 8 January 2017).

174   Demsetz, H. (1964) The Exchange and Enforcement of Property Rights, Journal of Law and Economics, Vol. 7, pp. 11-26

Klein, K. (1987) Employee Stock Ownership and Employee Attitudes: A Test of Three Models, Journal of Applied Psychology, Vol. 72, No. 2, 319-332

175   Hogan, M. (2016) How Much Is Music Really Worth? ONLINE: https://pitchfork.com/features/article/9628-how-much-is-music-really-worth/

176   Miller, G. (2001) The Mating Mind: How Sexual Choice Shaped the Evolution of Human Nature. Anchor Books, pp. 528, ISBN 9780385495172

Simler, K. a Hanson, R. (2018) The Elephant in the Brain: Hidden Motives in Everyday Life. Oxford University Press, pp. 416, ISBN 978-0190495992

177   Crosetto, P. a T. Regner (2015), 'Crowdfunding: Determinants of Success and Funding Dynamics', Working Paper 2015-02, Grenoble Applied Economics Laboratory (GAEL).

178   Mollick, E. (2014) The Dynamics of Crowdfunding: An Exploratory Study. Journal of Business Venturing 29(1):1–16 DOI: 10.1016/j.jbusvent.2013.06.005

179 Tabarrok, A. (1998) The private provision of public goods via dominant assurance contracts: Public Choice 96,pp. 345-362, ONLINE: https://mason.gmu.edu/~atabarro/PrivateProvision.pdf

180 Cason, T. N. a Zubrickas, R. (2017) Enhancing fundraising with refund bonuses. Games and Economic Behavior, 101, pp. 218-233.

181 Zandt, D. E. (1993) The Lessons of the Lighthouse: „Government" or „Private" Provision of Goods. The Journal of Legal Studies, Vol. 22, No. 1 (Jan. 1993), pp. 47-72, ONLINE: https://www.jstor.org/stable/3085633

182 Bertrand, E. (2006) The Coasean analysis of lighthouse financing: myths and realities. Cambridge Journal of Economics, Vol. 30, No. 3 (May 2006), pp. 389-402, ONLINE: https://www.jstor.org/stable/23601678

183 Candela, R. a Geloso, V. (2018) The Lightship in Economics: Public Choice vol. 176, no. 3 (2018), pp. 479-506, ONLINE: https://papers.ssrn.com/sol3/papers.cfm?abstract_id=3157100 Candela, R. a Geloso, V. (2018) The Lighthouse Debate and the Dynamics of Interventionism: The Review of Austrian Economics, Forthcoming, pp. 44, ONLINE: https://papers.ssrn.com/sol3/papers.cfm?abstract_id=3179536

184 Hof, K. V. (1868), Dějiny Velkého Národního Divadla v Praze: Od Prvnich Počátkův Až Do Kladení Základního Kamena, Praha: Nákl. slavnostního výboru. (The History of the National Theatre in Prague: From the Begginnings to Cornerstone Laying)

185 Hof, K. V. (1868), Dějiny Velkého Národního Divadla v Praze: Od Prvnich Počátkův Až Do Kladení Základního Kamena, Praha: Nákl. slavnostního výboru. (The History of the National Theatre in Prague: From the Begginnings to Cornerstone Laying)

186 Cowen (1985) Public Goods Definitions and their Institutional Context: a Critique of Public Goods Theory, pp. 62 ONLINE: http://philpapers.org/rec/DEMTPP

187 Brubaker, E.R., 1975, Free ride, free revelation, or golden rule? Journal of Law and Economics 18, 147-161.

188 Military Budger, ONLINE: https://www.globalsecurity.org/military/world/ukraine/budget.htm

189 Wood, G. R. (2019) Crowdfunding defense: Publich Choice, Volume 180, Issue 3-4, pp. 451-467, ONLINE: https://link.springer.com/article/10.1007%2Fs11127-019-00648-w

190 Gorlov, D. M., & Korniesky, O. A. (2015). Volunteer movement: Global experience and Ukrianian civic practices. National Institute for Strategic Studies. https://web.archive.org/web/20160415001030/http://www.niss.gov.ua/content/articles/files/volonter-697e4.pdf.

https://web.archive.org/web/20160415001030/http://www.niss.gov.ua/content/articles/files/volonter-697e4.pdf.

191 Davies, R. (2014) Civic Crowdfunding: Participatory Communities, Entrepreneurs and the Political Economy of Place, pp. 173

192 People's Project auditor: I heard no one say „what you are doing is bullshit", ONLINE: https://www.peoplesproject.com/en/articles/people-project-auditor-i-heard-no-one-say-what-you-are-doing-is-bullshit/

193 Fike, R. a Gwartney, J. (2015) Public Choice, Market Failure, and Government Failure in Principles Textbooks: The Journal of Economic Education, vol. 46, issue 2, pp. 207-218

Coyne, C. a Lucas, D. S. (2016) Economists Have No Defense: A Critical Review of National Defense in Economics Textbooks: The Journal of Private Enterprise, winter 2016

CONCLUSION – REFLECTIONS

Eyzaguirre, H. a kol. (2014) Textbook Confessions: Government Failure: Journal of Private Enterprise, Fall2014, Vol. 29 Issue 3, pp. 159-175

194 Somin, I. (2013) Democracy and Political Ignorance: Why Smaller Government Is Smarter. Palo Alto: Stanford University Press, pp. 280, ISBN 978-0804786614

195 Caplan, B. (2008) The Myth of the Rational Voter: Why Democracies Choose Bad Policies. New Jersey: Princeton University Press, pp. 296, ISBN 978-0691138732

196 Vasilko, T. (2016) Kto volil Kotlebu a prečo? Nie, nie je to len pre utečencov (Who voted for Kotleba and why? No, the answer is not immigrants): Denník N, 6. marca 2016, ONLINE: https://dennikn.sk/395557/volil-kotlebu-preco-nie-nie-su-utecencitito-ludia-volili-kotlebu-tychto-dovodov/

197 Caplan, B. (2008) The Myth of the Rational Voter: Why Democracies Choose Bad Policies. New Jersey: Princeton University Press, pp. 296, ISBN 978-0691138732

198 Lupia, M a McCubbins, D. (1998) The Democratic Dilemma. Cambridge: Cambridge University Press.

199 Wicksell, K. 1958. A New Principle of Just Taxation, in R. A. Musgrave and A. T. Peacock, eds., Classics in the Theory of Public Finance, London, UK: Macmillan and Co., pp. 72-118.

200 Samuelson, P. A. (1954) The Pure Theory of Public Expenditure:The Review of Economics and Statistics, Vol. 36, No. 4, pp. 387-389.

Buchanan, J. (1999) The demand and supply of public goods. Indianapolis: Liberty Fund,

Baumol, W. J. (1967) Welfare economics and the theory of the state. G. Bell & Sons.

201 Schmidtz, D. (1871) The Limits of Government: An Essay on the Public Goods Argument. Westview

Friedman, D. (1989) The Machinery of Freedom: Guide to a Radical Capitalism. Open court, pp. 267, ISBN 978-0812690699

202 Minton, A. (2017) Civic crowdfunding is privatisation masquerading as democracy, ONLINE: https://www.theguardian.com/cities/2017/oct/24/civic-crowdfunding-erode-democracy-local-authority

203 Glott, R., Schmidt, P. a Ghosh, R., 2010. Wikipedia survey—overview of results, United Nations University UNU-Merit, March. ONLINE: https://www.merit.unu.edu/wp-content/uploads/2019/03/Wikipedia_Overview_15March2010-FINAL.pdf [last accessed 28 August 2012].

204 Redaktor:Jetam2, ONLINE: https://sk.wikipedia.org/wiki/Redaktor:Jetam2

205 Safner, R. (2016) "Institutional Entrepreneurship, Wikipedia, and the Opportunity of the Commons,": Journal of Institutional Economics, 12 (4) 743–71

206 Safner, R. (2016) "Institutional Entrepreneurship, Wikipedia, and the Opportunity of the Commons,": Journal of Institutional Economics, 12 (4) 743–71

Dourado, E. a Tabarrok, A. (2015) Public Choice Perspectives on Intellectual Property: Public Choice, 163 (1), pp. 129–51

207 Ľuboš Blaha: História revízií. Wikipédia, ONLINE: https://sk.wikipedia.org/w/index.php?title=%C4%BDubo%C5%A1_Blaha&action=history

208 Hoffman, D. A. a Mehra, S. K. (2010) Wikitruth Through Wikiorder, Emory Law Journal, Vol. 59, 2010, ONLINE https://papers.ssrn.com/sol3/papers.cfm?abstract_id=1354424.

209 Tim O'Reilly (2017) WTF?: What's the Future and Why It's Up to Us. New York: HarperBusiness, pp. 448, ISBN 978-0062565716.

LAW AND ORDER IN INTERNET ANARCHY

210 Buchanan, J. (1974). Review of The machinery of freedom: Guide to a radical capitalism. Journal of Economic Literature, 12, 914–915.

211 Williamson, O. (2005) The Economics of Governance. American Economic Review. VOL. 95, NO. 2, MAY 2005 (pp. 1-18) ONLINE https://www.aeaweb.org/articles?id=10.1257/000282805774669880

212 Smith, A. (1982) Lectures on Jurisprudence. Edited by R. L. Meek, D. D. Raphael, and P. G. Stein. Indianapolis: Liberty Fund.

213 Boehm, Ch. (2001) Hierarchy in the Forest: The Evolution of Egalitarian Behavior. Cambridge: Harvard University Press, pp. 304, ISBN 978-0674006911

214 Scott, J. C. (2010) The Art of Not Being Governed: An Anarchist History of Upland Southeast Asia. New Haven: Yale University Press, pp. 464, ISBN 978-0300169171,

Leeson, P. T. (2006) Efficient anarchy: Publich Choice (2016) 130, pp. 41-53

215 Hoebel,E. A. (1954) The Law of Primitive Man: A Study in Comparative Legal Dynamics. Cambridge: Harvard University Press, pp. 368, ISBN 978-0674023628

Turnbull, C. M. (1961) Forest People. New York: Simon & Schuster, pp. 295, ISBN 978-0671200312

Benson, M. J. (1989) The Academic Listening Task: A Case Study: Tesol Quarterly, Volume 23, Issue 3, pp. 421-455

216 Gouldner, A. W. (1960) The Norm of Reciprocity: A Preliminary Statement: Journal Article, Vol. 25, No. 2, pp. 161-178;

Trivers, R. L. (1971) The Evolution of Reciprocal Altruism: The Quarterly Review of Biology, Vol. 46, No. 1, pp. 35-57

Taylor, M. (1987) The Possibility of Cooperation (Studies in Rationality and Social Change), Cambridge University Press

217 Axelrod, R. (2006) The Evolution of Cooperation. New York: Basic Books, pp. 264, ISBN 978-0465005642

218 Nowak,MA a Sigmund, K. (1998) Evolution of indirect reciprocity by image scoring: Nature 393, July 1998, pp. 573-7.

219 Dixit, Avinash (2004). Lawlessness and Economics: Alternative Modes of Governance. Princeton: Princeton University Press.

220 Skarbel, D. (2014) The Social Order of the Underworld: How Prison Gangs Govern the American Penal System. Oxford: Oxford University Press, pp. 240, ISBN 978-0199328505

221 Buchanan, J. M. (1965) An Economic Theory of Clubs: Journal Article, Vol. 32, No. 125, pp. 1-14

222 Stringham, E. P. a kol. (2008) Are Regulations the Answer for Emerging Stock Markets?: Quarterly Review of Economics & Finance, Vol. 48, pp. 541-566

CONCLUSION – REFLECTIONS

Stringham, E. P. (2002) The Emergence of the London Stock Exchange as a Self- Policing Club, Journal of Private Enterprise 17(2)

Stringham, E. P. (2003) The extralegal development of securities trading in seventeenth-century Amsterdam The Quarterly Review of Economics and Finance Volume 43, Issue 2, Summer 2003, Pages 321-344

223   Bernstein, L. (1992) Opting out of the Legal System: Extralegal Contractual Relations in the Diamond Industry: The Journal of Legal Studies, Vol. 21, No. 1, pp. 115-157, ONLINE: https://www.jstor.org/stable/724403

Richman, B. D. (2006) How Community Institutions Create Economic Advantage: Jewish Diamond Merchants in New York: Law & Social Inquiry, Volume 31, Issue 2, pp. 383-420, ONLINE: https://scholarship.law.duke.edu/cgi/viewcontent.cgi?article=2335&context=faculty_scholarship

Richman, B. D. (2017) Stateless Commerce: The Diamond Network and the Persistence of Relational Exchange. Cambridge: Harvard University Press, pp. 240, ISBN 978-0674972179

224   Stringham, E. P. (2007) Anarchy and the Law: The Political Economy of Choice

Stringham, E. P. (2005) Anarchy, State And Public Choice (New Thinking in Political Economy)

Stringham, E. P. a Powell, B. (2009) Public choice and the economic analysis of anarchy: a survey

225   Leeson, P. T. (2011) The Invisible Hook: The Hidden Economics of Pirates, Princeton University Press, pp. 288, ISBN 978-0691150093.

226   Grief, A. (1993) Contract enfoceability and economic institutions in early trade? The Maghribi traders' coalition: American Economic Review, 83, pp. 525-48

Benson, B. L. (1989) The Spontaneous Evolution of Commercial Law: Southern Economic Journal

227   Landa, J. T. (1994) Trust, ethnicity, and identity: beyond the new institutional economics of ethnic trading networks, contract law, and gift-exchange. Ann Arbor: University of Michigan Press

228   Clay, K. (1997) Trade without Law: Private-Order Institutions in Mexican California: Journal of Law, Economics & Organization, Vol. 13, No. 1, pp. 202-231

229   Leeson, P. (2010) Social Distance and Sel-Enforcing Exchange: Journal of Legal Studies, Vol. 37, No. 1 – heteregonostou

230   Anderson, T. L. a Hill, P. J. (2004) The Not So Wild, Wild West: Property Rights on the Frontier. Stanford Economics and Finance.

231   Ellickson, R. C. (1991) Order without Law, pp. 316, ISBN 9780674641693

232   Dixit, A. (2003) On Modes of Economic Governance

Landa, J. T. (1994) Trust, ethnicity, and identity: beyond the new institutional economics of ethnic trading networks, contract law, and gift-exchange. Ann Arbor: University of Michigan Press

Grief, A. (1993) Contract enfoceability and economic institutions in early trade? The Maghribi traders' coalition: American Economic Review, 83, pp. 525-48

233   Bernstein, L. (1992) Opting out of the Legal System: Extralegal Contractual Relations in the Diamond Industry: The Journal of Legal Studies, Vol. 21, No. 1, pp. 115-157, ONLINE: https://www.jstor.org/stable/724403?seq=1#page_scan_tab_contents

CONCLUSION – REFLECTIONS

234 Richman, B. D. (2009) Ethnic Networks, Extralegal Certainty, and Globalisation: Peering Into the Diamond Industry: Empirical Studies and Theoretical Debates on Institutional Support for Global Economic: Exchanges, pp. 31-49, ONLINE: https://scholarship.law.duke.edu/faculty_scholarship/1605/

235 North, D. C. (1991) Institutions, Institutional Change and Economic Performance. Washington, ISBN 9780521397346

236 Skarbek, D. (2014) The Social Order of the Underworld: How Prison Gangs Govern the American Penal System, ISBN 9780199328499, ONLINE: http://www.oxfordscholarship.com/view/10.1093/acprof:oso/9780199328499.001.0001/acprof-9780199328499

237 Skarbek, D. (2014) The Social Order of the Underworld: How Prison Gangs Govern the American Penal System, ISBN 9780199328499, ONLINE: http://www.oxfordscholarship.com/view/10.1093/acprof:oso/9780199328499.001.0001/acprof-9780199328499

238 Skarbek, D. (2014) The Social Order of the Underworld: How Prison Gangs Govern the American Penal System, ISBN 9780199328499, ONLINE: http://www.oxfordscholarship.com/view/10.1093/acprof:oso/9780199328499.001.0001/acprof-9780199328499

239 Greif, A. (2006) History Lessons: The Birth of Impersonal Exchange: The Community Responsibility System and Impartial Justice: Journal of Economic Perspectives, Volume 20, Number 2, Spring 2006, pp. 221-236, ONLINE: https://pubs.aeaweb.org/doi/pdfplus/10.1257/jep.20.2.221

  Greif, A. (2001) Impersonal Exchange and the Origin of Markets: From the Community Responsibility System to Individual Legal Responsibility in Pre-Modern Europe, ISBN 9780199241019, ONLINE: http://oxfordindex.oup.com/view/10.1093/0199241015.003.0001

240 Greif, A. (2004) Institutions and Impersonal Exchange: The European Experience: Stanford Law and Economics Olin Working Paper No. 284, pp. 40, ONLINE: https://papers.ssrn.com/sol3/papers.cfm?abstract_id=548783

241 Ransom, G. (2009) Oral history - The 1978 UCLA Interviews With Friedrich Hayek, ONLINE: http://hayekcenter.org/?p=628

242 NCTA (2017) The Price per Megabit per Second has Gone Down 90 Percent, ONLINE: https://www.ncta.com/whats-new/the-price-per-megabit-per-second-has-gone-down-90-percent

243 Dimitriy, M., Meyer, U. a Tadelis, S. (2015) Canary in the e-Commerce Coal Mine: Detecting and Predicting Poor Experiences Using Buyer-to-Seller Messages. Proceedings of the Sixteenth ACM Conference on Economics and Computation.

244 Nosko, Ch.a Tadelis, S. (2015) Consumer Heterogeneity and Paid Search Effectiveness: A Large Scale Field Experiment: NBER Working Paper No. 20171

245 Li, L. I. a Xiao, E. (2014). Money talks: Rebate mechanisms in reputation system design. Management Science, 60(8):2054–2072.

  Li, L. a spol (2018) Buying Reputation as a Signal of Quality: Evidence from an Online Marketplace. ONLINE: http://faculty.haas.berkeley.edu/stadelis/Taobao.pdf

246 Dimitriy, M., Meyer, U. a Tadelis, S. (2015) Canary in the e-Commerce Coal Mine: Detecting and Predicting Poor Experiences Using Buyer-to-Seller Messages. Proceedings of the Sixteenth ACM Conference on Economics and Computation.

CONCLUSION – REFLECTIONS

Ott, M. a spol. (2011) Finding deceptive opinion spam by any stretch of the imagination. In Proceedings of the 49th Annual Meeting of the Association for Computational Linguistics: Human Language Technologies, pages 309–319. Association for Computational Linguistics.

Hovy, D. a Spruit, S. (2016) The Social Impact of Natural Language Processing. ONLINE: https://www.aclweb.org/anthology/P16-2096

247 Pollman, E. a Barry, J. M. (2017) Regulatory Entrepreneurship, ONLINE: https://www.ifrogs.org/PDF/CONF_2016/Pollman_Barry_2016.pdf

Smith, H. (2015) Uber, Lyft, and the growing problem of temp jobs, ONLINE: https://grist.org/business-technology/uber-lyft-and-the-growing-problem-of-temp-jobs/

Gallagher, L. (2017) The Airbnb Story: How Three Ordinary Guys Disrupted an Industry, Made Billions…and Created Plenty of Controversy. Boston: Houghton Mifflin Harcourt, pp. 256, ISBN 978-0544952669

248 Tucker, J. A. (2017) Greyball: Uber's Super Cool App to Subvert Trolls, ONLINE: https://fee.org/articles/greyball-uber-s-super-cool-app-to-subvert-trolls/

249 Tracy you for mailonline (2016) Would YOU use an Uber driver who looks like this? Ghost accounts with zombie-like profiles scare and scam passengers in China, ONLINE: https://www.dailymail.co.uk/news/peoplesdaily/article-3804003/Uber-s-ghost-drivers-zombie-like-profiles-scare-scam-passengers-China.html

McGoogan, C. (2017) Uber drivers gang up to cause surge pricing, research says, ONLINE: https://www.telegraph.co.uk/technology/2017/08/02/uber-drivers-gang-cause-surge-pricing-research-says/

Adegoke, Y. (2017) Uber drivers in Lagos are using a fake GPS app to inflate rider fares, ONLINE: https://qz.com/africa/1127853/uber-drivers-in-lagos-nigeria-use-fake-lockito-app-to-boost-fares/

Murgia, M. (2015) Can Uber's surge pricing be gamed? ONLINE: https://www.telegraph.co.uk/technology/uber/11964956/Can-Ubers-surge-pricing-be-gamed.html

250 Price, R. (2018) Uber is reportedly making a new service to provide short-term jobs in security, hospitality, and more, ONLINE: https://www.businessinsider.com/uber-works-short-term-job-service-2018-10

251 Hayek, F. A. (1960) The Constitution of Liberty, University of Chicago Press. ISBN 0226320847

252 Stiglitz, J. E. (1982) National Bureau of Economic Research: NBER working paper series, No. 954, ONLINE: https://core.ac.uk/download/pdf/6707647.pdf .

Caplan, B. (2001) Standing Tiebout on his head: Tax capitalization and the monopoly power of local governments: Public Choice 108, pp. 101-122, ONLINE: http://econfaculty.gmu.edu/bcaplan/pdfs/standingtiebout.pdf

Buchanan, J. a Goetz, Ch. J. (1972) Efficiency limits of fiscal mobility: An assessment of the tiebout model: Journal of Public Economics, vol. 1, issue 1, pp. 25-43, ONLINE: https://econpapers.repec.org/article/eeepubeco/v_3a1_3ay_3a1972_3ai_3a1_3ap_3a25-43.htm

253 Friedman, D. D. (1989) Machinery of freedom.Open Court, pp. 267, ISBN 978-0812690699

254 Demsetz, H. (1968) "Why Regulate Utilities?": Journal of Law and Economics, Vol. 11, No. 1, pp. 55-65

Habtemariam, D. (2018) How Uber & Lyft Market Share Changed in 2017, ONLINE: http://www.businesstravelnews.com/Transportation/Ground/How-Uber-and-Lyft-Market-Share-Changed-in-2017

Ride Sharing Forum (2017) Lyft aimed at controlling 33 % of US Rideshare Market in 2017, ONLINE: https://www.ridesharingforum.com/t/lyft-aimed-at-controlling-33-of-us-rideshare-market-in-2017/355

Molla, R. a Bhuiyan, J. (2017) Uber hasn't recovered its business in San Francisco and New York since #deleteUber, ONLINE: https://www.recode.net/2017/11/8/16617798/uber-delete-uber-lyft-market-share-sales

Rodriguez, A. (2019) Lyft says it nearly doubled its market share since 2016. Here's how much that cost in marketing ONLINE: https://qz.com/1563547/lyft-nearly-doubled-market-share-since-2016-heres-what-it-cost/

255 Bloomberg Technology (2017) How Bolt Distinguishes Itself From Uber, ONLINE: https://www.youtube.com/watch?v=ZsrRhVdQAYQ

256 McDermid, R. (2017) With HomeAway growing like crazy, Expedia closes in on Airbnb for market share, ONLINE: https://www.bizjournals.com/austin/news/2017/07/25/with-homeaway-growing-like-crazy-expedia-closes-in.html

257 Buchanan, J. (1978) A CONTRACTARIAN PERSPECTIVE ON ANARCHY, American Society for Political and Legal Philosophy, ONLINE: https://www.jstor.org/stable/24219037

258 Locke, J. (1980) Second Treatise of Government. Massachusetts: Hackett Publishing Company,pp. 100-120, ISBN 978-0915144860

259 Rawls, J. (1971) Teória spravodlivosti. Harvard University Press, pp. 607

260 Buchanan, J. a Tullock, G. (1999) The Calculus of Consent. Liberty Fund, pp. 376, ISBN 978-0865972186

261 Tucker, A. (2015) Panarchy: Political Theories of Non-Territorial States (Routledge Studies in Social and Political Thought). Abingdon: Routledge, pp. 282, ISBN 978-1138884847

262 Tucker, A. (2015) Panarchy: Political Theories of Non-Territorial States (Routledge Studies in Social and Political Thought). Abingdon: Routledge, pp. 282, ISBN 978-1138884847

263 Jackson, E. M. (2012) The Paypal Wars: Battles with eBay, the Media, the Mafia, and the Rest of Planet Earth. WND Books, pp. 350, ISBN 978-1936488599

264 Stringham, E. P. (2017) Entrepreneurial As Opposed to Legalistic, Solutions for. Mitigating Fraud and Facilitating Online Commerce in the Digital Age, currently under peer-review in California Management Review

265 Al-Mahmood, S. Z., a Larano, C. (2016) "From the Fed to the Philippines: Bangladesh's Stolen-Money Trail.": Wall Street Journal, March, 18.

Citované v Stringham, E. P. (2017) The Fable of the Leeches, or: The Single Most Unrealistic Positive Assumption of Most Economists: Review of Austrian Economics, Vol. 40, No. 4, ONLINE:

266 Brooks, G., Button, M. a Frimpong, K. (2009). Policing fraud in the private sector: a survey of the FTSE 100 companies in the UK, International Journal of Police Science and Management, 11 (4), pp. 493-504.

CONCLUSION – REFLECTIONS

	Brooks, G. a Button, M. (2011). The police and fraud investigation and the case for a nationalized solution in the United Kingdom, The Police Journal, 84, pp. 305-319.
267	Stringham, E. P. (2017) Entrepreneurial As Opposed to Legalistic, Solutions for. Mitigating Fraud and Facilitating Online Commerce in the Digital Age je momentálne pod peer-review v časopise California Management Review
268	Stringham, E. P. (2017) Entrepreneurial As Opposed to Legalistic, Solutions for. Mitigating Fraud and Facilitating Online Commerce in the Digital Age je momentálne pod peer-review v časopise California Management Review
269	Katsh, E. a Rabinovich-Einy, O. (2017) Digital Justice: Technology and the Internet of Disputes. ISBN-13: 9780190464585
270	Palumbo, G. a kol. (2013) Judicial performance and its determinants: a cross-country perspective: OECD Economic Policy Papers No. 05, ONLINE: https://www.oecd.org/eco/growth/FINAL%20Civil%20Justice%20Policy%20Paper.pdf
	Narasappa, H. (2016) The long, expensive road to justice, ONLINE: https://www.indiatoday.in/magazine/cover-story/story/20160509-judicial-system-judiciary-cji-law-cases-the-long-expensive-road-to-justice-828810-2016-04-27
	Doshi, V. (2016) India's long wait for justice: 27m court cases trapped in legal logjam, ONLINE: https://www.theguardian.com/world/2016/may/05/indias-long-wait-for-justice-27-million-court-cases-trapped-in-a-legal-logjam
	Lasseter, T. (2015) India's Stagnant Courts Resist Reform, ONLINE: https://www.bloomberg.com/news/articles/2015-01-08/indias-courts-resist-reform-backlog-at-314-million-cases
271	Chen, J. a spol. (2015) Big data based fraud risk management at Alibaba, ONLINE https://www.sciencedirect.com/science/article/pii/S2405918815000021
272	Liu, L. a Weingast, B. R. (2018) Taobao, Federalism, and the Emergence of Law, Chinese Style, ONLINE: http://www.minnesotalawreview.org/wp-content/uploads/2018/06/LiuWeingast_MLR.pdf
	Katsh, E. a Rabinovich-Einy, O. (2017) Digital Justice: Technology and the Internet of Disputes. Oxford University Press, pp. 264, ISBN 978-0190675677
273	Erickson, J. (2014) How Taobao is Crowdsourcing Justice in Online Shopping Disputes, ONLINE: https://www.alizila.com/how-taobao-is-crowdsourcing-justice-in-online-shopping-disputes/
274	Liu, L. a Weingast, B. R. (2018) Taobao, Federalism, and the Emergence of Law, Chinese Style, ONLINE: http://www.minnesotalawreview.org/wp-content/uploads/2018/06/LiuWeingast_MLR.pdf
275	McKinsey Global Institute (2013) Disruptive technologies: Advances that will transform life, business, and the global economy: McKinsey & Company
276	Stoll, C. (1995) Why the Web Won't Be Nirvana. ONLINE: https://www.newsweek.com/clifford-stoll-why-web-wont-be-nirvana-185306
277	Cohen, A. (2008) The Perfect Store: Inside eBay. Back Bay Books
278	Liu, L. a Weingast, B. R. (2017) Law, Chinese Style: Solving the Authoritarian's Legal Dilemma Through the Private Provision of Law, ONLINE: https://www.lizhiliu.com/uploads/6/0/9/8/60987819/liu-weingast.main_tbo.ms__apsa2017.pdf Schultz, T. (2008) Private legal systems: What cyberspace might teach legal theorists: Yale Journal of Law and Technology, Volume 10, Issue 1, ONLINE: https://pdfs.semanticscholar.org/252a/d8d7b-867651b4a1ea76de618af474a3ee0f1.pdf

CONCLUSION – REFLECTIONS

279 Liu, L. a Weingast, B. R. (2018) Taobao, Federalism, and the Emergence of Law, Chinese Style, ONLINE: http://www.minnesotalawreview.org/wp-content/uploads/2018/06/LiuWeingast_MLR.pdf

280 Kapor, M. ONLINE: https://www.brainyquote.com/quotes/mitch_kapor_690443

281 Boettke, P. J. (2010) Anarchism as a Progressive Research Program in Political Economy: Anarchy, state and publich choice, Edward Elgar Publishing, pp. 206-219, ONLINE: https://papers.ssrn.com/sol3/papers.cfm?abstract_id=1538490

Stringham, E. P. (2007) Anarchy and the Law: The Political Economy of Choice (Independent Studies in Political Economy). Tansaction Publishers/ Independent Institute, pp. 698, ISBN 978-1412805797

Powell, B. a Stringham, E. P. (2009) Public Choice and the Economic Analysis of Anarchy: A survey, ONLINE: https://papers.ssrn.com/sol3/papers.cfm?abstract_id=1324407

282 https://en.wikipedia.org/wiki/Tor_(anonymity_network)

283 Tarquin (2019) What is the Dark Web? How to Access it Secretly (10 Simple Steps), ONLINE: https://darkwebnews.com/help-advice/access-dark-web/

284 Harford, T. (2017) Fifty Inventions That Shaped the Modern Economy. New York: Riverhead Books, pp. 336, ISBN 978-0735216136

285 Dearing, C. (2017) Nobel Laureate Milton Friedman Predicted Bitcoin Era 17 Years Ago, ONLINE: https://cointelegraph.com/news/nobel-laureate-milton-friedman-predicted-bitcoin-era-17-years-ago

286 Nakamoto, S. (2008) Bitcoin: A Peer-to-Peer Electronic Cash System

287 3Blue1Brown (2017) Ever wonder how Bitcoin (and other cryptocurrencies) actually work?, ONLINE: https://www.youtube.com/watch?v=bBC-nXj3Ng4

288 Ammous, S. (2018) The Bitcoin Standard. New Jersey: Wiley-Blackwell, pp. 304, ISBN 9781119473862

289 Ammous, S. (2018) The Bitcoin Standard. New Jersey: Wiley-Blackwell, pp. 304, ISBN 9781119473862

290 Shukla, V. (2018) Monero Is Replacing Bitcoin On The Dark Web. Are you surprised? ONLINE: https://www.valuewalk.com/2018/01/monero-replacing-bitcoin-dark-web/

291 Hill, K. (2014) Secret Money: Living On Bitcoin In the Real World, ONLINE: https://www.goodreads.com/book/show/20638336-secret-money

Daily Mail Reporter (2013) Bitcoin newlyweds: Couple will live first 90 days of married life on virtual currency, ONLINE: https://www.dailymail.co.uk/news/article-2339759/Bitcoin-newlyweds-Couple-live-90-days-married-life-virtual-currency.html

Prague Convention Bureau (2018) Prague is the Number One Bitcoin City, ONLINE: https://www.pragueconvention.cz/hot-news/prague-is-the-number-one-bitcoin-city

292 Haig, S. (2017) Afghan Entrepreneur Empowers Women Through Bitcoin, ONLINE: https://news.bitcoin.com/afghan-entrepreneur-empowers-women-through-bitcoin-in-afghanistan/

293 Santos, M. (2018) How this refugee is using Bitcoin to change lives in Afghanistan, ONLINE: https://99bitcoins.com/how-this-refugee-is-using-bitcoin-to-change-lives-in-afghanistan/

CONCLUSION — REFLECTIONS

294   Kunt, A. D. a kol. (2017) The Global Findex Database, ONLINE: World Bank

The Economist (2014) Beyond cows: Coaxing does more to boost saving than compelling, ONLINE: https://www.economist.com/news/finance-and-economics/21618900-coaxing-does-more-boost-saving-compelling-beyond-cows

Salmon, F. (2015) Why Bitcoin's male domination will be its downfall, ONLINE: https://splinternews.com/why-bitcoins-male-domination-will-be-its-downfall-1793847330

295   Tran, K. (2017) A startup is making a $30 smartphone in Africa, ONLINE: https://www.businessinsider.com/onyx-connect-making-30-dollar-smartphone-in-africa-2017-5

296   Wikipedia (2019) Global Internet usage, ONLINE: https://en.wikipedia.org/wiki/Global_Internet_usage

297   Market Mad House (2017) UN Food Program Adopting Ethereum and Bitcoin, ONLINE: https://marketmadhouse.com/un-food-program-adopting-ethereum-bitcoin/

Techzim (2018) UN Using Blockchain To Improve The World Food Programme Initiative, ONLINE: https://www.techzim.co.zw/2018/10/un-using-blockchain-to-improve-the-world-food-programme-initiative/

298   Romero, L. (2018) With 1,000,000% inflation, Venezuela is slashing five zeroes from its currency, ONLINE: https://qz.com/1341092/venezuela-is-slashing-five-zeroes-from-the-bolivar/

299   Laya, P. (2018) Bolivar to Bitcoin Market Hits Record $1 Million Per Day, ONLINE: https://www.bloomberg.com/news/articles/2018-04-18/bolivar-to-bitcoin-market-hits-record-1-million-per-day

Emem, M. (2018) Soaring Inflation Sends Bitcoin Trading Volume to [Another] New High in Venezuela, ONLINE: https://www.ccn.com/as-inflation-soars-bitcoin-trading-volumes-rise-to-record-highs-in-venezuela/

Coin Dance: LocalBitcoins Volume (Venezuela), ONLINE: https://coin.dance/volume/localbitcoins/VES/BTC

300   Campbell, R. (2018) Discussions In Place For Dash To Be Accepted At KFC Venezuela, ONLINE: https://www.forbes.com/sites/rebeccacampbell1/2018/12/07/discussions-in-place-for-dash-to-be-accepted-at-kfc-venezuela/#52919d335d38

301   Dash Help (2018) Dash Text Incredible New Feature!! Integration with POS system! ONLINE: https://www.youtube.com/watch?time_continue=25&v=keXxT_PvTe0

302   Ormsby, E. (2014) Silk Road. Sydney: Macmillan Australia, pp. 352

303   Ormsby, E. (2014) Silk Road. Sydney: Macmillan Australia, pp. 352

304   Franceschi-Bicchierai, L. (2013) The Silk Road Online Drug Marketplace by the Numbers, ONLINE: https://mashable.com/2013/10/04/silk-road-by-the-numbers/?europe=true

305   Hardy, R. A. a Norgaard, J. R. (2015) Reputation in the Internet black market: an empirical and theoretical analysis of the Deep Web.

306   Li, L. a spol. (2016) Buying reputation as a signal of quality: Evidence from online marketplace. NBER Working Paper No. 22584

307   All Things Vice (2012) The Great 420 Scam, ONLINE: https://allthingsvice.com/2012/05/30/the-great-420-scam/

CONCLUSION – REFLECTIONS

308 Branwen, G. (2013) Darknet Market Mortality Risks, ONLINE: https://www.gwern.net/DNM-survival

309 European Monitoring Centre for Drugs and Drug Addiction and Europol (2017) Drugs and the darknet: Perspectives for enforcement, research and policy, EMCDDA – Europol Joint publications, Publications Office of the European Union, ONLINE: https://www.europol.europa.eu/sites/default/files/documents/drugs_and_the_darknet_-_td0417834enn.pdf

310 Ormsby, E. (2014) Silk Road. Sydney: Macmillan Australia, pp. 352

311 Caudevilla, F., Ventura, M., Fornís, I., Barratt., Vidal, C., Lladanosa, C.G., Quintana, P., et al. (2016), 'Results of an international drug testing service for cryptomarket users', International Journal of Drug Policy 35, pp. 38-41

312 Caudevilla, F. a kol. (2016) Results of an international drug testing service for cryptomarket users: International Journal of Drug Policy, pp. 4, ONLINE: https://energycontrol-international.org/wp-content/uploads/2016/04/Results-of-an-international-drug-testing-service-for-cryptomarket-users.pdf

313 UNITED STATES DISTRICT COURT (2013) ONLINE: https://antilop.cc/sr/files/Silk_Road_JTAN_com_Search_Warrant.pdf

314 Christensen, C. M. a kol. (2011) Disrupting Class: How Disruptive Innovation Will Change the Way the World Learns, New York, McGraw Hill

315 Ormsby, E. (2014) Silk Road. Sydney: Macmillan Australia, pp. 352

316 Jarvis, N. (2016) What Happens if You're Caught Getting Drugs in the Mail? ONLINE: https://www.vice.com/en_au/article/zn8xm3/what-happens-if-youre-caught-receiving-drugs-in-the-mail

317 Branwen, G. (2019) Silk Road 1: Theory & Practice, ONLINE: https://www.gwern.net/Silk-Road

318 Forman, J. (2017) Second Circuit Upholds Harsh Life Without Parole Sentence for Silk Road's Ross Ulbricht, ONLINE: http://www.drugpolicy.org/blog/second-circuit-upholds-harsh-life-without-parole-sentence-silk-roads-ross-ulbricht

319 Branwen, G. (2012) Tor DNM-related arrests, ONLINE: https://www.gwern.net/DNM-arrests.page

320 Taleb, N. N. (2013) Antifragile. London: Penguin Books, pp. 519, ISBN 9780141038223

321 Bergmann, Ch. (2017) Nearly Half of the Darknet Drug Trading Happens in the EU, but the Scope of the Market Remains Insignificant, ONLINE: https://btcmanager.com/nearly-half-of-darknet-drug-trading-happens-in-eu-but-scope-remains-insignificant/

322 European Monitoring Centre for Drugs and Drug Addiction and Europol (2017) Drugs and the darknet: Perspectives for enforcement, research and policy, EMCDDA-Europol Joint publications, Publications Office of the European Union, ONLINE: https://www.europol.europa.eu/sites/default/files/documents/drugs_and_the_darknet_-_td0417834enn.pdf

323 Lupták, P. (2018) Anonymita v kryptoanarchii a jej dramatický dopad na spoločnosť, ONLINE: https://paralelnapolis.sk/anonymita-v-kryptoanarchii-a-jej-dramaticky-dopad-na-spolocnost/

324 Tullock, G. (1970) Private Wants, Public Means: An economic analysis of the desirable scope of government. New York: Basic Books, Inc, 1970.

325 May, T. (1992) The Crypto Anarchist Manifesto, ONLINE: The Crypto Anarchist Manifesto (activism.net)

CONCLUSION – REFLECTIONS

326   OpenBazaar (2018) Verified Moderators, ONLINE: https://medium.com/openbazaarproject/verified-moderators-c83ea2f2c7f3

         Patterson, S. (2018) OB1 Announces Verified Moderators on OpenBazaar, ONLINE: https://medium.com/openbazaarproject/ob1-announces-verified-moderators-on-openbazaar-ff881d3b892d

327   OpenBazaarModerators, ONLINE:https://www.reddit.com/r/OpenBazaarModerators/

328   Scott, A. (2016) Top 5 Things People Are Buying on OpenBazaar, ONLINE: https://news.bitcoin.com/top-5-products-openbazaar/

         Munkachy, A. (2018) The Strangest Things People Sell on OpenBazaar's Anarchic Peer-to-peer Marketplace, ONLINE: https://coiniq.com/openbazaar-decentralized-marketplace/

329   Szabo, N. (1994) Smart Contracts, ONLINE: http://www.fon.hum.uva.nl/rob/Courses/InformationInSpeech/CDROM/Literature/LOTwinterschool2006/szabo.best.vwh.net/smart.contracts.html

330   Rooney, K. (2018) Ethereum falls on report that the second-biggest cryptocurrency is under regulatory scrutiny, ONLINE: https://www.cnbc.com/2018/05/01/ethereum-falls-on-report-second-biggest-cryptocurrency-is-under-regulatory-scrutiny.html

331   Mahler, T. A. (2018) 13 Ethereum – The World Computer, ONLINE: https://medium.com/blockwhat/13-ethereum-the-world-computer-bd22cecbc0d

332   Mamoria, M. (2017) Everything you've ever wanted to know about Ethereum patiently explained, ONLINE: https://thenextweb.com/contributors/2017/11/28/ultimate-2000-word-plain-english-guide-ethereum/

333   Waters, R. (2016) Automated company raises equivalent of $120M in digital currency, ONLINE: https://www.cnbc.com/2016/05/17/automated-company-raises-equivalent-of-120-million-in-digital-currency.html

334   Schelling, T. C. (1980) The Strategy of Conflict (Reprint, illustrated and revised. ed.). Harvard University Press. p. 309. ISBN 978-0-674-84031-7. Retrieved September 21, 2010.

335   AlTawy, R. a kol. (2017) Lelantos: A Blockchain-based Anonymous Physical Delivery System, ONLINE: https://eprint.iacr.org/2017/465.pdf

336   Wikipedia (2020) Dead drop, ONLINE: https://en.wikipedia.org/wiki/Dead_drop

337   Logan, J. (2018) Dropgans, or the future of darknet markets, ONLINE: https://opaque.link/post/dropgang/

CONCLUSION – REFLECTIONS

338   Barlow, P. (1996) A Declaration of the Independence of Cyberspace, ONLINE: https://paralelnapolis.sk/institute-of-cryptoanarchy/a-declaration-of-the-independence-of-cyberspace/

339   Hayek, F. A. (1960) The Constitution of Liberty, University of Chicago Press. ISBN 0226320847

FOOTNOTE REFERENCES

A1 McAfee, A. a Brynjolfsson, E. (2017) Machine, Platform, Crowd: Harnessing Our Digital Future

A2 Farrell, D. a Greig, F. (2016) Paychecks, Paydays, and the Online Platform Economy: Big Data on Income Volatility

A3 Hall, J. a Krueger, A. (2015) An Analysis of the Labor Market for Uber's Driver-Partners in the United States, ONLINE:https://irs.princeton.edu/sites/irs/files/An%20Analysis%20of%20 the%20Labor%20Market%20for%20 Uber%E2%80%99s%20Driver-Partners%20in%20the%20 United%20States%20587.pdf

A4 (Haggag et al 2017). Haggag, K., McManus, B. a Paci, G. (2017). Learning by Driving: Productivity Improvements by New York City Taxi Drivers. American Economic Journal: Applied Economics 9 (1), 70–95.

A5 Loan, P. (2018), ONLINE: https://www.facebook.com/paul.loan.7/posts/856427861196322

A6 Fagerstrøm a kol. That personal profile image might jeopardize your rental opportunity! On the relative impact of the seller's facial expressions upon buying behavior on Airbnb, Computers in Human Behavior Volume 72, July 2017, Pages 123-131 ONLINE: https://www.sciencedirect.com/science/article/pii/S0747563217301012

Ert, E. a kol. (2016) Trust and reputation in the sharing economy: The role of personal photos in Airbnb Tourism Management, 55 (2016), pp. 62 73,

A7 Silverglate, H. (2011) Three Felonies A Day: How the Feds Target the Innocent. New York: Encounter Books, pp. 392, ISBN 978-1594035227

A8 The Box: How the shipping container made the world smaller and the world economy bigger. New Jersey: Princeton University Press, pp. 400, ISBN 978-0691136400

A9 Elert, N. a Henrekson, M. (2014) Evasive Entrepreneurship: IFN Working Paper No. 1044, pp. 34

Pollman, E. a Barry, J. M. (2016) Regulatory Entrepreneurship: Loyola Law School, Los Angeles Legal Studies Research Paper No. 2017-29

A10 http://journal.fsv.cuni.cz/storage/146_004_111_125.pdf

SAMUELSON, P. A. – NORDHAUS, W. D. (1991): Ekonomie. 13. vydání. Praha, Svoboda, 1991.

SOJKA, M. (1995): Přístupy k interpretaci díla J. M. Keynese v neokeynesovské literatufie. Politická ekonomie, 1995, ā. 5, ss. 690–702 (Interpretation Approaches to the works of J.M.Keynese in the neokeynesian literature)

SAMUELSON, P. A. (1954): The Pure Theory of Public Expenditure. Review of Economics and Statistics, XXXVI, November 1954, pp. 387–389.

MUSGRAVE, R. A. – MUSGRAVEOVÁ, P. B. (1994): Vefiejné finance v teorii a praxi. Praha, Management Press, 1994 – pfietisk z: Finance a úvûr, 1992–94.(Public Finance in Theory and Practice)

A11 Andreoni, J. a R. Petrie (2004), 'Public Goods Experiments without Confidentiality: A Glimpse into Fund-Raising', Journal of Public Economics, 88(7–8): 1605–1623

A12 Mail Foreign Service (2010) eBay buyer sued for defamation after leaving negative feedback on auction site, ONLINE: https://www.dailymail.co.uk/news/article-1265490/eBay-buyer-sued-defamation-leaving-negative-feedback-auction-site.html

CONCLUSION – REFLECTIONS

A13   Hirschman, A. O. (1970) Exit, Voice, and Loyalty. Harvard University Press, pp. 176.

A14   Beito, D. T. (2009) The Voluntary City: Choice, Community, and Civil Society. Oakland: Independent Institute, pp. 480, ISBN 978-1598130324

A15   Fuller, C. (2019) Is the market for digital privacy a failure?, Public Choice, ONLINE: https://link.springer.com/article/10.1007/s11127-019-00642-2

A16   Katsh, E. a Rabinovich-Einy, O. (2017) Digital Justice: Technology and the Internet of Disputes. Oxford University Press, pp. 264, 978-0190675677

A17   Karpiš, J. a Vlachynský, M. (2017) Prečo zachovať hotovosť Why should we keep cash, ONLINE: http://iness.sk/sites/default/files/media/file/pdf/INT/INT_3-2017_Preco_zachovat_hotovost.pdf

A18   May, T. C. (1994) Cyphernomicon, ONLINE: https://archive.org/details/cyphernomicon

A19   Brekke, J. K. (2018) Disassembling the Trust Machine: An introduction to a political economy of blockchain: The New Centre for Research and Practice

A20   Blockchain (2018) Transaction, ONLINE: https://www.blockchain.com/btc/tx/cff2dd0918b-4243b6c98148ad139473bc1a7603057f9df6844529bc3cf73dc38?fbclid=IwAR2I4xpRpDnXz8ruJ-d9oeoh3DW35_q8kwRNlTw6IhpK7kNfevOFJWuYunc4

A21   https://www.amazon.com/Silk-Road-Eileen-Ormsby-ebook/dp/B00HTWDEK0

A22   Ormsby, E. (2014) Silk Road. Sydney: Macmillan Australia, pp. 352

A23   Van Hout, M. and Bingham, T. (2013) 'Surfing the Silk Road: a study of users' experiences': International Journal of Drug Policy 24, pp. 524-529

Barratt, M., Ferris, J. and Winstock, A. (2014) 'Use of Silk Road, the online drug marketplace, in the United Kingdom, Australia and the United States': Addiction 109, pp. 774-783.

A24   Henrich, J. (2015) The Secret of Our Success: How Culture Is Driving Human Evolution, Domesticating Our Species, and Making Us Smarter. Princeton University Press, pp. 464, ISBN 978-0691166858

A25   Friedman, D. D. (1989) Machinery of freedom.Open Court, pp. 267, ISBN 978-0812690699

Rothbard, M. N. (2009) Man, Economy, and State with Power and Market. Ludwig von Mises Institute, pp. 1506

Urza (2018) Anarchokapitalizmus, pp. 244, ISBN 978-80-270-1648-8.

A26   Leeson, P. T. (2007) Better off stateless: Somalia before and after government collapse, ONLINE: http://www.peterleeson.com/Better_Off_Stateless.pdf
Powell, B. a kol. (2006) Somalia After State Collapse: Chaos or Improvement? Independent Institute Working Paper Number 64, ONLINE: http://www.observatori.org/paises/pais_74/documentos/64_somalia.pdf

We would like to thank all the supporters who made the publication of this book possible:

NOTES

NOTES

Printed in Poland
by Amazon Fulfillment
Poland Sp. z o.o., Wrocław